JOURNAL FOR THE STUDY OF THE OLD TESTAMENT
SUPPLEMENT SERIES
132

Editors
David J.A. Clines
Philip R. Davies

JSOT Press
Sheffield

CONTEXTS FOR AMOS

Prophetic Poetics in
Latin American Perspective

Mark Daniel Carroll R.

Journal for the Study of the Old Testament
Supplement Series 132

Al hombre de maíz
en la tierra de la eterna primavera
y al pueblo de Dios
que nace en su seno.

Published by JSOT Press
JSOT Press is an imprint of
Sheffield Academic Press Ltd
The University of Sheffield
343 Fulwood Road
Sheffield S10 3BP
England

Printed on acid-free paper in Great Britain
by Billing & Sons Ltd
Worcester

British Library Cataloguing in Publication Data

Carroll, M.D.
   Contexts for Amos.—(JSOT Supplement
   Series, ISSN 0309-0787; No. 132)
   I. Title II. Series
   224.806

ISBN 1-85075-297-4

CONTENTS

PREFACE

This work is a slight revision of a thesis presented for the PhD in Biblical Studies at the University of Sheffield in March 1990. The revision consists primarily of minor corrections and of an updating of the footnotes based on further reading over the last year. This study, like the original thesis, is a product of the desire to understand better how to allow the Old Testament to speak within Latin America and reflects the twin focii of this interest: on the one hand, the locating of biblical study and theological reflection within the *complex cultural realities* of that continent; on the other, the articulating of a possibly fruitful *textual method*. In both areas my study has been motivated to a certain extent by the conviction of the need to offer alternative approaches to those of Latin American liberation theologians. Hopefully, this dialogue and interaction with that broad modern current can demonstrate both an appreciation of its theoretical and methodological insights, as well as facilitate discussion in new areas.

A word is in order about the reading of the prophetic text. No original translation of the Hebrew text is offered. In general the wording of the RSV is followed, except where the exegesis suggests changes. The transliteration reproduces only the consonants of the Masoretic Text.

This effort would not have been possible without the help of many people too numerous to mention here. I would like to single out, however, three groups of people to whom I owe a particular debt. First, a word of appreciation is due to the Biblical Studies Department at the University of Sheffield, whose openness to new ideas and concern for methodology make for a creative environment within which to work. I offer a special word of thanks to my advisor, Professor John Rogerson, who models an exemplary integration of careful Old Testament scholarship, a keen interest in ethics, and a commitment to the Christian church.

Second, I would also like to express my gratitude to the assistance granted by friends in Guatemala. Kelvin St John graciously dedicated untold hours on his computer to help get the thesis ready for submission and its revision for publication. Gary Williams, despite his heavy administrative load as rector of El Seminario Teológico Centroamericano and his own thesis preparation, interacted with the reading of Amos. David Suazo J. and Guillermo W. Méndez, two Guatemalan colleagues and dear friends, have been constant and stimulating companions in a shared pilgrimage to bring the Bible to life in our context.

Lastly, and most importantly, I thank from the depths of my heart my two sons, Matthew and Adam, who have been so patient with a father who has been too busy, and my wife Joan, without whose faithful encouragement and support this project never would have been completed.

M. Daniel Carroll R.
Guatemala City
April 1991

ABBREVIATIONS

1. *Journals and Series*

AA	*Acta antiqua academiae scientarum hungaricae*
AB	The Anchor Bible
AJSL	*American Journal of Semitic Languages and Literature*
AmAnth	*American Anthropologist*
AmJSoc	*American Journal of Sociology*
AmSocRev	*American Sociological Review*
AnnRevAnth	*Annual Review of Anthropology*
AOAT	Alter Orient und Altes Testament
ArEurSoc	*Archives européenes de sociologie*
ASTI	*Annual of the Swedish Theological Institute*
ATANT	Abhandlungen zur Theologie des Alten und Neuen Testaments
BA	*Biblical Archaeologist*
BARev	*Biblical Archaeology Review*
BASOR	*Bulletin of the American Schools of Oriental Research*
BBB	Bonner Biblische Beiträge
Bib	*Biblica*
BibNot	*Biblische Notizen*
BTB	*Biblical Theology Bulletin*
BolTeol	*Boletín teológico*
BRev	*Bible Review*
BSac	*Bibliotheca Sacra*
BT	*The Bible Translator*
BZ	*Biblische Zeitschrift*
BZAW	Beihefte zur ZAW
CahRRRel	*Cahiers de recherche et réflexion religieuses*
CalvTJ	*Calvin Theological Journal*
CBQ	*Catholic Biblical Quarterly*
CLAR	Confederación Latinoamericana de Religiosos
ConBOT	Coniectanea Biblica Old Testament Series
Conc	*Concilium*
CritInq	*Critical Inquiry*
CrSoc	*Cristianismo y sociedad*
CuadTeol	*Cuadernos de teología* [Argentina]
CultHerm	*Cultural Hermeneutics*
CurrAnth	*Current Anthropology*

CurTM	*Currents in Theology and Mission*
EcuR	*The Ecumenical Review*
EI	*Eretz Israel*
EstBib	*Estudios bíblicos*
ETR	*Etudes théologiques et religieuses*
EvT	*Evangelische Theologie*
ExpTim	*The Expository Times*
FRLANT	Forschungen zur Religion und Literatur des Alten und Neuen Testaments
HAR	*Hebrew Annual Review*
HebSt	*Hebrew Studies*
HorBT	*Horizons in Biblical Theology*
HTR	*Harvard Theological Review*
HUCA	*Hebrew Union College Annual*
Int	*Interpretation*
IrTQ	*Irish Theological Quarterly*
JAAR	*Journal of the American Academy of Religion*
JANESCU	*Journal of the Ancient Near Eastern Society of Columbia University*
JAnthRes	*Journal of Anthropological Research*
JAOS	*Journal of the American Oriental Society*
JETS	*Journal of the Evangelical Theological Society*
JJS	*Journal of Jewish Studies*
JNWS	*Journal of North West Semitic Languages*
JRoyAnthI	*Journal of the Royal Anthropological Institute*
JPhil	*Journal of Philosophy*
JPopCul	*Journal of Popular Culture*
JRelEth	*Journal of Religious Ethics*
JSOT	*Journal for the Study of the Old Testament*
JSOTSup	*Journal for the Study of the Old Testament* Supplement Series
JSS	*Journal of Semitic Studies*
JTS	*Journal of Theological Studies*
LARR	*Latin American Research Review*
ModChm	*Modern Churchman*
ModTh	*Modern Theology*
NICM	*National Institute of Campus Ministries Journal*
NLH	*New Literary History*
NSys	*Neue Zeitschrift für systematische Theologie und Religionsphilosophie*
OBO	Orbis Biblicus et Orientalis
OTS	*Oudtestamentische Studiën*
OTWSA	*Die Outestamentiese Werkgemeenskap in Suid-Africa*
PerspRelSt	*Perspectives in Religious Studies*
Prot	*Protestantesimo*

PSB	*Princeton Seminary Bulletin*
RB	*Revue biblique*
Rel	*Religion*
ReStR	*Religious Studies Review*
RestQ	*Restoration Quarterly*
RevPol	*Review of Politics*
RevBíb	*Revista bíblica* [Argentina]
RSR	*Recherches de science religieuse*
RIBLA	*Revista de interpretación bíblica latinoamericana*
RivBiblt	*Rivista Biblica Italiana*
RLT	*Revista latinoamericana de teología* [El Salvador]
SBLDS	Society of Biblical Literature Dissertation Series
SBLSP	*Society of Biblical Literature Seminar Papers*
ScEs	*Science et esprit*
SH	*Scripta Hierosolymitana*
SJT	*Scottish Journal of Theology*
SocComp	*Social Compass*
SocRes	*Social Research*
SOTSMS	Society for Old Testament Study Monograph Series
SWBAS	Social World of Biblical Antiquity Series
TBT	*The Bible Today*
ThEv	*Theologia Evangelica*
ThSt	*Theological Studies*
TTod	*Theology Today*
TLZ	*Theologische Literaturzeitung*
TZ	*Theologische Zeitschrift*
UF	*Ugarit-Forschungen*
VPens	*Vida y pensamiento* [Costa Rica]
VT	*Vetus Testamentum*
VTSup	*Vetus Testamentum* Supplements
ZAW	*Zeitschrift für die alttestamentliche Wissenschaft*
ZDPV	*Zeitschrift des deutschen Palästina-Vereins*
ZRGG	*Zeitschrift fur Religions- und Geistesgeschichte*

2. Reference Works

BDB	Brown, Driver and Briggs, *Hebrew and English Lexicon of the Old Testament*
GKC	*Gesenius' Hebrew Grammar*, ed. E. Kautzsch, trans. A.E. Cowley
KB	Koehler and Baumgartner, *Lexicon in Veteris Testamenti libros*

TDNT	Kittel and Friedrich (eds.), *Theological Dictionary of the New Testament*
TDOT	Botterweck and Ringgren (eds.), *Theological Dictionary of the Old Testament*

3. *Versions*

BHS	*Biblia hebraica stuttgartensia*
JB	*Jerusalem Bible*
LXX	*Duodecim prophetae. Septuaginta* (ed. J. Ziegler)
NEB	*New English Bible*
NIV	*New International Version*
RSV	*Revised Standard Version*
BLA	*Biblia Latinoamericana*
FC	*Sagrada Biblia Fuster-Colunga*
RVA	*Reina Valera Actualizada*

Chapter 1

RELATING THE TEXT AND THE WORLD:
INTRODUCTION AND FRAMEWORK

Throughout its history the Christian church has constantly wrestled with how to use the Bible properly to speak out relevantly and effectively in society. The hermeneutics and sociopolitical models have been many and varied, and within the same historical contexts different approaches have competed for biblical justification and ecclesiastical allegiance.

The Old Testament prophetic office and literature in particular have always attracted those who have desired to carry such biblical themes as pure religion, holiness and justice beyond the confines of the Christian communities and into the national and international arena. Moved by the biblical message, and indignant at the prevailing social situation, 'prophets' from a wide theological and ideological spectrum across the centuries have spoken out and attempted to challenge the status quo. Theirs has been no mere academic interest in the biblical literature, but rather a passion to change the very structures of society.

In the mid-sixteenth century, for example, the Marian exiles—Puritans who had fled the Catholic persecution in England to seek out and emulate the Reformed social experiment in Calvin's Geneva—envisioned themselves as called out to denounce

> the counterfayte Christians this day, which everie where (but especially in our miserable countrie) imprison, famishe, murther, hange, and burne their own countriemen, and deare children of God at the commandement of furious Jesabel, and her false Priestes and Prophetes, the bloudie Bishopps and shavelynges. . . [1]

At the time of the exiles' departure, the British Isles were ruled by

1. C. Goodman in E. Morgan (ed.), *Puritan Political Ideas 1558–1794* (Indianapolis, IN: Bobbs–Merrill, 1965), p. 7.

Catholics (even worse, by women!), who in their sight promoted a false faith and oppressed true religion. In the prophetic office they found the justification for public censure and the call for national repentance and reformation.[1] John Knox could write: 'We in this our miserable age are bounde to admonishe the world and the tyrannes thereof, of their sodeine destruction, to assure them, and to crie unto them, whether they list to heare or not'.[2] The Geneva Bible, which they published in 1560,[3] was to become the most popular version in England for a century. Its opening dedication to Elizabeth I and the notes to certain biblical passages left no doubt that the Bible was a political document and that ministers, like Old Testament prophets, had both the right and the duty to remind rulers of their solemn obligations.[4]

1. M. Walzer, *The Revolution of the Saints: A Study in the Origins of Radical Politics* (London: Weidenfeld & Nicolson, 1965), pp. 99-109. Taking the French Huguenots and especially the English Puritans as his case studies, Walzer proposes looking at Calvinism as a powerful ideology (not in the Marxist sense) of transition into the modern era and as a model of radicalism which has features in common with other social movements. See also H.G. Reventlow, *The Authority of the Bible and the Rise of the Modern World* (trans. J. Bowden; London: SCM Press, 1984), pp. 143-44.

2. J. Knox, *The First Blast of the Trumpet Against the Monstrous Regiment of Women—1558* (ed. E. Arber; London: n.p., 1878), p. 5.

3. B. Hall, *The Geneva Version of the English Bible* (London: The Presbyterian Historical Society of England, 1957); F.F. Bruce, *History of the Bible in English* (3rd edn; London: Lutterworth, 1979), pp. 86-92; L. Lupton, *A History of the Geneva Bible*. III. *Truth* (London: Compton Press, 1972), pp. 76-87.

4. H. Craig, Jr, 'The Geneva Bible as a Political Document', *Pacific Historical Review* (1938), pp. 40-49; Lupton, *A History of the Geneva Bible*. IV. *Travail*, pp. 140-44. There were some inconsistencies in the political thrust of the notes reflecting the struggle to ascertain the proper limits of submission and civil disobedience. Their published writings were more straightforward and condemnatory.

The criticism of the monarchy in Great Britain on the basis of prophetic texts did not disappear with the passing of the Puritans. Note these words from early in this century by J.E. McFayden, *A Cry for Justice: A Study of Amos* (Edinburgh: T. & T. Clark, 1912).

(1) Paraphrasing 7.7-9: 'Your ancient cathedrals and your beautiful churches—Canterbury, York, Westminster, St Paul's, and a hundred others—will be laid in ruins, and the dynasty of King George will perish by the sword' (p. 97).
(2) On 9.7: 'We, too, who have sometimes spoken as if the kingdom of God and the cause of God were indissolubly associated with the British Empire, may do well

The Puritan ideals not only led to reformation in Scotland and eventually to the Cromwellian revolution in England, but also had a formative influence in the founding and shaping of the American republic. There, too, ministers functioned as prophets to keep the young nation on what was judged to be the correct road for the discharge of its sacred mission: 'The purpose of their jeremiads was to direct an imperiled people of God toward the fulfillment of their destiny, to guide them individually toward salvation, and collectively toward the American city of God'.[1] This powerful prophetic rhetoric, the American jeremiad, forged a sense of national identity and, even after the failure of the New England theocracy and the secularization of its aims, contributed to the shaping of a pervasive civil religion and ideology.[2]

Interest in the prophetic, then, is not new. Today there is also renewed interest in a 'prophetic' ministry and church that concern themselves with unjust social realities. How the 'prophetic' is understood and what can serve as its theoretical basis, however, can vary.[3]

On the one hand, for example, are those who turn to sociological studies, often using the pioneer work of Max Weber on the prophetic charisma as the starting point of discussion.[4] This orientation can

---

to listen, with chastened hearts, to the challenge of Amos. . . and to remind ourselves that the only empire that will live is that which seeks good and not evil. . .' (p. 133).

1. S. Bercovitch, *The American Jeremiad* (Madison: University of Wisconsin Press, 1978), p. 9.

2. Bercovitch's thesis is that the American jeremiad is inexorably linked to the North American ideals of limitless progress as well as to the middle-class free enterprise consensus. It should be mentioned that the Puritans and their 'heirs' used other portions of the Old Testament besides the prophets. For other studies of the texts used and the hermeneutical methods of typology and analogy that they employed, see Reventlow, *Authority of the Bible*, pp. 92-184; M.I. Lowance, *The Language of Canaan: Metaphor and Symbol in New England from the Puritans to the Transcendentalists* (Cambridge, MA: Harvard University Press, 1980).

3. For other modern understandings not considered here, see the discussions and surveys in T.W. Overholt, *Channels of Prophecy: The Social Dynamics of Prophetic Activity* (Minneapolis, MN: Fortress Press, 1989), ch. 7; G.M. Tucker, 'The Role of the Prophets and the Role of the Church', in *Prophecy in Israel* (ed. D.L. Petersen; Issues in Theology, 10; Philadelphia: Fortress Press, 1987), pp. 159-74.

4. S.N. Eisenstadt (ed.), *Max Weber on Charisma and Institution Building— Selected Papers* (Chicago: University of Chicago Press, 1968), pp. 48-65; M. Weber, *Economy and Society: An Outline of Interpretive Sociology*, II (ed.

refer to the varied role of religion in politics or more specifically to action based on the ethical and social implications of the Christian faith. Here the key to 'prophetic' religion is the claim of a transcendent authority by which it can either question or legitimize a given regime.

Other perspectives can make more direct reference to the biblical material, but once again there exists a whole spectrum of approaches. Michael Walzer, for instance, does allude to a particular prophet, Amos, but not in detail, as part of a larger theoretical framework to establish his notion of the 'connected critic'—that is, one committed to the socially constructed world of his community, who is, however, at enough distance (on the periphery perhaps, but not detached) to challenge the accepted morality and vision of life.[1] The biblical data serve to illustrate and confirm his thoughts on how that kind of critical, yet constructive, practice might be imitated in the modern world.

This concept of modern prophecy can be contrasted with others in more distant latitudes which seek other bridges of continuity with the Old Testament prophets. Ndiokwere points out that in Africa the prophets of the Independent Churches, while often in touch with social issues, also see parallels in their experience of the ecstatic and the miraculous, the Zion-Jerusalem imagery, and messianic expectations.[2]

G. Roth and C. Wittich; New York: Bedminster Press, 1968), pp. 439-68. For a modern use see, e.g., R. Gill, *Prophecy and Praxis: The Social Function of the Churches* (London: Marshall, Morgan & Scott, 1981); T.E. Long, 'Prophecy, Charisma, and Politics: Reinterpreting the Weberian Thesis', in *Religion and the Political Order*. I. *Prophetic Religion and Politics* (ed. J.K. Hadden and A. Shupe; New York: Paragon House, 1986), pp. 3-17; *idem*, 'A Theory of Prophetic Religion and Politics', in *Religion and the Political Order*. II. *The Politics of Religion and Social Change* (ed. J.K. Hadden and Anson Shupe; New York: Paragon House, 1988), pp. 3-16.

1. M. Walzer, *Interpretation and Social Criticism* (Cambridge, MA: Harvard University Press, 1987). For Amos, see pp. 80-94.

2. N.I. Ndiokwere, *Prophecy and Revolution: The Role of Prophets in the African Churches and in Biblical Tradition* (London: SPCK, 1981). For a declaration dealing specifically with South Africa and concerned with the political understanding and commitment of the Christian church, not indigenous cultural expressions, see The Kairos Document, *Challenge to the Church: A Theological Comment on the Political Crisis in South Africa* (Grand Rapids: Eerdmans, 1985). For the prophetic theology, see pp. 36-46. Cf. C. Rowland and M. Corner, *Liberating Exegesis: The Challenge of Liberation Theology to Biblical Studies* (Biblical Foundations in

In this case, within the myriad of autochthonous religious movements the modern prophets are considered to have a more direct link with the biblical personae.

This book, however, is primarily interested in how the 'prophetic' is being formulated within Latin America. On that continent in recent decades, especially in Liberation Theology circles, there has arisen a clarion call to assume a prophetic stance in a context of injustice and oppression, to reformulate the Christian ministry according to the *proyecto histórico* of liberation.[1] This social task entails the changing of the existing political and economic structures and the creation of a different kind of society.

This challenge to be prophetic can be taken to apply to various levels: to individuals,[2] to the religious orders,[3] and to the Christian church in the challenging task of 'doing theology'.[4] How, though, can this charge be understood? What would be the concrete features of such a commitment?

On the basis of the pictures of prophets within the Bible this liberation perspective would hold that fundamental to the prophetic option is the concept of *mission*, which begins with solidarity with the poor, life among the poor, and sacrificial service in the struggle to eradicate oppression. In addition, this vocation proclaims a powerful *message*, a word in season aware of the sociopolitical realities of the continent. The prophetic word is a denunciation of the injustice, but involves,

Theology; London: SPCK, 1990), pp. 173-88.

1. E.g. N.O. Miguez, 'Profecía y proyecto histórico', in *Misión profética de la iglesia* (ed. P.N. Rigol *et al.*; Mexico: CUPSA, 1981), pp. 69-83.

2. J.S. Croatto, *Exodus: A Hermeneutics of Freedom* (trans. S. Attansio; Maryknoll: Orbis Books, 1981), ch. 4; and 'Palabra profética y no-conversión: la tematización bíblica del rechazo al profeta', *Vox Evangelii* ns 1 (1984), pp. 9-20; J.V. Pixley, 'Hacia una teoría de la profecía', in *Misión profética de la iglesia*, pp. 87-103; E. Dussel, *Ethics and Community* (trans. R.R. Barr; Tunbridge Wells: Burns & Oates, 1988), ch. 9.

3. Equipo Teólogos, CLAR, *Tendencias proféticas de la vida religiosa en América Latina* (CLAR, 24; Bogotá: Secretariado General de la CLAR, 1975); D. Brunelli, *Profetas del reino. Grandes lineas de la actual teología de la vida religiosa en América Latina* (CLAR, 58; Bogotá: Secretariado General de la CLAR, 1987).

4. R. Avila, 'La profecía en América Latina', in *Misión profética de la iglesia* pp. 87-103; G. Gutiérrez, *Hablar de Dios desde el sufrimiento del inocente. Una reflexión sobre el libro de Job* (Salamanca: Ediciones Sígueme, 2nd edn, 1988), chs. 4-6.

too, both the assignment of raising the consciousness of the people as
well as the announcement of the hope of a better world.

As in other times and situations, the elaboration of a 'prophetic'
ministry or church within Latin America can be grounded either in
broader philosophical and sociological considerations separate from
or loosely attached to the biblical material, or in a study of the
prophetic text itself. This book purposes to investigate the biblical
text. One prophetic book in particular will serve as the object of
study: Amos. This text has always excited much interest throughout
the history of the Christian church, and even earlier among the
Qumran sect. Today, its harsh demands for justice have found special
resonance.[1]

I want in this book to move beyond vague references to the
'prophetic' that can lead to rather sweeping statements about the biblical prophets in the attempt to seek modern applications. What can the
prophetic text actually offer in terms of details regarding the
prophets' lifestyles and mission? How should the prophetic literature
be read for moral life today?

These sorts of questions refer to more than the ascertaining of a
prophetic book's content, data in this case from Amos; the concerns
are also hermeneutical, because *how to read* a text involves both the
textual method and the *contextual situatedness* of the reader. The
sweep of this thesis, therefore, will be rather broad and will follow
this twin set of hermeneutical tracks in its reading of Amos. In
addition, because I live and work in Latin America, the forays into
contextualization will center on that geographical area and will enter
into dialogue with the theologizing being done there by liberation
theologians. It is hoped, however, that whatever insights might be
gleaned from this study would be profitable in some measure
elsewhere, too.

This book is an extensive essay in method, an exploration in how to
use the Bible in moral reasoning within a given context. The next
chapter begins the discussion with a look at various attempts to reconstruct the life and message of the prophet Amos. Is this the most
profitable way to proceed? After an analysis of possible shortcomings
of this approach, in the succeeding chapters the book will propose a

---

1. R. Martin-Achard, *Amos: l'homme, le message, l'influence* (Geneva: Labor et
Fides, 1984), pp. 161-271.

different direction: *a poetic reading within a rich understanding of the cultural context.*

In the many efforts to contextualize the prophetic message, all sorts of extremes can surface and often the stakes are high, but Martin-Achard's words are a fitting motivation to take up the challenge:

> Certain abuses, however, should in no way keep us from listening to the prophets and, in this case, to Amos, as we know moreover that every reading, here as in other pages of Scripture, involves a risk which is worth taking.[1]

---

1. Martin-Achard, *Amos*, p. 168.

Chapter 2

THE WORLD BEHIND THE TEXT:
SOCIOLOGICAL STUDIES AND THE OLD TESTAMENT

Any attempt to employ the prophets in the sociopolitical realities of the modern world could logically begin with a study of the prophetic contexts with an eye to discovering the thrust of their message and the essence of their activity. That is, this pragmatic concern would try to push research beyond the interest in the possible sources upon which prophetic ethics drew.[1] Even form-critical studies, which have sought to locate the prophets in their societies by identifying underlying traditions, have proven inadequate.[2] These attempts have often confused the possible original setting of language with its actual use and have not dealt with the sociopolitical issues and tensions so prominent in that language.

Interest in the political ideas and activity of the prophets is currently growing. Yet, despite impressions to the contrary, serious investigation into the political and social convictions and loyalties of the prophets,[3] as well as the use of the social sciences in the study of the

---

1. E.g. the well-known essays by N.W. Porteous, 'The Basis of the Ethical Teaching of the Prophets', in *Studies in Old Testament Prophecy Presented to Professor Theodore H. Robinson* (ed. H.H. Rowley; Edinburgh: T. & T. Clark, repr. 1957), pp. 143-56; and E. Hammershaimb, 'On the Ethics of the Old Testament Prophets', *VTSup* 7 (1959), pp. 75-101. More recently E.W. Davies, *Prophecy and Ethics: Isaiah and the Ethical Tradition of Israel* (JSOTSup, 16; Sheffield: JSOT Press, 1981).

2. R.R. Wilson, *Prophecy and Society in Ancient Israel* (Philadelphia: Fortress Press, 1980), pp. 3-14.

3. Surveys of studies on prophetic politics include N.K. Gottwald, *All the Kingdoms of the Earth: Israelite Prophecy and International Relations and the Ancient Near East* (New York: Harper & Row, 1964), pp. 350-65; J.A. Soggin, 'Profezia e rivoluzione nell' Antico Testamento. L'opera di Elia e di Eliseo nella

Old Testament, are in no way a new development.[1] Because of its strident social message, Amos in particular has consistently generated scholarly discussion.[2]

valutazione di Osea', *Prot* 25 (1970), pp. 1-14; B. Albrektson, 'Prophecy and Politics in the Old Testament', in *The Myth of the State* (ed. H. Brezais; Stockholm: Almqvist & Wiksell, 1972), pp. 45-56; L. Ramlot, 'Prophétisme', in *Supplément au dictionnaire de la Bible*, VIII (ed. H. Cazelles and A. Feuillet; Paris: Letouzey & Ané, 1972), pp. 1050-58; B. Lang, *Monotheism and the Prophetic Minority: An Essay in Biblical History and Sociology* (SWBAS, 1; Sheffield: Almond Press, 1983), pp. 83-91; J. Dearman, *Property Rights in the Eighth-Century Prophets* (SBLDS, 106; Atlanta: Scholars Press, 1988), pp. 2-16. Other studies not mentioned in these surveys include J.S. Holloday, 'Assyrian Statecraft and the Prophets of Israel', *HTR* 63 (1970), pp. 29-51; M.A. Cohen, 'The Prophets as Revolutionaries: A Sociopolitical Analysis', *BARev* 5 (1979), pp. 12-19; J.K. de Geus, 'Die Gesellschaftskritik der Propheten und die Archäologie', *ZDPV* 98 (1982), pp. 50-57; B. Uffenheimer, 'Ancient Hebrew Prophecy—Political Teaching and Practice', *Immanuel* 18 (1984), pp. 7-21.

1. J.W. Rogerson takes the use of sociological thought back to Josephus in 'The Use of Sociology in Old Testament Studies', *VTSup* 36 (1985), pp. 245-56. Helpful surveys include H.H. Hahn, *The Old Testament in Modern Research* (Philadelphia: Fortress Press, 1966), pp. 157-84; J. Blenkinsopp, *A History of Prophecy in Israel: From the Settlement in the Land to the Hellenistic Period* (Philadelphia: Westminster Press, 1983), pp. 38-46; J.W. Rogerson, *Anthropology and the Old Testament* (Sheffield: JSOT Press, 1984); J.L. Sicre, *'Con los pobres de la tierra'. La justica social en los profetas de Israel* (Madrid: Ediciones Cristiandad, 1984), who presents a survey as well as his own reconstruction of developments leading up to the eighth century (pp. 48-83); L. Epsztein, *Social Justice in the Ancient Near East and the People of the Bible* (trans. J. Bowden; London: SCM Press, 1986), pp. 45-82. For a recent anthology see B. Lang (ed.), *Anthropological Approaches to the Old Testament* (London/Philadelphia: SPCK/Fortress Press, 1985). It is interesting to note that in R.R. Wilson's survey (*Prophecy and Society*, pp. 1-19) there is no mention of sociological studies that have been geared toward exploring political, structural, and economic issues. This lacuna is reflected in his research: any social concern is ultimately limited to the relation of religious groups to religious centers.

2. For good surveys, see Martin-Achard, *Amos*, pp. 83-88; Gottwald, *All the Kingdoms*, pp. 94-119; Sicre, *'Con los pobres'*, pp. 141-68; A.G. Auld, *Amos* (Old Testament Guides; Sheffield: JSOT Press, 1986), pp. 60-72; G. Fleischer, *Von Menschenverkäufern, Baschankühen und Rechtsverkrern. Die Sozialkritik des Amosbuches in historisch-kritischer, sozialgeschichter und archäologischer Perspektive* (BBB, 74; Frankfurt am Main: Athenäum Verlag, 1989), pp. 284-301, 346-70, 402-23.

It is undeniable, however, that there has been a recent explosion in the number and variety of sociological studies and methods employed. Each project has been an attempt to probe certain aspects of the reality of the ancient world and has, with the utilization of a particular approach, attempted to reconstruct that world. For example, comparative studies by Thomas W. Overholt and Burke O. Long have sought analogies between Israelite and more modern prophetic movements regarding the fundamental problem of legitimation, whether of the prophet himself[1] or of the prophetic office and tradition.[2] T.R. Hobbs has suggested the society-as-drama perspective of V. Turner,[3] and Martin J. Buss has brought forward the various possible contributions of social psychology[4] to probe the prophetic consciousness. Terry Giles offers insights from voluntary social movements to try to explain the cultic language and social influence of the prophet Amos.[5] Robert P. Carroll draws upon the theory of cognitive dissonance to posit a re-working of the prophetic material in light of the disconfirmation of predictions.[6] Robert R. Wilson's extensive work uses both parallels to ancient Near Eastern and modern prophetic movements for a tentative historical and geographical understanding of

1. T.W. Overholt, 'Commanding the Prophets: Amos and the Problem of Prophetic Authority', *CBQ* 12 (1979), pp. 517-32; 'Prophecy: The Problem of Cross-Cultural Comparison', *Semeia* 21 (1982), pp. 55-78; 'Seeing is Believing: The Social Setting of Prophetic Acts of Power', *JSOT* 23 (1982), pp. 3-31; and especially *Channels of Prophecy: The Dynamics of Prophetic Activity* (Minneapolis, MN: Fortress Press, 1989).

2. B.O. Long, 'The Social Setting of Prophetic Miracle Stories', *Semeia* 3 (1975), pp. 46-63; 'Prophetic Authority as Social Reality', in *Canon and Authority: Essays in Old Testament Religion and Theology* (ed. G.W. Coats and B.O. Long; Philadelphia: Fortress Press, 1977), pp. 3-20.

3. T.R. Hobbs, 'The Search for Prophetic Consciousness: Comments on Method', *BTB* 15 (1985), pp. 136-41.

4. M.J. Buss, 'The Social Psychology of Prophecy', in *Prophecy: Essays Presented to Georg Fohrer on his Sixty-fifth Birthday 6 September 1980* (BZAW, 150; Berlin: de Gruyter, 1980), pp. 1-11.

5. T. Giles, 'An Introductory Investigation of Amos by Means of the Model of the Voluntary Social Movement', *Eastern Great Lakes Biblical Society Proceedings* 8 (1988), pp. 135-53.

6. R.P. Carroll, *When Prophecy Fails: Reactions and Responses to Failure in the Old Testament Prophetic Traditions* (London: SCM Press, 1979). See especially pp. 111-28.

biblical prophetic groups and traditions.[1]

The concern here, however, is to explore the sociopolitical interests of the prophets, an area not really grappled with in the aforementioned sociological research. For that reason, this chapter will look instead at Max Weber's *Ancient Judaism*,[2] David L. Petersen's *The Roles of Israel's Prophets*,[3] and Bernhard Lang's *Monotheism and the Prophetic Minority*.[4] The first has provided by far the most comprehensive model of the three: Weber's is a work designed to explain the evolution of Judaism. The other two are the works of biblical scholars, who focus on the prophets and apply particular sociological approaches. Each was selected for a reason: Weber's as representative of a macro-model, albeit a dated one (but this will be an important point as will become clear later); Petersen's and Lang's as types of modern, more specialized studies, but also because of their interest in Amos.

The ultimate aim is to clarify what social theories actually do and what they can offer for the modern context—in other words, this is a discussion of sociological method. What follows, therefore, is separated into two large sections, each of which is sub-divided into two parts. The first major section is a brief summary of these scholars' views, and this under the headings 'the prophet as a model for action' and 'the object of prophetic denunciation'. These captions clearly overstep the intended compass of the authors, but that is by design. These are the categories which are today being defined on the basis of biblical allusions or parallels. But then the question arises: how viable is historical reconstruction? Hence the second section will evaluate the potential for modern application. To begin with, there are presented general, practical, and common-sense issues that any sociological theory must negotiate; a more rigorous examination of one of the three models follows as an attempt to encourage more careful

---

1. Wilson, *Prophecy and Society*.

2. M. Weber, *Ancient Judaism* (trans. H. H. Gerth and D. Martindale; Glencoe: The Free Press, 1952).

3. D.L. Petersen, *The Roles of Israel's Prophets* (JSOTSup, 17; Sheffield: JSOT Press, 1981).

4. This book is actually a collection of essays dealing with different issues. The first, for instance, is his reconstruction of the history of the prophetic movement. This study will concentrate on the chapter entitled 'The Social Organization of Peasant Poverty in Biblical Israel', in *Monotheism*, pp. 114-27.

consideration as to how social theories should be constructed and as to
how usable they can actually prove to be.

1. *Fundamental Categories*

a. *The Prophet as a Model for Action*
Weber's *Ancient Judaism* is a detailed reconstruction of Jewish
history[1] with the stated purpose of trying to ascertain why and how
the Jews had become a 'pariah people'.[2] This sociological problem, of
course, is also an aspect of his larger concern to understand the practical economic consequences of religious belief.[3] Interest in Weber's
views of prophets has often centered on his discussions of the distinctions between charismatic, legal and traditional authority and the
differences between the several kinds of religious leaders.[4] It is in
Ancient Judaism, however, that we move beyond the 'ideal types' to a
particular reconstruction;[5] and it is the monarchical prophets that are
of primary interest here.

According to his scheme, from the earlier war ecstatics of the tribal
confederacy there developed various kinds of prophets due to the
sociopolitical shift to the monarchy and the subsequent demilitariza-

---

1. Helpful summaries include F. Raphaël, 'Max Weber et le judaïsme antique',
ArEurSoc 11 (1970), pp. 297-336; D.L. Petersen, 'Max Weber and the Sociological
Study of Ancient Israel', in *Religious Change and Continuity* (ed. H. Johnson; San
Francisco: Jossey-Bass, 1979), pp. 117-49; T. Fahey, 'Max Weber's *Ancient
Judaism*', *AmJSoc* 88 (1982), pp. 62-87.

2. Weber, *Ancient Judaism*, pp. 3-5. Cf. A. Momigliano, 'A Note on Max
Weber's Definition of Judaism as a Pariah-Religion', *History and Theory* 19 (1980),
pp. 313-18.

3. C. Camic, 'Weber and the Judaic Economic Ethic: A Commentary on Fahey',
AmJSoc 89 (1983), pp. 1417-20.

4. See the references to Weber in the discussion of the 'prophetic' in Chapter 1.
Petersen traces the application of these ideas to biblical studies in *Israel's Prophets*,
pp. 9-15.

5. D. Emmett in 'Prophets and their Societies', *JRoyAnthI* 86 (1956), pp. 13-23,
contrasts Weber's ideal types with biblical data, yet ignores or is unaware of *Ancient
Judaism*. Contrast P.L. Berger, 'Charisma and Religious Innovation: The Social
Location of Israelite Prophecy', *AmSocRev* 28 (1963), pp. 949-50. Also note the
interaction with Weber's reconstruction by A. Neher, *Amos. Contribution a l'étude
du prophétisme* (Bibliothèque d'histoire de la Philosophie; Paris: Librarie
Philosophique J. Vrin, 2nd rev. edn, 1981), pp. 156-60, 237-50.

tion of the peasant class. Soon a professional *nebiim* group emerged who were preachers of good fortune and attached to the monarchy. But there was also a group of free *nebiim* who were to evolve into the 'classical prophets', the intellectual leaders of the opposition against the royal house.[1]

Although they came from diverse backgrounds, these free prophets agreed on a passionate ethical message directed against the many changes brought on by the monarchy. Weber describes them as 'political demagogues' and 'pamphleteers', for they were an intellectual elite, not political partisans or defenders of any particular social class. The masses were incapable of governing themselves, and hence the call for committed and competent leadership. Their support base was not among the masses (indeed the people were often hostile because of the prophetic attack on popular religion), and obviously not among the ruling classes and cultic institutions they criticized, but rather among those who defended pure Yahwism—that is, individual pious houses and the Levites. These free speakers championed a set of values and tried to redirect the conscience of the nation; as ideologues they offered no practical steps, no sociopolitical programs; they participated in no revolution.[2]

Petersen, in his recent study, utilizes role theory[3] to try to elucidate the various levels of the intensity of prophetic involvement (chapter 2) and to explain how roles require various skills and engender certain expectations (chapter 6). The larger part of his work, however, is devoted to trying to sort out the various biblical designations (role labels) for the prophets and to locate different kinds of prophets geographically and socially (chapters 3, 4). Although he admits that the titles get mixed together after the fall of the northern kingdom, through word studies and critical distinctions, he believes his reconstruction can be substantiated.

His thesis is that the category *hozeh* refers to prophets in Judah, *nabî'* to those in Israel. Basically this is asserted by appealing to Mic. 3.5-12 and to what he considers to be authentic Isaianic passages (Isa. 3.1-3; 28.7) where the *nabî'* is viewed by these southern prophets in a

---

1. Weber, *Ancient Judaism*, pp. 90-117.
2. *Ancient Judaism*, pp. 267-96.
3. Lang also appeals to role theory in *Monotheism*, pp. 104-13 (although he utilizes Sundén's role psychology).

negative light. His interpretation of Amos 7.12-15 is crucial. Because of the north–south distinction, these verses are taken to mean that both Amaziah and Amos are recognizing the geographically specific label distinction, but that the prophet is claiming the right to enact his prophetic role in Israel because of Yahweh's call. Accordingly then, Amos 2.11-12 refers to Israel's rejection of specifically northern prophets. The possibility of including Amos among the *hanneb î'îm* in 3.7 is eliminated because of the secondary nature of the verse.[1]

Both the *hozeh* and the *nabî'* are, in his estimation, 'central morality' prophets. These would be those related to important social institutions and whose task it was to legitimate public morality according to a particular symbolic universe. According to his proposal, the central prophets in Judah and Israel, two very distinct societies, appealed to two distinct (and mutually exclusive) theological traditions.[2] In sum, therefore, although complex biblical material confronts the interpreter, role theory permits one to appreciate the variety of prophetic experience and titles, and reconstruction allows (now necessary because of the subsequent mixing of terms in the later redactions of biblical texts) further geographic distinctions while maintaining some similarity in function.

The reconstructions by these two scholars locate the prophets socially in different manners. In Weber's case the classical prophets are political ideologues on the periphery criticizing the central authorities; for Petersen the *hozeh* and *nabî'*, at least, are somehow more closely tied to the monarchy, yet can maintain a critical posture based on their particular moral universe. In both cases prophets are neither politically partisan nor socially involved, and their activity is motivated primarily by religious concern.[3]

---

1. Petersen, *Israel's Prophets*, pp. 52-63. Wilson's study is more judicious with the evidence in *Prophecy and Society*, pp. 136-38, 254-56, 266-70.

2. Petersen, *Israel's Prophets*, pp. 63-88.

3. Lang also discusses the prophetic role in politics, but in a different section of his book than with which this study is concerned (*Monotheism*, pp. 60-91). In light of much recent conviction that the prophets lived in and spoke for solidarity with the poor, his reconstruction yields an interesting result (p. 68):

> In fact, all the prophets belong to the landowning nobility and so to the social stratum from which highly placed stated officials are recruited. . . the only groups exercising influence on the king are the land-owning upper classes and those prophets belonging to them. . . The prophet belongs to the nobility and can be seen as its commissioner.

b. *The Object of Prophetic Denunciation*

Weber's thesis is that the prophets were fighting against a change in the nation's way of life:

> Through all prophecy sounded the echoes of the 'nomadic ideal' as the tradition of the literati idealized the kingless past. . . Compared to the luxurious and therefore haughty present which was disobedient to Yahweh, the desert times remained to the prophets the truly pious epoch.[1]

The prophets railed against the professionalization of the army, the bureaucratization of the state, and the concentration of wealth and power in the urban centers. The tribal organization had been replaced by new social forms. Even though before the institution of the monarchy there had been class tensions and conflict between the urban patricians and the rural proletariat, Yahwism and the covenant had provided a religious cohesion. Now that faith was being challenged by new social and religious developments.

The prophetic criticism, however, was not limited to these threatening institutions and potent classes, but was also directed at the popular religion of the masses and the popular culture that was continually being influenced by Israel's neighbors. With the Levites they make a concerted effort to shape faith toward a more rational and ethical orientation.[2]

The element of Weber's complex presentation that was picked up by several subsequent biblical scholars was the idea of the social changes and conflicts due to the transition from rural and tribal life to the centralized urban civilization of the monarchical system,[3] from the

Lang never coordinates this perspective with his study of Amos in 'The Social Organization of Peasant Poverty'.

1. Weber, *Ancient Judaism*, p. 285.

2. For interaction with foreign ideas and morality, see Weber, *Ancient Judaism*, pp. 194-218; for the movement toward a more rational faith, pp. 219-34, 297-335. Weber also discusses the contribution of the prophets to exilic and postexilic Judaism with its pariah orientation (pp. 336ff., 380-82), but that topic lies beyond the scope of this study.

3. E.g. J. Lindblom, *Prophecy in Ancient Israel* (Philadelphia: Fortress Press, 1962), pp. 344-46; E. Neufeld, 'The Emergence of a Royal Urban Society in Ancient Israel', *HUCA* 31 (1960), pp. 31-53. Though Hahn links A. Causse to this 'nomadic ideal' approach (*The Old Testament in Modern Research*, p. 168), S.T. Kimbrough, Jr, asserts that Causse's concern with that idea depended more on a 'primitive mentality' perspective; the prophets in Causse's scheme serve as a transi-

collective solidarity of early Israel to the 'paganization' of the state.[1]

Lang's study, on the other hand, identifies the object of Amos's wrath as 'rent capitalism'. He is not the first to label the socio-economic system of Israel capitalistic,[2] but his work goes beyond a vague economic reference to an attempt to explain how that oppressive and exploitative system actually functioned.[3] Drawing upon social anthropolitical studies, he describes Israel as a 'peasant society'. In the particular arrangement known as 'rent capitalism' the peasant classes are dependent on urban money-lenders and merchants, and through exploitation, the ownership of land and labor are separated. In this kind of economic order the urban creditor has no sense of obligation to the rural debtor or tenant.

---

tional element from primitive collectivism and solidarity to a more ethical, individualistic, and rational faith (*Israelite Religion in Sociological Perspective: The Work of Antonin Causse* [Wiesbaden: Otto Harrasowitz, 1978], pp. 54-72, 102-105, 110-13). Raphaël details the legacy of Weber among Old Testament scholars who have explored the social world of ancient Israel in 'Max Weber et le judaïsme antique', pp. 330-36. Fahey is not so generous: 'it is easy to exaggerate his impact on biblical studies. . . In general, the style of institutional analysis favored by Weber has had at best merely a tributary influence on the mainstream of Bible studies' ('Max Weber's *Ancient Judaism*', p. 65 n. 5).

1. This term is taken from G.E. Mendenhall, who offers his own version of the sociopolitical and religious developments in 'The Monarchy', *Int* 29 (1975), pp. 155-70.

2. For example, F. Dijkema ('Le fond des propheties d'Amos', *OTS* 2 [1943], pp. 18-34) uses the term 'le capitalisme croissant' (p. 20); J.-L. Vesco ('Amos de Teqoa, defenseur de l'homme', *RB* 87 [1980], pp. 481-543), 'le capitalisme naissant' (p. 511); J.L. Mays ('Justice: Perspectives from the Prophetic Tradition', *Int* 37 [1983], pp. 5-17), 'early capitalism' (p. 9).

3. This approach of 'rent capitalism' had been used earlier by O. Loretz, 'Die prophetische Kritik des Rentcapitalismus: Grundlagen-Probleme der Prophetenforschung', *UF* 7 (1975), pp. 271-78, and more recently by R.B. Coote, *Amos among the Prophets: Composition and Theology* (Philadelphia: Fortress Press, 1981), pp. 24-39, and D.N. Premnath, 'Latifundialization and Isaiah 5:8-10', *JSOT* 40 (1988), pp. 49-60. Sicre appreciates the insights of this approach, although he recognizes limitations as well ('*Con los pobres*', pp. 82-83). Note the criticisms of Dearman, *Property Rights*, pp. 15, 133-35; and Fleischer, who himself proposes a hypothesis (based on studies by the French historian E. LeRoy Languedoc), which focuses on population growth, inheritance problems, and changes brought about by the development of the monarchy (*Menschenverkäufern*, pp. 359-62, 365-90).

In eighth-century Israel the ethos associated with this kind of society is reflected in the self-indulgent lifestyle of the rich townspeople. The oppression of the poor is evident in the treatment of indebted peasants. Lang turns to Amos 8.6 and 2.6 to reconstruct the debt system in Israel. Stating that the 'standard translations are misleading' (they usually have an ambiguous 'for'), he proposes consistently to read the *beth*'s in both verses as causal. These verses, therefore, give the reason for reducing the peasants to bond slavery as their debts. 'Because of money' would refer explicitly to a money debt, and 'because of a pair of sandals' would deal with a debt agreement (as pictured in Ruth 4.7; Ps. 60.8 [Heb. 60.10]). Amos 8.6 would describe the poor falling into abject dependency on the merchant: the inability to pay in the market place results in their being 'bought'—that is, their losing financial independence by being reduced into 'slave-like bondage' to the upper class. Amos 2.6, according to ancient parallels, would picture their sale overseas.[1]

In both studies the object of prophetic invective is in some sense the socioeconomic and political system, although the mechanics of the system's 'transgression' are understood differently. Weber focuses primarily on values, Lang on the structural organization itself.[2]

2. *Problems and Limitations in Method*

a. *Basic Criteria*

The evaluation of these explanatory models will proceed on two levels. First, how viable are these constructs in light of the data available, and how are the data themselves handled? Secondly, what sort of

---

1. Lang, *Monotheism*, pp. 121-27; *idem*, 'Sklaven und unfreie im Buch Amos (II 6, VIII 6)', *VT* 31 (1981), pp. 482-88. For a similar interpretation of 8.6, see J. Pons, *L'oppression dans l'Ancien Testament* (Paris: Letouzey & Ané, 1981), p. 72. Sicre also opts for this view but would take the verse literally, not metaphorically ('*Con los pobres*', pp. 140-41 n. 71).

2. Petersen does not really detail the object of the prophet's wrath. Consistent with his North–South hypothesis is his discussion of the disparate symbolic universes of the two nations that their respective prophets legitimate (*Israel's Prophets*, pp. 64-68, 79-88). There is no mention of nor investigation into the sharp clashes, both theological and social, that these 'central *morality*' prophets (emphasis added) had with their alleged symbolic universes and the structures that these would sustain.

distinctions and clarifications are necessary to assess the value of a theory for developing a 'prophetic model' today? Instead of critiquing point by point the multiple claims of each study, this initial part will pick out certain elements within the framework of two general methodological weaknesses that are inherent in any reconstruction project.

The problem of the availability of data. Weber's massive study has been criticized for various reasons, but one liability which clearly stands out is simply its age. Old Testament studies have moved on, and new insights from comparative studies of ancient and modern societies and fresh perspectives on biblical faith have changed the picture of the prophets commonly held early in this century. Although Weber differed from those of his time who would have seen the prophets as originators of a monotheistic ethic, he still, like many others, posited, among other things, too much of a cleavage between priest and prophet.[1] Weber was openly dependent on much of Wellhausen's work,[2] yet some of those positions can no longer be sustained.

It is not that Weber's study is of no value. Many of his insights still hold, and some of his hypothesis was before its time, but it, like any theory, is a child of its time. This limitation is compounded by the very comprehensiveness of his work: the broader the model, the greater the danger of multiple errors and the 'ripple effect' of misjudgment or lack of data throughout the model.

The availability of data has another dimension, because one is dealing with two disciplines, biblical studies and sociology. Weber was a sociologist, not a biblical scholar. His use of biblical data was determined by his acquaintance with biblical research. This problem obviously works both ways. Biblical scholars trying to use sociological

1. For developments and how they would affect Weber's thesis see H. Cazelles, 'Bible, histoire et sociologie du prophétisme', *CahRRRel* 3 (1973), pp. 7-15; C.S. Rodd, 'Max Weber and Ancient Judaism', *SJT* 32 (1979); Berger, 'Charisma and Religious Innovation'. Though J.G. Williams criticizes Berger's view, the point made still holds ('The Social Location of Israelite Prophecy', *JAAR* 39 [1969], pp. 153-65).

2. 'Wellhausen brilliantly utilized methods which he brought to highest systematic perfection' (Weber, *Ancient Judaism*, p. 426 n. 1). Cf. J.A. Holstein's critical assessment in 'Max Weber and Biblical Scholarship', *HUCA* 46 (1975), pp. 159-79.

methods can be at the mercy of an inadequate exposure or understanding of sociological theory (in all its depth and variety) and
procedure.[1] Efforts at reconstruction, therefore, not only are children
of their time, but can very well be confused offspring of ignorance. In
his evaluation of this sociologist's work, Lang comments:

> Because Weber accepts the exegetical opinion of a particular contemporary
> theologian, his description must remain unsatisfactory; in many points it is
> out of date to the same extent as the literature used by him is obsolete.[2]

In addition to the issues of time and expertise is the question of
exactly just how much data are at hand to build a model. Lang, for
instance, to postulate 'rent capitalism' in Amos marshalls evidence
from four strands: the opulent lifestyle of the rich, exploitation of
tenants, debt-bondage, and the corn trade as a source of income of the
upper classes. Although these evils might exist in such an economic
system, they are in no way necessarily limited to it. His proposal concerning debt-bondage and the selling of slaves is based on two verses
(8.6; 2.6) and depends on a particular interpretation of the preposition
beth, about which there exists no universal agreement.[3] The text gives

---

1. Wilson, *Prophecy and Society,* pp. 15-16; *idem, Sociological Approaches to
the Old Testament* (Guides to Biblical Scholarship; Philadelphia: Fortress Press,
1984), pp. 28-29; D. Fiensy, 'Using the Nuer Culture of Africa in Understanding
the Old Testament: An Evaluation', *JSOT* 38 (1987), pp. 73-83. Rogerson's
Anthropology and the Old Testament is a mine of case studies dealing with this very
problem.
2. B. Lang, 'Max Weber und Israels Propheten: Eine kritische Stellungnahme',
ZRGG 36 (1984), p. 161. After giving an overview of Weber's view of the
prophets, Lang criticizes him for reflecting too much the views of the last century and
then contrasts the reconstruction with his own. In his book, however, Lang does
offer appreciative comments on Weber, employs his ideas regarding various kinds of
authority, and approves of his grasp of the political use of prophetic writing
(*Monotheism,* pp. 12, 65-67, 80-82, respectively).
3. The *beth* is often taken as *pretii.* In the case of 2.6 sometimes the phrase is then
taken to refer to the bribing of the judge (in both cola, or only in the first) or to the
compensation to creditors for the debt owed, whether large or small. For discussions
with bibliography of the various viewpoints see Sicre, *'Con los pobres',* pp. 105-
107 (2.6), 140-41 (8.6); J.A. Soggin, *The Prophet Amos: A Translation and
Commentary* (trans. J. Bowden; London: SCM Press, 1987), *ad loc.* For these uses
of *beth* (causal, *pretii*), see GKC 119p; B.K. Waltke and M. O'Conner, *An
Introduction to Biblical Hebrew Syntax* (Winona Lake, IN: Eisenbrauns, 1990),
11.2.5d, e.

precious little detail for reconstructing the particular market system; what clearly is registered are abuses, but how far can those data take us? Though Lang begins with the confident assertion that Amos's 'literary legacy provides us with much evidence for the economic and social situation that obtained in his society',[1] at the end of his essay he makes an honest, but surprising, admission:

> In saying all this I am well aware that I am going slightly beyond the information given in the biblical sources. But read in the light of anthropology, the scattered bits of economic and social information fit into a definite and clear picture known as rent capitalism.[2]

The related question about what kind of reliable evidence the text can provide us with has been the source of much recent debate.[3]

All of these problems are heightened by the impossibility of anything more than tenuous verification. The distance is too great and evidence too meager to substantiate with absolute certainty the kind of self-confident claims of many of these theories. Rodd concludes:

> My plea is that there is a world of difference between sociology applied to contemporary society, where the researcher can test his theories against evidence which he collects, and historical sociology where he has only fossilized evidence that has been preserved by chance or for purposes very different from that of the sociologist. It is a cardinal error to move promiscuously between the two.[4]

The problem of the arbitrary use of the data. Related to the issue of how much material is available is the matter of how it is used to formulate a theoretical construct. At a very fundamental level this is a philosophical dilemma. Research is affected by a whole set of inter-

---

1. Lang, *Monotheism*, p. 115.

2. *Monotheism*, p. 127. Fleischer criticizes the Loretz–Lang effort precisely because of the lack of hard evidence (*Menschenverkäufern*, pp. 265-67).

3. Note J.M. Sasson's distinction between two sets of 'facts' and 'visions' (i.e. those of the Hebrew writer and those of the modern scholar) in 'On Choosing Models for Recreating Israelite Pre-Monarchic History', *JSOT* 21 (1981), pp. 3-8, and the more radical program of K.W. Whitelam, 'Recreating the History of Israel', *JSOT* 35 (1986), pp. 45-70. Lang himself in his opening essay questions the reliability of the biblical sources in various places (*Monotheism*, pp. 25, 26, 28, 30, 39).

4. C.S. Rodd, 'On Applying a Sociological Theory to Biblical Studies', *JSOT* 19 (1981), p. 105.

related presuppositions, whether cultural, ideological, intellectual, or socioeconomic. This phenomenon has been effectively underscored by liberation theologians as well as other theologians from the Two-Thirds World in their telling criticisms of western theology and theologizing.[1] Sasson, Dearman and Herion have all pointed out in recent articles how Old Testament scholarly work and approaches have reflected the particular contexts of scholars.[2] In an observation with great implications for those who are trying to use sociological approaches to derive guidelines for modern praxis, Sasson points out:

> Thus, whenever a scholar compares kingship, democracy, absolutism, etc., in the Ancient Near East and in the OT, his comparison is understood by his audience—and by him, for that matter—not so much because he has recreated the political realities in Israel and in the Near East, but because he is using currently understood models as frames of reference.[3]

Models 'ring true' because they are our creations. One cannot help but be struck by the differences that exist between Weber's solitary demagogues, Petersen's neatly packaged central morality prophets, and Lang's socially well-placed spokesmen for the nobility. . . and how far removed these all are from the thundering denouncers of injustice envisioned by some non-western theologians!

Besides this inherent and inescapable arbitrariness of perspective is the arbitrariness of the utilization of the data, or the tyranny of the 'infallibility complex'. Theories try to say too much and go to great

---

1. The issue of pre-understandings from the Latin American perspective will be explored more fully in the next chapter.

2. Sasson, 'On Choosing Models', pp. 8-17; J.A. Dearman, 'Hebrew Prophecy and Social Criticism: Some Observations for Perspective', *PerspRelSt* 9 (1982), pp. 131-43; G.A. Herion, 'The Impact of Modern and Social Science Assumptions on the Reconstruction of Israelite History', *JSOT* 34 (1986), pp. 3-33; note also the comments by S. Holm-Nielsen, 'Die Sozialkritik des Propheten', in *Denkender Glaube: Festschrift Carl Heinz Ratschow* (ed. O. Kaiser; Berlin: de Gruyter, 1976), pp. 8, 12, 22. It is interesting to note recent ideological criticisms that have been levelled at Weber: Holstein sharply criticizes Weber for his supposed objectivity and the subsequent handling of the text ('Max Weber and Biblical Scholarship'); Gottwald specifically criticizes Weber's notion of 'elective affinity' and 'co-determination' of religion and economics. Gottwald himself takes an explicitly, historical-materialistic approach (*The Tribes of Yahweh: A Sociology of the Religion of Liberated Israel, 1250–1050 BCE* [Maryknoll: Orbis Books, 1979], pp. 627-31).

3. Sasson, 'On Choosing Models', p. 8.

lengths to appear comprehensive and irrefutable. Again Petersen can serve as an illustration. To make his North–South distinction he points to Amos 7.12 and a few verses in Micah and Isaiah that give negative pictures of the *nabî'* (the part of Isa. 29.10 that would similarly portray the *ḥozeh* is eliminated from consideration as a deutero-prophetic commentary). He goes on to say that in Isaiah only the *ḥozeh* and *roeh* are viewed positively, and that therefore these are the Judaic prophets. Incredibly, this conclusion is based on only one verse in Isaiah (30.10) and ignores the fact that the mere mention of the *nabî'*, in whatever light, demonstrates the active presence of his northern 'central morality' functionaries in Judah. Moreover, although Petersen concedes that Isaiah's contemporary, Micah, lumps both *ḥozeh* and *nabî'* together in a condemnation (Mic. 3.5-8), he refuses to allow the passage to have any bearing on his reconstruction. Tucked away in a footnote is the admission that verses in both prophetic books 'demonstrate that the title *nabî'* could be used to label prophetic figures in Judah'.[1] How then can he maintain his tight distinctions (especially when he stresses to such a great degree the differences in context and theology), if both kinds in these verses are admitted to be crossing borders and are being situated in both centers of national activity? Not only does Petersen's hypothesis suffer from a paucity of data, it is also not altogether consistent in its presentation.

There is yet another serious issue crucial to this enterprise of historical reconstruction. Arbitrariness can also be manifest in the employment of the social sciences. Several have wisely warned against too facile and uninformed a use of sociological theories,[2] but what has usually not been provided is a guide as to how to articulate properly a hypothetical construct. It is this problem of the methodology of social theory that the next section will examine.

b. *Constructing a Social Theory*
It is not sufficient to use a given sociological approach because of the

1. Petersen, *Israel's Prophets*, p. 111 n. 21 (Mic. 2.9-12 should be corrected to Mic. 3.9-12). This is just one example of caveats and changes to fit his argument. Note, for instance, the suggestion to change the word order of the Masoretic text in 2 Kgs 17.13. This alteration, which does have some support, serves to parallel his reconstruction (p. 109 n. 4).

2. See the earlier discussion in this chapter entitled 'The problem of the availability of data'.

intriguing and illuminating parallels or insights it can provide for elucidating the biblical data and proposing an explanatory model. What is so often lacking in the multitude of sociological studies that are appearing in many fields of biblical research is a circumspect reflection on exactly how such an approach should be pursued. Helpful in this regard is W.G. Runciman's *A Treatise on Social Theory*, which discusses the four tasks which should be distinguished, but are often confused, in social theories.[1] Bernhard Lang's 'The Social Organization of Peasant Poverty in Biblical Israel' will serve as a test case.

The first point for consideration is what Runciman labels *reportage*,[2] which involves the description of the actions, attitudes or states of affairs to be investigated. This level of 'primary understanding' gives priority to the account given by the agents under study (as does each subsequent one). The theorists' own observations and final report should be acceptable to these agents and other rival observers.[3] In addition, whether the report is couched in the form of a narrative, generalization, aphorism or pattern, the dangers to be avoided are the use of what he calls 'pre-emptive taxonomies' and the selective or manipulative presentation of the available data.

It is often the case that a particular report can be pre-empted by other reports, so that the present one follows from the others indisputably ('the deductive mode'), logically but still with a high degree

---

1. W.G. Runciman, *A Treatise on Social Theory*. I. *The Methodology of Social Theory* (Cambridge: Cambridge University Press, 1983). Rogerson gives a helpful summary of the various parts of Runciman's book and utilizes his approach to evaluate the work of some biblical scholars ('The Use of Sociology', pp. 250-56).

2. Runciman, *Treatise*, ch. 2.

3. This approach is not the same as the useful observations of M. Harris, 'History and Significance of the Emic/Etic Distinction', *AnnRevAnth* 5 (1976), pp. 329-50; both the emic and the etic perspectives (i.e. of those observed and of the observer) are part and parcel of the whole process of constructing a social theory:

> At the risk of repetition, let me insist that the problem is not that of reconciling the viewpoint of the observer with that of those whose behaviour he observes—the 'emic/etic' distinction. . . It is true that the relation between observers' and agents' categories is inherently problematic. But the problem will not be resolved by keeping them apart, since the necessary distinction between reportage of agents' behaviour on the one hand and its explanation, description and evaluation on the other depends from the outset on the inclusion in reportage of enough (but not too much) of what goes on 'inside the natives' heads' (Runciman, *Treatise*, p. 119).

of certainty ('the semi-deductive mode') or less assuredly, because of dependence on other reports not directly given and which themselves may be open to question ('the quasi-deductive mode').

How does Lang's study measure up to these various requirements? An obvious problem with his hypothesis, which was mentioned earlier, is the lack of hard data for the report. Actually, the section preceding the presentation of the biblical data sets the scene for the reader, yet these pages are drawn from modern investigations and reports. The textual information that can be gleaned from Amos is simply attached as illustrative material to the 'rent capitalism' society already provided (and this of only a few items). Although others might all agree on the existence of oppression, is the market system envisaged by Lang sufficiently convincing to quell doubts satisfactorily?

The problems are multiplied when the other criteria are brought to bear. For instance, although Lang records observations from his source, Amos, has he incorporated the breadth of the social critique and the complexity of its vision of Israelite society? Could not the entire nation stand under moral condemnation, and not just the privileged? For example, Marlene Fendler's study on the social problems in Amos is much more sensitive at this point and suggests that the dynamics of the market place, with all its intrigue and desperation, absorbs the gamut of social classes.[1] On the other hand, might there not also exist the possibility that the prophet's vocabulary assumes distinctions among the oppressed and actually singles out one particular group (say, the poor peasantry) to defend?[2]

There is also the problem of a 'pre-emptive taxonomy'. Lang bases his hypothesis to a large degree on peasant studies, but interestingly, this term for Runciman illustrates the very issue at stake:

Its application depends, as all observers will agree, on some shared con-

1. M. Fendler, 'Zur Sozialkritik des Amos: Versuch einer wirtschafts- und sozialgeschichtlichen Interpretation alttestamentlicher Texte', *EvT* 33 (1973), pp. 32-53. Cf. Fleischer's critique of Fendler, *Menschenverkäufern*, pp. 295-99.

2. Sicre, '*Con los pobres*', pp. 145-52. He also analyzes Fendler's option. Of course, there is the possibility that Amos is not directing his criticism (only) at an avaricious wealthy class. Dearman, for example, lays the blame for much of the injustice at the feet of a state judicial and land grant system (*Property Rights*). Cf. Fleischer on Dearman's hypothesis, *Menschenverkäufern*, p. 294.

ception of what it is that a 'peasant' typically does. The trouble is not that the constitutive intentions and beliefs of what he does are problematic. . . But no such convention will be of any help in bringing sociologists, anthropologists and historians of rival schools into agreement with one another, for the disagreements between them are not over what the 'peasants' were doing but over why, or more importantly, why not. 'Peasant', in other words, is another of those standard sociological terms which can only be theory-neutrally construed if either so loosely or so restrictively defined as to defeat the purpose of introducing it in the first place.[1]

This reality is readily apparent by checking the sources cited by Lang in his footnotes: the peasant studies of Robert Redfield,[2] Eric R. Wolf,[3] and George Dalton.[4] Each of these is very different from the other two: Redfield focuses on peasant culture, its ideological process, symbolic communication and world views; Wolf, while appreciative of Redfield's insights, criticizes him for ignoring the socioeconomic, class and power tensions and conflicts inherent in all societies;[5] Dalton, for his part, takes issue with Wolf's 'misleading generalizations' of peasant economic life, and is sharply answered in reply.[6] The differences between them are recognized by others as well. The Marxist anthropologist Maurice Godelier approvingly quotes Wolf and then goes on to say:

Peasants then, do not form a 'society', nor even a 'subsociety', a sub-culture (in Redfield's terminology), but a 'dominated class' and the nature and role of this class differs according to specific relations of production which make them dependent on the ruling class. One has, therefore, to

1. Runciman, *Treatise*, p. 125.
2. R. Redfield, *Peasant Society and Culture: An Anthropological Approach to Civilization* (Chicago: University of Chicago Press, 1956).
3. E.R. Wolf, *Peasants* (Englewood Cliffs, NJ: Prentice–Hall, 1966).
4. G. Dalton, 'Peasantries in Anthropology and History', *CurrAnth* 13 (1972), pp. 385-407.
5. E.R. Wolf, *Anthropology* (New York: Norton, 2nd edn, 1974), pp. 58-61, 82-84. Cf. E.R. Wolf, *Europe and the People without History* (Berkeley: University of California Press, 1982), pp. 3-24.
6. Dalton, 'Peasantries', pp. 401-402. Wolf's reply appears on pp. 410-411. Redfield is criticized at several points in Dalton's article, but is not given an extended treatment as is Wolf.

characterize these relations of production each time and that is what Eric
Wolf has tried to do. . . [1]

On closer inspection, Lang relies on Wolf's socioeconomic thrust,
an orientation perhaps hinted at by his opening his essay with a quote
from Marx. His, then, is a 'quasi-deductive' report—that is, dependent
on other reports, which themselves are open to further scrutiny.

At this most fundamental level of *reportage*, therefore, Lang's study
is in a precarious position. Handling inadequately perhaps what little
data the text of Amos does provide, he has apparently not scrutinized
sufficiently the problematic nature of the area of sociological research
to which he appeals.

Runciman moves on to discuss the next concern in social theory,
that of *explanation*.[2] Explanation, 'secondary understanding', goes a
step further than reportage and tries to account for causes, social
structures and relationships; in short, to construct a conceptual model.
What makes for good explanations? Runciman observes that:

> first they specify an antecedent which, given a set of initial conditions and
> constraints which rival observers can check for themselves, can be
> claimed to have made the decisive difference; and second, they furnish a
> plausible answer to the question why the chosen antecedent should have
> the capacity to be decisive in the first place.[3]

But this necessitates that any model must be transparently frank:

> The reader who is presented with an explanation which is consistent with
> the reported evidence and a theoretical grounding claimed to underlie it
> must be told not only what sort of evidence might have invalidated the
> initial hypothesis but also what sort of evidence might show that the cause
> was not a cause for the reason claimed—in which case the theory is the
> wrong one or the ' "refutable" protective belt' has indeed been refuted.[4]

1. M. Godelier, *Perspectives in Marxist Anthropology* (trans. R. Brain;
Cambridge Studies in Social Anthropology, 18; Cambridge: Cambridge University
Press, 1977), p. 31. For Wolf's use of Marxism, see *Europe*, pp. 19-24, 73-100,
400-404, and more recently 'An Interview with Eric Wolf', *CurrAnth* 28 (1987),
pp. 107-18, especially 109, 112-17.

2. Runciman, *Treatise*, ch. 3.

3. *Treatise*, p. 175.

4. *Treatise*, p. 186. By the ' "refutable" protective belt' he means the researcher's
theory that had been built around the untestable presuppositions which underlie his
social theory. Thus, either the choice of theory was mistaken or the theory itself is
untenable. See his discussion, pp. 186-93.

Lang mentions three kinds of domain described in Wolf's study—
patrimonial, prebendal, and mercantile—and then centers on and illustrates a particular kind of system of the last type, 'rent capitalism'.[1]
To return to Runciman's first criterion for a successful explanation,
however, is to be immediately confronted precisely with the lack of 'a
set of initial conditions and constraints which rival observers can
check for themselves'. What is more, the general data found in the
text could fit in several different systems. Amos never discloses in any
detail the actual workings of the market place nor of the economic
relationships between the rich and poor; in short, the biblical text
never explains why and how things are happening the way they are in
Israel. Must rent capitalism then be the one 'decisive antecedent',
the only possible cause, of that exploitative socioeconomic system? Does
the paucity of textual information with its limited economic indicators
demand this choice? Correlation in some details cannot validate or
prove an explanation.

These questions lead on to the second requisite, namely the capability to demonstrate why this explanatory approach is superior to other
rival theories. Yet Lang never explains why the other two domain
categories (patrimonial and prebendal) are not viable. The prebendal
arrangement, for example, where land is handed over to state officials
as grants of income or the tax collection is centralized and in which
ceremonial ritual plays a crucial role, could also be a candidate for a
monarchical society. More important is Wolf's observation that these
forms of domain usually coexist in a variety of combinations; indeed,

---

1. Wolf, *Peasants*, pp. 50-57. As does Wolf, Lang mentions Hans Bobeck, 'The
Main Stages in Socioeconomic Evolution from a Geographic Point of View', in
Readings in Cultural Geography (ed. P.L. Wagner and M.W. Mikesell; Chicago:
University of Chicago Press, 1962), pp. 233-40. Loretz's article ('Die prophetische
Kritik des Rentcapitalismus') is heavily dependent on Bobeck. Though Coote cites
Wolf, he mistakenly assigns rent capitalism to the prebendal arrangement (*Amos*,
p. 29). Mention should also be made of the possible problems of applying a
twentieth-century theory to Old Testament times. It is true that this is the only kind of
tool that is available and that this theory can help in illuminating the text, yet Dalton's
position is that peasant societies change through time and that different configurations
develop in different latitudes and epochs. How adequate then could Wolf's theory
be? Note Lang's caveat, *Monotheism*, p. 167 n. 218, and the quote from Rodd, at
the end of the earlier discussion in this chapter entitled 'The problem of the
availability of data'.

rent capitalism arises out of a particular configuration of the three![1]

A third aspect of social theory Runciman calls *description*.[2] This 'tertiary understanding' should not be confused with *reportage*, the recording of observations. Here the aim is to ascertain what life is really like, to explore the agent's *Weltanschauung*, to so conceptualize the investigated society that both the agents and the reader judge the description as comprehensible and authentic.

Amos reports the attitudes and lifestyle of the privileged in several passages, but never gives equal details of peasant life. Lang notes the former, but to fill in the gaps of the latter he brings in descriptions of contemporary peasant societies. Using more modern parallels to convey a desired description to contemporary readers methodologically is not necessarily unsound. It is in fact often unavoidable. But again the fundamental problem of the available data rears its head: there is nothing in the text with which Lang can bridge the 'experience gap' between the biblical and the modern worlds.

But even if one were to grant the representability of these descriptions for a society almost three millennia ago, can they be said to be a comprehensive and authentic portrayal of peasant life? In his desire to underline the differences between the urban rich and rural poor in a specific realm, the economic, Lang fails to mention the common ground between them, a fact that Redfield's peasant study does emphasize.[3] The relationship between these two groups is seen to be complex, dynamic, and dialectical. Both can share, in their own way, in a common symbolic world and traditions, and both integrate a common history. Moreover, no morality can be limited to just one social stratum because of the influences on character due to the vigorous nature of cultural reality and socioeconomic conditions. Thus

1. Wolf, *Peasants*, pp. 54-55. Dearman's thesis of a land grant system would come under the prebendal category.

2. Runciman, *Treatise*, ch. 4.

3. Redfield, *Peasant Society*, pp. 67-104, 129-42. He makes a pertinent comment in a section dealing with shared values:

> It will not do to describe these relations between the urban and rural population only as relations of ruler and ruled or of exploiter and exploited, although these elements are likely to be present. The student will want also to describe the prestige or contempt, the feelings of superiority and inferiority, and the examples of excellence to be imitated or of baseness to be avoided that may be present in the relations between peasant and elite (p. 64).

morality is never class-specific. One important implication of this observation is that the 'morality of abuse' can also be found among the poor, not just suffered by them.

Lang, therefore, has confused *description* with *explanation* by reducing peasant life to his neat economic model of rural–urban/ poor–rich tensions. Even Wolf, upon whom Lang depends so much for economic insights, details the complex religious and ideological bonds between the peasantry and the larger social order.[1] Lang has fallen into two errors of misapprehension in description: incompleteness and oversimplification.[2]

Runciman's last distinction is the issue of *evaluation* in social theory.[3] Basically the point here is to judge whether the researched behavior, events or state of affairs are good or bad, again with a sensitivity to keeping separate the agents' own evaluation from the investigator's. The pitfalls here involve, for instance, unconsciously preempting the former by the latter or deliberately manipulating and misconstruing the report, explanation or description according to a hidden ideological agenda of whatever sort.

Lang's study does convey the evaluation of the life of the wealthy by Amos, whose condemnation is part and parcel of that picture of life in Israel. At this point, one perhaps would question whether Lang, however, has passed on to his readers the full scope of the text's denunciation. The essay's primary concern, however, is in providing an explanation of the socioeconomic system of Israel, so there is no

1. Wolf, *Peasants*, pp. 96-106.

2. Still another possibility is the error of 'ahistoricity', which 'typically arises where the researcher forgets that a set of reports about the behaviour of the members of an earlier society all of which may be perfectly accurate as they stand will be a misdescription if so presented as to imply that they were capable of conceptualizing their own experience in the idiom of a later one' (Runciman, *Treatise*, p. 246). The other major kind of mistake mentioned by Runciman is 'mystification', which also has its sub-categories (*Treatise*, pp. 246-49). Lang never considers the possibility of an inauthentic description on Amos's part, even though he elsewhere had placed the prophet within a particular class and specific ideological and religious process in his 'Yahweh-alone' proposal. Cohen, on the other hand, will say that the prophetic message was deliberately exaggerated and simplistic in accordance with its anti-establishment aims ('Prophets as Revolutionaries').

3. Runciman, *Treatise*, ch. 5. There is no question in Lang's work of a misevaluation (because of 'false consciousness' or 'bad faith') by Amos or the text. For a discussion of these forms of error, see Runciman, *Treatise*, pp. 312-18.

elaboration of the fuller evaluation in Amos, which would entail mentioning, for instance, the many judgment passages in the book. Lang's own evaluation can be only construed indirectly: his apparent approval of the prophet's accusations (e.g. his introducing discussions of the relevant biblical passages with phrases such as 'shameless luxury' and 'ruthlessly exploited'), the initial quote from Marx, and his mention of more contemporary abuses.[1] Any possibility of accusing him of a pre-emptive evaluation would have to prove the skewing of his work according to a certain economic ideology or class commitment. Such an appraisal is unobtainable from the essay itself.

In summary then, Runciman calls for distinguishing *reportage*, *explanation*, *description* and *evaluation* in the construction of social theories. Each aspect appeals to different criteria, and to confuse these four levels is to muddle the hypothetical construct itself. Each of the theories studied in this chapter could be accordingly scrutinized. In Lang's case, a report is almost impossible to make because of the lack of data; the explanation, in the final analysis, is more projected upon the text than capable of being deduced from it; the description is an inadequate picture of peasant life and actually betrays its dependence upon and entanglement with the explanation; the evaluation, although secondary to the primary purpose of the essay, is generally faithful to the text and fair to the reader, although perhaps more restrictive than the prophet himself might have intended.

3. Conclusion and Challenge

This chapter has sought to raise questions concerning the use of sociological research in biblical studies. Although these approaches can each help interpret particulars within the text, much care must be taken in offering a reconstruction of the social world of ancient Israel. The variety of models and proposals testifies to the difficulty of understanding and construing the data. This picture of disparate, and sometimes conflicting, reconstructions would be even more complex if mention were made of the wide range of form-critical hypotheses and historical studies attempting to identify the prophet's vocation, theological traditions and broader setting (see Appendix 1).

---

1. The two headings mentioned appear in *Monotheism*, pp. 121, 124 respectively. For more modern parallels see pp. 120-21, 123.

The hazards in sociological reconstructions are multiple, as has been demonstrated on a broad level in the twin tests of the availability of data and their arbitrary use, and on a more rigorous plane according to the methodological distinctions presented by Runciman. Each of these evaluative procedures demonstrates the tenuousness of much of the work that has been done by biblical scholars.

Clearly what is needed is not only methodological clarity and honesty, but also an awareness of how sociological approaches can best serve biblical research. Some can be manifestly helpful in illuminating different aspects of the biblical material: the explanatory hypotheses can generate deeper insights not only as they explore and pinpoint textual particulars, but also as they might suggest clues as to the myriad of possible causes behind them.

All of these efforts should be encouraged. There is yet another responsibility, however, that has not been mentioned but which is crucial to my enterprise. Though related to warnings at each level of the dangers of the possible pre-emptive intrusion of the researcher's own values and theories, this next step would extend the concern to clarify parameters for proper sociological method to include the *utilization* of the results of sociological inquiry. Care here would need to be taken to avoid the proposing or defending of a particular point of view because of the supposed 'unavoidable conclusions of scientific research'.[1]

In the case of biblical studies, this move could involve, for instance, a supposed rigorous and objective investigation with a sociological tool to reconstruct and evaluate the ancient world and then the subsequent appropriation of the gleaned 'insights and truths' with a view towards their modern contextualization—analogically, for example, to a parallel situation (e.g. oppression) or historical process (e.g. liberation).[2] This sort of application has already been made and

---

1. Runciman, *Treatise*, pp. 318-41.

2. For example, Rogerson faults Gottwald for having confused Runciman's third and fourth categories ('The Use of Sociology', pp. 254-55). Although Gottwald does distinguish between 'emics' and 'etics' (*Tribes of Yahweh*, pp. 785-86 nn. 558, 564), one could still apply Runciman's tests of 'misdescription' (e.g. 'inauthenticity') to his description of the life and faith of pre-monarchic Israel. Gottwald's ultimate concerns go much beyond a simple investigation of pre-monarchic Israel, however, to modern struggles of liberation (*Tribes of Yahweh*, pp. 700-709).

For a recent example utilizing Amos: Michael Walzer in his use of Amos has

cannot but be increasingly so as attempts to make the Old Testament sociopolitically relevant continue to increase.

Methodological confusion and abuse can arise because of the powerful combination of respect for detailed inquiry and the moral authority of the Bible. The danger of misapplication is thus compounded in this wedding of science and Scripture. In other words, not only can social studies be used to elucidate the text, but then these and the resulting reconstructed world (with the attending biblical authority, as it were) can claim to clarify the present and provide norms for action. This 'sociohermeneutical' circle can entail the elaboration of novel approaches or the 'plundering of the Egyptians', where other studies are brought in to substantiate one's claims and model. In the latter case, the original scope of a work is set aside to assist in the formulation of a larger construct and program.[1] Herion correctly points out:

> Here the past becomes an authoritative vehicle for expressing and legitimizing contemporary concerns. . . When the authority of 'the past' is combined with the authority of 'science'—not to mention the additional authority that in certain religious circles adheres to any statement made about the Bible or ancient Israel—an interdisciplinary study combining history, social science and biblical studies becomes ripe for ideological exploitation. One is no longer certain whether the study is an objective accounting of the 'real' past or a partisan advocacy of a desirable future.[2]

Others then have also pointed out how arbitrary (though still useful) sociological approaches can be. What has not been said, but is stressed

---

appropriated some of Weber's model in *Ancient Israel* to help describe what he would consider to be the 'social practice' of the 'connected critic'—i.e., one who is committed to the socially constructed world of his community, although who is at enough distance to challenge the accepted morality and vision of life. The prophet Amos, for Walzer, provides an image of a repeatable practice (*Interpretation and Social Criticism* [Cambridge, MA: Harvard University Press, 1987]. For his use of Weber see pp. 71-72, 79-80, 91).

1. E.g. Gottwald's critical use of Noth and Mendenhall. From a different angle, note J.P. Miranda's use of biblical scholarship to separate the exodus from covenant and so make Yahweh's response solely one of action against (any) social injustice, then and now (*Marx and the Bible: A Critique of the Philosophy of Oppression* [trans. J. Eagleson; Maryknoll: Orbis Books, 1974], pp. 78-103). C. Rowland and M. Corner explain how Liberation Theology has utilized critical studies in work on the New Testament (*Liberating Exegesis*).

2. Herion, 'Impact', p. 26.

here, is that an uncertain model, when it is taken out of the safe intellectual confines of the university and is used in real-life struggles for liberation and freedom, can be a potent ideological tool sanctified with biblico-religious authority. The stakes are high, and sociological studies are no longer just 'interesting'; they are part of an ideological and social commitment. The claims made by these approaches must therefore be humble and tentative and handled with an acute sense of responsibility.

Indeed, one could go further and state that reconstruction models cannot provide the kind of information required to posit confidently and with a high degree of certainty either a model for modern 'prophetic' sociopolitical activity or the identification of a specific system for 'prophetic' denunciation. What this inspection of Weber, Petersen and Lang does demonstrate is that the data are too scanty and complex to allow the consideration of using any reconstruction model in some ethically *prescriptive* way. These models are, in the final analysis, potentially *illuminative* of textual particulars and context; they can be nothing else.

If the text cannot guarantee constructs based on historical reconstructions, in what alternative ways, if any, can sociological approaches provide guidance for moral activity in the present? Is there any manner of addressing the particular concern to gain insights from the prophetic literature as to how one is to function sociopolitically within modern cultural reality and processes of change? The next chapter will attempt to begin to formulate an answer to these questions.

Chapter 3

A WORLD WITHIN THE WORLD:
RELIGION AND MORALITY IN CONTEXT

To attempt to apply the prophetic concerns to modern realities according to a historical reconstruction has been shown not to be methodologically viable. The data cannot permit anything substantial enough to postulate with much detail the system which is the object of prophetic invective. What is decried can be generalized as 'oppression', 'judicial abuse' and 'exploitation', but the precise mechanisms of these social evils for the most part elude the researcher. Ascertaining, with any rigor, a consistent, coherent and clear picture of prophetic activity and social class within that system is also beyond reach. Accordingly, to try to bridge the gap of millennia on a system level (for example, by claiming that now as 'then' capitalism is the culprit), or by a behavior-imitation claim, is untenable.

What can be the utility, therefore, of the social sciences in the effort by the Christian church to bring the prophetic material to bear upon the exigencies within the broader milieu? Perhaps the solution to this query lies in approaching the task from another perspective, in asking a question of a very different sort. My proposal is that a key to unleashing the critical power of the text lies not in seeking to reconstruct the system the prophets might have attacked, but rather in trying to ascertain how the prophetic text functions in a given context. The goal then is to attempt to clarify *the use of the Bible in the moral life of the Christian community in today's world*. The focus of the study, therefore, is no longer the identification of an elusive historical construal (perhaps with modern parallels), but instead an exploration of Christian moral life and ethical discourse in a particular socio-cultural setting, of a way of looking at and living in the world.

To present this different approach the chapter is divided into three major parts. The first, instead of beginning with sociological studies of the Old Testament, utilizes interpretive anthropology, the sociology of knowledge, and narrative ethics as the theoretical foundation for studying life today. From within this framework, the nature of religion and the complex make-up of morality will be explained with a view to elucidating their role in the construction, maintenance and challenging of social structures.

This investigation of religion and ethical life in general, and of Christian moral life in particular, has implications for theological method. A contextual approach will have as its priority and commitment the elaboration and incarnation of a theology from within, and for, a certain setting. Such an enterprise must recognize and distinguish the contributions from the particular religious tradition, local culture, and ideologies.

On the basis of this theoretical groundwork, there follows in the second part of the chapter an attempt to offer an understanding of the Christian church in Latin America. This starting point affects how theologizing can be done in that context. To better expound the issues raised by the proposal, certain method-conscious liberation theologians, especially Enrique Dussel and Juan Luis Segundo, will be used as foils. The point is neither to argue with or defend others also committed to Christian involvement in the process of change in Latin America; rather, the contrast will serve to clarify my method.

The last large section of this chapter returns to the Old Testament, not for a historical reconstruction, but to look at moral life in antiquity from the interpretive point of view presented in the first section. Perhaps that approach can shed light on *the textual data* and begin to raise the pertinent questions as to *the textual function* that will be the topic of the next chapter.

What the discussion of this chapter tries to suggest is *a way of seeing*, a manner of comprehending religious and moral life both in Latin America and ancient Israel. How is the existence of the community of faith to be understood now and back then, here and over there? Only on the basis of this initial step will the decision on how the biblical text should be used make sense.

1. *Religion and Moral Life in Context*

a. *Geertz: Interpretive Anthropology and the Nature of Culture*
In several places the introduction mentions 'culture' when referring to

a context. The term 'culture', however, has been perennially difficult
to define. Different theories and schools have appeared successively
during this century, and all have had their defenders and detractors.[1]

Within the last few decades a distinct orientation to anthropological
studies has increasingly gained prominence. This new perspective has
heralded a paradigm shift away from the classical positivistic
approach of explanation based on general laws and empirical
verification toward conventions and methods arising out of a very
dissimilar conceptual framework.[2] Clifford Geertz, perhaps the best
known of these ethnographers, claims in his essay, 'Blurred Genres:
The Refiguration of Social Thought', that:

> there has been an enormous amount of genre mixing in intellectual life in
> recent years, and it is, such blurring of kinds, continuing apace. . . many
> social scientists have turned away from a laws and instances ideal of
> explanation toward a cases and interpretations one. . . analogies drawn
> from the humanities are coming to play the kind of role in sociological
> understanding that analogies drawn from the crafts and technology have
> long played in physical understanding.[3]

1. See the different summaries and evaluative postures of R.M. Keesing,
'Theories of Culture', *AnnRevAnth* 3 (1974), pp. 73-97; M. Harris, *Cultural
Materialism: The Struggle for a Science of Culture* (New York: Vintage Books,
1979), pp. 117-341. K.A. Rice offers a helpful discussion of the various types of
theories (nominal, essentialist, real, explicative) and the components (focal, phenomenal, temporal, situational) that can serve to distinguish theories of culture, in *Geertz
and Culture* (Anthropology Series: Studies in Cultural Analysis; Ann Arbor:
University of Michigan Press, 1980), pp. 3-25.

2. For the concept of a 'paradigm' see T. Kuhn, *The Structure of Scientific
Revolutions* (International Encyclopedia of Unified Science, 2.2; Chicago: University
of Chicago Press, 2nd edn, 1970); G.E. Marcus and D. Cushman, 'Ethnographies
as Texts', *AnnRevAnth* 11 (1982), pp. 25-69. G.E. Marcus and M.M.J. Fischer
place this shift within a broader framework of a general crisis in methodology within
the social sciences and other disciplines, in *Anthropology as Cultural Critique: An
Experimental Moment in the Human Sciences* (Chicago: University of Chicago
Press, 1986), chs. 1 and 2. B. Scholte testifies to the initial impact of Kuhn's book
and suggests how anthropology could now even enhance the paradigm idea in
'Cultural Anthropology and the Paradigm-Concept: A Brief History of their Recent
Convergence', in *Functions and Uses of Disciplinary Studies*, VII (ed. L. Graham,
W. Lepensies and P. Weingart; n.p.: Reidel, 1983), pp. 229-78.

3. C. Geertz, 'Blurred Genres: The Refiguration of Social Thought', in *Local
Knowledge: Further Essays in Interpretive Anthropology* (New York: Basic Books,
1983), p. 19. He speaks of a new set of guiding analogies, such as game theory,

In an earlier, now famous, piece which is seminal for this alternative approach, Geertz introduced the explication of this method with
these oft-quoted words:

> The concept of culture I espouse, and whose utility the essays below
> attempt to demonstrate, is essentially a semiotic one. Believing, with Max
> Weber, that man is an animal suspended in webs of significance he him-
> self has spun, I take culture to be those webs and the analysis of it to be
> therefore not an experimental science in search of law but an interpretive
> one in search of meaning.[1]

Central to this enterprise is ascertaining codes of meaning and their
social ground and importance. He distances himself from what he considers the various extremes of giving 'culture' a reified existence and
power removed from concrete realities and limitations (idealism), of
reducing it to predictable behavior patterns (materialism), of
understanding it as a mental and psychological phenomenon (cognitive
anthropology), or of treating it simply as a symbolic system. Culture
is now seen as 'interworked systems of construable signs', as structures of significations within and for human experience. Consequently,
there is no dichotomy between material life and cognition, because
culture, thus understood, is articulated through, and also affected by,
action and existence. Ultimately, the concept of culture is inseparable
from one's notion of the nature of man:

> I want to propose two ideas. The first of these is that culture is best seen
> not as complexes of concrete behavior patterns—customs, usages, tradi-
> tions, habit clusters. . . but as a set of control mechanisms—plans,
> recipes, rules, instructions. . . for the governing of behavior. The
> second idea is that man is precisely the animal most desperately dependent
> upon such extragenetic, outside the skin mechanisms, such cultural pro-
> grams, for ordering his behavior.[2]

---

drama, text. More recently, *idem*, 'History and Anthropology', *NLH* 21 (1990),
pp. 321-35.

1. Geertz, 'Thick Description: Toward an Interpretive Theory of Culture', in *The
Interpretation of Cultures: Selected Essays* (New York: Basic Books, 1973), p. 5.
For a detailed study of most of his published work, see Rice, *Geertz and Culture*. An
excellent summary based on the analytical grid developed on pp. 3-25 of his work
appears on pp. 211-38.

2. Geertz, 'The Impact of the Concept of Culture on the Concept of Man', in *The
Interpretation of Cultures*, p. 44.

Meaning, however, is problematic and not easily transparent to the observer. To get at how a group or population understands and shapes life requires that anthropology be an interpretive, even an imaginative, exercise that gives primacy to the 'native point of view'. To understand and explain an institution, ritual, event, act or any other cultural expression from the actor's perspective is to provide 'thick description' grounded in his meanings, not a 'thin description' of alleged objective data and detached observation. The change in approach, then, clearly requires an epistemological conversion, as it were. One must always recognize, moreover, the incompleteness and indeterminateness of the task of moving toward deeper and clearer comprehension in what could be conceived of as a sociohermeneutical spiral.[1]

How has the interpretive program of this anthropological method, and Geertz in particular, been received? What is often faulted in interpretive anthropology is precisely the paradigm shift away from more traditional canons of investigation. Remonstrances arise because of the difficulty of 'predictability, replicability, verifiability, and law-generating capacity'.[2] The cultural materialist Marvin Harris classifies this approach as 'cognitive idealism'[3] (a label Geertz eschews) and favors a more 'scientific' method:

> The aim of cultural materialism in particular is to account for the origin, maintenance, and change of the global inventory of socio-cultural differences and similarities. Thus cultural materialism shares with other scientific strategies an epistemology which seeks to restrict fields of inquiry to events, entities, and relationships that are knowable by means

1. Geertz, 'Thick Description', pp. 3-30; *idem*, '"From the Native's Point of View": On the Nature of Anthropological Understanding', in *Local Knowledge*, pp. 55-70. Marcus and Fischer document the new approaches in ethnography seeking even more authentic description and effective translation (*Anthropology as Cultural Critique*, ch. 3).

2. P. Shankman, 'The Thick and the Thin: On the Interpretive Program of Clifford Geertz', *CurrAnth* 25 (1984), p. 264.

3. Harris, *Cultural Materialism*, pp. 278-86. Keesing clearly distinguishes Geertz's approach from cognitive anthropology in 'Theories of Culture', especially pp. 79-81, and in 'Models, "folk" and "cultural": Paradigms Regained?', in *Cultural Models in Language and Thought* (ed. D. Holland and N. Quinn; Cambridge: Cambridge University Press, 1987), pp. 369-93, *passim*.

of explicit, logico-empirical, inductive-deductive, quantifiable public procedure or 'operations' subject to replication by independent observers.[1]

He adds categorically:

> No other way of knowing is based on a set of rules explicitly designed to
> transcend the prior belief systems of mutually antagonistic tribes, nations,
> classes, and ethnic and religious communities in order to arrive at knowl-
> edge that is equally probable for any rational human mind.[2]

The aim here is not to engage in (let alone resolve) the centuries old debate between the 'materialist' and 'idealist' strains in the social sciences.[3] Two comments, however, are in order. First, an interpretive orientation would question the possibility of a purely objective stance (in Harris's case, of a cadre of scientists), untouched by any kind of pre-understanding factors and unconditioned by context.[4] Data

---

1. Harris, *Cultural Materialism*, p. 27. For a helpful survey of Harris's theory and method see M.K. Taylor, *Beyond Explanation: Religious Dimensions in Cultural Anthropology* (Macon, GA: Mercer University Press, 1986), pp. 139-70, 190-203. For critiques see H.D. Heinen, 'On Cultural Materialism, Marx, and the Hegelian Monkey', *CurrAnth* 16 (1975), pp. 450-56, and P.J. Magnarella, 'Cultural Materialism and the Problem of Probabilities', *AmAnth* 84 (1982), pp. 138-46.

2. Harris, *Cultural Materialism*, p. 28.

3. Taylor traces the history of the debate (*Beyond Explanation*, ch. 2), yet in his approach assumes that human inquiry involves not a dichotomy of these two ideals of understanding and explanation, but rather a dialectical relation between them (p. 73). Cf. J.T. O'Meara, 'Anthropology as Empirical Science', *AmAnth* 91 (1989), pp. 354-69. Marcus and Fischer would suggest

> in anthropology, the situation is often pictured as the challenge of newer, inter-
> pretive programs of research to reigning positivist ones. Our perspective is that at
> the current moment, interpretive perspectives, although still 'anti-establishment'
> in ethos, are as much an accepted and understood part of contemporary discourse
> as are positivist perspectives (*Anthropology as Cultural Critique*, p. x).

4. Besides the interpretive anthropologists mentioned, see also D. Nash and R. Wintrob, 'The Emergence of Self-Consciousness in Ethnography', *CurrAnth* (1972), pp. 527-42. Scholte, who had earlier in his career embraced uncritically a neo-Marxist anthropology without recognizing its situatedness and cultural relativity, calls Harris's absolutist claims for science a case of ethnocentric and arrogant 'bourgeois rationalism' ('Cultural Anthropology', p. 269 n. 32). Note also the discussion of anthropology and its relationship to local sociopolitical issues in J. Spencer, 'Writing within: Anthropology, Nationalism, and Culture in Sri Lanka', *CurrAnth* 31 (1990), pp. 283-300, and K. Hastrup and P. Elsass, 'Anthropological Advocacy: A Contradiction in Terms?', *CurrAnth* 31 (1990), pp. 301-11; 32 (1990), pp. 387-90.

is not only recorded, but also construed: strategies select the 'facts' to be observed, and the theoretical givens can determine how these are to be understood. Anthropological theories themselves, in other words, are constructions of 'reality' grounded in and reflecting particular, supposedly transcendent, universes of discourse. Harris's nomothetical program, for example, is also driven by the moral imperative of righting injustice; his is an attempt to identify root causes of wrong as the first step toward change.[1] His quest for the true, the real, and the good, therefore, exposes what Mark Kline Taylor labels the 'religious dimension' of Harris's work.[2] Harris's explanations, in other words, are also interpretations.

Secondly, in the presentation of his method Harris makes a helpful distinction that underscores the change in perspective and can serve to clarify further the priorities of interpretive anthology. Harris distinguishes between 'emics' and 'etics'—that is, 'the native point of view' as opposed to the categories and analysis of the observer.[3] Each perspective provides, in his opinion, different information: 'the test of the adequacy of emic analyses is their ability to generate statements

These authors recognize how values can determine how anthropological data can be used in the political arena and are wary of possible pitfalls if 'facts' and 'values' are not adequately differentiated. By way of contrast, note the call to involvement by T.B. Ehlers in 'Central America in the 1980s: Political Crisis and the Social Responsibility of Anthropologists', *LARR* 25.3 (1990), pp. 141-55.

1. See Taylor's helpful treatment of this dimension of Harris's work in *Beyond Explanation*, pp. 164-70, 227-38, 245-49.

2. For Taylor's understanding of this term see *Beyond Explanation*, pp. 61-65, 216-49. In an earlier article he had used the word 'symbol' ('Symbolic Dimensions in Cultural Anthropology', *CurrAnth* 26 [1985], pp. 167-85; note Harris's sharp response on p. 175), but perhaps has now revised his terminology because of its status as, to use Runciman's label, a 'preemptive taxonomy'. Taylor, in his book, focuses specifically on anthropologies of 'explanation' (singling out Lévi-Strauss and Harris) to demonstrate this dimension. Geertz has recently discussed the studies of Lévi-Strauss, Evans-Pritchard, Malinowski, and Benedict as works of the imagination with particular perspectives and convictions, and so with different literary strategies, in *Works and Lives: The Anthropologist as Author* (Stanford: Stanford University Press, 1988).

3. M. Harris, 'Why a Perfect Knowledge of All the Rules One Must Know to Act Like a Native Cannot Lead to the Knowledge of How Natives Act', *JAnthRes* 30 (1974), pp. 240-51; *idem*, 'History and Significance of the Emic/Etic Distinction', pp. 329-50; *idem, Cultural Materialism*, pp. 32-56. See Taylor's discussion, *Beyond Explanation*, pp. 158-63.

the native accepts as real, meaningful, or appropriate', whereas 'the test of etic accounts is simply their ability to generate scientifically productive theories about the causes of socio-cultural differences and similarities'.[1] He differentiates the etic behavioral components of the infrastructure (the modes of production and reproduction), structure (domestic and political economies) and superstructure (for example, art, rituals), from the corresponding emic components.

Harris feels, though, that emic descriptions may suffer from mystification, are culture-specific, and can lead finally to a 'total relativism'. They are thus excluded from investigation of more 'objective' realities:

> rather than distinguish the mental and emic components according to the strength of their relationship to specific etic behavioral components, I shall lump them together and designate them in their entirety as the *mental and emic superstructure*.[2]

Harris defends the principle of infrastructural determinism, and so looking at emics is only the 'ultimate recourse when no testable etic behavioral theories can be formulated or when all that have been formulated have been decisively discredited'.[3] The 'emic superstructures' have little power to alter society and can serve only as a feedback process to either slow down or facilitate change determined ultimately by the infrastructure.[4]

Interpretive anthropology, on the other hand, puts a greater emphasis on emics in order to understand man. Yet this construal of meaning is not simply an 'internal' exercise, as Harris suggests, but also a social and public activity available for observation and analysis by the social scientist. Its contention is that emics cannot be so easily set aside in a discussion of social change. How people construe their lives can be a powerful factor in how they shape them.

How is religion to be understood in interpretive anthropology? Could semiotic analysis and description of culture offer a fresh perspective on how religion functions and on its relation to morality? Moreover, how helpful could this approach be in grappling with political life, particularly the role of ideology, in a given context?

1. Harris, *Cultural Materialism*, p. 32.
2. *Cultural Materialism*, p. 54 (emphasis Harris's).
3. *Cultural Materialism*, p. 56.
4. *Cultural Materialism*, pp. 70-75.

These issues, central to the concerns of this thesis, can indeed be illuminated by this focus on meaning and will now be handled in turn.

In a well-known essay, 'Religion as a Cultural System', Geertz defines religion as:

> (1) a system of symbols which acts to (2) establish powerful, pervasive, and long-lasting moods and motivations in men by (3) formulating conceptions of a general order of existence and (4) clothing these conceptions with such an aura of factuality that (5) the moods and motivations seem uniquely realistic.[1]

Rather than presenting religious beliefs and rituals as, say, superstition or indicative of a 'primitive mentality', he observes that religion brings an ethos together with a particular world-view, gives a coherence of explanation to everyday existence as well as to the various threats of anomie, and legitimizes a certain morality. Religion, through sacred images and rituals, can provide models both of and for life that gain additional power as part of the culturally constructed world which is apparently congruent with reality. Morality is, therefore, not only common sense; it is also ordained. As Geertz points out:

> Never merely metaphysics, religion is never merely ethics either. The source of its moral vitality is conceived to lie in the fidelity with which it expresses the fundamental nature of reality. The powerful coercive 'ought' is felt to grow out of a comprehensive factual 'is', and in such a way religion grounds the most specific requirements of human action in the most general contexts of human experience.[2]

Religion can be an influential force, then, in articulating, substantiating and affirming the right and the true. Yet religion can be but one of several inter-connected cultural elements generating and reflecting significations[3] that define and enforce moral norms and that help resolve moral quandaries. The 'ideal-type' description of religion cited earlier is in no way intended to ignore or mask the complexities

---

1. Geertz, 'Religion as a Cultural System', in *The Interpretation of Cultures*, p. 90. Besides this essay also see in the same volume 'Ethos, World-View, and the Analysis of Sacred Symbols', pp. 126-41. R.J. Schreiter also develops a semiotic approach in *Constructing Local Theologies* (Maryknoll: Orbis Books, 1985), especially ch. 3.

2. Geertz, 'Ethos, World-View', p. 126.

3. See the various essays in *Local Knowledge* that deal with common sense, art, and law.

of social meaning systems.[1] Different structures of meaning with their own formal and popular mechanisms are operating, sometimes in conjunction, sometimes at odds, to prescribe moral principles and produce moral vision. From a fascinating collection of essays edited by Adrian C. Mayer on the interplay of culture and moral dilemmas in South East Asia[2] what vividly emerges is the role of culture both in defining the issues that are perceived as morally problematic and in setting the conditions and limits, whether conceptual or social, of their solutions: the struggle between ascetic mysticism and material body is incomprehensible apart from Hindu faith and practice; the various kinds of large-scale efforts to redefine moral values and social relationships make no sense apart from the deep-seated prejudices of all groups (low and high) in the caste system; strike rhetoric and success is unclear unless viewed against a conflict between overlapping and competing meaning systems (Christianity, caste, ethnicity) and their institutions; the varying congruence between religiously sanctioned and popular morality is incomprehensible if not explicated from an appreciation of the complex interplay between ritual drama, with its ethical ideals, and the moral conventions and social pressures of everyday household and caste life. The fact of the inseparability of cultural and moral life is evident at every level (personal, familial, caste, village, nation), in every sphere (conjugal, educational, religious, labor, political), and in all sort of configurations (maintenance of the status quo, mild and radical reform movements). Yet the 'culture' is no single entity or single monolithic meaning system, but rather a jigsaw puzzle of shared world-views, ethos, and symbols cutting across sexual, class and group boundaries in all manner of ways.[3]

1. Note the criticisms made by T. Asad in 'Anthropological Conceptions of Religion: Reflections on Geertz', *Man* ns 18 (1983), pp. 237-59. Geertz, however, distinguishes the religious perspective from other judgments integral to how humanity understands its world—the commonsensical, the scientific, the aesthetic. Neither is ritual always totally convincing and determinative for daily life, nor is it solely religious; it may be public, political.
2. A.C. Mayer, *Culture and Morality: Essays in Honour of Christoph von Furer-Haimendorf* (Delhi: Oxford University Press, 1981). Cf. C.J. Greenhouse, 'Looking at Culture, Looking for Rules', Man ns 17 (1982), pp. 58-73.
3. Note also Geertz's discussion of legal logic and systems in 'Local Knowledge: Fact and Law in Comparative Perspectives', in *Local Knowledge*, pp. 167-234.

At least one problem arises out of this comprehension of morality. If morality is so context-specific, how can there be any communication or application of morality across time and space boundaries and cultural frontiers? This enigmatic question is at once relevant for a community such as the Christian church, which is so separated from biblical times and is now scattered around the globe. Moral interchange does in fact take place.

In 'Found in Translation: On the Social History of the Moral Imagination', Geertz deals with the paradox of works of art (itself a cultural system) of the past which, though context-bound, continue to speak to moral sensibility.[1] His essay then is actually the study of the moral function of a text. How can a text still impact moral vision? Using the description of a ritual in Bali and a novel by Jane Austen, he first points out how this process of cross-cultural reach and appropriation should not be construed:

> Neither the recovery of literary intentions ('what Austen wished to convey') nor the isolation of literary responses ('what Columbian students contrive to see in her'), neither the reconstruction of intra-cultural meaning ('Balinese creation rites as caste drama') nor the establishment of cross-cultural uniformities ('the theophanous symbolism of mortuary fire') can by itself bring it to proper focus.[2]

The move to the here-and-now is not easily explicated, nor can it be simplistically reduced to a they-are-just-like-us (whether in mind or social position) equation. Rather a text works on its reader's moral vision:

> This is how anything imaginational grows in our minds, is transformed, socially transformed, from something we merely know to exist or have existed, somewhere or other, to something which is properly ours, a working force in our consciousness. . . When major cultural lines are transversed in the process of interpretive reworking, a different sense of

Laws, too, he says, 'do not just regulate behavior, they construe it. . . Law. . . is local knowledge; local not just as to place, time, class, and variety of issue, but as to accent—vernacular characterizations of what happens connected to vernacular imaginings of what can' (p. 215).

1. C. Geertz, 'Found in Translation: On the Social History of the Moral Imagination', in *Local Knowledge*, pp. 36-54 (note also in the same volume 'Art as a Cultural System', pp. 94-120).

2. Geertz, 'Found in Translation', p. 45.

discovery is produced: one more of having come across something than of having remembered it, of an acquisition than of inheritance.[1]

The text is found to be real, authentic, true to existence, yet at once different; what then was lived is now a living metaphor. What Geertz does not articulate is how a text claims its reader or how a reader should respond to a text. His primary concern in the long run is apparently more epistemological than ethical.[2] Still, his focus on the moral function of a text in and across contexts hints at a discussion later in this chapter and in the next on the biblical text, which, though ancient and foreign, is the moral text of the Christian church.

The last area of particular interest is the formulation of the nature of ideology also as a realm of culture. As Geertz explains it, generally speaking, there are two principal approaches to the notion of ideology—one, the 'interest theory', emphasizes the class structure and political manipulations and portrays ideology as an instrument of power; the other, the 'strain theory', is less doctrinaire and views ideologies as reactions, with a wide range of possible functions, to various degrees of social tension. Geertz, however, would point out what he perceives as a fundamental weakness of both theories:

> Both interest and strain theory go directly from source analysis to conse-
> quence analysis without ever seriously examining ideologies as systems
> of interacting symbols, as patterns of interworking meanings. . . The
> problem of how, after all, ideologies transform sentiment into significance
> and so make it socially available is short-circuited by the crude device of
> placing particular symbols and particular strains (or interests) side by side
> in such a way that the fact that the first are derivatives of the second seems
> more common sense—or at least post-Freudian, post-Marxian common
> sense. . . The connection is not thereby explained but merely educed.
> The nature of the relationship between the sociopsychological stresses that
> incite ideological attitudes are given a public existence is much too compli

---

1. 'Found in Translation', pp. 47-48.
2. See G. Gunn, 'The Semiotics of Culture and the Interpretation of Literature: Clifford Geertz and the Moral Imagination', *Studies in Literary Imagination* 12 (1977), pp. 109-28, especially pp. 125-28. Marcus and Fischer would fault Geertz for not bringing his anthropological insights more directly to bear on a critique of modern American society, a process they call 'repatriation' (*Anthropology as Cultural Critique*, pp. 141-42, 145-46).

cated to be comprehended in terms of a vague and unexamined notion of
emotive resonance.[1]

The success and power of an ideology, then, is grounded in social
and political factors as well as in the strength of its metaphors and
symbols (which could in some cases also have a religious base) and in
the many connections these have with multiple spheres of social life.
Ideology is not merely social manipulation or resolution; it is 'itself a
social process': 'The function of ideology is to make an autonomous
politics possible by providing the authoritative concepts that render it
meaningful, the suasive images of which it can be sensibly grasped'.[2]
A particular ideology gains collective credence and loyalty to the
extent that it offers a more adequate and compelling image of sociopolitical reality than the reigning one and thus demands 'truer' and
more 'realistic' (and thereby necessary) courses of action and solutions. All of this is not to deny the actuality of social needs and abuses;
it is rather an attempt to elucidate the cultural activity of all
ideologies.

Can the interpretive approach provide helpful insights into the
dynamics of the conflictive situations and the role of religion in the
Two-Thirds World? Harris, in his usual biting style, has been particularly derisive of this (incorrectly labelled) 'cognitive idealism':

> Never has there been a strategy less suited to the study of conflict and
> political process. The subjects prohibited to 'modern cultural anthropol-
> ogy' are the guts of contemporary life. No amount of knowledge of
> 'competent natives'' rules and codes can 'account for' phenomena such
> as poverty; underdevelopment; imperialism; the population explosion;
> minorities; ethnic and class conflict; exploitation, taxation, private prop-
> erty. . . These phenomena, like everything else that is important to
> human beings, are the consequences of intersection and contradictory
> vectors of belief, will, and power. They cannot be scientifically under-
> stood as manifestations of codes or rules.[3]

Harris is not alone in his criticism. Others, who also underline the
contribution of Marxist approaches which highlight class interests but
avoid too 'vulgar' a view of the social function of ideology, have also

---

1. C. Geertz, 'Ideology as a Cultural System', in *The Interpretation of Cultures*,
p. 207.
2. 'Ideology as a Cultural System', p. 218.
3. Harris, *Cultural Materialism*, p. 285.

pointed out that the theme of power is crucial in any description of ideology: meanings are not just shared, they are created and defined, distributed and controlled.[1]

Interpretive anthropologists are increasingly sensitive to this issue and to its implications for investigative strategies and conventions of description. This recognition, however, does not mean abandoning the approach. As Marcus and Fischer point out:

> The usual objection to interpretive anthropology is that 'cold', 'hard' issues of power, interests, economics, and historical change are elided in favor of portraying the native point of view as richly as possible. . . What makes representation challenging and a focus of experimentation is the perception that the 'outside' forces in fact are an integral part of the construction and constitution of the 'inside', the culture unit itself, and must be registered at the most intimate levels of cultural process. . . [2]

Have these phenomena been ignored by Geertz? A closer look at 'Ideology as a Cultural System' demonstrates that he is more aware of the 'contradictory vectors of belief, will, and power' than is sometimes supposed. Geertz's discussion speaks of the intense conceptual battle of rival ideologies, not only in a general sense but also in the specific case of Indonesia, as they try to provide an adequate symbolic framework for dealing with changing sociopolitical realities. The factors in this social process are sociological and cultural; the analysis necessarily both emic and etic:

1. E.g. Asad, 'Anthropological Conceptions'; R.G. Walters, 'Signs of the Times: Clifford Geertz and Historians', *SocRes* 47 (1980), pp. 537-56; W. Roseberry, 'Balinese Cockfights and the Seduction of Anthropology', *SocRes* 49 (1982), pp. 1013-28; R.M. Keesing, 'Anthropology as Interpretive Quest', *CurrAnth* 28 (1987), pp. 161-76. The last three authors criticize the text metaphor that Geertz has employed because it can lead to an overemphasis on the 'reading' of culture at the expense of perceiving the processes that led to the creation and reproduction of that 'text'. Of the three, Walters recognizes that this impression sometimes has more to do with unfortunate language in Geertz than with intention. Still, the danger remains. In 'Blurred Genres', Geertz lists this metaphor, however, as but one of several being utilized today. In addition, he admits its problematic nature and does mention the aspects of intention, construction, and reference (*Local Knowledge*, pp. 30-33). What is more, this metaphor is but one piece of a larger theoretical construct and to limit criticism to this one point is unfair.

2. Marcus and Fischer, *Anthropology as Cultural Critique*, p. 77. Cf. Schreiter, *Constructing Local Theologies*, pp. 70-73.

> Ideologies do make empirical claims about the condition and direction of
> society, which it is the business of science (and, where scientific language
> is lacking, common sense) to assess. The social function of science vis-à-
> vis ideologies is first to understand them—what they are, how they work,
> what gives rise to them—and second to criticize them to come to terms
> with (but not necessarily to surrender to) reality.[1]

A perusal of other essays that go into much more detail of the
Indonesian situation illustrates the dynamic historical interplay, for
example, between older traditions and newer ideologies, between
different religions which share some common moral grounds but that
are groping toward political awareness and are competing for power
locally and nationally, and between a government striving somehow to
mold a national consensus around new symbols and celebrations
against this complex cultural background.[2]

To stress meaning is not to mystify social reality or to negate history. Indeed, it should naturally lead to an inspection of the creation,
perpetuation and exploitation of meaning in the ideological conflict.
What this approach does do, however, is react against theoretical
models in which culture is minimized and is presented as just an
obstacle (or stimulus) to change or as, more recently, a 'collective
illusion' masking exploitation:

> It is not economic analysis itself that is the problem, any more than it is
> quantification. It is economism: the notion. . . that a determinate picture
> of social change can be obtained in the absence of an understanding of the
> passions and imaginings that provoke and inform it. Such understanding
> is inevitably limited. . . And the determinateness it brings is inevitably
> partial. . . But without it there is nothing but polemic, schematicism and
> endless measurements of amorphous magnitudes: history without temper,
> sociology without tone.[3]

1. Geertz, 'Ideology as a Cultural System', p. 232.
2. C. Geertz, 'Conflict and Integration', in *The Religion of Java* (London: The
Free Press of Glencoe, 1960), pp. 355-81; *idem*, 'Ritual and Social Change: A
Javanese Example', 'The Politics of Meaning' and 'Politics Past, Politics Present:
Some Notes on the Uses of Anthropology in Understanding the New States', in *The
Interpretation of Cultures*, pp. 142-69, 311-26, and 327-41, respectively; *idem*,
'Centers, Kings, and Charisma: Reflections on the Symbols of Power', in *Local
Knowledge*, pp. 121-46; *idem*, 'Culture and Social Change: The Indonesian Case',
Man ns 19 (1984), pp. 511-32.
3. Geertz, 'Culture and Social Change', p. 523.

In addition, an insight, which those who might claim (mistakenly) that interpretive anthropology does not provide an adequate exposition of the forces inhibiting social change often miss, is that this approach would point out that every ideology, whether oppressive or liberative, can be subjected to semiotic analysis. Any absolutist's posture in the name of ideological purity or realism is hereby to some degree relativized. The charge of political naivety in the end can come back full circle to be levelled at those who only see the manipulation of meaning by the 'the other side':

> though both the structure and the expressions of social life change, the inner necessities that animate it do not. Thrones may be out of fashion, and pageantry too; but political authority still requires a cultural frame in which to define itself and advance its claims, and so does opposition to it.[1]

In sum, interpretive anthropology offers a distinct perception of humans and their world. The contributions of Geertz posit that the construal of meaning is integral to human experience. This section has explored the nature of religion, morality and ideology and their interplay within the complicated meaning systems of social life and process. By allowing for both emic and etic components in the task of social description and explanation, a semiotic approach can be a helpful instrument for probing moral life within the changing realities of society by underscoring how people perceive, and so live, in their world.

It is within the 'webs of significance' that make up cultural existence that the Christian faith and moral task must be understood. In the search for a more just 'world', the church must see itself as a smaller world within a larger culture, recognize the contextual framing of ethical problems and solutions, and admit the relative value of any ideology. The challenge is to present a faith at once culturally authentic and morally true; the danger, so to identify with the context that those 'webs' choke its ethical life and calling.

b. *Berger: Sociology of Knowledge and Sociological Methodology*
The sociology of Peter L. Berger draws upon several sources. Though some have considered his work to be primarily phenomenological, a

---

1. Geertz, 'Centers, Kings, and Charisma', p. 143.

look at what he has written requires that this label be qualified.[1] Berger himself has consistently enumerated those from whom he has gleaned insights, whether substantive or methodological.[2] His contribution to this discussion on faith in context will be twofold. First, his focus on the centrality of meaning in social experience will reinforce the preceding section on anthropology, as well as provide the opportunity to explore other pertinent areas. Secondly, his concern for methodological clarity and its consequent political implications will serve to pursue further the pragmatic concerns of this book.

The social construction of reality. Though defining 'culture' differently from Geertz,[3] Berger, too, sees humans as creatures who strive for order in their existence and stand in a dialectical relationship with their context both as world builders and products. There is, therefore, a similar concern to understand subjective meanings and intentions and their complex relationship to the social milieu. The object of study is more the realm of everyday life than that of philosophical discourse:

> The sociology of knowledge must concern itself with whatever passes for 'knowledge' in a society regardless of the ultimate validity or invalidity (by whatever criteria) of such 'knowledge'. And in so far as all human 'knowledge' is developed, transmitted and maintained in social situations,

1. R. Wuthnow *et al.*, 'The Phenomenology of Peter L. Berger', in *Cultural Analysis: The Work of Peter L. Berger, Mary Douglas, Michel Foucault, Jurgen Habermas* (London: Routledge & Kegan Paul, 1984), pp. 21-76; S.C. Ainlay, 'The Encounter with Phenomenology', in *Making Sense of Modern Times: Peter L. Berger and the Vision of Interpretive Sociology* (ed. J.D. Hunter and S.C. Ainlay; London: Routledge & Kegan Paul, 1986), pp. 31-54.

2. P.L. Berger, *Invitation to Sociology: A Humanistic Perspective* (Garden City, NY: Doubleday, 1963), pp. 177-86; the extensive notes in *The Sacred Canopy: Elements of a Sociology of Religion* (Garden City, NY: Doubleday, 1969), pp. 187-205; *The Capitalist Revolution: Fifty Propositions about Prosperity, Equality, and Liberty* (New York: Basic Books, 1986), pp. 6-7, 27-31; P.L. Berger and T. Luckmann, *The Social Construction of Reality: A Treatise in the Sociology of Knowledge* (Harmondsworth: Penguin Books, 1967), pp. 15-30; P.L. Berger and H. Kellner, *Sociology Reinterpreted: An Essay on Method and Vocation* (Harmondsworth: Penguin Books, 1981), pp. 9-23, 167-70.

3. Berger never really elaborates this concept, but does say at one point, 'culture consists of the totality of man's products. Some of these are material, others are not' (*The Sacred Canopy*, p. 6).

the sociology of knowledge must seek to understand the processes by which this is done in such a way that a taken-for-granted 'reality' congeals for the man in the street. In other words, we contend that *the sociology of knowledge is concerned with the analysis of the social construction of reality.*[1]

As in interpretive anthropology, care is taken to avoid the twin dangers of 'idealism' or of a determinist materialism by highlighting the inseparable, yet variegated, connection between individual and social consciousness and material life.[2]

Humans, as fundamentally social creatures, both construct and develop within a society which to a great extent determines their self-understanding and perception of the manifold dimensions of life. Society is an objective reality—external to them, visualized in surrounding institutions, incarnated in representative roles, and substantiated by various means. Society is also a subjective reality—absorbed into the consciousness through a complex process of socialization. In other words, 'man is in society' and 'society in man'.

Reality is socially constructed through such things as language, divisions of capital and labor, typification of roles, and the structuring of an institutional order. Every society has some common stock of knowledge and shared convictions that permit practical competence in everyday life. The intricate social relationships and commitments generated from labor, class, racial, linguistic, historical, religious and ideological bonds serve to give a measure of cohesiveness to any society and a certain sense of comprehensive validity:

> The social world intends, as far as possible, to be taken for granted.
> Socialization achieves success to the degree that this taken-for-granted
> quality is internalized. It is not enough that the individual look upon the
> key meanings of the social order as useful, desirable or right. It is much

1. Berger and Luckmann, *Social Construction*, p. 15 (authors' emphasis).

2. For what follows, see Berger, *The Sacred Canopy* and *Invitation to Sociology* (chs. 4, 5, 6); Berger and Luckmann, *Social Construction*. For a detailed survey of Berger's work, see N. Abercrombie, 'Knowledge, Order, and Human Autonomy', in Hunter and Ainlay (eds.), *Making Sense of Modern Times*, pp. 11-30. For other 'sociology-of-everyday-life' approaches see J.D. Douglas, 'Understanding Everyday Life', in *Understanding Everyday Life: Toward the Reconstruction of Sociological Knowledge* (ed. J.D. Douglas; London: Routledge & Kegan Paul, 1970), pp. 3-44 (though Douglas is critical of Berger, pp. 34, 43) and A.J. Weigert, *Sociology of Everyday Life* (New York: Longman, 1981), especially pp. 20-47.

better (better, that is in terms of social stability) if he looks upon them as inevitable, as part and parcel of the universal 'nature of things'.[1]

The legitimation of this socially constructed reality occurs at various levels—that is, through customs, traditions, theories and symbolic universes. All of these generate and perpetuate meanings: this is what life *is* like. Their function, though, is more than cognitive. It is also normative: this is what life *should be* like. Part of the facticity of this social world, therefore, is a set of mores and moral values, of proper and improper behavior, of sins and virtues. The created nomos of any society sets the boundaries of social deviance and impropriety. The violation of what are taken as self-evident norms and ethical principles condemns the guilty and ultimately, if left unchecked, can expose society to the terror of anomie and moral disruption. The ordering of experience consequently includes as well the ordering of morality, and the various moral mechanisms of a society can serve as powerful restraints upon behavior.[2] Social morality becomes an integral and intuitive component of the created reality.

The success and maintenance of this nomization process depends in part upon the credibility of symbolic universes, which are defined as

> bodies of theoretical tradition that integrate different provinces of meaning and encompass the institutional order in a symbolic totality. . . . To reiterate, symbolic processes are processes of signification that refer to realities other than those of everyday experience.[3]

These universes transcend yet ground existence. Religion has traditionally proven to be a powerful world-legitimizer because it can add divine sanction to the multiple institutions, roles, and mores of this created world. Religion can help provide a heightened sense of finality and universality through various legitimizing traditions and canons and the rituals that re-enact and bring to remembrance the basic meanings of life. Here, as within any sphere of everyday life and discourse, there are degrees of sophistication of theoretical (here, theological) knowledge. Both formal and popular theology can adhere to the same symbolic universe and its

1. Berger, *The Sacred Canopy*, p. 24.
2. *The Sacred Canopy*, pp. 19-24. See also R. Bierstedt, *The Social Order* (New York: McGraw–Hill, 4th edn, 1974), pp. 215-49, where he distinguishes varieties of moral norms (e.g. folkways, mores, taboos).
3. Berger and Luckmann, *Social Construction*, p. 113.

institutional and sacramental framework.[1]

This constructed reality depends upon what Berger calls 'plausibility structures', the communities in which the legitimations have credence and in which the designated world finds acceptance and incarnation. The size of a plausibility structure depends, in turn, upon the extent, in the case of a religious symbolic universe, of the 'sacred canopy'. These communities are the context of social relationships and interactions. In any society tensions can arise between dominant plausibility structures and those of minority groups. Moreover, the interplay is complicated because no community is immune from influences from others as activity and allegiances cross blurred boundaries.[2]

In the modern world, where secularization can appear so all-embracing, religion can increasingly be marginalized—that is, plausibility itself becomes the crucial challenge of the times. On the one hand, Berger has discussed his perception of the various theological and organizational strategies employed to engage this dilemma,[3] but he has also offered another helpful theoretical construct which actually would call for the necessity of religion. To counter the alienation and anomie of modernity Berger points to the existence of what he labels 'mediating structures': 'those institutions which stand between the individual in his private sphere and the large institutions of the public sphere'.[4]

These structures (the family, the church, voluntary associations) are said to be basic for providing meaning, stability, and identity. More importantly, however, these mediating structures, of which religion is one, are essential in providing moral values within and for the larger society:

1. For this paragraph see Berger, *The Sacred Canopy*, ch. 2. For this final point, see *The Sacred Canopy*, p. 40; Berger and Luckmann, *Social Construction*, pp. 128-30; R. Wuthnow, 'Religion as a Sacred Canopy', in Hunter and Ainlay (eds.), *Making Sense of Modern Times*, pp. 121-42.

2. Berger, *The Sacred Canopy*, pp. 45-51, 123-25; idem, *A Rumor of Angels: Modern Society and the Rediscovery of the Supernatural* (New York: Doubleday, rev. edn, 1990), ch. 2. See a critique by R. Gill, 'Berger's Plausibility Structures: A Response to Professor Cairns', *SJT* 27 (1984), pp. 198-207.

3. Berger, *The Sacred Canopy*, chs. 5–7, Appendix II; idem, 'Secular Theology and the Rejection of the Supernatural: Reflections on Recent Trends', *ThSt* 38 (1977), pp. 39-56; P.E. Hammond, 'Religion in the Modern World', in Hunter and Ainlay (eds.), *Making Sense of Modern Times*, pp. 143-58.

4. P.L. Berger, 'In Praise of Particularity', *RevPol* 38 (1976), p. 401.

The megastructures, and especially the state, must depend for, let us say, 'moral sustenance' on institutions or social formulations that are 'below' them. They must do so, to be exact, unless coercion is to replace moral authority as the basis of the political order.[1]

This is neither the place to identify nor evaluate the particular religious vision or program he champions.[2] Rather, the key point is to stress that in his view the public square cannot be left naked[3]—that is, without transcendent values: religion, even if seemingly peripheral to the dominant social world, has a moral responsibility to its context.

Especially relevant to the practical commitment of this book to the problems of Latin America is the question of the assistance Berger's work can offer to the comprehension of social change. At first glance, his construct emphasizes order and reality-maintenance and so apparently can offer little. There are, however, several ways in which Berger does address the issue.

One of the overriding concerns of Berger is the analysis of 'modernity', that is, a process of change apparent in contemporary Western society with the collapse of the (sacred) canopy. A more uniform social construction of reality is disintegrating under the various features of this twentieth-century phenomenon. There is no need here to survey his analysis,[4] other than to emphasize that in one respect the focus of Berger's program has been about change.

In addition, the drive toward modernity is not only evident within Western democratic nations. In *Pyramids of Sacrifice*, Berger looks at

---

1. 'In Praise of Particularity', p. 403.

2. See J. Mechling, 'Myth and Mediation: Peter Berger's and John Neuhaus' Theodicy for Modern America', *Soundings* 62 (1979), pp. 338-68.

3. This phrase is drawn from the title of the book by R.J. Neuhaus, *The Naked Public Square: Religion and Democracy in America* (Grand Rapids: Eerdmans, 1984). He argues that religion is crucial for the democratic experiment and that the challenge is learning how to present a moral vision and interact responsibly with competing ones. In 'Biblical Religion and Social Sciences in the Modern World', *NICM Journal* 6 (1981), pp. 8-22, R.N. Bellah speaks of 'demonstration communities where elementary decencies can be maintained and handed down, humanizing a bad situation as it exists, and providing seedbeds for larger efforts at social amelioration when that becomes possible' (pp. 21-22).

4. See A.C. Zijderveld, 'The Challenges of Modernity', and J.D. Hunter, 'The Modern Malaise', in Hunter and Ainlay (eds.), *Making Sense of Modern Times*, pp. 57-75 and 76-100, respectively.

the efforts of Brazil (capitalism) and China (Marxism) to 'improve' society.[1] In both cases the attempt has led to the brutal sacrifice of a generation. In a manner much more concrete than his generalized theoretical discussions, Berger demonstrates that socioeconomic and political changes are indivisible from the complex matter of meaning:

> It is valid and useful to understand modernization as an institutional process. However, one must also understand it as a process on the levels of meanings and consciousness. At its very heart, modernization is a transformation of the meanings by which men live, a revolution of the structures of consciousness.[2]

This conflict of symbolic universes and their legitimations runs along a spectrum from more uniform societies with large-scale consensus to revolutionary situations. Even societies with high coherence are constantly battling against competing and deviant constructs. Any discussion of meaning, as a result, will necessarily include (though cannot be limited to) an examination of interests and power that maintain the institutional and conceptual machineries. The possible responses by those in control and by those in the minority are also multiple and can range from mutual accommodation to violent confrontation.[3]

Another aspect of Berger's sociology of knowledge dovetails with the reality of legitimation conflict. Socialization is never total; humans are still intentional creatures, and the manifest influence of social determinants cannot negate the fact that they still rebel against their given 'world'. The two perspectives are to be kept in tension:

> *Man's freedom is not some sort of hole in the fabric of causality.* Put differently, *the same act that may be perceived as free may also and at the same time be perceived as causally bound.* Two different perceptions are involved then, the first being attentive to man's subjective self-understanding as free, the second being attentive to the various systems of determination. The two perceptions are not logically contradictory, but they are sharply discrete.[4]

1. P.L. Berger, *Pyramids of Sacrifice: Political Ethics and Social Change* (London: Allen Lane/Penguin Books, 1976).

2. *Pyramids of Sacrifice*, p. 199.

3. Berger and Luckmann, *Social Construction*, pp. 125-46. See also the earlier remarks in this section regarding plausibility structures.

4. Berger and Kellner, *Sociology Reinterpreted*, p. 96. Cf. W.M. Lafferty, 'Externalization and Dialectics: Taking the Brackets off Berger and Luckmann's

The beliefs in freedom, as well as their social context and results, are a distinct (though related) sphere of study from that of the sociopolitical options that might be available.

Another example of the difficulty of total socialization is the phenomenon of the duplication of consciousness—that is, of the incongruity between objectivation and internalization, resulting both in internal and external tensions for the individual.[1] Although Berger does not develop the point, this eventuality could be a motivation for change. Disquiet can breed discontent with the status quo and hope for something better in the future.

Over against this phenomenon stands alienation, where humanity is no longer aware of its potentialities within its context. The social construction of reality now assumes particular force for it is accepted unquestionably as one with nature, and the sense of freedom is diminished in the face of this reified world. Religion has always been a powerful agent of alienation, yet it would be false to categorize all religion as alienating, as generative of false consciousness and bad faith. Even as religion can mystify meaning, it can also relativize any social construction precisely because of the 'otherness' and omnipotence of the deity.[2] Consequently,

> Such a 'debunking' motif can be traced all through the biblical tradition, directly related to its radical transcendentalization of God, finding its classic expression in Israelite prophecy for continuing in a variety of expressions in the history of the three great religions of the biblical orbit. This same motif accounts for the recurrent revolutionary use of the Biblical tradition, against its. . . employment for conservative legitimation.[3]

In sum, Berger's aim, as that of the interpretive anthropologists, is to emphasize the manner in which man understands and structures his world. Working from within a different scientific discipline obviously means that another taxonomy is employed, resulting perhaps in a bit more technically precise labeling of similar phenomena. Both realms

Sociology of Knowledge', *CultHerm* 4 (1977), pp. 139-61; D.L. Redfoot, 'The Problem of Freedom', in Hunter and Ainlay (eds.), *Making Sense of Modern Times*, pp. 101-18.

1. Berger, *The Sacred Canopy*, pp. 83-85.
2. *The Sacred Canopy*, pp. 85-101. For his points of agreement with and dissent from Marxist formulations of alienation, see pp. 197-99.
3. *The Sacred Canopy*, p. 99.

of discourse, however, depend on second-order constructs: the social scientist's studies 'must be meaning-adequate. . . that is, they must retain an intelligible connection with the meaningful intentions of the actors in the situation'.[1] In both interpretive anthropology and Berger's sociology of knowledge it is also apparent that this concentration on meaning, whether dealing with life in general or religion in particular, does not lead either to the ignoring of material life and social structure or to a functionalist fixation on order. The fact that these approaches seek to probe *how* humanity orders its existence does not imply that humans do not or cannot seek change, that this order is a monolithic homogeneity, or that these perspectives cannot factor changes into its systems.

The task and limits of sociology. Like Geertz, Berger has also always demonstrated a great methodological self-awareness; indeed, he sometimes seems to be crusading for what he feels is the proper exercise of sociology. There is also attention given to the political ramifications of sociology, and Berger is keen to set what he considers to be the justifiable boundaries of sociological research.

An approach that highlights meaning requires that these meanings be given respect and the right of expression. Such a practice necessitates a certain kind of 'relevance structure', a particular mode of procedure: objectivity. This is not the objectivity, however, of positivism, and, at the same time, it is a reaction to those who would claim that objectivity is impossible to achieve. Berger's sociology of knowledge will not allow for an acontextualized observer. Although there is a body of accepted data, study is always conducted from within a theoretical and institutional framework:

> Objectivity, then, does *not* mean that the sociologist reports on 'raw facts' that are 'out there' in and of themselves. Rather, objectivity means that the sociologist's conceptual scheme is in a dialectical relationship with the empirical data.[2]

---

1. Berger and Kellner, *Sociology Reinterpreted*, p. 45. The concern to take into consideration the 'native point of view' and the interest in methodology echoes many of the concerns and observations of Runciman (*Treatise*) discussed in the preceding chapter.

2. *Sociology Reinterpreted*, p. 53.

In the study of social constructions of reality this method means that the sociologist should strive for 'value-freeness'. Does this not return one, though, to the acontextualized observer? Not at all. Values and motivations are patently part of one's being:

> That is not the point. Rather the point is that once these sociologists embark on their scientific inquiry they must 'bracket' these values as much as possible—not, needless to say, in the sense of giving them up or trying to forget them, but in the sense of controlling the way in which these values might distort the sociological vision.[1]

This commitment is obviously an ascetic ideal, but only in this manner can others' meanings be given a hearing; only in this way can sociologists be ruthlessly honest with their work in the effort to better comprehend social reality, be open even to the data that might falsify their own hypotheses.

Not only is the alternative of the 'technocrat' rejected, but also that of the extreme relativizers. Those who deny empirical and theoretical objectivity often do so from a position of certainty. Berger directs his attack here especially at those Marxists who have tried to exempt themselves from the sociopolitical implications of the relativity of a sociology of knowledge by positing epistemological impunity either to a class (the proletariat) or to a cognitive elite.

Indeed, the Marxist dialogue with phenomenology does have a long history.[2] The formulated options, however, are more than the two options of the proletarian class consciousness (a position most often associated with Lukács)[3] and of the organic intellectuals (a stance made famous by Gramsci)[4] that Berger mentions. Gramsci, for example, is also known for his formulation of 'praxis' whereby true

---

1. *Sociology Reinterpreted*, p. 56.
2. See F.R. Dallmayr, 'Phenomenology and Marxism: A Salute to Enzo Paci', in *Phenomenological Sociology: Issues and Applications* (ed. G. Psathas; New York: John Wiley & Sons, 1973), pp. 305-56; P. Hamilton, *Knowledge and Social Structure: An Introduction to the Classical Argument in the Sociology of Knowledge* (International Library of Sociology; London: Routledge & Kegan Paul, 1974), pp. 15-74.
3. G. Lukács, *History and Class Consciousness: Studies in Marxist Dialectics* (trans. R. Livingstone; London: Merlin Press, 1971), ch. 2.
4. A. Gramsci, *Selections from the Prison Notebooks of Antonio Gramsci* (ed. and trans. Q. Hoare and G. Nowell-Smith; London: Lawrence & Wishart, 1971), pp. 3-24.

knowledge is gained in purposeful action.[1]

Still, Berger's point that some Marxist approaches can betray a hidden positivism is well taken. Sociological research cannot claim a transcendent finality solely on the basis of its data. This sober realism, grounded in an honest acceptance of the relativity inherent in the sociology of knowledge, demands an 'ethic of responsibility': the modest admission that sociology cannot be *prescriptive*, but rather simply *prognostic* of social probabilities.[2]

The never finally attainable ideal goal of scientific 'neutrality', however, in no way implies ethical neutrality or moral indifference. *Value-freeness* does not mean *valuelessness*. What Berger seeks is methodological lucidity in the distinction between understanding and political action. Without this differentiation sociological *data* can be used to legitimate a course of action (of the right or left), when in truth this decision is motivated by the sociologist's *values*.[3] There is a

1. *Prison Notebooks*, pp. 323-419.

2. Berger and Kellner, *Sociology Reinterpreted*, pp. 72-85; Berger, *The Capitalist Revolution*, pp. 216-18; *A Rumor of Angels*, ch. 8. Cf. R.N. Bellah's distinction between 'practical social science', which is committed to moral prudence and reflection, and 'technological social science', which claims to be ideologically free and grounded in facts ('Social Science as Practical Reason', *The Hastings Center Report* 12 [1982], pp. 32-39).

3. As a demonstration of his application of his method, one can turn to *The Capitalist Revolution*, where Berger presents first a discussion centered on fifty propositions which he believes demonstrate the preferability of capitalism to socialism. At the start he says:

I want to stress, as emphatically as I can, that *each one of these propositions is to be understood as a hypothesis within on ongoing empirical inquiry*. The book constitutes a prima facie argument for these propositions. It follows, though, that *each proposition is, in principle, falsifiable*. My own view of the likelihood of this happening varies from case to case (p. 8).

It is only after the presentation of these propositions that he turns to the issue of values (pp. 216-21). He mentions seven and would hold that capitalism is the better option (it should be noted that in the case of at least one, equality, he would say that capitalism does not fare well). Interestingly, instead of juxtaposing the same set of values as does Berger, Marxist sociologist Tom Bottomore contrasts what he feels are the different sets of values held by each system (*Sociology and Socialism* [Brighton: Wheatsheaf Books, 1984], pp. 147-52, 155-56). Cf. The distinction between 'anthropological advocacy' and 'anthropologist's advocacy' made by Hastrup and Elsass in 'Anthropological Advocacy: A Contradiction in Terms?'.

precarious and an 'enormous tension between detachment and engagement',[1] but the alternative is still more dangerous:

> The sociologist who would make of the discipline that kind of exclusionary programme will logically have to excommunicate from sociology (or from its 'true' segment that he alone represents) all those who do not agree with the programme or who do not have the ascriptive status of the 'true' in-group. Once such a procedure begins in earnest, sociology ceases to be itself. It becomes a sect or a tribe. When this happens, not only are the methodological presuppositions of the discipline violated. Ironically, its *political* usefulness comes to an end. Caught in sectarian or tribal particularisms, it can no longer represent itself as *anything but* an ideological legitimation of these particular interests.[2]

The power of a partisan sociology (of whatever political persuasion) is multiplied when the positivistic certainty of the technocrat is joined to the fervor of the ideologist, for now 'scientific rigor' buttresses the 'utopian hope'. Berger is appreciative of much of Marxist sociology and openly embraces many of its insights,[3] yet he fears its totalistic claims and the subsequent distortion of the sociological enterprise. The relationship between theory and action is not as direct as some imagine; the data (the 'is') cannot prescribe the moral solution (the 'ought'). It is precisely here, though, that some Marxist approaches demonstrate their attractiveness: options are simplified, and sociology becomes redemptive.[4]

---

1. Berger, *Pyramids of Sacrifice*, p. 255.

2. Berger and Kellner, *Sociology Reinterpreted*, p. 119 (authors' emphasis). The authors claim to be embracing a Weberian approach. Alvin W. Gouldner critiques Weber's effort to separate fact from value. Though he respects this formulation, Gouldner at the same time disagrees with it, and condemns as well how this notion has been abused in sociology (*For Sociology: Revival and Critique in Sociology Today* [London: Allen Lane, 1973], ch. 1).

3. 'The sociology of knowledge inherited from Marx not only the sharpest formulation of its central problem, but also some of its key concepts' (Berger and Luckmann, *Social Construction*, p. 18). See also the many references in the extensive notes in this book and *The Sacred Canopy*, as well as the list of contributions in *Sociology Reinterpreted* (p. 138).

4. Berger and Kellner, *Sociology Reinterpreted*, pp. 136-42. Berger would say that for several reasons intellectuals in particular are prone to be attracted to the 'socialist myth' (by myth he means a powerful explanation of the nature of reality): 'The Socialist Myth', *The Public Interest* 44 (1976), pp. 3-16; *idem*, *The Capitalist Revolution*, ch. 9. In contrast, from a Marxist perspective Bottomore would lament

3. A World within the World

Berger's method carries at least three important political implications. First, there is a commitment to democracy as a system that ideally can allow for 'the freedom of ordinary people against the dictatorial ambition of these cognitive elites (from "scientific" social workers to "scientific" revolutionaries)'.[1] To opt for and defend a particular political system is beyond the bounds of this book. What is important here, however, is to emphasize that meanings and their mediating structures are important and are to be valued in any consideration of sociopolitical change.

Secondly, because a sociology of knowledge exposes the fact that humans do construct their world and their morality as well as their legitimizing symbolic universes, it desacralizes society and programs. Its relativizing power, what Berger calls its 'debunking potentiality', underscores its subversive capacity. Sociology demonstrates 'the *makability* of the world: *Not only is the world not what it appears to be, but it could be different from what it is*'.[2] In terms of political options, this realization allows for exposing the unreflective arrogance and unjustifiable abuse of a regime, but utopian aspirations also are tainted. Revolutions, too, in time can become reified:

> Sociological understanding leads to a considerable measure of disenchantment. The disenchanted man is a poor risk for both conservative and revolutionary movements; for the former because he does not possess the requisite amount of credulity in the ideologies of the *status quo*, for the latter because he will be skeptical about the utopian myths that invariably form the nurture of revolutionaries.[3]

Lastly, sociologists, according to their own particular values and vision of the good, can work fervently for change (even revolution).[4] In this task their data can help them grasp contextual realities in all their breadth and with all their complex contradictions. At the same,

their lack of radicalization (*Sociology and Socialism*, pp. 152-55).

1. Berger and Kellner, *Sociology Reinterpreted*, p. 104. See also Berger, *Pyramids of Sacrifice*, ch. 6; idem, *The Capitalist Revolution*, pp. 216-17.
2. Berger and Kellner, *Sociology Reinterpreted*, pp. 13-14 (authors' emphasis). See also Berger, *Invitation to Sociology*, chs. 1, 2, 7, 8.
3. Berger, *Invitation to Sociology*, p. 162.
4. Berger, *Pyramids of Sacrifice*, p. 249; Berger and Kellner, *Sociology Reinterpreted*, pp. 114-16. Berger's *The Capitalist Revolution* is his attempt qua sociologist (i.e. according to his understanding of that role) to present a positive theoretical framework to better understand 'economic culture'.

time, respect for others and their informed skepticism should weigh heavily on the 'calculus of pain' and the 'calculus of meaning'.[1] In the end, he must keep clear in his mind the limits of each of his roles, that of a sociologist-researcher and of a citizen-activist.

The sociology of knowledge, like interpretive anthropology, grants significance to humanity's meanings and its comprehension of life. Humanity's sociopolitical behavior and plausibility structures are inseparable from its symbolic universes. Its moral life is inexorably linked with its world-view and to its 'world'. Religious institutions can be a major socializing and legitimizing agent and, even when in conflict with other (perhaps dominant) 'constructed realities' and structures, can function as moral leaven and an ethical alternative.

Like Geertz, Berger stresses that meaning systems be factored into any discussion of ideology and social change. Berger pursues the relativization further by explaining more explicitly the political ramifications for the researcher: the option for a system that would respect meaning and an aversion of extremism.

c. MacIntyre, Hauerwas and Narrative Ethics

The preceding two sections emphasized humanity's penchant for constructing systems of meaning that are fleshed out in the many institutions, structures and artifacts of everyday life. These systems are not static, nor are they neatly uniform. Humanity lives within a 'web of significances' that has a dialectical relationship with material life.

Germane to the burden of this book are the implications this theoretical framework has for religion and moral life. As has been pointed out, religion can play an important role in the construction of meanings, their legitimation and maintenance, as well as, on occasion, their demystification. Religion also has a part in the definition, promotion and sanctioning of morality.

This section studies in much more detail moral behavior and belief and the relationship between an ethic and a particular community. The work of Alasdair MacIntyre and Stanley Hauerwas can provide

---

1. These are the titles to chs. 5 and 6, respectively, in *Pyramids of Sacrifice*. The former refers to the calculation of the cost in terms of human misery and lives in any postulated program of social change; the latter to the awareness of the inevitable clash of meanings and its possible consequences. In contrast to his earlier ambivalence, in *The Capitalist Revolution*, Berger would still hold to these criteria, yet now opt for capitalism (pp. 12 and 242 n. 32).

greater insight into the dynamic of the morality of a religious community—both its formulation within that association, and its function within the larger society. The discussion that follows considers first the apparent status of morality in general within modern pluralistic societies. Then the fruitful term 'narrative' is explicated to better elucidate the various dimensions of any specific morality. Lastly, this inquiry into ethical discourse will point out the hermeneutical implications of such a narrative approach.

To begin with, what can be said of the state of morality today? The condition of morality itself must be clarified before turning to that of a certain group, such as the Christian church, within the modern world. At first glance, moral coherence has collapsed; chaos and contradiction apparently reign. MacIntyre has recently explored the extent of moral confusion and ethical disagreement in the Western world. His thesis is that the theoretical foundations for moral consensus have been destroyed and abandoned, and that

> What we possess, if this view is true, are the fragments of a conceptual sphere, parts which now lack those contexts from which their significance derived. We possess indeed simulcra of morality, we continue to use many of the key expressions. But we have—very largely, if not entirely— lost our comprehension, both theoretical and practical, of morality.[1]

Consequently, the hope for substantial agreement on moral issues and solutions to pressing social problems is finally an illusion:

> It follows that our society cannot hope to achieve moral consensus. . . It is not just that we live too much by a variety and multiplicity of fragmented concepts; it is that these are used at one and the same time to express rival and incompatible social ideals and policies *and* to furnish us with a pluralistic rhetoric whose function is to conceal the depth of our conflicts.[2]

1. A. MacIntyre, *After Virtue* (Notre Dame, IN: University of Notre Dame Press, 2nd edn, 1984), p. 2. For fuller discussions see *After Virtue*, especially chs. 2, 6–9, 17, and his more recent *Whose Justice? Which Rationality?* (Notre Dame, IN: University of Notre Dame Press, 1988), chs. 1, 18–20. Note also his 'Moral Philosophy: What Next?', in *Revisions: Changing Perspectives in Moral Philosophy* (ed. A. MacIntyre and S. Hauerwas; Notre Dame, IN: University of Notre Dame Press, 1983), pp. 1-15, and 'Does Applied Ethics Rest on a Mistake?', *The Monist* 67 (1984), pp. 498-513.

2. MacIntyre, *After Virtue*, pp. 252-53. This is not to say that there can be no communication between rival traditions. See his discussion of how traditions interact

MacIntyre carefully documents this pessimistic assessment by presenting a historical account of the shifting basis of moral thought; his is a 'dramatic narrative'[1] that tries to make logically and historically intelligible the demise of the traditional consensus and the impossibility of shared moral vision. In his view, the present moral crisis reflects an epistemological one. The solution, in broad terms, lies in 'the construction of local forms of community within which civility and the intellectual and moral life can be sustained through the new dark ages which are already upon us'.[2] For MacIntyre it is the tradition of the virtues, articulated so ably by Aristotle and which has also had its own diachronic development, that is to be nurtured in these communities and that provides the soundest hope for the future.

How is the pluralism-as-predicament quandary to be addressed? Without negating the fact of moral disagreement and its emotive character within Western society, one is not necessarily left with MacIntyre's pessimistic assessment. Modern pluralism does not have to imply total moral entropy. Henry David Aiken's study of the levels of moral discourse can aid here in clarifying the nature of moral con-

and mature and how his perspective differs from what he would call modern 'liberalism', in *Whose Justice?*, chs. 1, 17–20.

1. He anticipates this method in an earlier essay, 'Epistemological Crises, Dramatic Narrative and the Philosophy of Science', *The Monist* 60 (1977), pp. 453-72.

2. MacIntyre, *After Virtue*, p. 263. Others who take the same view of the modern context propose quite distinct solutions. For example, B. Mitchell, citing earlier work by MacIntyre, urges Christian ethics to enter the fray confidently in *Morality: Religious and Secular—The Dilemma of the Traditional Conscience* (Oxford: Clarendon Press, 1980); B. Williams, while recognizing the moral pluralization, investigates the nature of ethical disagreement itself and posits a more confident hope in the possibility of agreement centered on conceptions of human need in *Ethics and the Limits of Philosophy* (London: Fontana/Collins, 1985), pp. 132-73; note especially J. Stout's recent interaction with MacIntyre's position in *Ethics After Babel: The Languages of Morals and their Discontents* (Boston: Beacon Press, 1988), chs. 9–12. This is not, of course, totally to minimize the cultural disintegration that appears to be taking place. E.D. Hirsch, Jr, for example, laments the failure of the US educational system to transmit the community-specific and culturally shared information required for national coherence and for communication among citizens, for what he could call 'cultural competence' or 'cultural literacy' (*Cultural Literacy: What Every American Needs to Know* [Boston: Houghton Mifflin, 1987]).

sensus.[1] He mentions four levels: the expressive, moral rules, ethical principles, and finally the post-ethical. It is at least at the first two levels that conventional morality will find expression and popular agreement—that is, first, spontaneously and intuitively according to the 'nature of things' and, secondly, volitionally according to the constraints imposed by this constructed social reality. Sharp differences can occur at the other two levels over questions of ultimate validity, justification and authority. At the bottom levels, however, as has been pointed out by Geertz and Berger, more than specific moral philosophies are generating and defining ethical activity. Obviously, the fewer competing symbolic universes there are and the more extensive the theoretical homogeneity, the greater the amount of consensus. Yet, what is more, different moral theories themselves are not as exclusive as MacIntyre might sometimes imply, but can overlap and converge at different levels and on different issues; they can agree to similar courses of action and voice like concerns, even though the reasons may differ.

To limit the sphere of moral debate to the philosophical and academic, then, is to misread the very nature of social existence and everyday life. In Stuart Hampshire's words, 'there are two faces of morality: the rational and articulate side and the less than rational, the historically conditioned, fiercely individualistic, imaginative, parochial, the less than fully articulate side'.[2] The connections, moreover, are inescapable. Moral life is lived in the tension between the ideal (whether carefully thought out or not) and the pragmatic. In truth, to live consistently and solely on an ideal plane is impossible. Moral functionality requires the customary and the conventional, as well as the articulate.[3] Neuhaus, who refers to MacIntyre on several

---

1. H.D. Aiken, 'Levels of Moral Discourse', in *Reason and Conduct: New Bearings in Moral Philosophy* (New York: Alfred A. Knopf, 1962), pp. 65-87. See also Mitchell, *Morality: Religious and Secular*, pp. 98-106.

2. S. Hampshire, *Morality and Conflict* (Oxford: Basil Blackwell, 1983), p. 2.

3. W.K. Frankena points out that MacIntyre fails to distinguish a prevailing philosophical theory from the morality of a culture as a whole in his review of *After Virtue* ('MacIntyre and Modern Morality', *Ethics* 93 [1983], p. 583). Besides the references noted above that respond to MacIntyre's comment regarding 'the dark ages which are upon us', see also the more sensitive discussions by P.F. Strawson, 'Social Morality and Individual Ideal', in *Christian Ethics and Contemporary Society* (ed. I.T. Ramsey; The Library of Philosophy and Theology; London: SCM Press,

occasions in his treatment of modern North American society, makes this blunt, yet telling, remark: 'MacIntyre's dismal reading of our times is no doubt an accurate description of the *logic* of contemporary philosophical, moral, and legal reasoning. Fortunately, the world is not terribly logical.'[1]

Morality, therefore, as it is lived out 'on the ground' is a complex phenomenon. As Geertz and Berger also emphasize, it cannot be neatly categorized and limited to formal and tidy ethical theories. Societies possess competing and overlapping philosophies and world-views, as well as multiple arenas for social interchange. Any morality that might claim to be 'particular' cannot then pretend to be totally 'pure'; complete isolation is impossible, moral interaction inevitable.

Even if his understanding of the status of moral life can be questioned, MacIntyre's notion of 'narrative' can prove insightful in linking ethical traditions to communities. Because his employment of the term, however, is quite varied, the focus here will be only on those meanings pertinent to the concerns of this book.[2]

At one level the term can refer to the *history of ethical discourse*. This is the 'dramatic narrative' mentioned earlier, which plots the development of ethics over the centuries. His reconstruction would have to be evaluated, as indeed it already has been, according to its accuracy and comprehensiveness.[3]

1966), pp. 280-98; D. Emmett, *The Moral Prism* (London: Macmillan, 1973), pp. 115-24; Hampshire, *Morality and Conflict*, pp. 101-39.

1. Neuhaus, *Public Square*, p. 87 (author's emphasis).

2. See MacIntyre, *After Virtue*, ch. 15, for the various nuances of the term. For an analysis of these uses, see L.G. Jones, 'Alasdair MacIntyre on Narrative, Community, and the Moral Life', *ModTh* 4 (1987), pp. 53-69. For a survey of other ethicists who have also utilized aspects inherent in the concept without necessarily making use of the term itself, see P.T. Nelson, 'Narrative and Morality: A Theological Inquiry' (unpublished PhD thesis, Yale University, 1984), pp. 32-74.

3. E.g. Frankena, 'MacIntyre and Modern Morality'; J. Stout, 'Virtue Among the Ruins: An Essay on MacIntyre', *NSys* 26 (1984), pp. 256-73; R.J. Mouw, 'Alasdair MacIntyre on Reformation Ethics', *JRelEth* 13 (1985), pp. 243-57. MacIntyre himself allows, for example, that his earlier reading of Aquinas in *After Virtue* had been 'mistaken' (*Whose Justice?*, p. x). Mention should also be made of R.B. Reich's *Tales of a New America* (New York: Times Books, 1987). Reich would claim that North American society has structured its politics around four basic 'morality tales', and that both mainline political parties have interpreted them from their own perspective and utilized them. In other words, these stories are broadly

Another use refers to the nature of humans themselves. It is suggested that *the self has a narrative quality* and that humans have the need to order life according to stories, both 'mundane' and 'sacred'.[1] 'It is not enough' Amos Wilder says, 'for memory to expand the transient present by recall; it must structure this impermanence and "place" as in this or that reassuring pattern or chart or story which can thus also illuminate the present and the future'.[2]

Individual stories, however, are not isolated narratives, and so another aspect of the term's meaning can echo the earlier treatment of enculturation and socialization. These processes involve the creation and internalization of *a biography within a social context*:[3]

> in successfully identifying and understanding what someone else is doing we always move towards placing a particular episode in a context of a set of narrative histories, histories both of the individuals concerned and of the settings in which they act and suffer.[4]

Finally, another category to which the concept of narrative can be applied refers again to social identity, although now in terms of a certain community within society. In other words, the referent is now *a particular social context*. It may be recalled that MacIntyre's hope lies in 'local forms of community' that will embody and maintain ethical ideals. It is at this crucial juncture that vagueness blunts the force of his presentation. As Hauerwas and Wadell observe:

> Without some specification of what narrative MacIntyre espouses, his community offers little hope, and that's because, without a sense of who

shared by the public and yet are flexible enough to be reshaped and re-used through time. What is needed, he says, is a new version of the tales to meet the changing realities of modern politics and economics (see especially chs. 1–3, 20). His thesis is relevant because it would demonstrate that stories, especially ones shared by the larger populace, are much more widely appropriated, hardy and pliable than MacIntyre sometimes envisions.

1. S. Crites, 'The Narrative Quality of Experience', *JAAR* 39 (1971), pp. 291-311. See also A.N. Wilder, 'Story and Story-World', *Int* 37 (1983), pp. 353-64. For a critique of these sometimes sweeping claims, see T.L. Estess, 'The Inenarrable Contraption: Reflections on the Metaphor of Story', *JAAR* 42 (1974), pp. 415-34.

2. Wilder, 'Story and Story-World', p. 359.

3. E.g. P.L. Berger, 'Excursus: Alternation and Biography (Or: How to Acquire a Prefabricated Past)', in *Invitation to Sociology*, pp. 54-65; *idem*, *The Sacred Canopy*, *passim*; Weigert, *Sociology*, pp. 177-82.

4. MacIntyre, *After Virtue*, p. 211.

we are and what we are to become, it is difficult to determine what we ought to do. Until then, *After Virtue* remains trapped in the very tragedy it fears, and its retelling as a story of our lives is frightening.[1]

MacIntyre fails to identify his community of virtue, and so his vision of hope in the midst of perceived moral chaos remains empty—one could say bodiless. Where is this community to be found, nurtured, and sustained? Moreover, what relationship would it have with the other narratives, both shared and contending, of the larger context within which it would be embedded? Though these questions are not answered by MacIntyre, the concept of 'narrative' and the issues of community identity and existence can find fruitful application in the study of Christian ethics.

Recently, 'narrative theology' has arisen to probe the implications of this approach for the nature of Christian existence. This label, 'narrative theology', can be a very imprecise one, however, because of the far-ranging and diverse interests coming under this rubric.[2] Generally speaking, it is the attempt to understand reality and Christian life in terms of story—that is with characters, coherence, movement, and purpose set within the Christian communal and canonical framework.

Stanley Hauerwas has made a concerted effort to relate this narrative approach to Christian ethics. With MacIntyre he points to the contemporary moral confusion in society, which is 'living amid fragments'.[3] Hauerwas attempts to postulate a proper foundation for

1. S. Hauerwas and P. Wadell, review of *After Virtue*, *The Thomist* 46 (1982), p. 321.

2. For a comprehensive survey and critique, see M. Goldberg, *Theology and Narrative: A Critical Introduction* (Nashville: Abingdon Press, 1981); also G.W. Stroup, *The Promise of Narrative Theology: Recovering the Gospel in the Church* (Atlanta: John Knox, 1981), pp. 70-94; G. Fackre, 'Narrative Theology: An Overview', *Int* 37 (1983), pp. 340-52. Although G.A. Linbeck does not use the term 'narrative', his 'cultural linguistic' approach demonstrates similar concerns and perspectives (*The Nature of Doctrine: Religion and Theology in a Postliberal Age* [Philadelphia: Westminster Press, 1984], pp. 32-41).

3. S. Hauerwas, *The Peaceable Kingdom: A Primer in Christian Ethics* (London: SCM Press, 1983), pp. 1-15. Although more recently J.W. McClendon, who is very appreciative of the work of MacIntyre and Hauerwas, has also presented a narrative approach, this section will concentrate on Hauerwas. See McClendon, *Systematic Theology*. I. *Ethics* (Nashville: Abingdon Press, 1986), especially chs. 2, 6, 12. Note, too, B.C. Birch and L.L. Rasmussen, *Bible & Ethics in the Christian*

Christian moral life as over against both the modern assertion that morality is nothing more than free personal choice as well as the effort to transcend the chaos by appealing to some universal morality. Both postures are misguided: the former is selfish and manipulative; the latter is impractical and relativizes Christian convictions.

His thesis develops along several interrelated themes. One of his goals is to criticize the common deontological, teleological and situational models of moral discourse.[1] Usually, he claims, these methods tend to focus on moral 'quandaries', on the situations demanding a moral decision instead of on the character of the moral agent; they also remove morality from the broader communal context by trying to make ethics an objective rational enterprise that can appeal to universal norms, principles or ends; finally, they also misrepresent the bitter realities of moral dilemmas that seem to offer no hope of a painless solution by simplistically eliminating the problem through recourse to 'duty' or the 'common good'. A more appropriate ethic in his view must be grounded in the virtues—that is, in the formation of the moral character of the agent who can discern the appropriate course of action in any situation and who can remain faithful and committed to his moral vision.[2]

Crucial to the development of the virtues, then, will be the conceptual and experiential framework that provides the content and

Life (Minneapolis, MN: Augsburg, rev. edn, 1989).

1. S. Hauerwas with D.B. Burrell, 'From System to Story: An Alternative Pattern for Rationality in Ethics', in *Truthfulness and Tragedy: Further Investigations in Christian Ethics* (Notre Dame, IN: University of Notre Dame Press, 1977), pp. 15-39, and 'Casuistry as a Narrative Art', in *The Peaceable Kingdom*, pp. 116-34. (Cf. McClendon, *Systematic Theology*, I, pp. 332-46; Birch and Rasmussen, *Bible & Ethics*, chs. 3, 6.) For a critique from a non-narrative persuasion see J.W. Robbins, 'Narrative, Morality and Religion', *JRelEth* 8 (1980), pp. 161-76.

2. S. Hauerwas, *Character and the Christian Life: A Study in Theological Ethics* (San Antonio, TX: Trinity University Press, 1975), pp. 1-34. In 'Obligation and Virtue Once More' (*Truthfulness and Tragedy*, pp. 40-56) he distinguishes his understanding of an ethic of virtue from that of William K. Frankena. See Frankena, 'Conversations with Carney and Hauerwas', *JRelEth* 3 (1975), pp. 45-62. Note also the interchange between J.W. Robbins ('On the Role of Vision in Morality', *JAAR* 45 Supp. 1 [1977], pp. 623-42), and Hauerwas ('Learning How to See Red Wheelbarrows: On Vision and Relativism' in the same issue, pp. 643-55). Cf. McClendon, *Systematic Theology*, I, pp. 103-109, 169-73; Birch and Rasmussen, *Bible & Ethics*, chs. 4, 5.

context for those virtues. Every ethic, in other words, must be qualified, and accordingly a 'Christian' ethic will have a distinctive shape: 'The nature of Christian ethics is determined by the fact that Christian convictions take the form of a story, or perhaps better, a set of stories that constitutes a tradition, which in turn creates and forms a community'.[1]

A Christian morality, therefore, is a narrative ethic in the twofold sense of having a sociohistorical component (the Christian community), and a peculiar literary component (the Bible and tradition). This narrative foundation, which is both communal and canonical, provides a truthful vision of reality,[2] gives Christians an identity, shapes the character, and so determines how moral decisions are faced; casuistry, then, is not handled by rational argument according to a certain ethical theory, but rather by testing thoughts and behavior against how others, faithful to scriptural insights and within the community of moral discourse that is the church, have responded in the past. To try 'to deny the inherent historical and community-dependent nature of our moral convictions in the hopes that our "ethics" might be universally persuasive' by reducing the essence of religion to morality[3] or by supporting some sort of natural law[4] contradicts the distinctives fundamental to Christian faith. There is no room for eliminating or minimizing its particularistic aspects.

This vision of the moral life of the Christian and the church is compelling and insightful. A problem surfaces, however, precisely because of Hauerwas's stress on the radicalness of an ethic grounded in the Christian story. His concern to demonstrate the distinctive

---

1. Hauerwas, *The Peaceable Kingdom*, p. 24. See also *idem*, 'The Moral Authority of Scripture: The Politics and Ethics of Remembering', *Int* 34 (1980), pp. 356-70; *idem*, 'The Church as God's New Language', in *Scriptural Authority and Narrative Interpretation* (ed. G. Green; Philadelphia: Fortress Press, 1987), pp. 179-98; S. Hauerwas with W.H. Willimon, *Resident Aliens: Life in the Christian Colony* (Nashville: Abingdon Press, 1989), chs. 3, 4, 7.

2. For the criteria of a 'truthful' story see *Truthfulness and Tragedy*, pp. 34-39. (Cf. McClendon, *Systematic Theology*, I, pp. 348-56; Birch and Rasmussen, *Bible & Ethics*, chs. 7, 8.)

3. Hauerwas, 'On Keeping Theological Ethics Theological', in *Revisions*, p. 33. Cf. Hauerwas and Willimon, *Resident Aliens*, chs. 1, 2.

4. Hauerwas, *The Peaceable Kingdom*, pp. 50-64. See his alternative approach to natural law according to his ethics of virtues view: 'Natural Law, Tragedy, and Theological Ethics', *American Journal of Jurisprudence* 20 (1975), pp. 1-19.

nature of Christian morality has been consciously developed to contradict other attempts to find some kind of (lowest) common denominator with other moralities that do not share Christian convictions; usually the classical constructs have appealed to an independent realm of morality accessible by reason. What Hauerwas has rightly decried is the ensuing loss of particularity in attempting to find a universal morality, but has he sufficiently grasped the nature of morality in context or grappled with the 'moral overlap' that exists between other traditions and communities in a given society or between societies? How can the points of contact or moral convention be explained, even expected within his proposal? Hauerwas offers two possible solutions.

The primary task of the church in the world, he says, is to be the church, a community that tries to be a witness of God's kingdom and to help the world see itself truthfully, as it really is as God's redeemed though alienated creation.[1] The fact of this redemption points to a possible bridge to non-Christian moralities:

> That is why as Christians we may not only find that people who are not Christians manifest God's peace better than we ourselves, but we must demand that they exist. It is to be hoped that such people may provide the conditions for our ability to cooperate with others for securing justice in the world. Such cooperation, however, is not based on 'natural law', legitimation of a generally shared 'natural morality'. Rather it is a testimony to the fact that God's kingdom is wide indeed. As the church we have no right to determine the boundaries of God's kingdom, for it is our happy task to acknowledge God's power to make his kingdom present in the most surprising places and ways.[2]

This is a surprising, and apparently contradictory, statement in light of his passion to maintain a particularistic ethic shaped by a specific tradition and community

Another argument which is much more consistent with his general presentation posits, following Gustafson,[3] that all communities require certain sustaining 'natural' virtues.[4] Christian convictions, of course,

---

1. Hauerwas, 'The Politics of Charity', in *Truthfulness and Tragedy*, pp. 132-43; *The Peaceable Kingdom*, pp. 99-102; Hauerwas and Willimon, *Resident Aliens*, ch. 5.

2. Hauerwas, *The Peaceable Kingdom*, p. 101.

3. J.M. Gustafson, 'The Moral Conditions for Human Community', in *Christian Ethics and the Community* (New York: Pilgrim Press, 1979), pp. 153-63.

4. Hauerwas, 'Natural Law, Tragedy, and Theological Ethics'; *idem, The*

can give a different meaning and configuration to these common virtues. There can exist then, in some sense, shared virtues, but Hauerwas nowhere develops how this moral datum arises and is articulated in the social process.

Except for these short references to a possible broader consensus, his work tends to present the false alternatives of either a Christian ethic or a non-Christian morality. But how do Christians and the church actually perceive themselves and function within the larger society? Perhaps another formulation of a narrative ethic could be attempted which utilizes the positive contributions of Hauerwas as well as insights from the earlier sections of this chapter.

Narrative ethics is not only communal, it is also contextual. To start with, the levels of moral discourse mentioned above in connection with MacIntyre are relevant here: Hauerwas also seems to be doing his theoretical work at levels three (ethical) and four (post-ethical), where ethical principles are articulated and explicitly legitimated according to ultimate 'givens'. There is an apparent lack of an adequate sense of the more mundane and of the conventional. This lacuna is in part due to an insufficient grasp of the socialization process: the 'narrative' of any particular community and of any individual within it is actually intertwined with the larger 'narrative' (as well as many smaller ones) of society in a variety of ways. As Ogletree points out:

> if we are to speak of the *formation* of lives. . . then primacy must surely be granted not to beliefs and convictions in themselves, but to the various dynamics which make up human sociality—particularly the intersubjective constitution of selfhood as it interacts with basic instinctual energies, with specific patterns of social organization, and with a shared culture. Beliefs and convictions are a feature of the common culture, but they are effective in shaping lives only by way of the social processes which mediate, confirm, modify and reinforce them in human life.[1]

Specific communities are rarely, if ever, hermetically sealed entities immune from intercourse within the broader context; Christian identity, in other words, is tied to both Christian and larger traditions, associations and commitments. Christian moral understanding as well,

Peaceable Kingdom, pp. 69, 102-15. (Cf. McClendon, *Systematic Theology*, I, pp. 103-109.)

1. T.W. Ogletree, 'Character and Narrative: Stanley Hauerwas' Studies in the Christian Life', *RelStR* 6 (1980), p. 26 (author's emphasis). See also G. Outka, 'Character, Vision, and Narrative', *RelStR* 6 (1980), pp. 110-18.

then, will arise from several sources and be shaped in a variety of environments and challenged from different quarters. The problem, therefore, for *a Christian ethic in context* involves specifying its character according to its peculiar communal and canonical tradition, as well as defining or clarifying how this identity is to be comprehended within and related to the sociocultural world in which the church lives.[1] Hauerwas rightly criticizes supposedly ahistorical, objective, universal ethics by lobbying for a qualified ethic. This book also presses for a qualified ethic, but would hold that the label necessarily has two components: Christian and contextual. The order of the two qualifiers is important, for the goal is a *Christian* ethic. To interact with the many possible relationships between Christ and culture (to borrow the title from the book by H. Richard Niebuhr) lies beyond the compass of this book. The purpose here is simply to emphasize the priority of the 'Christian' specification and of its inseparableness from the local context.

The hermeneutical weaknesses inherent in Hauerwas's position are also immense. What is ignored is not only the social fact that any Christian community is situated within a larger setting, but also that that context can powerfully color the perception of the biblical narrative itself and the subsequent lifestyle that is labeled 'Christian'.

This awareness of the role of pre-understandings has become a major element of recent hermeneutical studies.[2] Theologians in the Two-Thirds World, however, and liberation theologians in particular, have especially underscored how determinative are the sociopolitical context and the (conscious or unconscious) ideological commitments of the theologian.

---

1. J.M. Gustafson, *Can Ethics Be Christian?* (Chicago: University of Chicago Press, 1975), pp. 145-79. Neuhaus, for example, grapples with this practically in trying to sort out how best the church should speak out in the public arena. In his argument he is critical of the means used by both the fundamentalists and the historical denominations (*Public Square*). To mention Neuhaus is not necessarily to agree with his point of view, but simply to recognize that the embeddedness of the church is a fact that must be wrestled with. Cf. G. Meilaender, 'Virtue in Contemporary Religious Thought', in *Virtue—Public & Private* (ed. R.J. Neuhaus; Encounter Series; Grand Rapids: Eerdmans, 1986), pp. 7-29, and Hauerwas's interaction, pp. 60-66, 72-73, 78-81.

2. For a helpful survey, see A.C. Thiselton, *The Two Horizons: New Testament Hermeneutics and Philosophic Description* (Grand Rapids: Eerdmans, 1980), pp. 103-14, 133-39, 136-39, 303-10.

The different social settings and commitments throughout the history of the Christian church have clearly affected the choice of controlling paradigms selected from the Bible by different individuals and ecclesiastical bodies[1] (even in this case, Hauerwas's selection of a servant-pacifist model),[2] and these constructs themselves can be in constant tension or dialogue.[3] Goldberg, in a critique of Hauerwas, makes the incisive observation:

> no theologian gets his understanding of the meaning of a narrative independent of any perspective whatsoever. To the extent that one's hermeneutic perspective has its roots in some tradition (religious or otherwise), and to the extent that each tradition is a narrative of sorts, one's choice of stories for theological significance as well as one's understanding of what significance such stories have will themselves be narrative dependent. In the end, traditions such as these establish the various primary conditions for the proper theological understanding of the meaning of a narrative.[4]

The decision to take a more comprehensive narrative approach also has political implications. Hauerwas's presentation of the Christian narrative relativizes commitment to and any identification with any specific sociopolitical system. On the one hand, the narrative perspec-

---

1. These studies can follow various approaches—e.g. a comparison of ecclesiastical models. The classic here, of course, would be E. Troeltsch, *The Social Teaching of the Christian Churches* (trans. O. Wyon; New York: Macmillan, 1931); or an investigation of the role of the Bible in political movements, such as E.R. Sandeen (ed.), *The Bible and Social Reform* (Philadelphia/Chico, CA: Fortress Press/Scholars Press, 1982). D.H. Kelsey's observation that different perceptions of the mode of God's presence among his people affect how the authority of Scripture is construed is appropriate here, as this would also pertain to how the corresponding ethic is formulated (*The Uses of Scripture in Recent Theology* [Philadelphia: Fortress Press, 1975], pp. 158-81). Cf. M.D. Carroll R., 'The Relevance of Cultural Conditioning for Social Ethics', *JETS* 29 (1986), pp. 307-15.

2. Hauerwas, *The Peaceable Kingdom*, pp. 87-91, 133-51. He admits his debt to J.H. Yoder, p. xxiv.

3. R.McA. Brown, perhaps because of his extensive interaction with liberation theology, is more aware of the challenge that comes from hearing the Christian story in a new way. See his 'My Story and "The Story"', *TTod* 32 (1975), pp. 166-73, and *Theology in a New Key: Responding to Liberation Themes* (Philadelphia: Westminster Press, 1978), chs. 2, 5, 6.

4. Goldberg, *Theology and Narrative*, p. 213. See also T.W. Ogletree's suggestion for 'historical contextualism' in *The Use of the Bible in Christian Ethics* (Philadelphia: Fortress Press, 1983), pp. 34-41.

tive would appear to tend to support some sort of democracy that would allow for plurality and freedom of expression.[1] Yet, at the same time, a democratic state is still a state, a human creation that can easily move in its own way toward hubris and cruelty:

> Democracies after all can be just as tyrannical in their claims on the loyalties of their citizens as totalitarian alternatives. Indeed, the tyranny may be all the more perverse because we have freely given the democratic state the right to command our consciences.[2]

The commitment to the ideals within Christian narrative must not tempt the church to compromise its unique identity by losing itself in a cause or a system:

> Rather, the call for the church to be the church means that the church is the only true polity we can know in this life. For the church, because it is a polity that fears not the truth, is also a community of friends that has the courage to form its citizens virtuously. . . Only by being such a people will we be able to resist the false choices—such as choosing between America and the Soviet Union—that would have us take sides in a manner that divides the Christian people from one another and their true Lord.[3]

This point of view generates its own 'narrative realism' and would question any wholesale embracing or advocating of any political campaign or program. Notice that what is *not* said is that the Christian should withdraw from society, or that he not make any political decisions or have preferences. Instead, what needs to be avoided is the granting of divine approbation or legitimation to any human government or ideology. The championing of Christian values, such as justice, must not ignore how the Christian ethic must be lived out, because the Christian narrative embodies both standards of morality and service. If the priority becomes *effectiveness*—that is, if the question becomes how well the ethic is working—then *faithfulness* to the narrative might be compromised, and ideological and political expediency thus override truthful living.[4]

---

1. E.g. McClendon, *Systematic Theology*, I, pp. 235-36.

2. S. Hauerwas, 'Reply to R.J. Neuhaus', *Center Journal* 1 (1982), p. 47. Cf. *The Peaceable Kingdom*, pp. 12-13, 111-15; Hauerwas and Willimon, *Resident Aliens*, pp. 30-36, 77-78.

3. Hauerwas, 'Reply to R.J. Neuhaus', p. 51.

4. Hauerwas, 'The Politics of Charity', in *Truthfulness and Tragedy*, pp. 132-46; *The Peaceable Kingdom*, pp. 102-106; Hauerwas and Willimon, *Resident*

If the strength of Hauerwas lies in his relativizing of politics, once again his weakness is contextual myopia. Although Christian perspectives and priorities can differ according to a particular history, story and life, the church cannot be isolated politically from its world. A review of Hauerwas's *The Peaceable Kingdom* concurs:

> Perhaps the biggest challenge to this position that insists upon the fundamental role of narrative for ethics is how it will enable those who adhere to it to participate in a moral dialogue with persons in other traditions, religious or secular, concerning public policy issues. There is no clear account of the ways in which public principles, or even public virtues, can be articulated and formed so as to provide a basis for members of different communities to communicate with each other for the common good of their shared society.[1]

Because of the recognition that the Christian church is embedded in other contextual narratives, a more comprehensive narrative approach, however, can enter into dialogue with others and can allow for involvement in the solving of public policy issues. Once again, this is not the place to specify how this responsibility should be defined or fleshed out; the crux is the awareness that religion and morality must be understood in context. This way of seeing, therefore, understands that the Christian church, the community of virtue of narrative ethics, exists within a broader sociocultural matrix which influences in some measure its faith and morality.

Hauerwas has rendered a valuable service in highlighting 'the *normative* frame of reference within which the moral quality of our lives is to be assessed'—namely, the Christian community and its Scripture.[2] What has been lacking is a better formulation of the *contextual* framework within which the Christian church lives and must act.

d. *Conclusion*

This first part of the chapter has attempted to present the theoretical basis for a different manner of understanding Christian morality in context. This orientation grounds its perspective in the contributions of certain social sciences and narrative ethics, which point out how

   1. M. Longwood, 'How Ethics Should Be Done', *Int* 40 (1986), p. 77.
   2, Ogletree, 'Character and Narrative', p. 26 (emphasis added).

any given context—and so the religion and morality within that setting—must be comprehended by focusing attention on the 'web of significances' that are a culture and a human society.

Interpretive anthropology and the sociology of knowledge explicate in part how humans construct (and are in turn molded by) their social reality and shape their relationships to material life and to their fellow human beings. They emphasize that meaning is relevant to analyzing society and to positing change.

Hauerwas, however, provides what Geertz and Berger do not: a normative reference point, amid the relativity of a world of constructed universes, in the Christian community and its sacred tradition. Geertz had spoken of the moral power of texts and Berger of the role of religious traditions, yet the narrative perspective more clearly specifies the sources—both relational and revelational, as it were—of the values for the commitment of the 'Bergerian' sociologist, who desires to be careful in his method yet constructive in his social action.

On the other hand, Geertz and Berger provide contextual realism to Hauerwas's abstract idealization: they demonstrate that the church is a culture within a culture, a community within a community, *a world within the world*. Importantly, all three would be wary of an absolutist program of change which might, on the one hand, manipulate meaning contexts and, on the other, evade the relativizing implications of the facts of its own particular formulation.

This book is ultimately concerned with discerning how Christian theology and morality are to be interpreted and articulated within Latin America. On the basis of the discussion thus far, the second part of this chapter suggests a way of looking at Latin America and the Christian church in that context. To clarify this approach, the proposal will interact with the hermeneutical and ideological commitments of several Latin American liberation theologians.

2. *Understanding Latin America*

This book has as its goal the articulation of a methodology that would offer guidelines for a sensitive use of the text in a context—sensitive in a double sense: to the biblical text's literary power and to the socio-cultural realities which that text is to impact. The first aspect is the topic of the next chapter. This section of the present chapter focuses on the second. Here a context is actually specified, because, though this is on the one hand a proposal of a general sort, ultimately my interests lie in Latin America, and even more particularly in Guatemala. The discussion that follows is divided into two parts, which deal in turn, from an interpretive perspective, with the Christian church in Latin America and theological method.

a. *Religion and Morality in Latin America*

Latin American culture is rich and blended, with roots in the great Amerindian civilizations that antedate the arrival of the Iberian explorers in the fifteenth century. These civilizations (in Guatemala's case, the Mayan) were defeated, ransacked for their wealth, and put into the service of the *conquistadores*. With the Spanish came not only a dominant language and a specific distribution of land and power by race and family, but also a whole set of values, an ethos, with its perspective on, among other things, work, women, race, and status, that was to hybridize with that of the native population.[1] Although the nature of the 'mix' of these civilizations is disputed,[2] their interfusion

---

1. Note the variety of interpretations of fifteenth- and sixteenth-century Spain and her Christian faith: the chapter entitled 'The Iberian Soul' in the classic work by J. Mackay, *The Other Spanish Christ: A Study in the Spiritual History of Spain and South America* (New York: Macmillan, 1932), pp. 3-22; E. Dussel, *A History of the Church in Latin America: Colonialism to Liberation* (trans. and rev. A. Neely; Grand Rapids: Eerdmans, 1981), pp. 37-61; S. Martínez Peláez, *La patria del criollo. Ensayo de interpretación de la realidad colonial guatemalteca* (San José, CR: EDUCA, 8th edn, 1981); J. Hawkins, *Inverse Images: The Meaning of Culture, Ethnicity and Family in Postcolonial Guatemala* (Albuquerque: University of New Mexico Press, 1984), ch. 2; F. Mires, *En nombre de la cruz. Discusiones teológicas y políticas frente al holocausto de los indios (período de conquista)* (San José, CR: DEI, 1986), chs. 1, 2, and *La colonización de las almas. Misión y conquista en Hispanoamérica* (San José, CR: DEI, 1987), ch. 1.

2. The traditional ideas are that what exists today is simply a new hybrid from the combination of the cultures, or that there are pre-Columbian elements surviving within the dominant Spanish culture. More recently, however, Hawkins has argued against

> simple notions of cultural syncretism, cultural separatism, or pre-Hispanic cultural continuity among the Indians by suggesting that many of the unique and un-Spanish aspects of Indian culture are an *inverse creation* of the overlord culture brought to America by the Spaniards. The deep premises of Indian life are a conceptual system primarily forged in response to Conquistador thought and action, rather than a system largely derived from the pristine Mayans and corrupted by subsequent Spanish influence (*Inverse Images*, p. 23; emphasis added).

has resulted in a culture unique to this continent.

The mosaic that is Latin America can be studied, on the one hand, diachronically, beginning with those pre-Hispanic peoples, moving through the conquest, to the present.[1] Latin American culture can also be viewed, however, synchronically and comparatively, by investigating individual national cultures (which each nurture their own particular customs and traditions)[2] as constituent parts within an overall continental culture.[3] Liberation historian and philosopher Enrique Dussel, while acknowledging the diversity, notes:

> Our national cultures can only be said to possess distinct personalities within a limited scope manifesting a certain consistency which could be legitimately designated by the name 'culture'. That is, our individual national cultures are constituent parts of the overall Latin American culture. Furthermore, these same regional cultures have for four centuries in one way or another—as all germinal cultures have—manifested secondary and marginal characteristics of European culture, and at the same time they have become consistently more autonomous. Despite the sociopolitical, economic, and technical underdevelopment, Latin America has become aware of its life-style and has tended to separate itself from European culture. Our hypothesis is, therefore, the following: to comprehend fully

For his part, Martínez Peláez would claim that the postcolonial Mayan culture was actually created by the Spanish to aid in the oppression of the Indians (Hawkins contrasts his own view with that of Martínez Peláez in *Inverse Images*, pp. 44, 80). The modern revolutionary project, he claims, would, therefore, no longer view their present culture as something to be preserved or valued as a national treasure, but rather would see its passing as part of the process of liberating the broader proletariat (*La patria del criollo*, pp. 394-618). Cf. Octavio Paz's thoughts on the resulting Mexican culture in 'Nueva España: orfandad y legitimidad', in *El ogro filantrópico. Historia y política 1971-1978* (México: Joaquín Mortiz, 1979), pp. 38-52.

1. E.g. P.H. Ureña, *A Concise History of Latin American Culture* (trans. G. Chase; London: Pall Mall Press, 1966); Dussel, *History*, especially pp. 21-35 (his various definitions appear on pp. 21-24, 262 n. 18). The former work actually details the 'cultural achievements' over time (e.g. art, literature).

2. E.g. for Guatemala: M.A. Carrera, *Costumbres de Guatemala. Cuadros de costumbres* (Guatemala: Edinter, 1986); V. Perera, *Rites: A Guatemalan Boyhood* (London: André Deutsch, 1986).

3. E.g. E.A. Nida, *Understanding Latin Americans, with Special Emphasis to Religious Values and Movements* (South Pasadena: William Carey Library, 1974); M.K. Mayers, *A Look at Latin America Lifestyles* (SIL Museum of Anthropology, 2; Dallas: SIL Museum of Anthropology, 1976); Dussel, *History*, ch. 2; E.A. Núñez and W.D. Taylor, *Crisis in Latin America: An Evangelical Perspective* (Chicago: Moody Press, 1989), ch. 5.

the individual national cultures, one must consider the structures of Latin American culture as a whole.[1]

Juan Carlos Scannone comments:

> The advocates of this line believe there is a Latin American culture; although this culture is neither uniform nor homogeneous nor without sharp contradictions, it has sufficient historical unity and similar nuclei to allow us to conceive it in terms of a pluralistic or analogical unity.[2]

Dussell makes further distinctions in his discussion of culture. On the one hand, he locates the national and broader continental cultures within the center-periphery dependency paradigm.[3] There exists, he says, cultural dependency: since the conquest, imperial and dominating cultural powers have invaded the continent and presented themselves as superior and universal. The traditional ruling elites have often absorbed and mimicked the foreign culture, and this cultural visitation has also often been linked with economic and political maneuvering and machinations.

This protest against cultural interference and imposition is not confined to liberationists. Latin Americans have often embarked on a quest to identify and celebrate a culture authentic to their context. The Mexican philosopher Leopoldo Zea decries the attempts in the past to deny Latin American reality and impose other values and systems:

> they tried, even though in vain, to change Latin American reality by using the frock coat, the silk hat, the railroad, the reading of the latest European book, the Constitution of the United States, and the imposition of the highest institutional forms of Western democracy and liberalism. Also useless was the adoption of positivism as an educational philosophy that tried to turn Latin Americans into southern Anglo-Saxons and their peo-

1. Dussel, *History*, p. 28.

2. J.C. Scannone, 'Evangelization of Culture, Liberation, and "Popular" Culture: The New Theological-Pastoral Synthesis in Latin America', in *The Church & Culture Since Vatican II: The Experience of North and Latin America* (ed. J. Gremillion; Notre Dame, IN: University of Notre Dame Press, 1985), p. 81.

3. E. Dussel, *Filosofía ética latinoamericana. 6/III. De la erótica a la pedagogía de la liberación* (Filosofía y Liberación Latinoamericana; México: EDICOL, SA, 1977), pp. 208-11; *History*, pp. 3-20. A Marxist attack published during the Allende regime in Chile, that has become a 'counter-culture' classic, hits at the invasion through the media of North American values and world-view into that context: A. Dorfman and A. Mattelart, *Para leer al pato Donald. Comunicación de masa y colonialismo* (Mexico: Siglo XXI, 28th edn, 1987), especially pp. 3-22, 151-60.

ples into a United States of the South. All of this was useless; the reality, no matter how hard they tried to hide it, was still there. The Indian and the *mestizo* were and still are there.[1]

The goal of this 'cultural process' has been freedom from foreign cultural domination and, ultimately, the establishment of socio-economic and political systems true to the constitution and color of Latin America. This sense of movement and unity of aspiration have characterized the continent since independence early in the last century. This feeling of purpose—even destiny—can reach universal dimensions, and Latin America has sometimes been envisioned as a source of inspiration for all mankind.[2]

1. L. Zea, *El pensamiento latinoamericano* (Bibliotheca de Ciencia Política; Barcelona: Editorial Ariel, 3rd edn, 1976), p. 451. See the fuller discussion on pp. 451-512 and also his chapter entitled 'Self-Discovery' in an earlier work, *Latin America and the World* (trans. F.K. Hendricks and B. Berler; Norman, OK: University of Oklahoma Press, 1969), pp. 3-16.

An early, now famous, essay published originally in 1900 by José Enrique Rodó (Uruguay) entitled *Ariel* endeavored to establish a Latin American identity vis-à-vis the United States. For modern interactions with this piece and the constant theme of the question of cultural identity, see the preface by Carlos Fuentes (Mexico) to a modern edition (*Ariel* [trans. M.S. Peden; Austin, TX: University of Texas Press, 1988], pp. 13-28), as well as R. González Echevarría, 'The Case of the Speaking Statue: *Ariel* and the Magisterial Rhetoric of the Latin American Essay', in *The Voice of the Masters: Writing and Authority in Modern Latin America* (Latin American Monographs, 64; Austin, TX: University of Texas Press, 1985), ch. 1; and C. Rangel, *Del buen salvaje al buen revolucionario. Mitos y realidades de América Latina* (San José, CR: Kosmos-Editorial, SA, 1986), ch. 4.

For this cultural tendency as personal quest, see C. Fuentes' essay, 'How I Began to Write', in *Myself with Others: Selected Essays* (New York: Farrar, Straus & Giroux, 1988), pp. 3-27. For other essays by well-known Latin American authors see A. Uslar-Pietri (Venezuela), 'El mestizaje y el Nuevo Mundo', in *Temas de filosofía de la historia latinoamericana* (ed. L.J. González Alvarez; Colección Antología, 6; Bogotá: Editorial El Buho, 1983), pp. 117-32; O. Paz (Mexico), 'Nueva España: orfandad y legitimidad', in *El ogro filantrópico*, pp. 38-52, and 'The Telltale Mirror', in *One Earth, Four or Five Worlds* (trans. H.R. Lane; San Diego: Harcourt Brace Jovanovich, 1985), pp. 137-57.

2. Zea, *Latin America*, chs. 5, 6; *El pensamiento*, pp. 513-40. Dussel says:

We should, therefore, place each of our nations *in* Latin America. . . not only so that we might understand ourselves as a people, but also so that we can participate with some influence and meaning in the world dialogue of cultures and in the integral development of our civilization (*History*, p. 31).

The Colombian writer, German Arciniegas, approvingly quotes Simon Bolivar: 'The freedom of America is the hope of the world'.[1] Of course, from a liberationist viewpoint this ideal would have its own particular content and expression.[2]

From the liberationist point of view, over against the cultural imperialism and elitist dependency would stand the 'popular culture'— that is, the culture of a group of peoples, a 'social block', who, according to Dussel, stand outside the capitalist system's circle of power brokers:

> 'Popular' culture is a specific culture, even more so Latin American popular culture. If 'the people' is not the nation as a whole. . . but rather the 'social block' of the oppressed, this indicates that in the innermost part of the 'people' are included the oppressed classes of the capitalist regime (salaried workers and peasants), as well as tribes, ethnic groups, the marginalized, the unemployed and other oppressed sectors (especially in the nations of the periphery, the dependent and underdeveloped ones of the international capitalist system). '*Popular* culture' is thus distinguished from transnational or imperial culture, from national culture, from the culture of the dominant classes and even from 'mass' culture.[3]

This 'popular' culture, Dussel claims, has demonstrated the capacity to resist, at least to some extent, capitalist cultural intervention and so exhibits liberative potential: '*Popular culture*, far from being a minor

1. G. Arciniegas, *The Green Continent: A Comprehensive View of Latin America by its Leading Writers* (trans. H. de Onis *et al.*; New York: Alfred A. Knopf, 1972), p. xvii. Contrast that upbeat note with the poignant depiction of the shattered hopes of the 'Liberator' at the end of his life as portrayed in G. García Márquez's recent historical novel, *The General in his Labyrinth* (trans. E. Grossmann; New York: Alfred A. Knopf, 1990).

2. Dussel, *History*, pp. 132-36. See the discussion in Chapter 6 of this book regarding the idea of cultural hegemony defended by G. Girardi (cf. P. Freire, *Pedagogy of the Oppressed* [trans M.B. Ramos; New York: Seabury , 1970], chs. 3, 4).

3. E. Dussel, 'Religiosidad popular latinoamericana, hipótesis fundamentales', *CrSoc* 88 (1986), p. 104. Cf. his *Filosofía ética latinoamericana*, pp. 211-25; *idem*, 'La cuestión popular', *CrSoc* 84 (1985), pp. 81-90; *idem*, *Ethics and Community* (trans. R.R. Barr; Tunbridge Wells: Burns & Oates, 1988), pp. 81-87, 199-208; cf. G. Girardi, *Sandinismo, marxismo, cristianismo: La confluencia* (Managua: Centro Ecuménico Antonio Valdivieso, 1986), pp. 159-210. See the helpful distinctions in J. Franco, 'What's in a Name? Popular Culture Theories and their Limitations', *Studies in Latin American Popular Culture* 1 (1982), pp. 5-14.

culture, *is the most uncontaminated and influential center of resistance of the oppressed against the oppressor*'.[1]

The issue of popular culture in Latin America can become more complex because of the problem of terminology: in Spanish *lo popular* is understood to refer to the poor masses. To the position of Dussel and this lexical complication an interpretive approach would respond in two ways. On the one hand, certain classes can have their own specific cultural expressions, yet, on the other hand, they participate in a larger cultural setting in which much is shared. The context is complex, with unique elements as well as common ones, and those that are common can perhaps be shaded differently by location, social station, race and religion. Dussel himself has admitted as much, but drops the global to emphasize the socioeconomic. Culture, however, cannot be so neatly compartmentalized.

To mention both the diachronic and synchronic perspectives is to recognize that the culture is influenced through time by all sorts of variables (be they religious, political, economic, social, historical) that continually shape a complex ethos. The culture then is not static and unchanging, yet there is always continuity with change, persistence with permutation, coherence with conflict.[2]

A detailed look at the 'world' as understood, valued, and shaped on this continent, obviously lies beyond the compass of this study. Each of its myriad autochthonous expressions is a study in itself.[3] Latin American literature, in particular the novel, continues to speak passionately of problems and hopes, yet *from within* and *according to*

1. Dussel, *Filosofía ética latinoamericana*, p. 22 (author's emphasis). Note these words by Julio de Santa Ana:

> though the people's systems of values, their artistic expressions, or their social organi-zations are influenced and shaped by powerful economic and ideological mechanisms, it is equally true that popular culture resists, survives and in some cases even grows strong, in spite of those very mechanisms of dominant groups. The survival of popular culture demonstrates that popular wisdom and philosophy develop remarkable forms of resistance to manipulation and destruction (*Towards a Church of the Poor: The Work of an Ecumenical Group on the Church and the Poor* [Maryknoll: Orbis Books, 1979], p. 48).

2. For a good blending of these two perspectives and its relation to politics, see G.A. Geyer, *The New Latins: Fateful Change in South and Central America* (Garden City, NY: Doubleday, 1970).

3. See *JPopCul* 14 (1980), pp. 405-534; 18 (1984), pp. 58-183, which discuss sport, comic strips, music, and television in Latin America.

the perceptions and interpretations of that continental reality.[1] However, because our ultimate concern is the interaction of the Christian church within the Latin American context, only one aspect of the culture, the religious component, will be highlighted briefly here.

Indeed, it is impossible to understand Latin American culture apart from the role of religion. Christianity came with the Spanish Roman Catholic *conquistadores*, with the cross and the sword. Spain believed herself chosen by God, not only to conquer, but also to propagate the

1. My Salvadoranean colleague E.A. Núñez once said in a conversation 'To understand Latin America it is important to read our novels'. For some thoughts on the relationship of Latin American literature to culture and politics by some of the continent's foremost writers, note the following essays by O. Paz, 'Latin American Poetry' and 'A Literature of Convergences', in *Convergences: Essays on Art and Literature* (trans. H. Lane; San Diego: Harcourt Brace Jovanovich, 1987), pp. 201-16 and 217-26, respectively; C. Fuentes, 'Gabriel García Márquez and the Invention of America', in *Myself With Others*, pp. 180-95. Regarding different genres: the Latin American fascination with politics, especially authoritarian rulers, has led to the development of the 'dictator novel' (see R. González Echevarría, 'The Dictatorship of Rhetoric/The Rhetoric of Dictatorship', in *The Voice of the Masters*, pp. 64-85); G. Arciniegas posits the centrality of the essay, which he feels best exhibits the character of the culture, in 'Nuestra América es un ensayo', in *Temas de filosofía*, pp. 95-110); from a Marxist literary critical perspective, J. Beverley and M. Zimmerman put forward the importance of poetry in the development of popular social consciousness in *Literature and Politics in the Central American Revolutions* (New Interpretations of Latin America Series; Austin, TX: University of Texas Press, 1990). The pathos of the 1954 coup in Guatemala and its eloquent cultural portrayal by the Guatemalan author and Nobel Prize winner M.A. Asturias testify to the dynamic interplay between national identity and foreign intervention (*Weekend en Guatemala* [Buenos Aires: Losada, SA, 1968]); see also his 'Guatemala (Cantata, 1954)', in *Torotumbo, La audencia de los confines, Mensajes indios* (Barcelona: Plaza & Janes, 1984), pp. 204-206 (cf. Pablo Neruda, 'Oda a Guatemala', in *Odas elementales* [Letras Hispánicas; Madrid: Ediciones Cátedra, SA, 2nd edn, 1985], pp. 130-37). For documented accounts of the coup, see S. Schlesinger and S. Kinzer, *Bitter Fruit: The Untold Story of the American Coup in Guatemala* (Garden City, NY: Doubleday, 1983) and J. Dunkerley, *Power in the Isthmus: A Political History of Modern Central America* (London: Verso, 1988), pp. 133-51. D.W. Foster reviews the various textual strategies *from within* Argentine culture that attempt to grapple with the debacle there early in this decade ('Argentine Sociopolitical Commentary, the Malvinas Conflict, and Beyond: Rhetoricizing a National Experience', *LARR* 22.1 [1987], pp. 7-34).

faith in the New World. Many Indians were 'converted' under threat of death, and colonial society was structured (note, for example, the *reducciones*, the concentrating of the native people in town centers) so as to facilitate colonial administration and Christianization.[1] Though there were a few, such as Bartolomé de las Casas,[2] who showed genuine concern for their welfare, the conquest can be generally viewed as an often brutal religious imposition.[3] Debate continues over whether the resulting religion be evaluated negatively as syncretistic or 'pagan',[4] or more positively as a sincere attempt to utilize native symbols and rites to communicate a genuine gospel.[5] The issue of the

1. For a discussion of this and other structures, see Martínez Peláez, *La patria del criollo*; Hawkins, *Inverse Images*, pp. 54-80; Mires, *En nombre de la cruz*, ch. 3, and *La colonización*, ch. 2.

2. De las Casas has been taken by some liberationists as a forerunner of modern liberation theologians. See Dussel, *History*, pp. 50-52; G. Gutiérrez, *The Power of the Poor in History: Selected Writings* (trans. R.R. Barr; Maryknoll: Orbis Books, 1983), pp. 194-97; Mires, *En nombre de la cruz*, chs. 4, 5, and *La colonización*, pp. 80-96, *passim*. Of course, De las Casas stood as a symbol of justice even before the rise of Liberation Theology and its particular perspective. Note, for example, the play by M.A. Asturias, 'La audencia de los confines (Crónica en tres andanzas)', in *Torotumbo*, pp. 75-173.

3. To say this is not to espouse what has been called the 'Black Legend', a totally negative view of the Spanish role. All sides acknowledge that much that was done in name of the Crown and Christ was lamentable.

4. E.g. J.A. Mackay, 'The Southamericanization of a Spanish Christ', in *The Other Spanish Christ*, ch. 7. J.J. Klor de Alva speaks of 'accommodation' versus 'conversion' in 'Spiritual Conflict and Accommodation in New Spain: Toward a Typology of Aztec Responses to Christianity', in *The Inca and Aztec States 1400-1800: Anthropology and History* (ed. G.A. Collier, R.I. Rosaldo and J.D. Wirth; New York: Academic Press, 1982), pp. 345-66.

5. For this generally more positive view, see L. Maldonado, who distinguishes *sincretismo* from *sincretización* (i.e. the process of affirming yet transcending native symbols) in *Introducción a la religiosidad popular* (Colección Presencia Teológica, 21; Santander: Editorial Sal Terrae, 1985), ch. 2. Dussel is more circumspect in his evaluation and labels the resulting liturgy an 'eclectic accumulation' and the level of Indian faith as that of an 'unfinished catechumenate' (*History*, pp. 66-71). Note these words from the official document of the Third Bishops Conference (Puebla, Mexico [1979]):

En la primera época, del siglo XVI al XVIII, se echan las bases de la cultura latinoamericana y de su real sustrato católico. Su evangelización fue suficiente profunda para que la fe pasara a ser constitutiva de su ser y de su identidad, otorgándole la unidad espiritual que subsiste pese a la ulterior división en diversas naciones, y a verse afectada

conquest is taking on increasing importance as the Roman Catholic Church and Spain move toward the commemoration of the five hundred year anniversary of the discovery of the continent. The celebration in 1992 will mark 'El Encuentro de Dos Mundos' ('The Meeting of Two Worlds').[1]

Though varying with each country, since the conquest Latin America has been a continent often strongly influenced, and sometimes dominated, by the Catholic Church at every level of life—from the political, institutional, and educational to the less formal realms of popular culture and morality. What has generally existed has been a Roman Catholic ethos and world-view with a pervasive sway across class lines and racial barriers. Although the religion of the Indian, the *mestizo* (or *ladino*: the mixture of the Spanish and the indigenous) masses, and the well-to-do are not strictly identical, there is still a sharing of common symbols and rituals (such as of the Virgin, and of the Crucified Christ and *procesiones* of Easter week) and allegiance to the Pope.[2] This broad, though variously thick, religious umbrella also

por desgarramientos en el nivel económico, político y social. (CELAM, *Puebla, La evangelización en el presente y en el futuro de América Latina*, III Conferencia General del Episcopado Latinoamericano [Bogotá: Editora L. Canal y Asociados, 3rd edn, 1979], para. 412, pp. 125-26).

1. Works critical of the role of religion in the conquest have begun to appear as 1992 approaches. For a liberationist perspective, see Mires, *En nombre de la cruz* and *La colonización*; E. Dussel, '¿Descubrimiento o invasión de América? Visión histórico-teológica', *Conc* 220 (1988), pp. 481-88; I. Ellacuría, 'Quinto centenario de América Latina ¿Descubrimiento o encubrimiento?' *RLT* 21 (1990), pp. 271-82. From an anthropological standpoint, Patricia Seed documents various ways in which this original 'encounter' was interpreted in 'Failing to Marvel: Atahualpa's Encounter with the Word', *LARR* 26.1 (1991), pp. 7-32.

2. For an excellent overview from the Roman Catholic perspective, see Maldonado, *Introducción,* chs. 3–5. For a case study, see S.R. Nelson, 'Bolivia: Continuity and Conflict', in *Religion and Political Conflict in Latin America* (ed. D.H. Levine; Chapel Hill: University of North Carolina Press, 1986), pp. 218-35. Note these words from the official document of the Third Bishops Conference (Puebla, 1979):

Esta religión del pueblo es vivida preferentemente por los 'pobres y sencillos'. . . pero abarca todos los sectores sociales y es, a veces, uno de los pocos vínculos que reune a los hombres en nuestras naciones políticamente tan divididas. Eso sí, debe sostenerse que esa unidad contiene diversidades múltiples según los grupos sociales, étnicos e, incluso, las generaciones (CELAM, *Puebla,* para. 447, pp. 131-32).

fosters and reinforces a certain element of moral coherence and consensus.

Loyalties are changing, to be sure. The Catholic Church is not the homogeneous entity it was several decades ago. Diversity and tensions are more apparent because of the rapid growth of the charismatic movement and growing secularism.[1] Liberation theologians, in particular, have clashed recently with Rome over the sociopolitical direction to be taken at the Bishops' conference of Puebla in 1979,[2] the censure of prominent theologians such as Leonardo Boff,[3] and the appearance of *la iglesia popular* in Sandinista Nicaragua.[4] Still, devo-

For a Latin American evangelical view of the Christs of the continent, see Nida, *Understanding Latin Americans*, chs. 6, 7; Núñez and Taylor, *Crisis in Latin America*, ch. 6; E.A. Núñez, *Liberation Theology* (trans. P.E. Sywulka; Chicago: Moody Press, 1985), ch. 8; and K. Yuasa, 'The Image of Christ in Latin American Popular Religiosity', in *Preaching Jesus in the Two-Thirds World* (ed. V. Samuel and C. Sugden; Bangalore: Partnership in Mission, Asia, 1983), pp. 61-85. From the liberationist viewpoint see the various contributions in *Faces of Jesus: Latin American Christologies* (ed. J. Míguez Bonino; Maryknoll: Orbis Books, 1984).

1. For example, for Guatemala see J.L. Chea, *La cruz fragmentada* (San José, CR: DEI, 1988). From an evangelical perspective see Núñez and Taylor, *Crisis in Latin America*, chs. 4, 7–10.

2. Contrast the optimism of G. Gutiérrez (*Power of the Poor*, pp. 125-65) with the more guarded view of Dussel (*History*, pp. 229-39) and the generally sober evaluation of J.L. Segundo (*Theology and the Church: A Response to Cardinal Ratzinger and a Warning to the Whole Church* [trans. J.W. Diercksmeier; Minneapolis, MN: Seabury/Winston Press, 1985]). Although there was much opposition to Liberation Theology at Puebla, Dussel sees in its documents the possibility of a 'popular appropriation', which could stimulate the base community movement ('La iglesia latinoamericana en la actual coyuntura (1972–1980)', in *Teología de liberación y comunidades cristianas de base* [ed. S. Torres; Salamanca: Ediciones Sígueme, 1982], pp. 93-122 [especially pp. 112-22]).

3. L. Boff, *Church: Charisma and Power—Liberation Theology and the Institutional Church* (trans. J.W. Dierksmeier; London: SCM Press, 1985). Note especially chs. 4–6, 8, 12, 13.

4. For a positive evaluation of the Sandinista government and Christian involvement in the Revolution see, for example, P. Richard and G. Meléndez (eds.), *La Iglesia de los pobres en América Central. Un análisis socio-político y teológico de la iglesia centroamericana (1960–1982)* (San José, CR: DEI, 1982), pp. 135-85; P. Berryman, *The Religious Roots of Rebellion: Christians in Central American Revolutions* (Maryknoll: Orbis Books, 1984), pp. 51-89, 226-67, and *Liberation Theology: Essential Facts about the Revolutionary Movement in Latin America and Beyond* (Bloomington, IN: Meyer-Stone Books, 1987), pp. 144-47, *passim*;

tion to the Pope and the institutional church runs deep, as evidenced by John Paul II's reception in visits to Latin America.

To look at Protestantism on the continent is to witness, on the other hand, a minority, and sometimes persecuted, religion. Their history has been relatively short, in Guatemala just over one hundred years.[1] Because of its planting and nurture by Anglo-Saxon (European and North American) missionaries the Protestant churches have often been directed by foreign leadership and occasionally characterized by doctrines, cultic patterns, and ideologies incongruous with the Latin culture.[2] Yet, for example, the spirit of *caudillismo* (charismatic 'boss

Girardi, *Sandinismo, marxismo, cristianismo*. For the contrary view see H. Belli, *Breaking Faith: The Sandinista Revolution and its Impact on Freedom and Christian Faith in Nicaragua* (Garden City, NY: The Puebla Institute, 1985). For a more non-partisan perspective, see S. Christian, *Nicaragua: Revolution in the Family* (New York: Random House, 1985), ch. 15, and D. Stoll, *Is Latin America Turning Protestant? The Politics of Evangelical Growth* (Berkeley: University of California Press, 1990), ch. 8. Note also my discussion in Chapter 6 of this work, that follows the analysis of the text of Amos.

1. V. Zapata A., *Historia de la iglesia evangélica en Guatemala* (Guatemala: Caisa, 1982). This is generally a triumphalist picture of the growth of the Protestant Church, yet is a good source for statistics and dates. Cf. V.G. Burnett, 'Protestantism in Rural Guatemala, 1874–1954', *LARR* 24.2 (1989), pp. 127-42. For a broader view of the history of the Protestant Church on the continent from an evangelical perspective, see Núñez and Taylor, *Crisis in Latin America*, pp. 146-78, and S. Escobar, *La fe evangélica y las teologías de la liberación* (El Paso: Casa Bautista de Publicaciones, 1987), chs. 2, 3, 6; for a liberationist perspective, see J.P. Bastian, *Breve historia del protestantismo en América Latina* (Mexico: CUPSA, 1986).

2. Evaluations vary as to the extent of the ideological motivation behind the missionary efforts over the last century. For critical, although not totally negative, appraisals, note O.E. Costas, *El protestantismo en América Latina hoy: ensayos del camino (1972–1974)* (San José, CR: Publicaciones INDEF, 1975), chs. 1, 2, and *Christ outside the Gate: Mission beyond Christendom* (Maryknoll: Orbis Books, 1982), pp. 58-70; A. Piedra S., 'Evaluación crítica de la actual coyuntura evangélica centroamericana', *VPens* 4 (1984), pp. 3-20, and 'Protestantismo y sociedad en América Central", *CrSoc* 103 (1990), pp. 87-106; C.R. Padilla, *Mission between the Times: Essays on the Kingdom* (Grand Rapids: Eerdmans, 1985), pp. 94-109. The foreign cultural element is now even more complicated because of the influence in some sectors of the 'Electronic Church'. For a liberationist view of the phenomenon see H. Assmann, *La iglesia electrónica y su impacto en América Latina* (San José, CR: DEI, 2nd edn, 1988). Stoll also points out the recent influence of the North American Religious Right (*Is Latin America Turning Protestant?, passim*).

rule'), a common cultural phenomenon,[1] has led to innumerable church and denominational conflicts and splits. The Protestant sub-culture, then, is a bit of a different hybrid than the dominant Roman Catholic one, yet at the same time indistinguishable in many ways.

Historically, except for a few early exceptions in some countries, the Protestant faith found access and response almost exclusively among the masses of poor and lower-middle class *mestizos*—a socio-economic factor that has had important consequences for the educa-tional level, the social outlook, and the economic and political possi-bilities of the Protestant churches. Until recently the Protestants were often marginalized. In Guatemala, however, with the inroads into the Indian groups and the phenomenal church growth, the breakthrough into the higher classes, the short presidency of General Efrain Rios

Some have gone so far as to develop conspiracy theories of certain missions as instruments of capitalist imperialism. Note the critique of this simplistic idea by J.P. Bastian, 'Para una aproximación teórica del fenómeno religioso protestante en América Central', *CrSoc* 85 (1985), pp. 61-68, and 'Religión popular protestante y comportamiento politico en América Central, clientela religiosa y estado patrón en Guatemala y Nicaragua', *CrSoc* 88 (1986), pp. 41-56 (these articles are more irenic than the account developed in his *Breve historia del protestantismo en América Latina*); J. Míguez Bonino, *Toward a Christian Political Ethics* (Philadelphia: Fortress Press, 1983), pp. 60-64. Note especially Stoll's *Is Latin America Turning Protestant?*, which has as one of its goals to dispel this idea, even though he recog-nizes how such an impression might arise and at the same time warns of that theory actually becoming a reality. David Martin believes that there are affinities between the 'spirit of capitalism' and Latin American Pentecostalism, but that no conspiracy exists. Indeed, he would trace the nature of this Pentecostalism back to early English Methodism and any clash or domination of cultures to within a framework of centuries of development; Latin American society, he says, is undergoing changes due to modernity and differentiation, and, as the traditional 'sacred canopy' shifts, Pentecostalism occupies the new free space (*Tongues of Fire: The Explosion of Protestantism in Latin America* [Cambridge, MA: Basil Blackwell, 1990], chs. 1, 3, 11, 13). This conspiracy theory appears, for example, in the pastoral letter pronounced by the Guatemalan Archbishop Próspero Penados del Barrio on 6 January 1989, which also attacks the 'non-Catholic sects' as being destructive of Guatemalan family, national and cultural life (*La Iglesia Católica en Guatemala. Signo de verdad y esperanza*, especially pp. 13-19).

1. For this cultural item, see Geyer, *The New Latins*, chs. 4 and 5; Nida *Understanding Latin Americans*, ch. 2; Núñez and Taylor, *Crisis in America*, pp. 203-205.

Montt in 1982–1983,[1] and the election of Jorge Serrano Elías in 1991, they are now struggling with how properly to harness their potential to impact national policy and to move out of their traditional pietistic ghetto. The challenge of *forjando nación* ('forging a nation') is to be concretely relevant to the structural issues and true to national (as well as broader Latin American) ideals, values and symbols—challenges complicated by the pressing need somehow to integrate properly the Indian populations into the dominant *mestizo* society.[2]

Each type of religion in Guatemala or any other Latin country, therefore, would in some way be reflecting, reinforcing or challenging values and social station, nurturing a particular spirituality, and confirming life itself through key rites of passage within a broad cultural matrix. The variegated popular morality, while in some ways reflecting religion, race and social interests, at the same time would mirror certain common traits.

The relevance of this discussion of Latin American culture and the relationship of religion to that culture is twofold. First, the Christian church must recognize that its ethical role must be understood and forged within a *cultural* context, and not purely from a *class* perspec-

---

1. There have been very disparate evaluations of the presidency of Ríos Montt. Note the breadth of evaluations recorded in Stoll, *Is Latin America Turning Protestant?*, ch. 7. For a positive evaluation, see J. Anfuso and D. Sczepanski, *Efrain Ríos Montt: Siervo o Dictador—La verdadera historia del controversial presidente de Guatemala* (Guatemala: Gospel Outreach, 1983). For a negative view, see Berryman, *Religious Roots*, pp. 217-19, 272-73. Núñez and Taylor offer a sympathetic yet balanced evaluation (*Crisis in Latin America*, pp. 172-74).

2. Latin American evangelicalism has often been criticized for being a- (or even anti-)political and recently for being committed to governments of the Right. Though the danger, especially among Pentecostals, to lean toward conservative status quo postures is stressed by Stoll, he also points out the variety within the broad camp (*Is Latin America Turning Protestant?*, pp. 156-57, 314-31, and *passim*). Martin is very sensitive to historical and regional differences, and he, like Stoll, underlines the fact that evangelicalism is endeavoring to create alternative, voluntary communities in a context of violence and corruption (*Tongues of Fire*, ch. 12, *passim*). For an overview and bibliography of the growing social awareness in Latin American evangelicalism, see M.D. Carroll R. and G.W. Méndez, 'Another Voice from Latin America: Concerned Evangelicals and the Challenge of a Continent in Crisis. An Introductory and Bibliographic Essay', *ModChm* 30.4 (1989), pp. 42-46; Núñez and Taylor, *Crisis in America*, chs. 12, 13 (ch. 12 deals specifically with Guatemala).

tive. To probe the problematic issues of this troubled continent means entering another world of meaning, another vista of how life is to be structured, lived and changed. A particular history has created a very different social and moral fabric than that of North America and Western Europe. Politics are therefore different, and these societies cannot function in like manner.[1] Some authors have recently suggested that even the problem of economic dependency should be approached from this realization.[2]

Yet several publications describing the options and commitments of the Guatemalan church within that harsh national context have tended to limit discussion to a particular perspective of the class struggle or

1. See Zea, *Latin America and the World*; idem, *El pensamiento latinamericano*; Geyer, *The New Latins*. Good discussions relating Latin American culture and politics are also found in *The Future of Democracy in Latin America: Essays by Frank Tannenbaum* (ed. J. Maier and R.W. Weatherhead; New York: Alfred A. Knopf, 1974) (Guatemala is discussed on pp. 90-93, 109-10); K.H. Silvert, *Essays in Understanding Latin America* (Philadelphia: The Institute for the Study of Human Issues, 1977); O. Paz, 'El ogro filantrópico', in *El ogro filantrópico*, pp. 85-100, and *One Earth, Four or Five Worlds*, pp. 116-213; Rangel, *Del buen salvaje al buen revolucionario*; H.C.F. Mansilla, 'La herencia ibérica y la persistencia del autoritarismo en América Latina', *CrSoc* 100 (1989), pp. 81-94. These stand in sharp contrast to other studies, such as the recent work by Dunkerley, *Power in the Isthmus*. His account is detailed and well-documented, but begins with the liberal reformers of the last century. The impact of the conquest and the values and structures that were then transmitted into the continent's political life are consciously minimized (see his comments on pp. xii-xiii). Note Gérard Chaliand's interesting comments on how the culture has affected the guerrilla movements in Latin America in *Revolution in the Third World* (trans. D. Johnstone; New York: Penguin Books, 1978), pp. 39-50.

2. M. Novak, *The Spirit of Democratic Capitalism* (New York: American Enterprise Institute/Simon & Schuster, 1982), pp. 182-86, 276-82, 298-307, 333-37; L.E. Harrison, *Underdevelopment Is a State of Mind: The Latin American Case* (Lanham, MD: The Center for International Affairs, Harvard University and University Press of America, 1985), for the theory, chs. 1, 7-9; for case studies, chs. 2-6. To cite these two North American authors is not to agree with all their arguments; rather the purpose is to point out that they are at least aware of the issues, whatever their construal of the problems and their solution. The Peruvian Hernando de Soto elaborates on the mercantile economy within Latin America that was inherited from Spain and that is perpetuated in different ways by both left- and right-wing governments on the continent, in *The Other Path: The Invisible Revolution in the Third World* (trans. J. Abbot; New York: Harper & Row, 1989), especially pp. 201-58.

economics.[1] Several possible dangers can arise. On the one hand, an inadequate representation of what is labeled the 'church' can be suggested, and no mention may be made as to what degree the broader Christian church (Catholic and Protestant) would actually agree with the stance defended therein.[2] A related issue is that such publications, because of simplistic categories, can mask the very real ambiguities and complexities of Christian responses and activity, whether of religious institutions and clergy or of laymen, vis-à-vis the social crisis.[3] Moreover, the approach of this book would again claim that the issue of how a people perceives its world and so incarnates its obligations in it is inseparable from quantitative studies of structures, whether national or international.

Latin America, therefore, has a complex culture, racially, religiously, economically and socially. To reduce the socioeconomic difficulties simply to rich versus poor or right versus left would be to

1. Richard and Meléndez, *La iglesia de los pobres*, pp. 195-250; Berryman, *Religious Roots*, pp. 163-220.

2. On the one hand, the 'church' is understood almost exclusively as the Roman Catholic Church: Richard and Meléndez do not discuss Protestantism in Guatemala, although Berryman does give it a brief mention (*Religious Roots*, p. 180). See also F. Bermúdez, *Death and Resurrection in Guatemala* (trans. R.R. Barr; Maryknoll: Orbis Books, 1986). Also, the ideological bias can tend not to speak of how much of a minority a liberationist perspective is. O.R. Sierra Pop, however, does admit:

> This Church demands pastoral forms, which in these [*sic*] moment might not necessarily include the majority of the population in Guatemala. Nevertheless, this church offers a more accelerated level of development relative to the advancement with the Revolutionary Process ('The Church and Social Conflicts in Guatemala', *SocComp* 30 [1983], p. 347).

He has offered a more circumspect analysis more recently in 'La iglesia católica entre el aperturismo democrático y el conflicto social en Guatemala', *CrSoc* 103 (1990), pp. 41-57. Stoll also underscores the fact that Liberation Theology has not found a broad popular following and that it could learn some lessons from the burgeoning Pentecostal movements (*Is Latin America Turning Protestant?*, ch. 10). Cf. the data in the discussion regarding base ecclesial communities in the Excursus.

3. J.L. Chea specifically singles out the works by Richard and Meléndez (*La iglesia de los pobres*) and Berryman (*Religious Roots*) as not adequately describing the response of the Roman Catholic hierarchy: 'no constituyen sino una fracción y una versión sobre los verdaderos orígenes del proceso de cambio de la Iglesia guatemalteca' (*La cruz fragmentada*, p. 37). Chea offers four categories: *los tradicionalistas, los desarrollistas, los rebeldes, los revolucionarios* (summarized on pp. 144-55).

ignore the moral dimension, the complicated and intricate interweaving of values, traditions and lifestyles; it would be to neglect the
shared mores and social habits (both good and bad) that cut across
social, political and religious boundaries. To underscore this cultural
reality is not to minimize or to deny the structural issues. Rather, the
challenge is to broaden the arena of debate and present another focus
to the moral issues and task at stake.

A second implication of the approach would be the suggestion of the
need to shift the usual sphere of the investigation of popular religion
in Latin America. Once more, because in Spanish the term *lo popular*
usually refers to the poor masses, the notion of *la religión* (or
religiosidad) *popular* ('popular religion') or *la iglesia popular* ('the
popular church') is taken 'as the beliefs and practices of the subordin-
ate classes, both peasants and urban workers, which are contrasted
sharply with the religion of the elite'.[1] In contradistinction to this
'terrain' concept of popular religion, there is an 'object' comprehension, which sees

> popular religion as a spontaneous and personal relationship between
> people and the supernatural; which, though it may be stronger in some
> social groups, can be found throughout the social structure.[2]

Maldonado would distinguish the two approaches in the following
manner: the first interpretation of 'the people' (*el pueblo*) he would
call 'partisan' (*partisana*), 'because it understands it [the people] as
divided. . . The "people" are the oppressed class, the proletariate, the
peasants, for whom one takes sides either for or against'.[3] The second
view cuts across class lines (*interclasista*) and is 'nationalistic'
(*nacionalista*):

1. T.A. Kselman, 'Ambivalence and Assumption in the Concept of Popular
Religion', in Levine (ed.), *Religion and Political Conflict*, pp. 24-25. For a helpful
discussion that presents the various theoretical approaches to popular religion, see
Schreiter, *Constructing Local Theologies*, ch. 6. For various perspectives from
within the Roman Catholic Church, compare the document of the Bishops
Conference at Puebla: CELAM, *Puebla*, paras. 444-469, pp. 131-36; P. Richard,
'Religiosidad popular en Centroamérica', in P. Richard and D. Irarrázaval, *Religión
y política en América Central. Hacia una nueva interpretación de la religiosidad
popular* (San José, CR: DEI, 1981), pp. 9-34; A. Shorter, *Toward a Theology of
Inculturation* (Maryknoll: Orbis Books, 1988).
2. Kselman, 'Ambivalence and Assumption', p. 25.
3. Maldonado, *Introducción*, p. 29.

> it has a global, inclusive, and unitary idea of 'the people'. The people are
> not a sector, a subgroup, a [social] fragment, a class. . . It is the collec-
> tive subject, owner and protagonist of a common history, tradition and
> culture.[1]

Liberation theologians have tended to take the *partisana* view. This
'subaltern approach', as Schreiter calls it,[2] would hold that the religion of the oppressed reflects cultural richness and resiliency in the
face of domination. This popular religion is said also to be the field of
battle where the poor strive to maintain their identity over against the
religion of the oppressor.[3]

At this point, the issue is not to explore the ecclesial form, the
'historical project', or the 'liberating potential' that some envision for
Latin American popular piety. That perspective will be explained and,
in light of the biblical study of Amos, evaluated in the last chapter of
this work. The crux here is the nature of popular religion.

As with popular culture, a broader semiotic approach would tend
toward the 'object' or *interclasista* concept, in which there is participation of all classes in the rites, some commonality of beliefs, and
shared religious traditions. All are part of a world of meaning and
symbols, with its lifestyles, mores, and structures, that is Latin
American culture. To take an apparently more unifying view in no
way implies the denial of particular expressions of popular piety by
certain groups or social strata, nor its manipulation by others.
Conflict, therefore, is not mystified, nor the poor ignored.[4] What can

---

1. *Introducción*.

2. Schreiter, *Constructing Local Theologies*, pp. 136-38. He links this view with
Gramsci as does Julio de Santa Ana (*Toward a Church of the Poor*, pp. 50, 53). For
Gramsci's notions of 'subaltern' and 'historical block', see *Selections from Prison
Notebooks* and *Selections from Cultural Writings* (ed. D. Forgacs and G. Nowell-
Smith; trans. W. Boelhower; London: Lawrence & Wishart, 1985), *passim*. Cf. A.
Nesti, 'Gramsci et la religion populaire', *SocComp* 22 (1975), pp. 343-54; F. Piñón
G., 'Antonio Gramsci y el análisis del fenómeno religioso', *CrSoc* 91 (1987),
pp. 63-79.

3. J. Míguez Bonino, 'Popular Piety in Latin America', in *The Mystical and
Political Dimension of the Christian Faith* (ed. C. Geffré and G. Gutiérrez; New
York: Herder & Herder, 1974), pp. 148-57; de Santa Ana, *Toward a Church of the
Poor*, ch. 4; Dussel, 'Religiosidad popular latinoamericana', pp. 106-12.

4. At this point Schreiter's discussion appears a bit simplistic. He tries to extend
the subaltern approach by suggesting that response to needs will be class-specific, so

be avoided, however, are facile categorizations.

In summary, to speak of religion and morality within Latin America from the theoretical position taken in this chapter is to suggest a more complex picture than is sometimes presented. Neither religion nor morality are strictly class or 'social block' specific. This sociocultural fact underlines the difficulty of formulating the faith and life of the Christian church in a way authentic to the Latin American context and faithful to the biblical tradition.

It is within the pregnant labyrinth that is Latin American culture, within the symbolic universe that is the warp and woof of everyday life, that the Christian church must flesh out its proper ethical lifestyle and make its moral demands. This approach places any discussion of the Christian church and its relationship to injustice, the market system, and oppressive structures within more than a purely structural analysis. These realities are in no way pushed aside, but rather looked at now in a different light. Our semiotic position focuses on a cultural discourse by asking another kind of question: *how can the church understand and incarnate its moral life in Latin America?*

This query points to another discussion beyond this one of culturo-religious identity. How is theology to be done contextually? Once more, interaction with certain liberation theologians will help make my proposal clearer.

b. *Doing Theology in the Latin American Context*
One of the major contributions of Latin American liberation theology has been its emphasis on the crucial relevance of contextual realities for the theological enterprise and pastoral practice. This focus on context has epistemological, hermeneutical and political implications. This section will first give a brief presentation of certain aspects of this method and then juxtapose it with the approach outlined up to this point.

To start with, liberation theology stresses that all theological constructs are in some way conditioned. They do not arise in a vacuum,

---

that each class will have its own 'popular religion'. Besides the fallacy of this kind of class response, there still remains the fact of shared popular religion. What is more, his is a method that compartmentalizes approaches depending on the interests of the observer. This, however, leads to the danger of justifying simplifications; each approach should rather be seen as necessarily complementary for a comprehensive understanding, although one might emphasize one perspective in particular.

but rather develop historically in specific situations and in response to what are felt to be the pressing needs and challenges of those times and places. Moreover, theologies do not exist in a vacuum either; they are sustained, implemented and reproduced in an institutional framework.

The different conditions and history of Latin America have generated, accordingly, a dissimilar 'Christendom' than that of Western Europe or North America.[1] What is more, the critical needs of Latin America now require a different theological formulation and agenda than what is found in other latitudes. The friction between liberation theology and other theologies is evident across the theological spectrum—from the rejection of conservative 'Right-Doctrine Protestantism' by Alves,[2] to the articulate response of Segundo to the Magisterium of the Vatican,[3] to the negative evaluations of the North American theology of secularization by Segundo[4] and of European theologies of hope and revolution by Assmann, Gutiérrez and others.[5]

The uniqueness of Latin American liberation theology, however, is ultimately due to more than geographic location or general historical differences. The crux of its innovation lies in a new starting point within society itself: from the 'underside of history', from the perspective of the poor. Gutiérrez remarks,

> The theology of liberation begins from the questions asked by the poor and plundered of the world, by those 'without a history', by those who are oppressed and marginalized precisely by the interlocutor of progressivist theology.[6]

1. See, e.g., Gutiérrez, 'Theology from the Underside of History', in *Power of the Poor*, pp. 169-221, and the section entitled 'El lenguaje profético', in *Hablar de Dios desde el sufrimiento del inocente. Una reflexión sobre el libro de Job* (Salamanca: Ediciones Sígueme, 1988), pp. 61-104.

2. R. Alves, *Protestantism and Repression: A Brazilian Case Study* (trans. J. Drury; rev. J. Wright; Maryknoll: Orbis Books, 1985).

3. Segundo, *Theology and the Church*. Cf. G. Girardi, 'Marxismo, Teología de la Liberación e "Iglesia Popular" en la lucha actual', *CrSoc* 100 (1989), pp. 19-42.

4. J.L. Segundo, *The Liberation of Theology* (trans. J. Drury; Maryknoll: Orbis Books, 1976), pp. 10-13.

5. E.g. H. Assmann, *Theology for a Nomad Church* (trans P. Burns; Maryknoll: Orbis Books, 1976), pp. 86-97; Gutiérrez, *A Theology of Liberation: History, Politics and Salvation* (trans. and ed. C. Inda and J. Eagleson; Maryknoll: Orbis Books, 1973), pp. 217-25, and *Power of the Poor*, pp. 178-85.

6. Gutiérrez, *Power of the Poor*, p. 212.

This new point of departure gives birth to new questions and insights and helps expose the irrelevancy of theology done 'from above', from within academia and comfortable conditions. Dussel can charge that:

> This theology of the 'center' has been conditioned in multiple ways of which the European and North American theologians show little or no awareness . . . It has been conditioned *liturgically*. . . It has been conditioned *culturally* by the fact that it has been developed by an intellectual elite. . . It has been conditioned *politically* by accommodating itself to and being a part of the metropolitan seat of power. It has been conditioned *economically* by the fact that for the most part it represents the value system of the oligarchy and the bourgeoisie of the neocapitalist world. . . Finally, it is conditioned *erotically* by these monks or celibates who lacked the experience to fashion an authentic theology of sexuality, marriage and family.[1]

This particular epistemological stance, moreover, involves not only the commitment to see from the perspective of the poor, but also the obligation to stand with and struggle for the poor. This choice for the poor, therefore, is at the same time a concrete political decision: 'The historical project of liberation entails a struggle against the historical project of oppression by the dominant classes. It is in that sense that solidarity with the poor is a class option.'[2] This 'epistemological break' grounded in a faith-commitment, then, is the fountainhead for active involvement in social action. Míguez Bonino states emphatically:

> For human beings. . . social location is a matter not merely of fate or circumstance but also of option and decision. We are *situated* in reality, to be sure—historically, geographically, culturally and most of all groupwise and classwise—but we can *position* ourselves differently in relation to that situation. . . an eschatological ethics of justice, which assumes solidarity with the poor as its historical mediation is the basis for this commitment. . . *Theological and social location for the Christian are one, unified in the specific commitment to the poor.*[3]

---

1. Dussel, *History*, p. 12 (emphasis added).
2. A. Cussianovich, *Religious Life and the Poor: Liberation Theology Perspectives* (trans. J. Drury; Maryknoll: Orbis Books, 1979), p. 97. The bibliography for this point is enormous. From the sources in English already cited see, for example, the essays by Gutiérrez in *Power of the Poor*, and Dussel, *History*, chs. 10, 12.
3. Míguez Bonino, *Toward a Christian Political Ethics* (author's emphasis), p. 44.

It is against this backdrop of commitment that Segundo's well-known 'hermeneutical circle' gains its critical force: contextual awareness and incisive criticism that unmask the mystifications of social reality and religion are inadequate unless accompanied by an engagement in changing both theology and the world.[1]

At this juncture liberation theology's use of the social sciences comes into play, for what is needed are tools to interpret Latin American life. Marxist analysis is claimed to provide the best insights into the realities of the continent. As Segundo points out:

> It is not strange then that the ideology (mistaken or not) which since the last century has made its center the search for more just structures should appear beside a theology that must move toward God by passing through the reality of a people subjected to terrible injustices. There is an undeniable affinity between the vision demanded by the Christian message in Latin America and any analysis that concentrates on explaining the injustice suffered by the people.[2]

Marxism has had a long history of diverse interpretations and applications among Latin American intellectuals throughout this century.[3] In the case of liberation theologians, the acceptance of Marxism has not been uncritical, and use would vary according to author.[4] There

1. Segundo, *The Liberation of Theology*, ch. 1.

2. Segundo, *The Liberation of Theology*, p. 90.

3. See the survey of the diverse Marxist thinking on the continent from a 'nonsectarian socialist perspective' in S.B. Liss, *Marxist Thought in Latin America* (Berkeley: University of California Press, 1984). Beside the general discussions (chs. 1, 2, 11), Liss offers a look at Marxist *pensadores* in ten countries. For thoughts on Liberation Theology, see pp. 282-86.

4. See the comments, for example, by Segundo in *Theology and the Church*, p. 96. In light of the evidence, Berryman's statement in *Religious Roots* that 'none of its major exponents have devoted systematic attention to Marxism as such' except for Miranda (p. 29) is surprising. More recently he has said, 'Contrary to a common stereotype in their writings liberation theologians do not devote much space to discussing Marxism directly' (*Liberation Theology*, p. 139), and does grant more 'head-on discussion' than previously by mentioning the work of Assmann and Hinkelammert (*Liberation Theology*, pp. 148-50). Míguez Bonino at an early stage devoted a whole book to the issue: *Christians and Marxists: The Mutual Challenge to Revolution* (Grand Rapids: Eerdmans, 1976). Perhaps Berryman has had only Roman Catholic authors in mind. Even so, Dussel, for example, has been very articulate—most recently: 'El concepto de fetichismo en el pensamiento de Marx: Elementos para una teoría general marxista de la religión', *CrSoc* 85 (1985), pp. 7-

has been, however, a resounding rejection of the atheism and the totalitarianism of orthodox (especially Soviet) Marxism.[1] Elements that have been appropriated would include, for example, the critique of religion and the concept of the class struggle (and with the latter the option for socialism).[2]

59; 'La cuestión popular'; 'Teología de Liberación y Marxismo', *CrSoc* 98 (1988), pp. 37-60. For a helpful discussion full of historical and bibliographic data as to how Marxist categories gained prominence, see S. Gotay, 'Las condiciones históricas y teóricas que hicieron posible la incorporación del materialismo histórico en el pensamiento cristiano en América Latina', *CrSoc* 84 (1985), pp. 25-48. More recently Segundo has shown his thorough acquaintance with Marxist discourse in *Faith and Ideologies, Jesus of Nazareth Yesterday and Today*, I (trans. J. Drury; Maryknoll: Orbis Books, 1984). See also Girardi, *Sandinismo, marxismo, cristianismo,* and 'Marxismo, Teología de la Liberación e "Iglesia Popular"'. Alistair Kee provides an overview of the use of Marxism by different liberationists in *Marx and the Failure of Liberation Theology* (London/Philadelphia: SCM Press/Trinity International Press, 1990), chs. 6–10.

1. Míguez Bonino, *Christians and Marxists*, chs. 3–6, 8; Segundo, *The Liberation of Theology*, pp. 57-62, and *Faith and Ideologies*, especially chs. 7–10; G. Gutiérrez, 'Teología y ciencias sociales', *CrSoc* 84 (1985), pp. 49-67; Girardi, *Sandinismo, marxismo, cristianismo*, pp. 99-136; Dussel, *Ethics and Community*. 17. In *Marx and the Failure of Liberation Theology*, Kee criticizes Latin American liberation theologians, on the other hand, for not taking Marx's critiques of religion (religion as reconciliation, reversal and ideology) seriously enough. He points out that the second critique is avoided or inadequately handled (chs. 6–10) and then proposes his own view of a more consistent appropriation (chs. 11, 12). It is interesting to read, as well, the evaluation of Liberation Theology by an 'orthodox' Marxist:

> In the last analysis, *liberation theology* is an absurd contradiction in terms. As laboring humanity liberates itself from all exploiters and masters on earth, it will have no need to recognize any master in the heavens. Once human beings achieve conscious control of their destiny—both collective and individual—they will scorn any idea of a god standing above society and manipulating its destiny. The liberation of humanity from all social oppression means the evaporation of all theology from the minds of men and women (D. Fogel, *Revolution in Central America* [San Francisco: Ism Press, 1985], p. 216).

2. For the socialist option, see, for example, J.L. Segundo, 'Capitalism–Socialism: A Theological Crux', in *The Mystical and Political Dimension of the Christian Faith*, pp. 105-23; Míguez Bonino, *Christians and Marxists*, chs. 1, 8; J.P. Miranda, *Marx and the Bible: A Critique of the Philosophy of Oppression* (trans. J. Eagleson; Maryknoll: Orbis Books, 1974), ch. 1, and *Communism in the Bible* (trans. R.R. Barr; Maryknoll: Orbis Books, 1982), ch. 1; H. Assmann (ed.), *El juego de los reformismos frente a la revolución en Centroamérica* (San José, CR:

How would the position taken in this thesis evaluate the methodological commitments mentioned thus far? In what ways would an interpretive and narrative approach echo or disagree with Latin American liberation theology?

There are, in fact, several areas of profound agreement. First, there would be the same conviction that epistemology is to a large extent contextually conditioned. This principle is foundational to my methodology. The most basic aim is to develop a theological ethic born in and true to Latin American culture.

To be even more specific, this orientation would also assent to the fact that the perspective of and from the poor would generate a new way of formulating theology. In light of the fact that the vast majority of the population is poor, this way of seeing and living should naturally be the horizon of pastoral practice and theological thinking for the Christian church if it is to do theology from 'the native point of view'! At the same time, as the previous section pointed out, the understanding of religious and moral life in context would also be aware of the links with the broader culture.

A semiotic approach would also emphasize the need of a methodological clarification in the use of the social sciences, and here the comments by Berger can prove helpful. It is precisely the recourse to Berger, however, that may bring protest. Although in *Pyramids of Sacrifice*, Berger condemns the cruel excesses of both capitalism and Marxism, he has more recently come out clearly in favor of the capitalist option for the Two-Thirds World.[1] This fact alone would disqualify him in the eyes of some because of the socialist commitment

DEI, 1981); Dussel, *History*, especially pp. 19, 127-32; *idem*, 'Cuatro temas en torno a teología y economía', *CrSoc* 87 (1986), pp. 67-91; *idem*, 'Teología de Liberación y Marxismo', pp. 59-60; *idem*, *Ethics and Community*, chs. 11–17; Girardi, *Sandinismo, marxismo, cristianismo*. For some, Cuba can serve as a model: Berryman, *Religious Roots*, pp. 16, 302, and *Liberation Theology*, pp. 87-93; G. Girardi, 'La revolución cubana en la historia de la esperanza', *CrSoc* 98 (1988), pp. 23-36. Note Novak's evaluation in *The Spirit of Democratic Capitalism*, ch. 17, and *Will It Liberate? Questions About Liberation Theology* (New York: Paulist Press, 1986), chs. 8, 9.

1. His position, however, is not altogether blind to the shortcomings and weaknesses of capitalism. Berger would claim that pragmatism and empirical evidence have driven him to take this system as the best option in the present. See Berger, *The Capitalist Revolution*, especially chs. 4–6; *idem*, 'Capitalism and the Disorders of Modernity', *First Things* 9 (1990), pp. 14-19.

within much of liberation theology. His affiliation with the American Enterprise Institute for Public Policy Research, a conservative think-tank in Washington, DC, would also for some disentitle him from consideration.[1] One can agree with his methodological insights, however, yet dissent from his analysis of the Two-Thirds World and his evaluations of socialism and capitalism.

It is precisely Berger's insights into the method and vocation of sociology that needs to be heard and that in fact allow his procedure to be distinguished from his politics. Berger harks back to the way of Weber who fought to maintain the ideal of keeping separate his descriptive analysis from his evaluative criteria.[2] Segundo criticizes Weber for this: 'Weber simply wants to make comparisons between different religious ideas insofar as they exert influence on different economic attitudes. There is no personal commitment involved.'[3] This sort of stance he claims is:

> the last systematic obstacle for any theology committed to human liberation. . . It is a certain type of academicism which posits ideological neutrality as the ultimate criterion; which levels down and relativizes all claims to absoluteness and all evaluations of some ideas over others.[4]

Yet Segundo has misunderstood Weber's (and so Berger's) methodology by not distinguishing the sociologist's technique from his moral stance. Berger in his seconding of Weber's explains that Weber:

> stated his positions on the 'value-freeness' of the social scientist and on the moral responsibility of the political actor. The two positions make the best sense when taken together. For the social scientist Weber insisted on one overriding obligation—that of looking at social reality with objectivity, without injecting his own values or taking into account his personal hopes or fears. For the political actor Weber insisted on the most painstaking moral responsibility, and especially the knowledge of being responsible for the consequences. . . The two positions are stated with equal passion. It is in this double passion that Weber's greatness lies. Both in his thought and in his life he tried to bear without flinching the

---

1. See Berryman's comments on this group *(Religious Roots*, pp. 303-309). Cf. J.M. Mardones, 'La razón económica capitalista y la teología política neoconservadora', *RLT* 21 (1990), pp. 283-306.

2. Berger and Kellner, *Sociology Reinterpreted*, cf. 1; Berger, *A Rumor of Angels*, ch. 8.

3. Segundo, *The Liberation of Theology*, p. 24.

4. Segundo, *The Liberation of Theology*, p. 25.

enormous tensions between detachment and engagement. And he had
contempt for those who sought relief from this tension, be it by denying
that moral options are real or by absolutely espousing one single option—
the psychological escape routes of, respectively the positivist and the doctrinaire ideologist.[1]

The point is that sociological analysis *per se* does not provide the
values for the evaluation of any given sociocultural context. Sociology's
only legitimate contribution is to provide an account of social reality;
it cannot be prescriptive. This was the issue that Weber sought to
clarify. At this descriptive and analytical level, Marxism has much to
offer (as Berger himself makes clear), and its value in helping to
understand Latin America's problems has been rightly appreciated.

A second related point is that the values of the sociologist must
come from outside sociology. This observation clarifies the nature of
value-freeness as an impossible but crucial ideal. Why 'crucial'? The
danger of a 'redemptive sociology' lies in that the cognitive elite who
possess the 'correct' view can become a political elite that brooks no
opposition and that either ignores or denies its own situatedness. From
the interpretive perspective every theoretical formulation and political
program involves a 'social construction of reality'—a fact that indeed
relativizes to some degree any and all constructs. This phenomenological actuality is vital to the Christian church which is looking for
sociopolitical options: in its traditions, both communal and canonical,
lie the sources from which to enable a critical and dialectical engagement (and if necessary, confrontation) with any sociological tool and
political project. As discussed earlier, this position does not imply a
purely objective position, for the church and its theology must always
be in dialogue with the context, but it does specify a *Christian* perspective with some sort of normative evaluative criteria.

Marxism has sometimes attempted in various manners to avoid the
implications of an interpretive approach by positing ideologically free
entities (such as the proletarian class or certain intellectuals) or
claiming the purity of praxis. Herein lies some ambivalence in liberation theology. Though many have properly criticized certain components and extremes of Marxism, there yet resonates from within some

---

1. Berger, *Pyramids of Sacrifice*, pp. 255-56. As an aside, Kee asserts that
Segundo in his discussion of the hermeneutical circle has not properly handled Cox,
Marx and Cone (*Marx and the Failure of Liberation Theology*, pp. 182-89).

of these theologians' writings the same notions: (a) Dussel speaks of the 'non-ideological', 'anti-ideological', and 'de-ideological' cries of the oppressed[1]—that is, those not tainted by 'ideology' (Dussel takes the term in the Marxist sense to refer to that which masks reality). Since the oppressed question the system, they are exempt. (b) Dussel and others speak of Gramsci's 'organic intellectual', who is involved in organizing and raising the consciousness of the popular classes on the road to social and cultural liberation, as the ideal for the liberation theologian.[2] (c) Lastly, praxis becomes 'objective' because of its liberative analysis, activity and goal.[3]

The interpretive view would question the absolutist claims of any class or cadre on several grounds. Is the 'program' a violation of a people's 'web of significances' and an imposition of other meanings? If so, will change take a culture into account? How? The ultimate question, of course, is: is change right? The answer again comes back to the methodological distinction between the proper limits of sociology and the sources of values and vision.

To simply condemn the social construction of reality by the 'other' side as does Alves in *Protestantism and Repression* is inadequate and self-deluding. He explicitly takes a sociology of knowledge approach to describe the meaning-schemes of conservative Presbyterians in Brazil and then denounces the private and social ethic of their 'world'. Without questioning here the value of his sociological data,[4] one must

1. Dussel, *History*, pp. 308, 313, 332, respectively. Cf. Dussel's idea of communities that live according to the 'Jerusalem Principle' in *Ethics and Community*, chs. 5, 8.

2. Gutiérrez, *A Theology of Liberation*, p. 13; *idem*, *Power of the Poor*, p. 212; Dussel, *History*, pp. 135-36, and his descriptions of the 'prophet' and the 'hero' in *Ethics and Community*, pp. 55-56, 72-73, 88-95, 178-79, 213-14, 227-28; J.F. Gómez G., 'El intelectual orgánico según Gramsci y el teólogo de la liberación en América Latina', *CrSoc* 91 (1987), pp. 95-109. Cf. Freire's description of the 'revolutionary leaders' in *Pedagogy of the Oppressed*, ch. 4. Gramsci's influence among Latin American intellectuals is discussed in Liss, *Marxist Thought in Latin America*, pp. 8-9, 28-30, 277-78.

3. Gutiérrez, 'Liberation Praxis and Christian Faith', in *Power of the Poor*, pp. 36-74.

4. For example, Alves's picture of the evangelical churches in Brazil is badly dated. A careful look at his sources shows them to be from the late fifties and the early sixties. Much has changed in the last twenty years! Across the Latin American continent there is a growing social concern among evangelicals. See my article

ask if all theologies and their communities do not in fact construct a reality; and if all of them do not in actuality convict those outside their circle and have institutional means of defending and legitimizing their cause. Alves himself does what he damns: he vehemently accuses, oversimplifies his opponent, and resorts to a power outlet (by publishing through an international publishing house). In other words, at the level of the observation of meaning systems all constructs are relativized because they are humanly-made fabrications.

An interpretive approach would consequently draw two conclusions at this point. First, it would be less sanguine about change. Liberation theologians might condemn this posture as an evasion, as an inadequate commitment to change. The response is that this perspective can be more constructively critical and responsible. As Berger says:

> if the foregoing is understood, then any totalistic concept of liberation becomes impossible. One will then recognize that any choice, however liberating when first made, will lead to new patterns that preclude other choices. Now this by no means implies that *therefore* there are no genuine liberations. There are, as we have seen. But not only will one's expectations about the final import of these liberating choices be relatively modest and modestly relativistic; one will not expect total liberation. . . There are costs to be weighed, probable consequences to be assessed, *institutions* to be envisaged.[1]

Secondly, this perspective would underscore that the source of values must be specified and that these cannot come from sociology. Interestingly, Segundo recently has actually made a similar fact–value distinction. He defines faith non-religiously as the meaning-structure (the 'fundamental anthropological dimension') that gives coherence to understanding and provides values, and ideology (the 'second anthropological dimension') as a 'system of means' that is used to analyze reality and implement a goal.[2] Segundo would hold that the two must be kept separate. They are complementary in that both are necessary;

' "Liberation Theology Come of Age": Clarifying an Assessment', *ExpTim* 98 (1987), pp. 170-71 and the earlier remarks and references in this section regarding how Protestants are beginning to wrestle with political issues.

1. Berger and Kellner, *Sociology Reinterpreted*, p. 112.

2. Segundo, *Faith and Ideologies*, ch. 1. This distinction had been mentioned earlier in *The Liberation of Theology*, ch. 4. Note Kee's criticism of this formulation vis-à-vis Marx's critique of religion as ideology, in *Marx and the Failure of Liberation Theology*, pp. 240-45.

each has a peculiar contribution to make. The danger can be twofold: either not recognizing that a faith cannot provide the concrete steps to implement its values, or failing to see that an ideology cannot be a metaphysics. In relationship to classic Marxist categories he says:

> precisely to the extent that they are confirmed (validated) by reality, neither historical materialism not dialectical materialism can claim to determine the value (the 'ought-to-be') possessed in and of themselves by premises which are, by definition, *self-validating*—that is, which belong to the realm of meaning.[1]

These two Marxist sociological tools can lead to a more realistic comprehension of and actuation in the world. But, at the same time,

> It should be clear that historical materialism cannot be a metaphysics, without betraying itself. It cannot propound general, atemporal statements about God or atheism, or even about basic, human anthropological faith. It was, it is, it always will be, a critical tool of any such faith.[2]

On the other hand,

> This realistic relocation of the dialectic likewise and inevitably entails the accentuation of some *predialectical* 'faith' in the sense I have been using the term faith. So dialectic can hardly attack the basis of such faith. It is not the dialectic that leads Marx to place himself on the side of the proletariat and his system to entrust the proletariat with the destiny of humanity once the division of labor has occurred. . . His option is an effort to change the world by establishing values.[3]

Segundo makes two other points that also parallel the methodological stance of this chapter. First, he emphasizes that a faith arises from within a tradition. Values depend, he says, on 'referential witnesses' on others in a particular community where people are taught how to learn to live their lives. For the Christian faith, the 'tradition' would embrace the history of those of the Christian religion in the past, its actual community, and the biblical text. All of these elements are sources of values and indispensable to the learning process within a cultural context.[4] Segundo, therefore, not only makes a distinction between sociology and values, he also specifies the community which will utilize his 'ideology' to effect the values it nurtures.

1. Segundo, *Faith and Ideologies*, p. 225.
2. Segundo, *Faith and Ideologies*, p. 194.
3. Segundo, *Faith and Ideologies*, pp. 234-35.
4. Segundo, *Faith and Ideologies*, pp. 74-82, 159-67, 269-70, 326-39.

Secondly, Segundo demonstrates the importance he places on meaning-structures in his treatment of violence in Latin America. There has been a cost paid for attempted change: revolutionary violence destroys what he calls the 'social ecology'.[1] He, too, then is less sanguine and more realistic about the revolutionary project, as more is involved than simply the 'liberation of the oppressed' and the creation of a 'new culture'. His stress on values and the social construction of reality move him into another sphere of discourse than others saying the struggle is humanized if the violence done to the oppressor is seen as part of a project of love,[2] or still others detailing the criteria for determining who are legitimate targets.[3]

No one would doubt Segundo's commitment to change. His alternative, however, is the creation and organization of Christian communities in which to transmit the values and meaning that would impact traditional church structures, as well as the rest of Latin American society and culture.[4]

1. Segundo, *Faith and Ideologies*, pp. 282-301. Cf. *The Liberation of Theology*, ch. 6, and *Theology and the Church*, pp. 107-32. It is interesting to note here David Martin's emphasis on the peaceableness among the growing evangelical/Pentecostal movement, partly as a reaction to the violence of the continent's history and current political and theological options, as well as because of the need to preserve and nurture their new communities (*Tongues of Fire*, pp. 12-13, 202-204, 267, 286-88).

2. Gutiérrez, *A Theology of Liberation*, pp. 272-79; Míguez Bonino, *Toward a Christian Political Ethics*, pp. 106-13. Also note Dussel's discussion from the just war perspective in which 'Christian ethical principles can function as norms to regulate and guide that exceptional praxis' that is the revolution (*Ethics and Community*, ch. 16; contrast this with his comments in *History*, pp. 164-76).

3. Berryman, *Religious Roots*, pp. 309-30 (cf. his comments in *Liberation Theology*, pp. 195-96). Contrast the views of Míguez Bonino, Dussel and Berryman with that of Helder Camara, *The Spiral of Violence* (London: Sheed & Ward, 1971). Cf. Núñez, *Liberation Theology*, pp. 267-72; Núñez and Taylor, *Crisis in America*, pp. 234-40; and the interaction between several liberationists and those of a pacifist persuasion in D.S. Schipani (ed.). *Freedom and Discipleship: Liberation Theology in an Anabaptist Perspective* (Maryknoll: Orbis Books, 1989).

4. Segundo, *Faith and Ideologies*, especially pp. 320-21, 334-39. The discussion in this section has remained at a general level in regards to the actual shape of a community in order to deal in a broad way with the issue of the relationship between the Christian church and context. At this juncture, however, some mention should be made of the *comunidades eclesiales de base* (CEBs, the 'base ecclesial communities') which are the focus of liberation theology ecclesiology. For more details see the

c. *Conclusion*

This second major part of this chapter has attempted to apply the theoretical position elaborated earlier to the Latin American context. Although actually clarifying how that culture can be understood rather than describing it in any detail, the first section of this part tried to articulate the implications of an interpretive approach for understanding religion and morality: the Christian church is immersed in a cultural ambient more extensive than any one class of social grouping. This cultural location and the church necessarily interact with and can mutually influence identity, morality and the shape of institutional structures.

The second section points out, to begin with, that for theology to be done from 'the native point of view' in Latin America means that it should arise from within that milieu. The other issue was the relationship between fact and value, between sociology and moral criteria. The stance of Berger was used to emphasize that, although sociology is necessary to comprehend a context and suggest action, it must be guided and controlled by a source of values and meaning outside that discipline.

The value of Segundo at this stage is that he has also defended the cruciality of this fact–value distinction and championed *the formation of communities that could transmit the values of the Christian tradition with a view toward social change.* In a general way Segundo's position concurs with that of this book: what is needed is a Christian ethic that arises from and is responsive to the Latin American contextual/cultural and canonical narratives and that is incarnated in the Christian community. These two narratives stand in a dialectical relationship, and the Christian community carries out its mission within this broader, shared setting. In this social process the biblical tradition plays a key role as a source for vision and virtues, for critique and the call for change.

Ideally, 'incarnation' and 'liberation' should reflect both narrative contexts. For Latin American liberation theology a test case is their understanding of and plans for popular religion. Only after a study of Amos and a look at the prophetic handling of the popular religion of ancient Israel will this book return to this theme. The goal of this

Excursus at the end of this chapter.

section has been to continue to seek methodological clarity, to focus again, yet from different angles, on systems of meaning. The third, and last, part of this chapter will employ this emphasis to probe the nature of old Testament morality, as well as return to the question of what textual method would be most appropriate for this approach.

3. *Israelite Morality and Old Testament Text*

Does the previous section have any relevance for Old Testament studies? Do the concept of culture as systems of meaning and the notion of the social construction of reality find a counterpart in ancient Israelite society? If the answer to these questions were to be in the affirmative, then, as now, it would be possible to explore the nature of moral life in antiquity. These issues of meaning and morality in the ancient world are the foci of this major section. At the same time, the following discussion will raise the question of how the approaches used to ascertain this sort of information might help in establishing a textual method that might be of use for ethical orientation in the present.

a. *Structural Anthropology and the Primitive Mentality*
Recent structural anthropology studies in the Old Testament provide corroborating evidence for humanity's inherent propensity to classify and arrange its reality. The research of Mary Douglas, in particular, with its focus on anomalies, underlines the 'natural codes' structured by religious cosmologies and reinforced by ritual and taboo. Her probing into the Old Testament material has centered on the ordered universe mirrored in and sanctioned by the dietary laws, the classification of clean and unclean animals, and social relationships.[1]

---

1. M. Douglas, 'In the Nature of Things', 'Deciphering a Meal' and 'Self-evidence', in *Implicit Meanings* (London: Routledge & Kegan Paul, 1975), pp. 210-19, 249-75, 276-318, respectively; 'The Abominations of Leviticus' in Lang (ed.), *Anthropological Approaches*, pp. 100-16. For an evaluation and the implications of structural anthropology for biblical studies see J.W. Rogerson, *Myth in Old Testament Interpretation* (BZAW, 134; Berlin: de Gruyter, 1974), ch. 8, and *Anthropology*, ch. 6. Rogerson has also reviewed the work of the anthropologists mentioned in this paragraph in 'Sacrifice in the Old Testament: Problems of Method and Approach', in *Sacrifice* (ed. M.F.C. Bourdillon and M. Fortes; London: Academic Press, 1980), pp. 54-58, and 'The Old Testament View of Nature: Some

Douglas Davies has attempted to extend the insights of her thesis to the moral question of leprosy. Sacrifice in this scheme functions socially not only to order life, but also to restore disrupted relationships within the covenant community.[1] Edmund Leach has sought to relate the spatial and temporal aspects of the tabernacle's construction and the consecration of the priests to a certain structuring of experience and the world.[2]

Two comments of Douglas's work are pertinent. First, the approach that stresses meaning and the created 'natural' order opens up new vistas regarding the possible significance of Old Testament rituals and regulations as boundary lines for the Israelite world. In 'The Abominations of Leviticus', she puts to one side the various explanations posited in the past to decipher the rules: as having medical justification, as being disciplinary to promote virtue or allegorical of virtues and vices, as protecting Israelites from foreign influence, or as finally being irrational. Douglas counters:

> Any interpretations will fail which take the Do-nots of the OT in piecemeal fashion. The only sound approach is to forget hygiene, aesthetics, morals and instinctive revulsion, even to forget the Canaanites and the Zoroastrian magi, and start with the texts. Since each of the injunctions is prefaced by the command to be holy, so they must be explained by that command. There must be contrariness between holiness and abomination which will make overall sense of all the particular restrictions.[3]

Once holiness is seen from the perspective of discrimination and meaning, it then embodies wholeness and perfection in a cosmic order. Accordingly,

> If the proposed interpretation of the forbidden animals is correct, the dietary laws would have been like signs which at every turn inspired meditation on the oneness, purity and completeness of God. By rules of avoidance holiness was given a physical expression in every encounter with the animal kingdom and at every meal. Observance of the dietary

Preliminary Questions', *OTS* 20 (1977), pp. 67-84.

1. D. Davies, 'An Interpretation of Sacrifice in Leviticus', in Lang (ed.), *Anthropological Approaches*, pp. 151-62.

2. E. Leach, 'The Logic of Sacrifice', in *Anthropological Approaches*, pp. 136-50.

3. Douglas, 'The Abominations of Leviticus', p. 109.

rules would thus have been a meaningful part of the great liturgical act of recognition and worship which culminated in the sacrifice in the Temple.[1]

Rogerson reinforces this observation

> By paying careful attention to the Israelite classification of the natural world, we shall get a better idea of how reality was structured for ancient Israelites into the holy, the ordered secular, and the disordered, and we shall be able to see how the sacrifices expressed and reinforced this system.[2]

Douglas's discussion is important not only because it supports my contention about the systematization of universes but also because of its subject matter. Sacrifice, the cultus, and social behavior are attacked harshly by the prophets, and this perspective can help explain why. These items would be inseparable, and one would thus expect that a perverse morality would be reflected in and sanctioned by an unacceptable worship.

Secondly, her work again brings to the fore the clash of paradigms mentioned earlier. Harris has criticized the structuralism of Douglas.[3] He singles out her essay 'Self-evidence' and its explanation of the classification of the pig. As a cultural materialist he can admit its anomaly, but then says, 'the source of this anomalous status is not the binary code of an arcane mental calculus; rather, it is the practical and mundane cost-benefit of raising pigs under marginal or inappropriate infrastructural conditions'.[4]

Though several of his points are well taken, Harris has again missed the issue of the breadth and power of meaning-construction. Even if he can explain (although his analysis would need to be scrutinized) this one case, can he so explain all the rules that occupy page after page in the biblical text? When Harris does try to extend his cultural materialistic explanations to the other taboo animals that would not have had an ecological importance, the weakness of his scheme is manifest. Regarding the list of prohibited birds he says:

---

1. Douglas, 'The Abominations of Leviticus', p. 116.
2. Rogerson, 'Sacrifice in the Old Testament', p. 56.
3. Harris, *Cultural Materialism*, pp. 190-97, and *The Sacred Cow and the Abominable Pig: Riddles of Food and Culture* (New York: Simon & Schuster, 1985), ch. 4.
4. Harris, *Cultural Materialism*, p. 192.

I suspect but again cannot prove that this list was primarily the result of a priestly attempt to enlarge on a smaller set of prohibited flying creatures. . . Perhaps the list was generated from this principle applied first to common local 'birds' and then extended to the exotic sea birds as a validation of the codifier's claim to special knowledge of the natural and supernatural worlds. But in any event, the list renders no disservice. Unless they were close to starvation and nothing else was available, the Israelites were well advised not to waste their time trying to catch eagles, ospreys, sea gulls, and the like, supposing they were more inclined to dine on creatures that consist of little more than skin, feathers, and well-nigh indestructible gizzards in the first place.[1]

Does resorting to the ego claims of the priests or to time-saving hunting tips adequately answer the challenge of how all the regulations were integrated into a system? Even if the origin of a rule can be specified, that datum cannot explain its significance in that meaning system nor its preservation or persistence over time once those initial material conditions have changed.

The implication, therefore, is that in ancient Israel, people also lived within a socially constructed reality, objectivized and internalized through a particular set of religious and sociopolitical factors and institutions. It is no longer possible, then, to speak of a 'primitive mentality' dissimilar from our own and incapable of a rational conceptualization of the world.[2] As Rogerson has pointed out, these earlier anthropological theories and those biblical studies based on them utilized inadequate definitions and so exaggerated a supposed dynamic view of 'nature'. They failed to distinguish natural laws of causation based on common observation from scientific laws of nature. In other words, 'primitives' may give different explications, but that does not mean that they are irrational or that theirs is a 'magical' world-view.

Moreover, these scholars did not differentiate the experience of the

1. Harris, *The Sacred Cow*, p. 82.
2. See J.W. Rogerson's helpful summaries and analysis in *Myth and Old Testament Interpretation*, pp. 85-100, 180-87; 'Primitive Mentality', in *Anthropology*, pp. 47-65; 'The Old Testament View of Nature', in *The Supernatural in the Old Testament* (London: Lutterworth Press, 1976), pp. 3-9; 'The World View of the Old Testament', in *Beginning Old Testament Study* (ed. J.W. Rogerson; London: SPCK, 1983), pp. 55-73. Cf. S. Wolfram, 'Basic Differences of Thought', in *Modes of Thought: Essays on Thinking in Western and Non-Western Societies* (ed. R. Horton and R. Finnegan; London: Faber & Faber, 1973), pp. 357-74.

ancient world from its theological explanation in the biblical text. Just
as it would be misrepresentative to confuse 'modern thought' with
academic theories, so too would it be to juxtapose, without any awareness of dissemblance, the thoughts and everyday perspectives of the
average Israelite citizen with the theology of the religious
'professionals' or of the biblical canon. Then, as today, people live
within a perceived and accepted 'nature of things' that is explained and
legitimated by a symbolic universe. The latter, however, would be
complex and variously understood and accepted.

b. *Moral Life in Ancient Israel and the Problem of the Text*

To probe the nature of moral discourse in Israel involves rethinking
some of the traditional approaches to Old Testament ethics. In this
regard, a series of articles by John Barton will prove fruitful in
clarifying the implications of my method.

To begin with, the term 'Old Testament ethics' must be elucidated:

> 'Old Testament ethics' can refer to two related but distinct things.
> Sometimes the study of 'Old Testament ethics' means the study of the
> historical development of ideas about morality, or of actual moral conduct,
> in ancient Israel. . . But the second thing we might be doing in studying
> 'Old Testament ethics' is to take the Old Testament essentially as a book
> that forms part of Christian Scripture, and to ask what, in its finished
> form, it has to say to us about ethical issues.[1]

Barton, although dividing the discussion into two general parts,
actually mentions three aspects: (a) the development of ethical constructs, (b) moral life itself, and (c) the use of the Old Testament
today. The first two actually go together, as both deal with ancient
Israel; the third turns its focus to the principal interest of this book,
modern appropriation. This subsection will deal with these three in
turn in relationship to the concern to come to grips with what kind of
textual approach might provide a firmer basis for the use of the
prophets as a moral guide for the church.

To begin with, Barton points out, attempts to detail the evolution of
ethical ideas in Israel seldom do justice to the complexity of moral
life. In 'Understanding Old Testament Ethics', Barton criticizes the
diachronic studies of Hempel and Eichrodt for oversimplifying syn-

---

1. J. Barton, 'Approaches to Ethics in the Old Testament', in *Beginning Old
Testament Study*, p. 114. Also see his 'Understanding Old Testament Ethics', *JSOT*
(1978), pp. 45-47.

chronic realities.[1] In the desire to present some sort of evolutionary scheme both tend to suppose that the morality of a certain group at a specific point in time was representative of the nation as a whole and limited to that historical juncture. Eichrodt is a good case in point, as he postulated, for example, the development from a popular morality of early Israel to the covenantal ethic and presupposes that this progression means as well the gradual supplanting of the former by the latter.[2] Ethical sophistication, in other words, would push out moral convention. But morality is more complicated than this and is as varied as society itself. To question his hypothesis, of course, is not to deny that there was moral development in Israel, but rather to doubt his understanding of moral life. The problem here, Barton says, is compounded by the small amount of data available in the text to reconstruct a history of ethical ideas, let alone the actual morality, of that society:

> One of the problems in trying to produce a *history* of ethics in Israel. . . is that in most periods we do not have evidence for more than a few of the various social strata that made up 'Israel', and often our evidence is for different groups in different periods.[3]

How, then, might a developmental approach contribute to ethical discourse in the present? The answer actually would depend on the nature of the evolutionary picture presented. In light of what he would perceive as the advance and later the corruption of moral thinking in Israel, Eichrodt posits a 'golden thread' visible throughout the nation's history:

> It is the loftiness of the obligation, the spirituality of the central good, the unconditional character of the Ought, and the perfect unity of these three aspects of moral conduct in the Thou as known in the gift of his favour, which give the ethics of the Old Testament their unique inner greatness.[4]

Does his reconstruction merely illustrate this moral truth, or is his thesis dependent on the reconstruction? If the former is more the case,

---

1. Barton, 'Understanding Old Testament Ethics', pp. 47-50, 52-56. (Cf. W. Eichrodt, *Theology of the Old Testament*, II [trans. J.A. Baker; Philadelphia: Westminster Press, 1967], pp. 231-67, 316-79; J. Hempel, 'Ethics in the OT', *IDB*, II, pp. 153-61.)

2. Eichrodt, *Theology*, II, pp. 317-26.

3. Barton, 'Approaches to Ethics', p. 118.

4. Eichrodt, *Theology*, II, p. 379.

although the reconstruction would have to be evaluated, the point
would actually be based on other grounds.[1] If his ethical stance were,
on the other hand, based upon the reconstruction itself, then the
affirmation would have to be much more tentative. The issue of the
paucity of evidence for reconstruction efforts was the topic of Chapter
2. It might be recalled that, because of the lack of available material
for a reconstruction, the results are best limited to elucidating data
and not to trying to establish an ethic.

Barton, however, does not take this state of affairs to imply that no
sure evidence is available for ascertaining a glimpse of moral life in
Israel, the second aspect of a study of Old Testament ethics. Appealing
to Dover's study on the ethics of Greece, he observes that speeches can
prove more helpful than narrative and legal material.[2] Moreover,
certain kinds of pieces designed for public delivery can reveal even a
clearer picture than others because they did not seek merely to entertain (drama) or to laud (epitaphs). The best sources then, in this view,
are forensic and political oratory. In both cases the speaker would
need to have some sort of common ground with his audience in order
to convince them of his point or contend with them. As Dover says,
'All we can claim in respect of the Athenians is that the available
material shows us what moral principles were enunciated or (more
often) taken for granted by a certain number of highly articulate men
in public utterance'.[3] Because of the speaking nature of prophetic
ministry, Barton would provisionally endorse the prophetic literature
as a viable source for probing the morality of ancient Israel.

He mentions specifically the appearance of quotations of the people's
beliefs and the possible popular assumptions behind the oracles against

1. For a good example of this see J.W. Rogerson, 'The Old Testament and Social
and Moral Questions', *ModChm* ns 25 (1982), pp. 28-35. Rogerson's argument
does not ultimately depend on his proposed reconstruction.

2. K.J. Dover, *Greek Popular Morality in the Time of Plato and Aristotle* (Oxford:
Basil Blackwell, 1974). Two other studies can also be mentioned: L. Pearson,
Popular Ethics in Ancient Greece (Stanford: Stanford University Press, 1962); W.
Den Boer, *Private Morality in Greece and Rome* (Leiden: Brill, 1979). Interestingly,
in contrast to Dover, Pearson does take the philosophical and poetical works as good
sources (pp. 1-33), but Dover's case is more telling. Also see H. McKeating,
'Sanctions against Adultery in Ancient Israelite Society, with Some Reflections on
Methodology in the Study of Old Testament Ethics', *JSOT* 11 (1979), pp. 57-72.
McKeating takes a more positive view of narrative.

3. Dover, *Greek Popular Morality*, p. 4.

the nations in the first two chapters of Amos.[1] His observation regarding a common ground for communication leads to the key distinction between popular morality and more sophisticated ethical discourse, between the ethical reasoning and moral life of the populace and the theological ethics of the prophets. The difference between the two was the reason that the prophets would denounce the people!

Rogerson makes the same point: 'One way of characterizing the Old Testament is to describe it as the story of the struggle between the God of Israel and the God of the Old Testament'.[2] The history of Israel is the account of the struggle between various expressions (and perversions) of the same faith, between popular religion and revealed faith, between, finally, common morality and divine ethics.[3] The symbolic universe in Israel, as in any culture, would not necessarily be a neat and monolithic construct. Various distinct, but interrelated, conceptions would co-exist. There would be, for example, an official dogma with its ideology and the more popular faith, each with a certain view of the world yet sharing in all manner of complex ways a common life and sacred tradition. Each would be influenced differ-

---

1. Barton, 'Understanding Old Testament Ethics', pp. 55-59, and *Amos' Oracles against the Nations: A Study of Amos 1.3–2.5* (SOTSMS, 6; Cambridge: Cambridge University Press, 1980), chs. 1, 6, 7.

2. Rogerson, *Beginning Old Testament Study*, p. 2.

3. This was a point recognized long ago. See, for example, J. Skinner, *Prophecy and Religion: Studies in the Life of Jeremiah* (Cambridge: Cambridge University Press, 1930), pp. 53-73. More recently, J.B. Segal, 'Popular Religion in Ancient Israel', *JJS* 27 (1976), pp. 1-22; Lang, *Monotheism*, ch. 1. (These historical reconstructions would have to be assessed, of course.) Recent archaeological evidence which apparently points to popular syncretistic religion in ancient Israel (although opinions differ regarding the interpretation of the evidence) has been uncovered at Kuntillet 'Ajrûd and Khirbet el-Qôm. For the former site see Z. Meshel, 'Did Yahweh Have a Consort? The New Religious Inscriptions from the Sinai', *BARev* 5 (March-April 1979), pp. 24-34; W.G. Dever, 'Recent Archaeological Confirmation of the Cult of Asherah in Ancient Israel', *HebSt* 23 (1982), pp. 37-43 and 'Asherah, Consort of Yahweh? New Evidence from Kuntillet 'Ajrûd', *BASOR* 255 (1984), pp. 21-39; and B. Margalit, 'The Meaning and Significance of the Asherah', *VT* 40 (1990), pp. 264-97. For the latter site, see Z. Zevit, 'The Khirbet el-Qôm Inscription Mentioning a Goddess', *BASOR* 255 (1984), pp. 39-47; J.M. Hadley, 'The Khirbet El-Qôm Inscription', *VT* 37 (1987), pp. 50-62; A. Lemaire, 'Who or What Was Yahweh's Asherah', *BARev* 10 (Nov-Dec 1984), pp. 42-51; B. Margalit, 'Some Observations on the Inscription and Drawing from Khirbet El-Qôm', *VT* 39 (1989), pp. 371-78.

ently by the faith and mores of the surrounding cultures, whether in
regard to sexual, economic, or political values and practices.

The prophetic message would sound into this kind of moral universe, finding points of agreement on various issues (such as the bar-
barity of the other nations) and levels (for instance, national promises
and election) but would nevertheless be at odds on other points. What
is more, concord on a moral issue would not necessarily imply
unanimity regarding the underlying theological argument. The
prophets are wrestling to redeem and transform a set of meanings and
the social life these embody.[1]

When Barton examines the common morality, however, some of
these important distinctions are sometimes lost. To probe the ordered
moral universe of ancient Israel, Barton turns to the evidence for
poetic justice. He refuses to go into much detail in discussing how
retribution may have been thought to work,[2] but rather postulates a
world-view lying behind that belief:

> [God's] justice is not simply a matter of definition, as in a wholly the-
> nomous ethical system in which justice simply means 'what God does or
> commands', but is a matter of empirical experience, when judged by the
> standards which men use in assessing the conduct of other men. And this,
> I would suggest means that the prophets who use the notion of poetic jus-
> tice are implicitly appealing to a human consensus about what sort of acts
> are just and unjust, which is not logically derived from the revelation of
> moral norms by God, but rests on ideas about ethics formed by reason—
> which one might conveniently refer to as natural law.[3]

Barton recognizes that to get at the moral life of Israel requires
more than isolating certain theological traditions in the text. With this
formulation, he goes beyond someone such as Davies,[4] who just shows

---

1. D.A. Knight is sensitive to the complexities of moral life in 'Jeremiah and the
Dimensions of the Moral Life', in *The Divine Helmsman: Studies in God's Control
of Human Events, Presented to Lou H. Silberman* (ed. J.L. Crenshaw and S.
Sandmel; New York: Ktav, 1980), pp. 87-105.

2. J. Barton, 'Natural Law and Poetic Justice in the Old Testament', *JTS* ns 30
(1979), pp. 1-14. See his comments on Koch's understanding of retribution
(pp. 10-11).

3. Barton, 'Natural Law', p. 12.

4. E.W. Davies, *Prophecy and Ethics: Isaiah and the Ethical Tradition of Israel*
(JSOTSup, 16; Sheffield; JSOT Press, 1981). Also see McKeating, 'Sanctions
Against Adultery'.

how no one tradition (whether law, covenant or wisdom) can explain all the data and that all would be at work to give a more cogent grasp of the social construction of reality.

There is much to commend in his point, but further clarification is needed because in ethical discourse 'human consensus' is not the same as 'natural law'. Human consensus is moral convention intrinsic to any symbolic universe; natural law is a philosophical or theological attempt to explain its existence and epistemology. The first is a phenomenological fact; the second a theoretical formulation. The confusion of the two categories is manifest in the introduction to the article just quoted:

> Natural law. . . may be viewed under two aspects; according as one is attending mainly to the moral norms as seen as 'natural law' in themselves or to the moral agents who 'naturally' perceive them to be valid. It is clear that for most systems of natural law this will be a methodological distinction rather than one of substance: the supposed universality of natural law rests on the notion that it is *inherent* to man, just as it is inherent in the world, not merely a matter of widely agreed convention.[1]

This theoretical muddle is carried on to the Old Testament material by merely asking whether the text is aware of or claims universal moral norms and it if holds that these norms are part of the 'nature of things'. These queries, however, are seeking theological explanations one step removed from the social realities of moral consensus itself.

In a study of Isaiah the same notion surfaces:

> The essence of morality is cooperation in maintaining the ordered structure which prevails, under *God's* guidance, in the natural constitution of things, and the keynote of the whole system is order, a proper submission to one's assigned place in the scheme of things and the avoidance of any action that would challenge the supremacy of *God* or to seek to subvert the orders *he* has established. Such is the basic premiss from which all *Isaiah's* thinking about ethical obligation begins.[2]

Nevertheless, the essential detail for the discussion here is: was the people's world-view the same as the prophet's? If so, in what way? If not, why not? The very fact that the nation and God's spokesman clashed would mean that each had dissimilar (though not wholly dispa-

---

1. Barton, 'Natural Law', p. 2.
2. J. Barton, 'Ethics in Isaiah of Jerusalem', *JTS* ns 32 (1981), p. 11 (emphasis added).

rate) notions about the 'natural constitution of things'. Communication was still possible, though conflict unavoidable.

In any case, Barton has helped clarify the nature of morality in ancient Israel by pointing to its multiformity and to different ways of acquiring evidence from the text. If one were to turn again, however, to the practical criterion of this work and ask how might the study of this aspect of Old Testament ethics provide ethical orientation in the present, what might be the response? In other words, in trying to better represent moral life in ancient Israel with a view to giving some moral light for today, what could be the method that might prove most helpful? If the answer were that the purpose would be to reconstruct the prophetic mission or specific target of denunciation, one returns once more to the methodological problems of any reconstruction approach in general and to the sort of theories criticized in Chapter 2 in particular. In addition, how well does the world pictured in the prophetic text match up with the actual world of ancient Israel?[1] This is not to say that it is impossible to glean any information at all on moral life in Israel or that such an effort is of no value; rather the pragmatic issue is still how sure a foundation can any reconstruction offer the church's ethical discourse. Again, the application of historical reconstruction must be limited to the role of illuminating textual particulars, in helping to explain what is being read, and not be extended to claim authority for moral direction. No hypothesis can confidently pretend such a broad jurisdiction.

The study of the first two aspects of Old Testament ethics (that is, the development of ethical ideas and the moral life in ancient Israel) leaves us with the dilemma of the conclusion of the preceding chapter; if reconstruction cannot be a firm basis, how then might *the text be handled for Christian ethics*, the third aspect mentioned by Barton?

---

1. Barton is a bit skeptical of how well the text represents the historical data. For example, in *Oracles of God: Perceptions of Ancient Prophecy in Israel after the Exile* (London: Darton, Longman & Todd, 1986) one of his purposes is to try to prove the discrepancy between the actual prophets of pre-exilic Israel and how they now appear in the text. He ends, however, on a rather ambiguous note regarding the success of the enterprise:

> It remains to ask whether modern scholarship can do better in establishing what the 'old prophets' were really like. I believe that it can, but that it is first necessary to see clearly how great an obstacle to the task the ages that succeeded them have placed in our way (p. 273).

On the one hand, Barton has presented his own historical and textual reconstruction of how the prophetic corpus came to be read as ethical instruction after the exile.[1] With this era came the tendency to see the prophets as teachers of the moral law and as models of righteousness. Vis-à-vis the most important part of the Jewish scriptures at that time, he says of the prophetic corpus:

> What happened to prophecy in the post-exilic age, then, is essentially no different from what happened to the Law, or from what happens to any other body of ancient texts that come to be venerated in classics in any religious system. People assumed that they would provide guidance for daily conduct in the present. The dominance of the Torah did not affect the way the prophetic texts *functioned*, though it did determine the status they had: as second-rank religious literature, prophecy could not in mainstream Judaism countermand principles laid down in the Torah, but only illustrate and amplify them.[2]

For Barton, the historical picture of the prophets as social critics was obscured once those texts were read with the presuppositions of postexilic Judaism. The portrait of the prophets in the final received collections of prophetic oracles and traditions that now make up the Old Testament, as well as other Jewish and Christian writings, for him is very different from the religious figures brought to light by critical scholarship. His attempt to distinguish the 'old prophets' of pre-exilic Israel, as he calls them, from the later representations and to plot the changes through time would naturally have to be evaluated as any other 'dramatic narrative'; his hypothesis, too, would be subject to the criticisms leveled at any reconstruction.

What is of interest here, however, is his mention of the prophets as *literature*, as a corpus *read* and *used* by a later community of faith. The fact is that the prophets did continue to live and speak to other generations through the received sacred text. Perhaps, therefore, a change in perspective that highlights *that* text, instead of looking for a foundation in a historical construal, might better serve the concerns of this study. Barton, however, is actually not totally averse toward granting value to the text as it now stands. In fact, in the quotation that began this subsection it might be remembered that Barton had said:

> But the second thing we might be doing in studying 'Old Testament ethics' is take the Old Testament essentially as a book that forms part of

1. Barton, *Oracles of God*, chs. 4 and 5, and pp. 266-73.
2. Barton, *Oracles of God*, pp. 171-72 (author's emphasis).

Christian Scripture, and to ask what, in its finished form, it has to say to us about ethical issues.[1]

The approach here is obviously very different, for now the focus can shift from *historical reconstruction* to *textual function*. In light of the various critical problems, Barton, for his part, suggests that the best means to appropriate the Old Testament text is to grasp its 'general drift' in order to support or question modern ethical positions:

> he purpose of the old Testament is not primarily to give information about morality. . . but to provide materials which, when pondered and absorbed into the mind, will suggest the pattern or shape of a way of life lived in the presence of God.[2]

Whether or not one agrees with his perspective, or whether he could agree with how our discussion will proceed, Barton has help-fully clarified the various aspects of Old Testament ethics and opened up the possibility of pursuing an investigation into a reading of a prophetic book as it now appears in the Bible. What can the text offer? It will be the task of the next chapter to explore in much more detail this option of studying the prophetic corpus as literature and the implications for its contribution to ethics. What has been demonstrated here is that there are different ways of handling the Old Testament for ethics and that, in agreement with the previous chapter, reconstruction schemes can be helpful tools for textual study but not definitive guides for ethics. History is not thereby ignored, but its place in this other perspective remains to be clarified. Another approach, therefore, is possible and perhaps may prove more fruitful for moral life in the modern world.

1 Barton, 'Approaches to Ethics', p. 114. Barton has also expressed the view that the new literary studies can be helpful (Reading the Old Testament: Method in Biblical Study [Philadelphia: Westminster Press, 1984]). He is not as sanguine, however, as some because of his commitment to a more historical critical method-ology. His book, moreover, is limited primarily to a discussion of structuralist and canonical approches in biblical studies and their relationship to New Criticism and does not explore other literary methods, such as poetics, which will be the focus of my next chapter.

2. 'Approaches to Ethics', p. 128. For a recent articulation of his views on bibli-cal authority and its relationship to his theological convictions and textual methods, see *People of the Book? The Authority of the Bible in Christianity* (Louisville: Westminster Press/John Knox, 1988).

c. *Conclusion*

This final part of the chapter began by showing that insights from interpretive anthropology, the sociology of knowledge, and narrative ethics can find an echo in the Old Testament through the work of Mary Douglas. Although she utilizes different conceptual tools, she demonstrates that ancient Israel, too, would have structured its world and constructed systems of meaning reflected in customs, lifestyles, and social structures and sustained by the stories of the community. Barton helpfully distinguishes, from another perspective, popular morality from prophetic ethics and so underscores the complexity of moral life in context. This third major section, therefore, supports the theoretical construct offered in the first part and then applied to Latin America in the second.

The issue of textual method was raised by looking at some of Barton's work on Old Testament ethics. As in Chapter 2, reconstruction theories surfaced, but it was suggested that taking the text in its finished form as Christian Scripture might offer another manner of focusing on the problem of the use of the text in modern ethical discourse.

4. *Conclusion*

The sweep of this chapter has been very broad indeed, moving from the social sciences and ethical theory to Latin America and lastly to the biblical text. The purpose of this multifaceted presentation has been to try to establish a new perspective for a different way of using the Old Testament in the moral life of the Christian church today. Each major section is an important building block in the laying of the foundation of this theoretical construct.

The first part presented the insights from Geertz's interpretive anthropology and Berger's sociology of knowledge in order to understand life in context—that is, in culture and in society. Religion and moral life are interwoven into contextual realities; so, although religious confession may be particular, social identity and moral behavior are to some extent still inseparable from the larger setting.

Narrative ethics centered even more particularly on the moral life of the Christian community. Hauerwas correctly emphasizes that the church's ethics must be qualified by its particular history and canon ical stories. The social sciences can provide greater realism to the narrative perspective by better explaining the complexity of context, but Hauerwas carries their general discussion a step further by specifying a particular people and a normative tradition. In other words, he contributes to our concern to explore not just any meaning system within a broader context, but *the Christian 'world' within the world*.

All three authors are concerned in their own way with method. Each would underscore both the importance of meaning from the native point of view and the relativity of ideologies. The latter, too, are meaning constructs and hence not absolute. Berger stresses as well the distinction between sociology and values; Hauerwas provides for us the locus and source of values within the Christian community.

From this starting point, the second major section turned to Latin America. An interpretive approach can give a rather different look at the Christian church on that continent. By taking a semiotic perspective, an exclusively class orientation to social and church life can be avoided as an oversimplification, yet without denying either the structural realities or some degree of a different outlook from the oppressed. Popular culture and religion, in spite of the Spanish term, is not entirely class specific.

Latin American liberation theologians have advocated the necessity of using the social sciences to understand that context. With this I would strongly agree, yet again the relativity of any ideology and the distinction between fact and value must be maintained. Segundo corroborates this stance and also speaks of the need for communities that would nurture and teach the necessary values for a new and more just world.

The last part of the chapter seeks to establish that life in ancient Israel would have also been structured by meaning systems and experienced moral complexity and conflict. Obviously, over these many centuries contextual configurations have changed, but the fact remains that context still intermeshes with religious and moral life.

This final section closes by focusing on textual method in the study of Old Testament ethics and posits the possibility of studying the received text as it now stands. The first two parts of this chapter also mentioned the text, but its role, not exegetical methodology. Geertz points out that a work of art can resonate across space and time because of its powerful effect on the moral vision. Hauerwas in particular underlines the fact that the Christian community has a sacred text that is its moral authority and a key in the shaping of the virtues. Segundo also is concerned with how the text should be used in order to inculcate values.

These twin concerns, the text in its finished form and the moral authority of Scripture, are hence juxtaposed. The task that remains for the next chapter is to expound a method that would embrace both aspects. With that step the theoretical basis for the study of Amos will be complete, for then it can perhaps be more clear *how the Bible could be used in the moral life of the Christian community in today's world.*

EXCURSUS

Several comments are in order to explain why the *comunidades eclesiales de base* (CEBs) have not figured in the theoretical discussion of this chapter. To begin with, they are primarily a Roman Catholic phenomenon. This new ecclesiology's emphasis on lay leadership and participation, therefore, should be seen against the background of the hierarchical structure of the Roman Catholic Church on the continent.[1] In contrast, there has always been a strong focus among Protestant groups on the laity and small group Bible study, though it must be admitted that the CEBs can have a different theological and social slant.[2]

Secondly, this movement is not numerically representative of the broader Roman Catholic Church, and even less so of the Protestant churches. Berryman admits as much regarding Catholic circles when he says that in El Salvador it 'incorporates only a minority of the people in an area', in Sandinista Nicaragua 'far less than 1 percent of the population participate in them', and in Brazil 'somewhat under 2 percent'.[3] Among Protestant groups the percentage would be even smaller.[4] The

---

1. See Segundo, *Theology and the Church*, ch. 4; Boff, *Church: Charism & Power*; Levine's articles 'Religion, the Poor, and Politics in Latin America Today' and 'Conflict and Renewal' in the volume he has edited, *Religion and Political Conflict*, pp. 3-23 and 236-55, respectively; and G. Meléndez, 'La iglesia católica centroamericana en la decada de los ochenta', *CrSoc* 103 (1990), pp. 19-40. For the statement by the hierarchy made at the Bishops Conference, see CELAM, *Puebla*, paras. 617-657, pp. 163-69.

2. Note, for example, the comments in Rowland and Corner, *Liberating Exegesis*, p. 14; and those by sociologist Martin in *Tongues of Fire*, pp. 227, 285-86.

3. For El Salvador, see P. Berryman, 'El Salvador: From Evangelization to Insurrection' in Levine (ed.), *Religion and Political Conflict*, p. 77; for Nicaragua and Brazil, *idem*, *Liberation Theology*, p. 72.

4. Gordon Spykman *et al.* estimate the total number of CEBs (Catholic and Protestant) in Guatemala to be 200 (*Let My People Live: Faith and Struggle in Central America* [Grand Rapids: Eerdmans, 1988], p. 221). Zapata in 1982 (*Historia de la iglesia en Guatemala*, p. 191) gives the total of Protestant churches and congregations as close to 7000 (to add to this number the total for

CEBs, therefore, are representative of a certain kind of approach, and not of the Christian church as a whole. This is not to minimize or discredit this approach, but rather to put it into perspective. What is more, it must be admitted that the term can mean different things to different groups in different countries.[1]

There is much to be appreciated and appropriated from this movement at a theoretical level—for example, lay leadership, communal readings, social concerns.[2] The possible trap of romanticizing the movement can be avoided by recognizing:

1. The readings are not always done 'spontaneously' by the people without the help and orientation of critical biblical scholarship and experts. The interaction between the scholars and the laity is, in fact, a constant challenge to the whole process.[3]

2. Some CEBs have been actively oriented (in some cases, felt forced) toward political, sometimes revolutionary, involvement by radical clergy. Once again, it needs to be asked how instinctive to the 'common people' such political commitments were in each situation. Pablo Richards comments:

> Popular religion thus appears as the place for producing a civil society which is an alternative to the dominant civil society, where class consciousness, popular organization and revolutionary political mobilization do not find an obstacle in the popular religion, but rather a place for development and fundamental motivation. . . The revolutionary conscience of the people thus develops without entering into a fundamental contradiction with the people's Christian conscience and its expression in the popular religion and the 'Popular Church'. What is more, there it [the revolutionary conscience] finds a place for growth and a dynamisms that enriches it.[4]

One well-known case of such an orientation is that of Ernesto Cardenal and the community he organized on the island of Solentiname. His commitment to armed struggle was fixed since his visit to Cuba in 1971:

---

the Roman Catholic Church would drive the percentage down even further). Of course, statistics would vary by country (with Brazil and Nicaragua being the exceptions).

1. Levine, *Religion and Conflict*, pp. 13-16.

2. For appreciative evaluations from an evangelical protestant perspective, see C.R. Padilla, 'La nueva eclesiología en América Latina' and G. Cook, 'La espiritualidad en las comunidades de base', in *BolTeol* 24 (1986), pp. 201-26 and 227-52, respectively.

3. Cf. Carlos Mesters, 'The Use of the Bible in the Christian Communities of the Common People', in N.K. Gottwald (ed.), *The Bible and Liberation*, pp. 119-33; Neftali Perez, 'La lectura biblica en las CEBs', *RIBLA* 1 (1988), pp. 8-29. Also see earlier references in this chapter to the 'organic intellectuals'. Note Berryman's comment: 'liberation theology is already at work in the selection of passages and the interpretive slant given them' (*Liberation Theology*, p. 46).

4. Richards, 'Religiosidad popular en Centroamerica', p. 33. Cf. Berryman's remarks on a country-by-country basis in *Religious Roots* and *Liberation Theology*, pp. 74-75, 130-31.

I arrived a reformer. We were in Solentiname for 12 years, and bit by bit we became politicized and radicalized. I already had a clear view of the revolution since my first visit to Cuba, and afterward because of the influence of Liberation Theology. And my community also evolved with me, because we made these reflections together, and then we read Che together, and Allende, Fidel, Lenin, etc.[1]

---

1.   Ernesto Cardenal, 'El Evangelio en Solentiname fue obra del pueblo', in *Nicaragua, trinchera teológica. Para una Teología de la Liberación desde Nicaragua* (ed. G. Girardi, B. Forcano and J.Ma. Vigil; Managua/Madrid: Centro Ecuménico Valdivieso/Lóguez Ediciones, 1987), p. 341. Note also Berryman, *Religious Roots*, pp. 7-24; Cardenal's comments cited by Girardi, *Sandinismo, marxismo, cristianismo*, pp. 330-31 n. 7 and pp. 350-51 n. 4; and the account of his progressive radicalization in Ernesto Cardenal, *Flights of Victory/Vuelos de Victoria* (ed. and trans. M. Zimmerman *et al.*; Willimantic, CT: Curbstone Press, 1988), pp. xiii-xvi. (This is expanded in Beverley and Zimmerman, *Literature and Politics*, pp. 82-87.)

Chapter 4

THE TEXT AND THE WORLD:
THE MORAL AUTHORITY OF SCRIPTURE
AND THE CALL FOR A RESPONSIBLE POETICS

How does a sacred text serve the moral life of a community? And, once its dynamics are appreciated, how should that text be studied and read? Chapter 2 pointed out that the option of a historical reconstruction as the basis for a biblical ethics is both tenuous and precarious. The tentative results and multiple hypotheses led to the suggestion of Chapter 3 to reorient the discussion. This different approach explored moral life in context, in particular the nature of the moral life of the Christian community within a given setting. What was hinted at there, but left unexplained, was the possibility of a method focusing on the received text, that prophetic corpus that has continued to impact its readers throughout the centuries. The purpose of this chapter, therefore, is to explicate how that canonical text can function as a moral authority for the Christian church within the realities of the modern world.

The discussion will try to steer a middle course between two other kinds of stances that attempt to make the biblical text relevant for contemporary life. On the one hand, there is the position, which is exemplified by Schreiter, that appreciates culture in a very sensitive and profound way and that champions the elaboration of 'local theologies'. Schreiter, then, echoes a number of the concerns of the previous chapter, yet his treatment of the role of the biblical tradition in context grants little space to the creative potential of the text.[1] For him, the canon functions as an authority which makes intelligible and sets the boundaries of acceptable belief and which contains resources

---

1. R.J. Schreiter, *Constructing Local Theologies* (Maryknoll: Orbis Books, 1985), ch. 5.

for mediating change. When it serves for 'normative guidance', Schreiter draws categories from Chomsky's transformational grammar and describes the Scripture as equivalent to a 'grammar of orthodoxy'.[1] While a sacred text can surely function as that, this chapter will highlight its generative possibilities and the dynamic interplay of text and context. The Scripture is no dead letter or simply a credal marker, but rather a living source of moral vision.

Another perspective is represented by the Old Testament scholar Walter Brueggemann who, unlike Schreiter, does champion the power of the biblical text. In a series of works he has expounded the transformational potency of the 'prophetic imagination'.[2] As does each major section of the Old Testament canon, the prophetic literature functions both to sustain self-identity and to challenge compromise, to maintain continuity and to present necessary discontinuity; ultimately to nurture an imagination faithful to a possible social order pleasing to Yahweh. Each part of the canon, however, offers a distinct epistemology and makes unique demands. In his opinion, the prophetic corpus in particular demonstrates a hermeneutics of suspicion by advocating an alternative vision to the reigning and oppressive rhetoric and constructed reality; a different rationality questions and de-legitimates dominant political claims and domesticated religion. This different reading of reality can serve today to generate a new consciousness and perception, and so open up possibilities of change through the language and symbols of hope.[3]

Brueggemann has captured well the potential of the prophetic text to question and subsequently shape the moral vision of the community of faith. In this, he is more sensitive to textual power than Schreiter.

---

1. The other possibility he mentions is that of the Scripture as a 'performance text' of early communities of faith, 'the first fruits of the church, the beginning and head of the tradition process' (*Constructing Local Theologies*, p. 117).

2. W. Brueggemann, *The Prophetic Imagination* (Philadelphia: Fortress Press, 1978); *The Creative Word: Canon as a Model for Biblical Education* (Philadelphia: Fortress Press, 1982), ch. 1; 'Imagination as a Mode of Fidelity', in *Understanding the Word: Essays in Honour of Bernhard Anderson* (ed. J.T. Butler, E.W. Conrad and B.C. Ollenburger; JSOTSup, 37; Sheffield: JSOT Press, 1985), pp. 13-36.

3. *The Prophetic Imagination*, chs. 1-4; *The Creative Word*, ch. 3; *Hopeful Imagination: Prophetic Voices in Exile* (Philadelphia: Fortress Press, 1986), pp. 1-7, 131-33; 'Prophetic Ministry: A Sustainable Alternative Community', *HorBT* 11 (1989), pp. 1-33.

Because of his textual and historical reconstruction, however, which only allows a choice between prophetic imagination *or* royal ideology, Brueggemann unnecessarily oversimplifies the biblical data and ethical reality.[1] Moral life, then and now, is never so neat. Systems of meaning and moral values and behavior cut across class and social lines; they are never as coherent or as closed as he would have his readers believe. The prophets are apparently utilizing the wide range of theological traditions available to the broad community, speak from several contexts, and aim their messages at a variety of audiences. It simply will not do to try to limit the prophet's lives and agendas to their ties to hypothetical 'peripheral communities'.[2]

Despite the claim to be more interested in the prophetic literature than in elusive prophetic personae,[3] Brueggemann's readings sometimes can be heavily dependent on his other historical reconstructions and are thus open to the criticisms brought to light in Chapter 2. What is more, these reconstructions allow him to make facile 'analogies' between Old Testament times and modern consumer society and its 'imperial ideology'. With the ethical lines tidily drawn and the prophetic vision summarily wedded to the stance of (his) 'serious believers', the divine purposes in history are easily discernible from and for modern marginal communities.[4]

On the basis of the previous two chapters, which point out in turn the weaknesses of reconstruction for an attempt to formulate an ethic and the complexities of moral life, the argument developed here will highlight instead the power of the received text apart from a heavy

1. *The Prophetic Imagination*, chs. 2–4; 'Trajectories in Old Testament Literature and the Sociology of Israel', *JBL* 98 (1979), pp. 161-85; *Revelation and Violence: A Study in Contextualization* (Milwaukee: Marquette University Press, 1986), pp. 36-54. In this last text Brueggemann builds on his interpretation of the significance of the phrase 'horses and chariots' in Josh. 11 and elsewhere. As K.L. Younger, Jr, points out, however, Brueggemann is not aware of these words' relationship to common ancient Near Eastern language for war, data that would contradict the sociotheological point that he is trying to make (*Ancient Conquest Accounts: A Study in Ancient Near Eastern and Biblical History Writing* [JSOTSup, 98; Sheffield: JSOT Press, 1990], pp. 254-56).

2. E.g. *The Prophetic Imagination*, pp. 24-25; *The Creative Word*, pp. 49-50.

3. *The Creative Word*, pp. 51-54: *Hopeful Imagination*, p. 11.

4. Although these notions are found throughout the cited works, see, for example, *The Prophetic Imagination*, pp. 41-53; *Hopeful Imagination*, pp. 5-7, 132-33; *Revelation and Violence*, pp. 54-60.

dependence on a possible historical or literary reconstruction and attempt to give voice to the breadth of its moral vision. The challenge is to appreciate and maintain both the compositeness of our context along with the imaginative potential of the text. A normative but sterile canon (Schreiter), as well as simplistic ethical distinctions (Brueggemann), represent twin dangers to be avoided.

This chapter is divided into two major sections. What follows first is a discussion of how to understand the moral authority of the biblical text from a functional and communal perspective. Secondly, the case for taking the received text is presented, along with the choice of what has been labelled 'poetics' for the method to be used in the next chapter's reading of Amos. This section closes with an investigation of the relationship between that text and various knotty issues of history and ideology. What needs answering is not only 'what' is to be read, but also 'how'.

1. *Textual Power: The Moral Authority of Scripture*

In contrast to the idea that authority always entails domination and the foreclosure of freedom, Gadamar offers a constructive notion of an authority earned and merited because of a more excellent insight and profound discernment. With this 'rehabilitation' of authority can also follow a more positive appreciation of tradition.[1] A living tradition is constantly renewed and finds continual resonance; its authority is at once celebrated and cherished.

In addition, understanding itself is always necessarily placed, whether recognized or not, within some stream of tradition. A pure objective historicism is impossible. Understanding takes place within a horizon shaped by a tradition; it is influenced by a set of pre-understandings. In the case of a text, comprehension cannot escape what Gadamer calls 'effective-history', that legacy of past interpretations and studies up until the present which impact the encounter with that text.[2] Understanding, in other words, rather than being immediate is

1. H.-G. Gadamer, *Truth and Method* (trans. and ed. G. Barden and J. Cumming; New York: Continuum, 1975). For what follows regarding tradition and effective history see pp. 245-53, 257-74. Cf. G.L. Bruns's helpful essay, 'What Is Tradition?', *NLH* 22 (1991), pp. 1-21.

2. Cf. H.R. Jauss, *Toward on Aesthetic of Reception* (trans. T. Bahti; Theory and History of Literature, 2; Minneapolis, MN: University of Minnesota Press,

inevitably mediated. What is required, therefore, is a consciousness of the hermeneutical situation and process.

This recognition of the formative influences on understanding parallels the sociocultural and ethical discussion of Chapter 3. Gadamer's terms 'tradition' and 'horizon' can find their counterparts, for example, in the concepts of 'narrative' and 'context', respectively. A Christian understanding of the biblical text, then, will be shaped in some degree by the various narratives of which it is a part and by the cultural setting within which it takes place. Consequently, interpretation needs to be contextually conscious.

Gadamer also speaks of certain texts, those 'classical examples', that can bridge the historical gap between the past and present by their quality of being able to present something ever-true.[1] A 'classical' text, although a product of the past, offers a world and a vision that transcends its own historical context and that illumines the present:

> it is a consciousness of something enduring, of significance that cannot be lost and is independent of all circumstances of time, in which we call something 'classical'—a kind of timeless present that is contemporaneous with every other age.[2]

The text captivates and informs the reader; the textual world continues to draw the reader into the reality offered in its pages: 'Our understanding will always include consciousness of our belonging to that world. And correlative to this is the fact that the work belongs to our world.'[3] Mexican author and critic Octavio Paz would call that textual potential to disclose and orient modern life through its world the 'consecration of the instant'.[4] The horizon of the text and that of the interpreter interact and 'fuse' within the broader horizon of human history. There can be no limiting the text's influencing possibilities to historicist reconstructions, although historical data are illuminative for proper understanding. Rather, the encounter with the text of the

---

1982), ch. 1, for a much more in-depth discussion of the continuing and changing reception of a text by the public over time.

1. Gadamer, *Truth and Method*, pp. 253-58.
2. Gadamer, *Truth and Method*, p. 256.
3. Gadamer, *Truth and Method*, p. 258.
4. Octavio Paz, *The Bow and the Lyre: The Poem. The Poetic Revelation. Poetry and History* (trans. R.L.C. Simms; Austin, TX: University of Texas Press, 1973), ch. 9.

past impacts the present, and the new insights are assimilated and applied.[1]

This functional perspective on literature is drawing increased attention within biblical studies. A pioneering study in this vein is the celebrated essay 'Odysseus' Scar' by Erich Auerbach.[2] What is of note at this juncture is not his argument that the Old Testament picture of life is more complex and profound than Homeric style; it is his claim that the text is autocratic in its demands that draws our attention here:

> The Scripture stories do not, like Homer's, court our favor, they do not flatter us that they may please us and enchant us—they seek to subject us, and if we refuse to be subjected we are rebels. . . it seeks to overcome our reality: we are to fit our own life into its world, feel ourselves to be elements in its structure of universal history.[3]

In other words, the biblical text can be perceived as a powerful 'classic' because of the world it portrays and the manner of that reality's presentation. Paul Ricoeur will speak of its 'poetic function', the 'manifestation' of truth through the redescription or representation of life offered through its language.[4] This mimetic function[5] explains the transcendent quality of the biblical text, the ability of the world unfolded by that the text to move from the moorings of the horizon of its production and initial reception to anchorage within life in the present.

Narrative ethics has focused on this functional perspective in its

---

1. Gadamer, *Truth and Method*, pp. 258-74. See also his discussion on application, pp. 274-305.

2. E. Auerbach, *Mimesis: The Representation of Reality in Western Literature* (trans. W. Trask; Garden City, NY: Doubleday, 1957), pp. 1-20.

3. *Mimesis*, p. 12. Auerbach also hits on other issues that will be brought up later in the chapter in more detail—e.g. history-likeness and the focus on the received form of the text.

4. P. Ricoeur, *Essays on Biblical Interpretation* (ed. L.S. Mudge; Philadelphia: Fortress Press, 1980), pp. 98-117.

5. For helpful discussions on mimesis, see C. Walhout, 'Texts and Actions', in R. Lundin, A.C. Thiselton and C. Walhout (eds.), *The Responsibility of Hermeneutics* (Grand Rapids: Eerdmans, 1985), pp. 31-77 (especially pp. 49-61); B.C. Lategan, 'Reference: Reception, Redescription and Reality', in B.C. Lategan and W.S. Vorster (eds.), *Text and Reality: Aspects of Reference in Biblical Texts* (SBL Semeia Studies; Atlanta: Scholars Press, 1985), pp. 67-93. The relationship between the text's world and the actual world will be explored below.

rendering of the moral authority of the Bible.[1] For Stanley Hauerwas this authority 'resides in the power to form a people able to live in accordance with it and witness to the God we claim to be the truth of existence'.[2] The canon is that set of texts which have been acknowledged by the Christian church as basic for self-understanding and the formulation of mission. The Scripture is the church's 'classic'.

A narrative approach would hold the biblical texts to be primarily identity documents—that is, those texts that offer to the community of faith depictions of a series of characters within a world. The primary character, of course, is God (or Jesus): it is from within the pages of the biblical accounts that the church can come to see what he is like, what he demands, and how he involves himself in personal lives, social realities and human history.

The Scripture also displays the life of the community which God creates, shapes and directs. This identity can appear either in a positive light or in a negative one, as a community of virtue and commitment

---

1. Although this book follows the notion of the functional authority of Scripture, the discussion does not claim that this is the only way that its moral authority can or should be perceived. For the various ways of construing the moral authority of the Bible see J. Gustafson, *Theology in Christian Ethics* (Philadelphia: Pilgrim Press, 1974), ch. 6; A. Verhey, *The Great Reversal: Ethics and the New Testament* (Grand Rapids: Eerdmans, 1984), pp. 153-65, 174-79, 187-96; Birch and Rasmussen, *Bible & Ethics*, pp. 142-43, 181-94.

This approach is actually a choice of a particular 'discrimen' according to a certain perception of the nature of the life of the church (i.e. a community of virtue). Every view of biblical authority is functional in this sense. See Kelsey, *Uses of Scripture*, chs. 6–9 (cf. Linbeck, *Nature of Doctrine*, ch. 6). It should be pointed out that the discussion here makes no more than a phenomenological observation on textual function, and statements regarding ontological aspects of the Bible (e.g. inspiration) are outside the purview of this book. Kelsey does keep his discussion within the parameters of his functional analysis (*Uses of Scripture*, pp. 207-16), but Verhey (*The Great Reversal*, pp. 169-74) and Birch and Rasmussen (*Bible & Ethics*, pp. 144-51) do make ontological statements.

2. Hauerwas, 'Moral Authority', p. 358. For this approach also see Hauerwas with Bonti and Burrell, *Truthfulness and Tragedy*, ch. 9; Hauerwas, *The Peaceable Kingdom*, especially ch. 5; McClendon, *Systematic Theology*, I, especially pp. 177-84, 212-30, 334-56. McClendon uses speech-act theory as a presupposition for his approach. Helpful explanations of this theory in relationship to the Bible can be found in Walhout, 'Texts and Actions', pp. 42-40, and in A.C. Thiselton's chapter in the same volume, 'Reader-Response Hermeneutics, Action Models, and the Parables of Jesus', pp. 79-113 (especially pp. 107-13).

or as a people rebellious to their God and malevolent even to their own. Finally, the text pictures a world to its readers and listeners: a reality at once strange yet familiar, of the past yet for the present, far away yet always attendant.

The canonical narrative, it is claimed, in and through its various genres provides a 'truthful' grasp of the divine, of the self and the church, and of social existence. The Bible has continually demonstrated its moral authority by the insights generated through the identities it renders for the common life of the church. Hauerwas comments:

> to claim the Bible as an authority is the testimony of the church that this book provides the resources necessary for the church to be a community sufficiently truthful so that our conversation with one another and God can continue across generations.[1]

The individual stories of the Bible, as well as its over-arching story, are no passive authority (if that were possible). These texts call to their reader, challenge alternative visions, invite participation in a different perception of life and initiation into a new community. These then are demanding texts, texts that not only grant perspectives for living, but that also require skills commensurate with their story. Therefore, the Scripture cannot properly function as Scripture unless learned and lived out within the context of the church. Only there can this moral vision be grasped, nurtured and sustained. The individual stories and the broader canonical story need 'growing into'—that is, training in the virtues, values, and duties correlative to that vision.

As the preceding chapter was at pains to point out, this process of building up of the character of the church in accordance with the narrative of the biblical tradition must also be aware of the other sociocultural traditions of the church's context. These other stories are inescapable. To claim the Bible as *the* moral authority of the church, however, is to declare that these writings do have a *privileged* role in establishing the identity of God's people and in influencing its moral deliberations.[2]

Others besides Brueggemann have also underscored this vision-

---

1. Hauerwas, 'Moral Authority', p. 362.

2. Though Hauerwas and McClendon do address this issue, for a fuller discussion see Verhey, *The Great Reversal*, pp. 166-69, 187-96; and Birch and Rasmussen, *Bible & Ethics*, pp. 152-55. Cf. Linbeck, *The Nature of Doctrine*.

shaping function of the Old Testament. David Clines can say of the Torah:

> The Pentateuch as a story therefore performs the function of creating a 'world' that is to a greater or lesser extent unlike the world of the reader, and that invites the reader to allow the horizons of his own world to merge with those of that other world. And to respond to that invitation is to allow oneself to be worked upon, influenced, by the story; that is, to expose oneself to the possibility of the story becoming one's own story (biography).[1]

Taking the Bible as a 'classic' and as scriptural authority allows the canon to reverberate within the life of the church:

> What is happening in imaginative literature such as a story and poem is the creation of worlds alternative to our own present reality. Though they bear a resemblance to our everyday world, we are aware that things are done differently there, values we recognize are differently esteemed, and our own personal security may be troubled as we realize that our way is not the only way for humans to be. If we are fascinated into acknowledging the alternative world as part, at least, of what we want to have as our own real world, two horizons merge: that of our prior world and that of the alternative world. In religious language, this is called 'hearing' Scripture.[2]

This approach has proved fruitful in the study of each major section of the Old Testament canon.[3] The next chapter explores the world of Amos, specifically its depiction of the faith and life of Israel. How can that rendering of an ancient worshipping community illuminate the church? How can the reality represented there impact moral life in context today? In light of what has been said thus far, the prophetic text can be said to serve as an identity document in two senses. First, the reading of Amos will *identify* the character of God and his people and the narrative world within which they act. Secondly, the biblical study will seek to probe how might the church's *identifying* with that representation guide its self-understanding and life as a community of

1. D.J.A. Clines, *The Theme of the Pentateuch* (JSOTSup, 10; Sheffield: JSOT Press, 1978), p. 102. For a fuller treatment see pp. 102-11.

2. D.J.A. Clines, 'Story and Poem: The Old Testament as Literature and as Scripture', *Int* 34 (1980), p. 127.

3. E.g. Brueggemann, *The Creative Word*; D.J.A. Clines, *I, He, We, & They: A Literary Approach to Isaiah 53* (JSOTSup, 1; Sheffield: JSOT Press, 1976), chs. 4, 5. See the works mentioned below in the discussion on poetics.

virtue. How is Amos to be read, though? The choice of a method and the implications of that option are the topics of the next section.

2. *Textual Method: Poetics and the Responsible Reader*

What has been suggested up to this point regarding the textual method to be employed in the reading of the prophetic text has been rather vague. All that has been proposed is that the study of Amos be based on the received text. What has not been specified, however, is a particular method, nor parameters for what might be called a relevant reading accountable to both the church and the wider context. The following discussion, accordingly, is divided into three parts. The first signals the selection of poetics as the textual approach for the reading of Amos; the second explores the relationship between the received text and history, along with its pertinence to the concern for contextualizing the Scripture. The chapter closes with a call for a 'responsible' reading.

a. *The Choice of Poetics*
The decision to adopt an approach focusing on the received text is no longer a novel one. In fact, there has been a quite an explosion in 'final form' studies. For some, the move away from more diachronic studies has been driven by a *polemical reaction* against professional restrictions and elitism. Walter Wink hits out at what he considers to be the 'false consciousness' of scholarly objectivism and bemoans the loss of the dialogue between text and interpreter and between the interpreter and the community.[1]

Others have felt forced to question the claims of source and form criticism and point out *perceived failures*. Rhetorical critics, for example, have called for going beyond form criticism in order to give more attention to the literary fabric of longer passages. Coherence and structural indicators now take precedence over supposed genres and hypothetical *Sitze im Leben*. The usual focus on repeatable forms tended to obscure the creativity and uniqueness of the passages under study.[2] From his canonical perspective, Brevard Childs would

---

1. W. Wink, *The Bible in Human Transformation: Toward a New Paradigm for Biblical Study* (Philadelphia: Fortress Press, 1973).
2. J. Muilenburg, 'Form Criticism and Beyond', *JBL* 88 (1969), pp. 1-18; M.

criticize form criticism for trying to base the theological issues of passages on a reconstruction, even if this 'runs directly in the face of the literature's explicit statement of its function within the final form of the biblical text'.[1] In other words, the present text sometimes no longer says what form critics believe the original portion once said.

Adele Berlin takes source and form criticism's criteria and assumptions to task and then uses *The Gilgamesh Epic* as evidence to demonstrate that editorial work in the ancient Near East apparently did not function as some critics have posited in the case of the biblical traditions.[2] In addition, some literary critics whose life work is beyond the realm of biblical studies, but who have given attention to the Bible, complain that what is taken for 'literary criticism' in biblical scholarship would be an anomaly in wider literary circles and actually demonstrates insensitivity to the nature of literature itself.[3] C.S. Lewis could say, 'First then, whatever these men may be as Biblical critics, I distrust them as critics. They seem to lack literary judgment, to be imperceptive about the very quality of the texts they are reading.'[4]

Kessler, 'An Introduction to Rhetorical Criticism of the Bible: Prolegomena', *Semitics* 7 (1980), pp. 1-27; *idem*, 'A Methodological Setting for Rhetorical Criticism', in *Art and Meaning: Rhetoric in Biblical Literature* (ed. D.J.A. Clines, D.M. Gunn and A.J. Hauser; JSOTSup, 19; Sheffield: JSOT Press, 1982), pp. 1-19.

1. B.S. Childs, *Introduction to the Old Testament as Scripture* (Philadelphia: Fortress Press, 1979), p. 75.

2. A. Berlin, *Poetics and Interpretation of Biblical Narrative* (Bible and Literature Series; Sheffield: Almond Press, 1983), ch. 5. Cf. Younger, *Ancient Conquest Accounts*, which compares ancient 'transmission codes' with how several Old Testament scholars have tried to formulate the composition of the biblical texts dealing with the conquest.

3. E.g. L. Ryken, 'Literary Criticism of the Bible: Some Fallacies', in *Literary Interpretations of Biblical Narrative* (ed. K.R.R. Gros Louis, J.S. Ackerman and T.S. Warshaw; Nashville: Abingdon Press, 1974), pp. 24-40; K.R.R. Gros Louis, 'Some Methodological Considerations', in *Literary Interpretations of Biblical Narrative*, II (ed. K.R.R. Gros Louis and J.S. Ackerman; Nashville: Abingdon Press, 1982), pp. 13-24; R. Alter, *The Art of Biblical Narrative* (New York: Basic Books, 1981), *passim*; M. Sternberg, *The Poetics of Biblical Narrative: Ideological Literature and the Drama of Reading* (Indiana Literary Biblical Series; Bloomington, IN: Indiana University Press, 1985), *passim*.

4. C.S. Lewis, 'Modern Theology and Biblical Criticism', in *Christian Reflections* (ed. W. Hooper; Grand Rapids: Eerdmans, 1967), pp. 152-66 (154).

Still others have no desire to attack diachronic approaches and would rather see synchronics simply as an *alternative perspective*, which answers a different set of questions and meets separate needs.[1] Barton would 'propose that we should see each of our "methods" as a codification of intuitions about the text which may occur to intelligent readers'.[2] Antagonism surfaces, he claims, when each approach seeks exclusive hegemony:

> Indeed, if there is one tendency of biblical criticism it has been my aim to call in question, it is this tendency to seek the normative, a tendency that crops up in every kind of criticism we have examined. Over and over again biblical critics seek *correct* methods, *prescriptive* answers to the question how we may read the Old Testament, *successful* procedures and techniques that will process the text and extract from it the answers that we *ought to* be looking for.[3]

This last posture is more amenable to my proposal, for it moves beyond polemics and debates over inadequacies of more traditional methods and posits the legitimacy of an approach which reads the received text. There is still, though, another voice emanating from biblical scholarship in favor of such a study. This is the vote of *pragmatism*.

What some are saying is that it is impossible to ascertain with much certainty the original setting of a message or to delimit the scope of an *Ur*-text. Textual reconstruction, in other words, is showing itself to be as tenuous as historical reconstruction.

In their recent commentary on Amos, Andersen and Freedman

---

1. Note Clines, who demonstrates his concern for both diachronics and synchronics, in *Theme of the Pentateuch*, chs. 9, 10; J.F.A. Sawyer, 'A Change of Emphasis in the Study of the Prophets', in *Israel's Prophetic Tradition: Essays in Honour of Peter R. Ackroyd* (ed. R. Coggins, A. Phillips and M. Knibb; Cambridge: Cambridge University Press, 1982), pp. 233-49. Sternberg would also distinguish the fields and contributions of what he labels 'source' and 'discourse' approaches (*Poetics of Biblical Narrative*, pp. 7-23). See also L. Alonso Schökel, 'Problemas hermenéuticos de un estudio literario de la Biblia' [originally appeared as 'Hermeneutical Problems of a Literary Study of the Bible', *VTSup* 28 (1975), pp. 1-15] and 'Modelos y métodos' (expanded version of 'Methods and Models', *VTSup* 36 [1985], pp. 3-13) in *Hermenéutica Biblica*. I. *Hermenéutica de la Palabra* (Madrid: Ediciones Cristiandad, 1986), pp. 163-76 and 177-93, respectively.

2. Barton, *Reading the Old Testament*, p. 5.

3. Barton, *Reading the Old Testament*, p. 207 (author's emphasis).

attribute a substantial portion of the book's material to that eighth-century prophet, but do not doubt the possibility of some editing and rewriting over centuries. Yet the difficulties in distinguishing the hypothetical layers of oracles and additions, coupled with the literary texture manifest in the thematic and lexical coherence and in the rhetorical creativity of the received text, have driven them to focus on the 'final form', on textual unity not supposed inconsistencies.[1]

Theirs is not a method that ignores historical settings and influences or that disregards the possible development of the canonical text of Amos. Rather, their textual study is grounded both in the practical admission of disagreements among critics and the arbitrariness of some more traditional approaches, as well as in an appreciation of the literariness of the prophetic piece.

This book seconds the pragmatism of that approach. One could mention yet again the results of Chapter 2 and the first Appendix regarding historical reconstructions in Amos, among which uncertainties and discrepancies abound. To this plethora of positions on historical issues can be added the plentiful theories concerning that prophetic book's composition.[2] Jeremias's words are pertinent:

---

1. F.I. Andersen and D.N. Freedman, *Amos* (AB, 24; Garden City, NY: Doubleday), pp. 3-18, 73-76, 141-49, *passim*. It should be noted that they presuppose substantial authenticity to the book, as well as a close relationship between prophet and editor.

2. For surveys of the many hypotheses see J.F. Craghan, 'The Prophet Amos in Recent Literature', *BTB* 2 (1972), pp. 243-46; Martin-Achard, *Amos*, pp. 52-74; Auld, *Amos*, ch. 5. More recent studies include Jorg Jeremias, 'Amos 3–6. Beobachtungen zur Entstehungsgeschichte eines Prophetenbuches', *ZAW* 100 (1988), pp. 123-38, and the broader discussion of W. Zimmerli, 'Vom Prophetenwort zum Prophetenbuch', *TLZ* 104 (1979), pp. 481-96. See also the more recent commentaries of Soggin (*Amos*), D. Stuart (*Hosea–Jonah* [Word Biblical Commentary; Waco, TX: Word Books, 1987]), J.H. Hayes (*Amos the Eighth-Century Prophet: His Times and his Preaching* [Nashville: Abingdon Press, 1988]), G.V. Smith (*Amos: A Commentary* [Library of Biblical Interpretation; Grand Rapids: Zondervan, 1989]), and Andersen and Freedman (*Amos*). Interestingly, G. Ebeling believes that the historical-critical method is necessary for an 'existentialist' interpretation and basic for an encounter with the word of God. Such an approach, however, if it were to seek detail, could flounder here because of the babel of voices. See his essays 'The Significance of the Critical Historical Method for Church and Theology in Protestantism' and 'Word of God and Hermeneutics', in *Word and Faith* (trans. J.W. Leitch; The Preacher's Library;

a reconstruction of the spoken words of Amos is only partially possible, and moreover often only by quite a complicated means and with surely a variable degree of probability.[1]

To this academic textual pragmatism must also be joined a *moral realism*: it is the received text that is most read and assimilated by Christians in local churches and in personal and group Bible reading. Far removed from academia, most of the community of faith know only that 'final form', and it is *that* text which moves and inspires them and which functions as their 'classic'. It is now time, Sawyer says, that this text be made the focus of careful study:

> In fact the context selected by many writers today, namely the final form of the text as understood by one or other of the religious communities that believe it to be in some way authoritative, happens to be a particularly interesting and important one, not only because of the influence it has had on the history of Western religious though but also because it has been neglected in mainstream Biblical scholarship for most of two centuries.[2]

The decision to study this form of the text is far removed from attempts to propose various stages of composition, each of which are then claimed to provide practical lessons for modern faith. Hypothetical actualizations become keys to application. Coote has done the most extensive work along these lines in Amos, which he divides into three stages—A: the edition of Amos and disciples; B: the Bethel edition of the seventh century; C: the exilic redactor. Each stage supposedly has a distinct message and thus carries different implications for the present. The weaknesses inherent in such an approach for moral reasoning in the church is obvious from the very beginning in this surprisingly contradictory caveat:

> It was possible to make such a selection of oracles of Amos only after a lengthy study of the book, with *a good deal of necessarily circular reasoning*. But now that we can read them in this way in a group, the distinctive features they have in common become *readily apparent.*[3]

What is at issue is how the biblical text should be read to nurture and shape the moral life of the community of faith in any given

London: SCM Press, 1963), pp. 17-61 and 305-32, respectively.
   1. Jeremias, 'Amos 3–6', p. 135.
   2. Sawyer, 'A Change of Emphasis in the Study of the Prophets', p. 243. Cf. Clines's comments on the Pentateuch in *Theme of the Pentateuch*, pp. 11-12.
   3. Coote, *Amos*, p. 15 (emphasis added).

context. This book distances itself from such reconstruction efforts in the moral enterprise, although (and this is an important balancing point) such efforts are in no way said to be somehow beyond the bounds of legitimate study. What is stressed here is that the Bible has and continues to function as a moral authority and to underscore that 'final form', as Sawyer rightfully points out, is both a natural and necessary task.

Behind the option for a method highlighting the received text, therefore, lies first the *practical admission* of what is conceived of as the written word of God by most of the Christian community around the globe.[1] At the same time, this choice is born of a *pastoral commitment* to make that text more intelligible and thus more clearly an ever-living word in context.

There are many available methods, however, that focus on the 'final form'—such as structuralism, canon criticism, and rhetorical criticism. The method that is chosen here, on the other hand, is what has been labelled poetics and has been associated in Old Testament studies with such scholars as Robert Alter,[2] Adele Berlin,[3] Meir Sternberg[4] and Harold Fisch.[5] Berlin has defined this approach in this way: 'Poetics, then, is an inductive science that seeks to abstract the general principles of literature from many different manifestations of those principles as they occur in actual literary texts.'[6]

Poetics, therefore, is committed to studying the biblical texts as literature according to literary principles. In actual practice, poetics observes not only structural markers and rhetorical devices, but also (and here it moves beyond rhetorical criticism) analyzes, for example, characterization and point of view. What is sought is *how* texts mean; and a fuller appreciation of literary art, it is claimed, can also yield a deeper understanding of *what* they mean.

---

1. Once more, the point is a phenomenological one. No attempt is made here to move into ontological categories concerning the nature of Scripture.

2. R. Alter, *Art of Biblical Narrative*, and *The Art of Biblical Poetry* (New York: Basic Books, 1985).

3. Berlin, *Poetics and Interpretation*.

4. Sternberg, *Poetics of Biblical Narrative*.

5. H. Fisch, *Poetry with a Purpose: Biblical Poetics and Interpretation* (Indiana Studies in Biblical Literature; Bloomington, IN: Indiana University Press, 1988).

6. Berlin, *Poetics and Interpretation*, p. 15 (this quote is part of a fuller discussion in her first chapter).

The goal, therefore, is more than the grasp of formal textual mechanics; it involves the world and characters of the text as well. This text, accepted as a sacred canon and understood in some way as God's word 'given', projects a reality that impacts the reader and makes its demands. To say as much is to move beyond mere aesthetics to what Sternberg calls the 'ideology' of the text, which seeks not just to entertain, but to persuade.[1] Rhetoric functions as a strategy to convince and to convert the reader; poetry is now purposive, and reading a drama.[2] The Bible, the authoritative written tradition of the people of God, confronts the reader. As Fisch says:

> In the end, it would seem that texts are sacred because they command and because we assent to their commands. . . This is what makes them 'Bible'. This has disturbing implications for the whole enterprise of leveling the Bible with other kinds of literature.[3]

But the sacred texts communicate their impact and weave their inescapable web through language and literary art:

> The Hebrew prophets and psalmists worked with words, fashioning them plastically to their needs, working with and sometimes against the grain of language. . . We can call this a species of metaphysical wit or we can call it a 'demonstration of spirit and power'. . . [4]

The next chapter offers a reading of chs. 3 through 6 of Amos. What contribution can a poetic approach to these chapters offer to the moral life of the Christian community in context? How can the representation of reality and the description of the identities of God and his people illuminate the present? The modern reader of faith is also drawn into that 'covenantal discourse'[5] pictured in that ancient text and, like the audience represented there, must respond to divine demands and guidance for life within history.

But how can a poetic approach be related to history? Is the 'final form' option to present the world of the text a vote to obscure, if not

---

1. Of those most associated with poetics Berlin appears as the one most limited to an aesthetic level. The others are deeply concerned with the demands made by the text through its poetic strategies.
2. This sentence is obviously a word-play taken from the sub-titles of the books by Sternberg and Fisch.
3. Fisch, *Poetry with a Purpose*, pp. 5-6.
4. Fisch, *Poetry with a Purpose*, p. 6.
5. This is Fisch's term (*Poetry with a Purpose*, pp. 118-20).

ignore, the relationship between the text and the ancient world in which it was produced? Is the text historically factual? These queries just begin to introduce a whole gamut of issues which the following section will seek to clarify.

b. *The Text and History*

To probe the relationship between the biblical text and history is to open up a discussion that actually has several components within recent scholarly debate. This study cannot hope to resolve these various issues (or tensions), but it is the purpose of this section at least to probe them and to set forth the stance to be taken in regard to Amos. Three items will be handled in turn: the notion of a self-contained text, the problem of historical reference, and the recently suggested history-likeness and historiography dichotomy.

Some literary critics, such as Kenneth R.R. Gros Louis, assume a self-contained work and accordingly push historical questions very much to the background or out of sight altogether:

> The text to us is not sacred, and whether the events it describes are historical is not relevant to our purposes. . . Our approach is essentially ahistorical; the text is taken as received, and the truth of an action or an idea or a motive, for literary criticism, depends on its rightness or appropriateness in context.[1]

Paul Ricoeur, who has done so much to introduce a functional focus on biblical literature, is himself admittedly vague on the issue of linking the text with the historical reality beyond the world represented within its pages.[2]

Such New Critical tendencies have been criticized by secular critics such as Robert Scholes. After helpfully charting the emphases of the various contemporary literary 'schools', Scholes presents his case for a semiotic approach that takes into account several interpretive codes—that is, the grammatical, semantic and cultural codes avail-

---

1. Gros Louis, 'Some Methodological Considerations', p. 14.
2. Ricoeur, *Essays on Biblical Interpretation*, pp. 44-45. (Robert Scholes takes Ricoeur to task for a false distinction between semiotics and semantics in *Semiotics and Interpretation* [New Haven: Yale University Press, 1982], pp. 44-46.) For a helpful survey of fundamental philosophic issues pertaining to the relationship between hermeneutics and history, see Thiselton, *Two Horizons*, ch. 3.

able.[1] An informed reading and interpretation of a text demands an awareness of these contextual variables, as well as an acquaintance with other concurrent texts.[2]

Sternberg specifically singles out Gros Louis's hermetic stance to point out that any literature is written according to linguistic and artistic codes.[3] Other literature from the ancient Near East can also prove to be an aid in recognizing literary conventions; by both comparison and contrast the uniquely biblical, as well as the shared cultural, elements can come in view.[4] Fisch believes, in fact, that this background demonstrates that the Old Testament texts are 'anti-literature', conscious efforts to undermine the mythological views of their time while using common forms.[5] Alter will even go so far as to claim that biblical narrative was a new form distinct from other ancient literature precisely because of its distinct theology.[6]

A poetic approach, therefore, *in theory* does not hold to a totally self-contained text, divorced from all conventions and codes. Such a radical stance would violate the basis of written and verbal communication. If the first point in the discussion is the philosophical assumption that no text (in this case Amos) can be understood in complete isolation, how is such a commitment to be worked out *in practice*? To what does the text actually refer?

For this second issue of historical reference, the critic Robert Scholes again can offer insight. To simplify a complex argument: Scholes points out that, although the relationship between signifier and signified is arbitrary, the signified is actually 'motivated by reference':

> Language, culture, our social frame of reference—all these exert a tremendous pressure on the selectivity of perception. But things are *there*, soliciting our attention. . . Language exists *in order* for us to talk about

---

1. Scholes, *Semiotics and Interpretation*, chs. 1, 2.

2. Scholes, *Semiotics and Interpretation*, ch. 3, and his *Textual Power: Literary Theory and the Teaching of English* (New Haven: Yale University Press, 1985), chs. 2, 3; and *Protocols of Reading* (New Haven: Yale University Press, 1989), ch. 1. Cf. Jauss, *Toward an Aesthetic of Reception*, pp. 22-28.

3. Sternberg, *Poetics of Biblical Narrative*, pp. 6-13.

4. E.g. Berlin, *Poetics and Interpretation*, pp. 129-34 (cf. her interaction with James Kugel in 'On the Bible as Literature', *Prooftexts* 2 [1982], pp. 323-32); Younger, *Ancient Conquest Accounts*.

5. Fisch, *Poetry with a Purpose*, pp. 2, 6, *passim*.

6. Alter, *Art of Biblical Narrative*, pp. 12, 24-29.

such things, among others. In every language there are words for certain
things not because language has 'chosen' arbitrarily to create those words
but because the things were sufficiently *there* to force language to accom-
modate them.[1]

Although the specific relationship between what is signified in the
text and the actual world outside the text will obviously vary, there
are (besides the unavoidable contacts through the codes mentioned
earlier) some sort of patterns within the text that parallel that world.[2]
Not only is a text not completely detached and autonomous, to hold to
such a conviction, in Scholes's view, would be destructive because the
power of a text to speak *into reality*, at its moment of production just
as now, is thereby foreclosed.[3]

These sentiments return the discussion to the earlier one regarding
the 'classical' and the merging of horizons. Contact with the actual
world is apparent at conception in the past and reception in the
present. That is why biblical texts continue to speak, and their world
to impact ours. They are 'real', in some way 'true' representations of
social life. To deny the referential connections of these texts could
abort their transforming power.

In the case of Amos the move from a general notion of 'reference'
to concrete items of 'referents' proves rather problematic. Chapter 2
and Appendix 1 point out the unsettled status of much of the historical
context of Amos. Yet, even though some referents can be given little
if any historical verification (even the prophet himself!), it is abun-
dantly clear that that book's world is linked with the actual world of
eighth-century Israel. This state of affairs echoes the conclusion of
those earlier discussions in this book: the historical data can serve to
illuminate textual particulars; to use the taxonomy of the preceding
paragraphs, reference and referents in Amos can provide guides to
understanding.[4]

1. Scholes, *Textual Power*, p. 97 (author's emphasis).
2. See the helpful discussion regarding mimesis in the works cited above, in the
discussion entitled 'Textual Power'.
3. Scholes, *Textual Power*, chs. 6, 7. See his distinction between 'metaphysical'
and 'pragmatic presence' in *Protocols of Reading*, pp. 59-77.
4. Notice this comment by Phillip J. King in the introduction to his *Amos, Hosea,
Micah—An Archaeological Commentary* (Philadelphia: Westminster Press, 1988):
'This book focuses on artifacts and other material remains recovered through excava-
tion and survey, with the hope that they may illuminate the eighth-century

Scholes's practical concern to argue for the notion of reference can serve as the transition to the third issue, the history-like/ historiography dichotomy. Several scholars have resorted to the category 'history-like' to underscore the power of the material that appears in apparently historical form in the Old Testament.[1] On the one hand, theirs is a pastoral concern:

> Perhaps our first need, then, is to be prepared to listen to (perhaps literally: but also to read) the stories. So often they have been pulled about, either in the interest of a particular form of literary criticism, or in the concern to establish a historical nucleus—'what actually happened'—that it has become all but impossible to see the story as a whole. In this way the role of the story as a vehicle of faith for the community of faith has been eroded, to a large extent by the sheer mass of historical knowledge now available.[2]

Although their interest lies primarily in biblical narrative, their desire to let the texts speak as texts, and not just function as specimens for historical scrutiny, is relevant to our own argument and obviously seconds the discussion up to this point. In the case of the prophetic literature, their history-likeness (their realistic depictions) allows them to speak across the centuries. Their world is not totally alien to the modern context, nor the message completely foreign to actual needs.

At this juncture Fernand Braudel's categories of levels of history can add more precision to clarifying the difficult relationship between text and history.[3] Braudel mentions three ways of looking at historical data. First, is the focus on *l'histoire évenementielle*, the history of

---

prophets. . . to demonstrate that the Bible is concerned with people who really lived' (pp. 23-24).

1. H.W. Frei, *The Eclipse of Biblical Narrative: A Study in Eighteenth and Nineteenth Century Hermeneutics* (New Haven: Yale University Press, 1974), pp. 1-16 for a preview of his argument; J.J. Collins, 'The "Historical Character" of the Old Testament in Recent Biblical Theology', *CBQ* 41 (1979), pp. 185-204; R.J. Coggins, 'History and Story in Old Testament Study', *JSOT* 11 (1979), pp. 36-46; J. Barr, 'Story and History in Biblical Theology', in *The Scope and Authority of the Bible* (Philadelphia: Westminster Press, 1980), pp. 1-17; R.E. Clements, 'History and Theology in Biblical Narrative', *HorBT* 4–5 (1982–1983), pp. 45-60; J.W. Rogerson, 'Old Testament History and the History of Israel', in *Beginning Old Testament Study*, ch. 3.

2. Coggins, 'History and Story', p. 43.

3. F. Braudel, *On History* (trans. S. Matthews; Chicago: University of Chicago Press, 1980), pp. 25-54.

events and moments; next is the *conjuncture*, broader and slower movements and cycles of socioeconomic developments over decades; lastly, there is the *longue durée*, the study of structures that are longer-lasting and which span centuries, which are determined by such things as geography, climate and culture.

Much of the archaeological and historical data that is utilized in the study of biblical material is of the first type, of artifacts and evidence for discrete items or persons; increasingly, sociological interest in Old Testament circles is pointing to the last two in order to explain better the social world of ancient Israel within the broader context of Near Eastern history.[1] What can be done, however, is to relate these categories to the history-like discussion, because then the moral relevance of the textual world to the actual world can become clearer.

For some, perhaps, the this-is-that conviction can take place at the level of events (category one): what is happening now is just like what happened back then. Historical disparities, however, would make such attempts at establishing close parallels difficult. Yet at levels two and three the bridge is easier precisely because the biblical data is vague and general enough to allow for the text to become a document that mirrors the modern world.[2] In Latin America, for example, where countries are often still largely agricultural societies and where open-air markets can be part of everyday life, the textual world can appear so very 'real', so history-like. Reference, therefore, works both ways: it grounds the textual world in eighth-century Israel, while at the same time pointing to actual socioeconomic structures and problems. Can one not then suggest yet a fourth category, *l'histoire constitutive*, those elements common to all societies throughout time: the exploitation and oppression that never disappear, but only change (so very slowly, so very little); the denunciation and hope that never die, and

1. E.g. F.R. Brandfon, 'Kinship, Culture and "Longue Durée"', *JSOT* 39 (1987), pp. 30-38.

2. By way of contrast, when one reads the works of Dickens (both his novels and articles), one is immediately impressed with the wealth and vividness of his detailed descriptions of nineteenth-century English (especially urban) life. While the amount of detail on the one hand paints a picture that horrifies, at the same time it forces the reader to realize that the world depicted is 'other'; there is, in other words, no room for the transcending of the particular context. For a sampling of Dickens's social commentary, see N. Phillip and V. Neuberg (eds.), *Charles Dickens: A December Vision and Other Thoughtful Writings* (New York: Continuum, 1987).

which always seem to echo the same themes.[1]

Such a methodological distinction could help clarify the nature of the text's ability to be relevant in human reality across the centuries, within varied cultural contexts, in different circumstances. Both textual and modern horizons, while both of a particular time and place, can thus merge together within human history. The 'classic' becomes truly ever-contemporary.

If those scholars who advocate a history-like approach do so in order that biblical narratives be allowed to exercise their theological aim, they sometimes also hold this view because they do not consider these documents to be proper historiography in the modern sense.[2] It is not within the scope of this work to enter into that difficult debate. To begin with, the prophetic texts do not fall within the genre of history writing. Nevertheless, one point is relevant, and can help reinforce the argument and also introduce the next major section.

It is my conviction that the prophetic material, as will become clear in the reading of Amos in the next chapter, is claiming to be not only morally correct; it is also claiming to be historically true, because of its repeated assertion of divine inspiration and revelation. The represented world is depicted as the actual state of affairs according to an authority granted from on high, and so the reader is allowed no escape from ethical decision. Whether and how this world in fact accords with archaeological findings is a matter to be decided at the historian's discretion, but *the textual claim* stands. To confuse form and factuality is a category mistake; on the one hand, because it is a false dichotomy, on the other, since such a notion ignores the ideological assumptions made by the text and communicated through its literary strategies.[3]

---

1. Cf. Alter's chapter entitled 'Character and the Connection with Reality', in *The Pleasures of Reading in an Ideological Age* (New York: Simon & Schuster, 1989), pp. 49-76 (especially pp. 75-76).

2. For the many new questions being asked concerning the study of the history of ancient Israel, see the collection of essays edited by P.R. Davies and D.M. Gunn, 'A History of Ancient Israel and Judah: A Discussion of Miller–Hayes (1986)', *JSOT* 39 (1987), pp. 3-63.

3. Sternberg, *Poetics of Biblical Narrative*, especially pp. 23-35, 41-57, 76-83. See his criticism's of Alter's term 'historicized prose fiction', pp. 24-30 (Alter, *Art of Biblical Narrative*, pp. 24, 32-35, 41), and his comments on Frei's history-like/historiography distinction, pp. 81-82. Also note Walhout, 'Texts and Actions',

In summary, the poetic approach followed in this study does not
hold to a self-contained prophetic text as the object of study. Not only
has it been suggested that this would be a naive presupposition because
of the interpretive codes embedded in the text, but also since the
concepts of reference and history-likeness demand some sort of
connection with the actual world, both ancient and modern.

The prophetic text, as a sacred 'classic', engages the reader and the
community of faith through the realistic representation of life and on
the basis of its claim to be true and historically informed. Aesthetics
and ideology are now wedded. If it can be said that a response is
summoned by the text, what sort is appropriate? To this question the
last section directs its attention.

c. *The Responsible Reader*

To speak of a 'responsible reader' is at once to imply that reading is
not a purely passive activity. The last chapter developed the idea of a
situated theology in touch with its communal and cultural context and
oriented by the biblical tradition. The discussion was entertained
within an anthropological, sociological and ethical framework. This
chapter has concentrated on the function of the Scripture from the
literary perspective. This last section will continue that approach.
Though some of what is said, especially at the close of this chapter,
might reflect in some measure the observations of that earlier
discussion, the insights from the literary disciplines can elucidate some
of the choices that must be made in the reading of a text. The concerns
are twofold: first, how one should respond to the ideology of the text
and, second, what might be the essence of a call for a responsible
reading.

No one has worked as extensively as Sternberg in the explication of
the ideology of the biblical text.[1] The Bible, he claims, not only holds
to monotheism and a certain ethic, but makes an absolute epistemolog-

pp. 69-77, and the incisive comments of G.O. West regarding the category con-
fusions in the work of some biblical historians and his use of 'secular' sources to
illuminate the discussion, in 'The Succession Narrative as History: A Critical
Discussion of the Debate in the Light of Recent Work in the Philosophy of History'
(unpublished MA thesis, University of Sheffield, 1986).

1. Sternberg, *Poetics of Biblical Narrative*. Although the interworking of aesthetics, ideology and the reading process are the concern of the entire volume, see ch.
3 for an introduction.

ical and capability claim for the deity: God is omniscient and omnipotent. This textual ideology is not communicated neutrally through the represented world, its characters, the plot unfolded within that reality, or the actuations of the divine; rather, rhetorical art transcribes an ideological imperative made upon the reader.

The over-arching ideology of a text should not be confused with too simplistic a notion of point of view.[1] Within any given piece several points of view can be operative and interacting. Multiple perspectives are transmitted through the text—such as God's, the author's, the narrator's, and the characters'.

Among these can exist all sorts of relationships,[2] but more importantly the literary technique and strategies force the reader to be a participant in the quest for knowledge and righteousness enacted within the textual drama. The many possible liaisons and the involvement the reader might have with any of the textual perspectives in the dynamics of reading are determined and mediated by the poetics.[3] Often the biblical presentation is not transparent nor amenable to facile reception by design. So reading, although compelling, can become complicated. Yet the text results not only in being a challenge to reader *skill*, but also, because of its ideological demand, a challenge to the reader's *world-view*. The text, therefore, aims at an appeal, and the narrator is committed to a mission:

> In the widest sense, 'rhetoric' embraces the whole discourse in its communicative aspect, as a set of means chosen and organized with an eye to an audience rather than to self-expression of pure making. . . But the term 'rhetoric' also has a stricter and more traditional sense, which

1. For a historical survey of the development of point of view in literature see J.W. Lotman, 'Point of View in a Text', *NLH* 6 (1975), pp. 339-52. Within biblical studies see especially Berlin, *Poetics and Interpretation*, ch. 3; Sternberg, *Poetics of Biblical Narrative*, chs. 4, 5. Alter places point of view in biblical narrative within the history of its development in literature in *Pleasures of Reading*, ch. 6.

2. Sternberg's discussion reveals more complexity in the biblical material than does Berlin's. See, for example, his discussion of the relationship between the narrator's point of view and his restraints vis-à-vis the overriding ideology (*Poetics of Biblical Narrative*, especially pp. 153-59 and ch. 13).

3. Besides Sternberg's discussion throughout his book, note also Fisch's observations on the relationship between a prophetic text (Hosea) and the reader in *Poetry with a Purpose*, pp. 48-53, 118-53, 118-20. Cf. H.R. Jauss, 'Levels of Identification of Hero and Audience', *NLH* 5 (1974), pp. 283-317.

narrows its range from communication as such to communication with persuasive intent. As a persuader, the rhetorician seeks not just to affect but to affect with establishing consensus in the face of possible demur and opposition. Success has only one meaning to him: bringing the audience's viewpoint into alignment with his own.[1]

What implications does this proposal have for a reading process committed to exploring the use of the Bible in the moral life of the Christian church? In actuality, two aspects of the issue of ideology have surfaced thus far, which could benefit from further clarification. First, when one speaks of the 'ideology of the text' to what does one refer and how can one 'get at it'? Secondly, is to claim the text to be ideologically demanding to suggest that what is communicated must be accepted blindly and without question?

To begin with, within literary criticism many would hold that inter-action with the text should not end at the initial steps of 'reading' (the comprehension of the textual material according to its cultural and linguistic codes) and 'interpretation' (the grasping of a text's themes and values). Robert Scholes, for example, as a professor of English literature, is committed to having his students not merely acquiesce before an author's text: 'An important part of the teacher's function in a literature classroom is to show students how to move from reading the text to interpreting and criticizing the codes that sustain the text's implications'.[2] 'Criticism', he says:

> is a way of discovering how to choose, how to take some measure of responsibility for ourselves and for our world. Criticism is our last best chance to loosen the bonds of textual powers in which we find ourselves enmeshed.[3]

Scholes's test case is Ernest Hemingway's *In Our Time*. Only after the aforementioned first stages does he move to 'criticism', because the text as text must be well understood before that final step. What is more, this critical examination of the ideology of that collection of short pieces is based on a careful reconstruction of Hemingway's life

---

1. Sternberg, *Poetics of Biblical Narrative*, p. 482.
2. Scholes, *Textual Power*, p. 61. These three aspects (reading, interpretation, criticism) are explained in ch. 2 of *Textual Power* and then expanded and illustrated in the rest of the book. Scholes also follows this same three-part pattern in *Protocols of Reading* in an appreciative yet critical interaction with deconstruction.
3. *Textual Power*, p. 73.

and writings. Scholes also notes that for criticism to be a socially constructive exercise it must be collective judgment.[1]

Before moving on, it is important to see what he is proposing. Note that Scholes's study would hold that criticism must come last, only after diligently trying to understand what the text is saying. The text is communicating an ideology. To get to the next step of scrutinizing and confronting textual assumptions and assertions requires a lot of background contextual information of a wide variety. Finally, because this move is a value decision, it must arise within and on behalf of a group engaged by the text.

The questioning of a vision and the unmasking of perceived hidden prejudices and agendas have been most often associated, of course, with Marxist literary critics. Frederic Jameson, for instance, calls not only for a materialist reading to expose the 'political unconscious' of the text, but also for a critical reading committed to collective social change within history.[2] His is not a simplistic Marxist theory of homologues and reflection, but instead an attempt to appreciate the very complex context of the literary act's production and emergence. His work analyzes individual works, as well as genres, which he too feels must be placed within the evolution of social conflict and recognized as 'original and meaningful protopolitical acts'.[3] Such an approach necessarily demands an informed reconstruction of a whole range of socioeconomic, historical, and literary influences and variables.[4] Jameson, too, therefore, is calling for getting 'behind' the text through

---

1. *Textual Power*, ch. 4; *Protocols of Reading*, ch. 3.

2. F. Jameson, *The Political Unconscious: Narrative as a Socially Symbolic Act* (London: Methuen, 1981), chs. 1, 6. Cf. E.W. Said, *The World, the Text, and the Critic* (Cambridge, MA: Harvard University Press, 1983). Note, however, Said's criticism of Jameson in 'Opponents, Audiences, Constituencies, and Community', *CritInq* 9 (1982), pp. 12-16, and Scholes's critique of Jameson in *Textual Power*, pp. 80-85. For another call by a Marxist literary critic for socially and politically committed literary criticism, see Terry Eagleton, *The Function of Criticism: From 'The Spectator' to Post Structuralism* (London: Verso Editions and NLB, 1984).

3. Jameson, *The Political Unconscious*, p. 149. Cf. Jauss, *Toward an Aesthetic of Reception*, pp. 22-28, 32-39.

4. In speaking of the interpretive process, Jameson mentions three 'concentric frameworks' of analysis (i.e. political history, society and the history of the modes of production), which each requires its own reconstruction (the text as a symbolic act, as an ideologeme, within an ideology of form, respectively). See *The Political Unconscious*, pp. 74-102.

a detailed reconstruction. In his case, the identification with the class struggle against capitalism prompts his criticism of textual ideology.

Within biblical scholarship, there are also those who point to the reader's role in producing meaning and cross-examining the ideology of the text. David Gunn criticizes Sternberg for overlooking this phenomenon. Although classifying his poetics as 'brilliant', Gunn observes that, 'there is no objective, ideologically sterile reader to appropriate an ideological prescription embedded in the text';[1] moreover, recent reader-oriented theories would relativize the reading process.[2]

A recent ambitious project to penetrate the text and reconstruct the settings for the production of biblical literature is Norman Gottwald's *The Hebrew Bible: A Socio-Literary Introduction*.[3] His is a sustained effort to establish how and where concepts were born, promulgated, and enscripturated according to several 'axes' (domain, sectorial, geographical).[4] For Gottwald,

> It is abundantly clear that the Hebrew Bible, far from presenting a body of fixed religious ideas or doctrines, gives us theological reflections embedded in historically changing social situations and articulated in concrete literary genres and genre complexes. The theology of the Hebrew Bible is thus both 'theology of social struggle' and 'theology of literary imagination'.[5]

According to this biblical scholar, the task of a modern reader of these texts is to discover their sociohistorical 'embeddedness' and recognize that they can but serve as testimonies of past reflection and provide possible orienting symbols for social change today.[6] His

---

1. D.M. Gunn, 'New Directions in the Study of Biblical Hebrew Narrative', *JSOT* 39 (1987), p. 68.

2. For helpful surveys see S.R. Suleiman, 'Introduction: Varieties of Audience-Oriented Criticism', in *The Reader in the Text: Essays on Audience and Interpretation* (ed. S.R. Suleiman and I. Crossman; Princeton, NJ: Princeton University Press, 1980), pp. 3-45; Thiselton, 'Reader Response Hermeneutics', pp. 90-106.

3. N.K. Gottwald, *The Hebrew Bible: A Socio-Literary Introduction* (Philadelphia: Fortress Press, 1985).

4. *Hebrew Bible*, pp. 596-607.

5. *Hebrew Bible*, p. 607.

6. *Hebrew Bible*, pp. 607-609. See also his 'The Theological Task after The Tribes of Yahweh', in *The Bible and Liberation: Political and Social Hermeneutics* (ed. N.K. Gottwald; Maryknoll: Orbis Books, 1983), pp. 190-200.

commitment to ideological discovery and critique, as those of the literary critics, would depend on an educated and complex reconstruction. His concerns also are not private, but are instead motivated by the desire for social justice. The text is questioned precisely because of this passion.

How well does Gottwald succeed in his undertaking? His discussion of the monarchic prophets, for example, is very vague and admits to difficulties that hinder achieving a solid reconstruction[1]—a conclusion I have also drawn earlier. On the other hand, Jobling criticizes his understanding of literature as simplistic and inadequate. Jobling, however, is sympathetic to Gottwald's effort and recommends the input that Jameson could provide for a better comprehension of textual production. But, even though those theoretical insights would enhance Gottwald's appreciation of literature, Jameson's stricter reconstruction demand would only complicate that biblical scholar's dilemma.[2]

Can these studies which base their ideological focus on reconstructions be coordinated with my suggested received text approach? If so, how? Walhout's sevenfold distinction about levels of analysis can provide the theoretical clarification which will help explain the option to be taken in the reading of the prophetic text. His levels are:

1. The examination of the formal elements of a text (e.g. vocabulary, imagery, figures of speech, style, plot).
2. The study of the imagined world projected by the text.
3. The inquiry into the apparent significance that the author gives to that projected world (i.e. textual point of view).
4. An analysis of the mimetic function of the text (i.e. its relationship to the actual world).
5. An evaluation of the projected world and the textual point of

---

1. Gottwald, *Hebrew Bible*, pp. 304-308 (esp. p. 308).
2. D. Jobling, 'Sociological and Literary Approaches to the Bible: How Shall the Twain Meet?', *JSOT* 38 (1987), pp. 85-93. Jobling is correct in saying that Gottwald obviously feels more secure in the postexilic period (Part IV of *Hebrew Bible*). He suggests that the reconstruction project begin there, yet one wonders if even that era can provide the same quantity and quality of data that Jameson seeks in order to propose his own reconstructions of much more recent literature (e.g. regarding Balzac: sociohistorical data, biographical conjectures, and the placing of Balzac within the history of forms which in turn is related to sociohistorical processes—*The Political Unconscious*, ch. 3).

view's encounter with the reader's world.
6.   The discovery of the intent of the text's production according
     to an historical reconstruction.
7.   An assessment of the modern uses of the text.[1]

A study such as Gottwald's turns its critical attention to step six with
an eye to the last issue, which should be the crucial target for any
approach concerned with the role of the Bible in the moral life of the
church. In deciding to utilize a poetic approach reading the received
text, however, this book pursues a different tack in its own concern to
explore the same pastoral problem. Poetics will highlight the first five
levels, but also with an interest in the last.

This choice to follow a poetic reading is, to begin with, a *procedural* one. It is procedural in the sense that Walhout's observations
point out that a close reading is a necessary step before the reconstruction critique should be made. In this, he parallels Scholes's stages.
Poetics emphasizes how the text has meaning. Therefore, even for one
committed to the reconstruction approach, the text must be given a
close hearing prior to that endeavor. Yet the choice is also based on
the *pragmatic* acknowledgement that a reconstruction effort cannot
provide a solid foundation for church ethics. The amount of data
required for a substantial study of this type is just not available. Such
a stance does not gainsay that effort, but does ask that its limitations
for ethics be recognized.

To return, therefore, to the question posed earlier about the text's
ideology and how to 'get at' it, the answer is that our poetics will not
depend on a reconstruction. Amos will be read and understood
according to its own textual strategies and the light offered by historical data. The ideology will be read off the text, not reconstructed
according to hypothetical factors of production lying behind the text.

It will be remembered that the second issue concerned responding
to the ideology of the text. The fact that it is demanding does not make
it necessarily acceptable. On the one hand, there is this reminder from
narrative ethics: the biblical text is a *privileged* text by virtue of the
confession of so much of the church. The reconstruction approaches
just mentioned underline the need to do their textual work from and
for a community. Our poetics does also. That is, from the narrative

---

1.   Walhout, 'Texts and Actions', pp. 61-69.

perspective the canonical stories and images are authoritative because
they have proven to offer a realistic and 'truthful' account of communal and social life. Any reading of the biblical text must acknowledge
the reality of this moral authority claim and at least grant the text the
opportunity to speak and present its world to the reader.[1] If the
church is truly interested in the 'prophetic voice', then it must first
hear its call. This, then, is an argument not for unquestioning acceptance, but rather for an initial respect.

To say as much is also not to ignore the fact that the canon might
present other sorts of worlds and images. The coordination of the different literature lies beyond the compass of this study.[2] The focus here
is on a particular prophetic voice, Amos, generally acknowledged to
be a socially powerful text. Finally, it must also be stressed that this
approach can in no way dictate beforehand how or to what degree the
biblical text will influence the world of the reader.

As an aside, the prophetic literature to date has not been questioned
to the same degree as have other parts of the Old Testament Scripture,
such as some wisdom material, which is charged by some with
reflecting the ethical mindset of well-to-do circles.[3] Quite the contrary, the value of the prophetic texts for *conscientización* has been
universally acclaimed. Birch and Rasmussen also make the observation
that liberation theologians have used a hermeneutics of 'retrieval' in
that they have tried to recover the message for the poor which has
been obscured by traditional interpretation, in contradistinction to
some feminist studies, whose 'suspicion' can extend to the text itself.[4]

---

1. Once more this book is holding forth a functional claim, not an ontological one.
2. Note these words by Hauerwas:

> The canon marks off as Scripture those texts that are necessary for the life of the church
> without trying to resolve their obvious diversity and/or even disagreement. . . these
> texts have been accepted as Scripture because they and they alone satisfy. . . our
> craving for a perfect story which we feel to be true ('Moral Authority', p. 364).

See also Kelsey, *Uses of Scripture*, pp. 100-108, 117-19, 196-97; Birch and
Rasmussen, *Bible & Ethics*, pp. 171-81. Cf. Brueggemann, *The Creative Word*.

3. E.g. J.D. Pleins, 'Poverty in the Social World of the Wise', *JSOT* 37 (1987),
pp. 61-78.

4. Birch and Rasmussen, *Bible & Ethics*, pp. 147-48. For feminist perspectives
see, for example, R.R. Reuther, 'Feminism and Patriarchal Religion: Principles of
Ideological Critique of the Bible', *JSOT* 22 (1982), pp. 54-66; D.N. Fewell,
'Feminist Reading of the Hebrew Bible: Affirmation, Resistance and

While this affirmation regarding liberation textual studies is true in some cases, there are, of course, exceptions to this generalization.[1] Textual methods, however, among liberation theologians vary. Appendix 2 presents a survey of the approaches that have been used by some liberationists in Latin America. The point is that the text continues to be a powerful medium.

A poetic approach, therefore, does not necessarily signal a retreat into textuality or indicate an escape into aesthetics. A serious consideration of the prophetic text cannot permit reading for enjoyment's sake; its ideological imperative demands an involved dialectic between its world and modern reality. As literary critic Edward Said explains, a text will not allow too simplistic a view of its challenge to the reader:

> The point is that texts have ways of existing that even in their most rarefied form are always enmeshed in circumstance, time, place, and society—in short, they are in the world, and hence worldly. Whether a text is preserved or put aside for a period, whether it is on a library shelf or not, whether it is considered dangerous or not: these matters have to do with a text's being in the world, which is a more complicated matter than the private process of reading.[2]

Some might fear that text-focused theories would grant too much relativity. Textual devices, however, will not allow an infinite number of arbitrary readings from every imaginable 'interpretive community'; language constrains interpretive options.[3] A functional focus on literature does not have to lead to interpretive license. To underscore the moral authority of the Bible for the Christian community is to stress its claim on the readers; to situate that text within that particu-

Transformation', *JSOT* 39 (1987), pp. 77-78.

1. In *Liberating Exegesis* one of the main points that Christopher Rowland and Mark Corner make is that Liberation Theology has often questioned the forces that have been operative in the production of biblical texts. Their examples are drawn primarily from New Testament studies.

2. Said, *The World, the Text, and the Critic*, p. 35.

3. *The World, the Text, and the Critic*, pp. 39-50, 144-57 (Said will also argue for the importance of ascertaining the genesis of a text to grasp better its constraints). Cf. Scholes, *Textual Power*, especially ch. 9, whose comments on 'reading' and 'interpretation' in *Textual Power* and *Protocols of Reading* are obviously relevant here, as is his discussion on coding and reference; Alter, *Pleasures of Reading*, ch. 7.

lar, as well as the larger sociocultural, context is to emphasize its potential resonance within modern realities. Reading, in other words, must be responsible.

Said faults literary critics in the United States who have been aligned, consciously or by default, with the status quo of a capitalistic regime.[1] He hits especially at those of the Left:

> we find that a new criticism adopting a position of opposition to what is considered to be established or conservative academic scholarship consciously takes on the function of the left wing in politics and argues *as if* for the radicalization of thought, practice, and perhaps even of society by means not so much of what it does and produces, but by means of what it says about itself and its opponents.[2]

Criticism often is but words and an attitude cultivated and perpetuated by professional consensus within institutional ghettoes. Yet the non-involved can slip into pontificating for a people and a context that they do not truly know: 'a rhetoric, a pose, a posture (let us at last be candid) claiming not so much to represent as *to be* the afflictions entailed by true adversarial politics'.[3] A responsible reading, therefore, entails more than taking up the rhetorical banner of a certain movement or party, of whatever stripe, for whatever causes. The temptation for the reader (and the writer), especially from within the comfortable confines of institutions, is either to parrot official voices or to bask in the popularity of radical chic.

From Latin America, Octavio Paz calls fellow intellectuals to account for not recognizing cultural factors that tend to make choices appear either black or white and every argument a crusade:

> Our intellectuals have successively embraced liberalism, positivism, and now Marxism-Leninism; nonetheless, in almost all of them, whatever their philosophy, it is not difficult to discern—buried deep but still alive— the moral and psychological attitudes of the old champions of Neo-Scholasticism. Thus they display a paradoxical modernity: the ideas are today's; the attitudes yesterday's. Their grandfathers swore by Saint

1. Said, 'Opponents, Audiences, Constituencies, and Community', and *The World, the Text, and the Critic*, ch. 8. Cf. Eagleton, *The Function of Criticism*.

2. Said, *The World, the Text, and the Critic*, p. 159 (author's emphasis).

3. *The World, the Text, and the Critic*, p. 160 (author's emphasis). Cf. Scholes's comments on the attraction of deconstruction for American critics and his negative evaluation of that school in its dialogue with feminist demands in *Protocols of Reading* (pp. 65-66 and ch. 3, respectively).

Thomas and they swear by Marx, yet both have seen in reason a weapon
in the service of a Truth with a capital T. . . Thus there has been perpetuated in our lands an intellectual tradition that has little respect for the
opinion of others, that prefers ideas to reality and intellectual systems to
the critique of systems.[1]

The contextual crisis, he says, is too complex to allow for simplistic
analysis and exclusivistic ideological reasoning.[2] Therein lies the
danger of well-intentioned intellectuals: before the coming of revolutionary change exists the temptation of constant, yet idealistic, critical acerbity; after its realization, domestication in service of an ideal
which does not really exist.[3] Paz eschews both the North American
structures and what he calls perverted socialistic models in Latin
America, and pushes for the maturing of democracy grounded and
nurtured within the cultural traditions and unique historical realities
of the continent.[4]

1. Paz, *One Earth, Four or Five Worlds*, p. 164.
2. *One Earth, Four or Five Worlds*, pp. 189-201.
3. See Paz's discussions entitled *La seducción totalitaria* and *Engañando*, which
form part of larger essays, in *El ogro filantrópico*, pp. 257-61 and 285-88,
respectively. Several Latin American intellectuals like Paz were disillusioned by the
events of the 'Prague Spring' in 1968—cf. Carlos Fuentes, 'The Other K', in *Myself
with Others*, pp. 160-79. R. González Echevarría comments on a work by the
Cuban writer G.C. Infante, who at first was 'an important cultural promoter' of the
Castro regime but later was disconcerted by its excesses and had to write in exile
(*The Voice of the Masters*, pp. 137-68). Contrast this perspective with that of
Gabriel García Márquez: his option for socialist politics and his friendship with Fidel
Castro, *El olor de la guayaba. Conversaciones con Pino Apuleyo Mendoza*
(Barcelona: Editorial Bruguera, 1982), pp. 139-51.
4. Paz, *One Earth, Four or Five Worlds*, pp. 116-213. For his political
views also see 'Polvos de aquellos lodos', 'Los centuriones de Santiago', and 'La
libertad contra la fe', in *El ogro filantrópico*, pp. 241-61, 271-76, 282-97,
respectively; 'Iniquitous Symmetries', in *Convergences: Essays on Art and Literature*
(trans. H. Lane; San Diego: Harcourt Brace Jovanovich, 1987), pp. 100-18.
Paz has been heavily criticized for his stance which is very critical of both sides
of the political spectrum, even though he would call himself a socialist. Commenting
on how his negative verdict on the Stalinist regime of the USSR was received, he
says:

La reacción de los intelectuales 'progresistas' fue el silencio. Nadie comentó mi estudio
pero se recrudeció la campaña de insinuaciones y alusiones torcidas comenzado unos
años antes por Neruda y sus amigos mexicanos. Una campaña que todavía hoy se
prosigue. Los adjetivos cambian, no el vituperio: he sido sucesivamente cosmopolita,

Whatever one might think of Paz's political option, his words of warning also could well serve those doing theology in Latin America.[1] The previous chapter pointed out the need for a situated theology from the 'native point of view', sustained within the community of faith, and orientated by values fostered by Christian tradition. This chapter highlights the authority of the biblical text in generating and shaping those values through its projected world. The call for a responsible reading echoes these convictions by championing active interaction with the text. Paz's point helps push the argument yet one step further: intellectual and moral integrity should not foreclose frank dialogue with the complex texture of the context; what is more, from the perspective of a narrative ethic, the text must be allowed to continue to speak in power at all times and in any political context, whatever one's ideological commitment. The textual world, to use biblical imagery, is not only a light unto the path of social change, but also a two-edged sword able to pierce as far as the division of both the left and the right.

3. *Conclusion*

This chapter has attempted to offer the theoretical basis for the textual reading of Amos. The discussion was divided into two major parts.

---

formalista, trotskista, agente de la CIA, 'intelectual liberal' y hasta ¡'estructuralista al servicio de la burguesía'! (*El ogro filantrópico*, p. 242).

1. E.g. R. Gibbons, 'Political Poetry and the Example of Ernesto Cardenal', *CritInq* 13 (1987), pp. 648-71. Gibbons would claim that Cardenal's partisan poetry after the fall of Somoza in Nicaragua lost its edge and idealized the Sandinista regime. Marc Zimmerman in his introduction to a collection of Cardenal's poetry recognizes how such a negative evaluation could arise, yet suggests that Cardenal was affected by the loss of available time to write poetry because of the demands of functioning as a minister in the Sandinista government and by the need to defend its accomplishments in the face of foreign aggression (Cardenal, *Flights of Victory/Vuelos de Victoria*, pp. xxviii-xxxi; cf. J. Beverley and M. Zimmerman, *Literature and Politics in the Central American Revolutions* [New Interpretations of Latin America Series; Austin, TX: University of Texas Press, 1990], which in chs. 1–4 places Cardenal's poetry within the ideological role of literature of the area and traces his influence through to the electoral defeat of the Sandinistas in February, 1990). Cf. the comments of Chapter 3 of this book regarding the possible loss of balance in some liberationist use of Marxism and the discussion in Chapter 6 about the danger of the identification of religion and the state.

The first presented a functional understanding of the nature of the moral authority of the Scripture. This authority was shown to reside in the ability to operate as an identity document for the Christian church through its images and alternative world. The biblical text demonstrates its power by this formative quality, by its continual influence on the self-understanding and social expression of the community of faith in the world.

The second section explained the option for poetics. Once a method is chosen for ethics, however, there are some hard issues that must be honestly faced. For that reason, this part of the chapter touched on the text's relationship to the actual world and on how to approach the ideology expressed in its literary art.

Reading a text with a view toward exercising its moral authority within the world must also be a responsible act. Especially within explosive contexts, the reader must accept that the text should not simply entertain; he or she must hear the text as it reverberates into social life. The temptation for readers committed to social change in any given context is to use the power of the text on others and for a political option. Its clarion voice, however, must not be manipulated or its power abused.

'Reading the Bible is not what is difficult', says L. Alonso Schökel, 'but rather knowing how to read'.[1] He is right. This chapter has suggested a way of reading, a way of allowing the moral imagination to be shaped and nurtured by the biblical text. The Scripture can do this because it is 'real' and 'true'. As this Spanish scholar goes on to explain:

> The most important works transcend the anecdote, full literary characters incarnate something of the human. And the Bible is written in the image and likeness of man: molded with the clay of human experience, with a spirit of life insufflated in it.[2]

But Alonso Schökel has not gone far enough. He calls for the reader to listen to, and to spend time alone with the text. But reading must be also done within and for a community in context—in our case, within the Christian community in Latin America. Reading must be careful,

---

1. L. Alonso Schökel, '¿Es difícil leer la Biblia?' (appeared originally in *Razón y Fe* 210 [1984], pp. 200-10) in *Hermenéutica Bíblica*, I, pp. 203-15.
2. '¿Es difícil leer la Biblia?', p. 206.

but hearing must be committed to bringing the biblical text into daily life.

The previous chapter appealed to a variety of disciplines to explore the nature of moral life in context. This chapter has utilized primarily literary studies to provide the final piece to the theoretical foundation for the reading of the prophetic text. It is to Amos that we must now turn.

Chapter 5

THE WORLD WITHIN THE TEXT:
POETICS AND THE SOCIAL IMAGINATION IN AMOS

On the basis of certain literary studies and narrative ethics, the last chapter suggested that as a 'classic' the biblical text through its language and style offers its readers a world, a world which can often be an alternative and powerful picture of reality that can challenge the present. Narrative ethics also proposes that this text be understood as an 'identity document', which depicts the person, activity, and demands of God as well as the life of the community that claims to be his people. The purpose of this chapter is to present a poetic reading of the received text of Amos, chs. 3–6, in order to explore its world and probe its characters.

In recent years several studies have focused on the literary structures evident within the canonical text of that prophetic book. By far the most detailed and extensive has been the work of a team at Hamburg under the direction of Klaus Koch.[1] They propose *eine Methode einer strukturalen Formgeschichte* which, while attentive to diachronics, attempts to investigate clues to the shape of the final composition suggested by various formulae and phrases.[2]

For his part, Coulot eschews a traditional exegesis that supposes the prophetic books to be but mere assemblage of *petites unités littéraires*. To demonstrate intertexual connections he suggests parallel structures

1. K. Koch, *Amos: Untersucht mit den Methode einer strukturalen Formgeschichte* (AOAT, 30; Neukirchen–Vluyn: Neukirchener Verlag, 1976). For summaries and interaction, see R.F. Melungin, 'The Formation of Amos: An Analysis of Exegetical Method', *SBLSP* 1978 (Missoula, MT: Scholars Press, 1978), pp. 369-91; A. van der Wal, 'The Structure of Amos', *JSOT* 26 (1983), pp. 107-108; and Auld, *Amos*, pp. 55-58.

2. For the diachronics (i.e. the work of the 'compositor[s]'), see Koch, *Amos*, II, pp. 105-25; for the detailed textual observations, pp. 126-59.

for chs. 3 and 4 and for 5.18-27 and ch. 6, as well as a chiastic framework for 5.1-17.[1] One work that tries to apply chiasm, or to use their
term, 'patterned recursion', to the whole of the book is the effort by
DeWaard and Smalley.[2] The chiastic framework of 5.1-17 is taken as
the center, with its peak at 5.8d, and then is expanded to include the
entire prophetic text.[3]

Spreafico has taken 4.6-13, which exhibits a solid cohesiveness
through its refrain and conclusion, as the starting point for the study
of the remaining two units of Amos chs. 3–6—that is, 3.1–4.5 and
5.1–6.14, respectively.[4] The former is marked by imperatives, the
latter especially by participles. Besides demonstrating the interlocking
structures within these two larger sections, he seeks to show how the
whole of those four chapters are tied together. In a short article van
der Wal has utilized the technique of *inclusio* to try to unlock the
organization of the first six chapters of this prophetic book.[5]

More recently, Andersen and Freedman's detailed study attempts to
offer an analysis at several levels. On the one hand, Amos is divided
into a number of major blocks; this more 'literary' reading would
include the Book of Doom (1.1–4.13), the Book of Woes (5.1–6.14),

1. C. Coulot, 'Prepositions pour une structuration du livre d'Amos au nivel
rédactionnel', *RSR* 51 (1977), pp. 169-86. His parallels perhaps demonstrate more
similarity in theme than in structure: to substantiate his juxtaposition of chs. 3 and 4
he omits 3.9-11, 13, 15 and 4.3-5; the parallels between 5.18-27 and 6.1-14 appear
quite lopsided and forced. His chiasm in ch. 5 leaves out 5.8, 13.

2. J. De Waard and W.A. Smalley, *A Translator's Handbook on Amos: Helps
for Translators* (New York: United Biblical Societies, 1979), especially pp. 189-
214.

3. The work on the chiasm in 5.1-17 appeared earlier in J. De Waard, 'The
Chiastic Structure of Amos V 1-17', *VT* 27 (1977), pp. 170-77, and was elaborated
on by N.J. Tromp, 'Amos V 1-17: Towards a Stylistic and Rhetorical Analysis',
OTS 23 (1984), pp. 56-84. De Waard and Smalley admit that the chiasm gets looser
as it extends beyond ch. 5 and that some verses (e.g. 3.1-2; 4.13; 5.1-3) do not fit
well into their scheme (*Amos*, pp. 192-94).

4. A. Spreafico, 'Amos: Struttura Formale E Spunti Per Una Interpretazione',
RivBiblt 29 (1981), pp. 147-76, especially pp. 151-65 on chs. 3–6.

5. Van der Wal, 'The Structure of Amos' (this effort, too, has its weaknesses—
e.g., his second part's delimitation [3.9–4.3] depends on a textual emendation in
4.3). Note that this analysis is carried further by a concordance study in A. van der
Wal and E. Talstra, *Amos: Concordance and Lexical Surveys* (Amsterdam: Free
University Press, 1984), pp. 105-36.

and the Book of Visions (7.1–9.6). The authors throughout their commentary make close observations concerning the structure of pericopes and the interlocking devices between passages and major sections. At another level, they suggest a chronological reconstruction, based in part on a study of the visions which would mirror the development of the prophet's career. This development, they believe, is discernible in the present arrangement of the book, with 5.14-15 being both the physical center and theological crux of the book.[1]

Besides these various structural studies, several other works have probed the text's literary devices. Mention can be made of Gese's observation of its propensity to exhibit fivefold sequences,[2] and Limburg's of seven,[3] as well as Moisés Chávez's full-length overview of its style and rhetoric.[4]

All of the works and approaches cited certainly contribute to the understanding of Amos. Each, however, emphasizes almost exclusively the skeleton, as it were, although this is accompanied sometimes by possible theological considerations suggested by the proposed patterns. What can often result is form without flow, framework without flesh. A poetic reading, on the other hand, attempts not only to grasp the text's shape, but also to comprehend the reality painted by the vocabulary, style, and structure.

Most works on poetics have focused on biblical narrative. Indeed, Sternberg dismisses prophetic rhetoric as 'naive' because of its often strict refusal to allow for other points of view.[5] Fisch and Alter, however, have helped to dispel that sort of misconception and faulty evaluation.[6] The prophetic text is immensely compelling because of its

1. For discussions regarding their various structural suggestions, see Andersen and Freedman, *Amos*, pp. 5-18, 73-88, 361-69. It should be mentioned that others have tried to correlate the career of the prophet with the structure of the book—e.g., R. Gordis, 'The Composition and Structure of Amos', *HTR* 33 (1940), pp. 239-51; J.D.W. Watts, 'The Origin of the Book of Amos', *ExpTim* 66 (1955), pp. 109-12, and *Vision and Prophecy in Amos* (Leiden: Brill, 1958), ch. 2.

2. H. Gese, 'Komposition bei Amos', *VT Sup* 32 (1980), pp. 74-95.

3. J. Limburg, 'Sevenfold Structures in the Book of Amos', *JBL* 106 (1987), pp. 217-22. Cf. S.M. Rosenbaum, *Amos of Israel: A New Interpretation* (Macon, GA: Mercer University Press, 1990), pp. 77-79.

4. M. Chávez, *Modelo de oratoria. Obra basada en el análisis estilístico del texto hebreo del libro de Amós* (Miami: Editorial Caribe, 1979).

5. Sternberg, *Poetics of Biblical Narrative*, p. 504.

6. Fisch, *Poetry with a Purpose*, especially chs. 4 and 8; Alter, *Art of Biblical*

literariness, in spite of what can be perceived as an univocal perspective. In truth, this very fact puts a heavy demand on the reader, who must accept or reject what is presented as the direct voice of God.

Alter mentions three overriding strategies manifest in prophetic texts: direct accusation, satire, and the 'monitory evocation of impending disaster'.[1] Each contributes to what he calls a 'rhetoric of entrapment', whereby—through frontal denunciation, the ironic dismantling of the pretensions of a world-view, and the announcement of imminent judgment—those addressed cannot escape the rightness of the divine verdict and the depth of their own guilt.

Amos is no exception. The task incumbent upon our reading will be to discern what (or whom) is being attacked in the world of the text and why. The challenge is to discover how this world is communicated through the book's poetics.[2] The reading singles out chs. 3–6. A

Poetry, especially ch. 6.

1. Alter, *Art of Biblical Poetry*, pp. 141-62. Also see L. Ryken for satire in Amos in *Words of Delight: A Literary Introduction to the Bible* (Grand Rapids: Baker Book House, 1987), pp. 329-37.

2. The following sources have proved especially helpful in the poetical reading of these chapters. They are listed here, because the rest of the footnotes will cite only Amos studies.

(a) Dynamics of parallelism: Alter, *Art of Biblical Poetry*, chs. 1-3, 6; W.G.E. Watson, *Classical Hebrew Poetry: A Guide to its Techniques* (JSOTSup, 26; Sheffield: JSOT Press, 1984), ch. 6; Fisch, *Poetry with a Purpose*, pp. 136-38; L. Alonso Schökel, *Hermenéutica de la Palabra. II. Interpretación literaria de textos bíblicos* (Madrid: Ediciones Cristiandad, 1987), pp. 69-85.

(b) Point of view: Berlin, *Poetics and Interpretation*, ch. 3; M. Sternberg, 'Point of View and the Indirections of Direct Speech', *Language and Style* 15.2 (1982), pp. 67-117, and *Poetics of Biblical Narrative*, *passim*.

(c) Characters and characterization: Berlin, *Poetics and Interpretation*, ch. 2; Alter, *Art of Biblical Narrative*, chs. 6–8; *idem, Pleasures of Reading*, ch. 2.

(d) Structure: Alter, *Pleasures of Reading*, ch. 5; Watson, *Classical Hebrew Poetry*, chs. 7, 8; Y.T. Radday, 'Chiasms in Hebrew Biblical Narrative', in *Chiasmus in Antiquity: Structures, Analyses, Exegesis* (ed. J. Welch; Hildesheim: Gerstenberg Verlag, 1981), pp. 50-115; H. Van Dyke Parunak, 'Oral Typesetting: Some Uses of Biblical Structure', *Bib* 62 (1981), pp. 153-68; *idem*, 'Some Axioms for Literary Architecture', *Semitics* 8 (1982), pp. 1-16; *idem*, 'Transitorial Techniques in the Bible', *JBL* 102 (1983), pp. 525-48.

quick and cursory glance at the book might give the impression that it breaks down naturally into three major sections: the oracles against the nations, chs. 1 and 2; the words of Amos, chs. 3–6; and the vision cycle of chs. 7 through 9. The part that is of interest here (3.1–6.14) can appear to be unified by the thrice-repeated formula 'Hear this word' (3.1; 4.1; 5.1) and the woes of chs. 5 and 6. Matters, of course, are not so simple, as attested by the reappearance of 'Hear this word' later in the text (8.4) and by the multitude of theories regarding the composition of Amos. The reading will attempt to show, however,

(e)   Sound: Watson, *Classical Hebrew Poetry*, ch. 9; Alonso Schökel, *Hermenéutica de la Palabra*, II, pp. 38-52; P.P. Saydon, 'Assonance in Hebrew as a Means of Expressing Emphasis', *Bib* 36 (1955), pp. 36-50, 287-304.

(f)   Imagery: Watson, *Classical Hebrew Poetry*, ch. 10; Alonso Schökel, *Hermenéutica de la Palabra*, II, pp. 118-67.

(g)   Poetic devices (e.g. repetition, key words, refrain, irony, rhetorical questions): Alter, *Art of Biblical Narrative*, ch. 5; Sternberg, *Poetics of Biblical Narrative, passim*; Watson, *Classical Hebrew Poetry*, ch. 11; Alonso Schökel, *Hermenéutica de la Palabra*, II, pp. 87-117, 168-228; G.J. Polan, *In the Ways of Justice toward Salvation: A Rhetorical Analysis of Isaiah 56–59* (American University Studies, Series VII: Theology and Religion, 13; New York: Peter Lang, 1986), *passim*; J. Muilenburg, 'A Study in Hebrew Rhetoric: Repetition and Style', *VTSup* 1 (1953), pp. 97-111; *idem*, 'The Linguistics and Rhetorical Usages of the Particle *KY*', *HUCA* 32 (1961), pp. 135-60; J.A. Thompson, 'The Use of Repetition in the Prophecy of Joel', in *On Language, Culture and Religion: In Honor of Eugene A. Nida* (ed. M. Black and W.A. Smalley; The Hague: Mouton, 1974), pp. 101-10; A. Schoors, 'The Particle *KY*', *OTS* 21 (1981), pp. 240-76; W.J. Claasen, 'Speaker-Oriented Functions of *KY*', *JNWS* 11 (1983), pp. 29-46; A. Aejmelaeus, 'Function and Interpretation of *KY*', *JBL* 105 (1986), pp. 193-209; R. Gordis, 'A Rhetorical Use of Interrogative Sentences in Biblical Hebrew', *AJSL* 49 (1933), pp. 212-17; W. Brueggemann, 'Jeremiah's Use of Rhetorical Questions', *JBL* 92 (1973), pp. 358-74.

(h)   General: L. Alonso Schökel, 'Die stilistische Analyse bei den Propheten', *VTSup* 7 (1959), pp. 154-64; J. Stek, 'The Stylistics of Hebrew Poetry', *CalvTJ* 9 (1974), pp. 15-30; S. Talmon, 'The Textual Study of the Bible—A New Outlook', in *Qumran and the History of the Bible* (ed. F.M. Cross and S. Talmon; Cambridge, MA: Harvard University Press, 1975), pp. 321-400.

that the section is in some measure a coherent conceptual unit.[1] The proof, to be sure, is in the reading.

Finally, 3.1–6.14 is not an isolated segment. The connections with the first two chapters have even led some to posit that 3.1-2 or 3.1-8 forms the conclusion to the oracles against the nations,[2] and there is certainly some common vocabulary and formulae. The same can be said of the chapters that follow our section as well. Koch for instance, proposes that the final large part of the book (excluding the closing promises of blessing, 9.7-15) extends from 5.1 to 9.6.[3] Although these links are not the primary concern of this study, allusion will be made when considered opportune. A poetic reading of the entire prophetic text, however, must remain for the future.

1. A Poetic Reading of Amos 3–6

The attempt to unfold the textual world can utilize for orientation some of the theoretical constructs of Chapter 3 of this study. On the one hand, cultural anthropology and the sociology of knowledge demonstrate that contexts are socially constructed. Different institutions, both secular and sacred, play a part in legitimizing a given context. Religion, through traditions, ritual and symbols, can sanctify that created universe so that that 'natural order of things' appears as a divine given and mandate. The structural anthropology of Mary Douglas corroborates the perspective by suggesting that the cult and taboos in Israel would function to help define and sanction a particular

1. Several authors have recently worked on these chapters as a unit (even if considered as the work of a redactor)—e.g. Coote, *Amos*, pp. 73-76; Spreafico, 'Amos: Struttura Formale'; J. Jeremias, 'Amos 3-6. Beobachtungen zur Entstehungsgeschichte eines Prophetenbuches', *ZAW* 100 (1988), pp. 123-38. Wolff, for his part, would say that these chapters contain the authentic 'words of Amos' (1.1a; J.W. Wolff, *Joel and Amos* [trans. W. Lanzen, S.D. McBride, Jr, and C.A. Muenchlow; Philadelphia: Fortress Press, 1977], p. 107). No authorial claims, however, are being made here.

2. For 3.1-2, see De Waard and Smalley, *Amos*, pp. 58, 193; for 3.1-8, see J. Vermeylen, 'Les relectures deutéronomistes des livres d'Amos et de Michée', in *Du prophete Isaïe à l'Apocaliptique. Isaïe 1-35, miroir d'un demi-millénaire d'expérience religieuse en Israël*, II (Paris: n.p., 1978), pp. 520-28; and van der Wal, 'The Structure of Amos'. Andersen and Freedman understand chs. 3 and 4 to be the elaboration and expansion of the themes of chs. 1 and 2 (e.g. *Amos*, pp. 357-77).

3. Koch, *Amos*, especially pp. 109-11.

understanding of life and history. If these ideas are applied to Amos, it can be posited that within the textual world, therefore, there can exist a 'world' of that community's making.

On the other hand, narrative ethics highlights the different stories by which and in which a people live and ground the meaning of their existence. The Israel within Amos, accordingly, could believe and defend the narrative(s) of its own 'world' or 'reality'. What remains to be seen is how that story and its interpretation stand in the light of the divine perspective.

This reading has as its primary goal the discovery of the picture of religion represented within Amos: its shape, its use, and its adherents. The prophetic text, however, not only offers a depiction of a 'world' within its world; it also evaluates it. The concomitant task, therefore, is to try to discern how and why this 'world' is either approved of or discredited, and how the text's literary strategies might move the reader to accept and echo its verdict.

a. *Two Tales of One City (3.1–4.3)*

The title of this subsection is taken from Fisch on Esther,[1] but also fits well here. Samaria, the capital of Israel, is pictured from two perspectives—the divine and the Israelite, both of which will be developed more fully throughout this reading. Sicre speaks of the *visión profética* and the *visión turística*, the distinction between how those called to observe in 3.9 might be repulsed or enraged through the evaluative lens of the deity, or impressed by the trappings of human achievement.[2] All of this, however, is to get ahead of the text itself, which prepares the reader for that setting through its introduction (3.1-8).

Amos 3.1-8. A new section of the book begins with the opening two verses of ch. 3.[3] For several scholars these two verses anticipate and summarize the contents of chs. 3–6 or even reflect the very heart of

---

1. Fisch, *Poetry with a Purpose*, ch. 1.
2. Sicre, '*Con los pobres*', pp. 118-19.
3. Several elements demonstrate this: the use of a different word for sin, the clear distinction made here between Israel and the nations, the 'Hear this word' formula is not found in chs. 1 and 2 (cf. Wolff, *Amos*; Hayes, *Amos*). There is a major break here with the opening formula because it has an accompanying relative clause (cf. 5.1), unlike 4.1. See especially Koch, *Amos*, pp. 107-109 (although my reading does not follow his view of the book's structure).

this prophetic message.[1] Is this true? Can these verses substantiate such a claim?

The opening verse, if considered in isolation, would seem to be an assurance and testimony of grace: those addressed are the 'sons of Israel' who had experienced deliverance from bondage by the personal intervention of God.[2] An allusion to Yahweh's singular relationship through his knowledge follows and is emphasized by the placement of 'only' (*rq*) and the declaration that 'all (*kl*) of the family (*hmšp hh*)'of Israel are somehow more special to him than 'all (*kl*) the families (*mšp hwt*) of the earth (3.2a).[3] Such apparently is the direct confession of God himself.

But these words cannot be read alone, for they continue the diatribe begun in ch. 2. Yahweh had raised up 'sons' from among these 'sons of Israel', but this nation had done its best to pervert the Lord's anointed (2.11-12); Israel was not the 'only' nation about whom Yahweh was concerned, or would judge (1.3–2.3); yes, he had

---

1. Wolff quotes Wellhausen: 'Whatever else he [Amos] says is a commentary on these words' (*Amos*, p. 178).

2. Several scholars view various elements of these first two verses as demonstrating deuteronomistic redaction. For the best summaries, see W.H. Schmidt, 'Die deuteronomische Redaktion des Amosbusches', *ZAW* 77 (1965), pp. 171-72 (however, note the observations by T.R. Hobbs, 'Amos 3.1b and 2.10', *ZAW* 81 [1969], pp. 384-87); Wolff, *Amos*; L. Markert, *Struktur und Bezeichnung des Scheltworts: Eine gattungskritische Studie anhand des Amosbuches* (BZAW, 140; Berlin: de Gruyter, 1977); Vermeylen, 'Les relectures deutéronomistes', pp. 543-54. For recent defenses of authenticity, see I. Willi-Plein, *Vorformen der Schriftexegese innerhalb des Alten Testaments—Untersuchungen zum literarischen Werden der auf Amos, Hosea und Micha zurückgehenden Bucher im hebräischen Zwölfprophetenbuch* (BZAW, 123; Berlin: de Gruyter, 1971), pp. 20-21; Smith, *Amos*; Andersen and Freedman, *Amos*; and Soggin's comment on the change of person (*Amos*). For a helpful summary of ch. 3's various critical issues see H.W. Wolff, *La hora de Amós* (trans. F. Martínez Goñi; Salamanca: Ediciones Sígueme, 1984), pp. 69-105, in the section entitled 'Introducción exegética para no exégetas'.

3. J. Vollmer (*Geschichtliche Rückblicke und Motive in der Prophetie des Amos, Hosea und Jesaja* [BZAW, 119; Berlin: de Gruyter, 1971], p. 30), and Markert (*Struktur*) propose that '*dmh* in 3.2a is a reference to 'cultivable land'. Vollmer's point, in light of 9.7, is that the verse speaks of Yahweh's involvement with this people in this particular place, and does not imply that he does not know the other nations of the earth. Note, however, that the terms are parallel in 3.5 and compare the use of '*rṣ* in 3.11. Soggin's response: 'this is useless pedantry' (*Amos*, p. 55).

brought them up out of Egypt (2.10), but now he would weigh them
down in judgment (2.13); 'all the family' would also include Judah,[1]
but it, too, lay within the circle of the condemned (2.4-5); 'all' of
them are to be punished for 'all' (*kl*) their sins (3.2bB). There is no
security, then, in these initial words in ch. 3. Grace appears inverted,
and now the relationship with God ominous.

There is no need to suggest that 3.2 is a quote from popular belief,
an echo of verse one celebrated by the nation.[2] Whatever the tradition
referred to here,[3] these are Yahweh's words, and the switch from the

---

1. There has been much discussion regarding the inclusiveness of the phrases
'the sons of Israel, against the whole family'. Some commentators take it as authentic
and understand it to refer to all the people of God, including Judah, although special
attention is directed at Israel (R.S. Cripps, *A Critical and Exegetical Commentary on
the Book of Amos* [n.p.: Klock & Klock, 2nd edn, repr. 1981]; J.L. Mays, *Amos: A
Commentary* [Old Testament Library; Philadelphia: Westminster Press, 1969];
Stuart, *Hosea–Jonah*; Smith, *Amos*; Andersen and Freedman, *Amos*). Others would
excise all or part of the phrase (S. Amsler, *Amos* [Commentaire de l'Ancien
Testament, 11a; ed. E. Jacob, K-A Keller and S. Amsler; Neuchâtel: Delachaux &
Niestlé, 1965]; Wolff, *Amos*; W. Rudolph, *Joel–Amos–Obadja–Jona* [KAT,
XIII.12; Gütersloh: Gerd Mohn, 1971]; Markert, *Struktur*; Soggin, *Amos*; Hayes,
Amos). Polley would consider the references to Judah as secondary according to his
theory that the prophet's goal is to call the nation back to the Davidic monarchy and
the legitimate religious shrines (M.E. Polley, *Amos and the Davidic Empire: A
Socio-Historical Approach* [New York: Oxford University Press, 1989], pp. 55-56,
94-95). At this point the debate surfaces over whether Amos limited his words to
Israel, with references to Judah being added later. References to Judah will appear
again, e.g., in 5.5; 6.1, 5. I am of the opinion that in Amos the term 'the sons of
Israel' may be a bit fluid and so in need of a modifier—cf. 3.12 (to distinguish from
3.1), 4.5 (no qualifier as meaning from the context is obviously the North). Koch
puts much stock on the variety of titles used of the people (*Amos*, pp. 118-20).
Andersen and Freedman have elaborated a very precise meaning for the 'geopolitical
terminology' (*Amos*, pp. 98-139). 'Israel' refers to the North, unless qualified, in
which case both North and South is meant; 'Jacob' to both kingdoms together;
'Joseph' and 'Isaac' to the North. Their hypothesis would bring Judah into more
contexts than those where that nation is not specifically mentioned.

2. Mays, *Amos*, and S.H. Blank, 'Irony By Way of Attribution', *Semitics* 1
(1970), p. 5. Koch notes that quotes are always introduced in Amos (*Amos*,
pp. 130-31). Cf. M.V. Fox, 'The Identification of Quotations in Biblical Literature',
ZAW 90 (1980), pp. 416-31.

3. See the discussion in Vollmer (*Rückblicke*, pp. 28-33), and Wolff (*Amos*).
Mention should be made here of the nature of allusion in literature. Alter suggests
that one should consider: (1) how the text signals an allusion, (2) its function within

initial third person (3.1a) to the first rhetorically expresses direct accusation. But what does Yahweh mean, 'Only you have I known'? Let these chapters explain, for in them unfolds the depth and significance of his knowing, and the willful obduracy of the nation's ignorance.[1] Here the verb *yd'* is tantalizingly ironic: what the sons of Israel might have considered redemptive knowledge through election is actually penetrative insight for chastisement; because he knows them, Yahweh must now 'visit' them. In other words, two different perceptions of the same tradition would be in conflict.

These first two verses introduce the theme of judgment in our section, but as they do, they also leave clues as to its nature. Will not 'all' the nation receive judgment for 'all' of its sins? Judgment then could very well be comprehensive and not only directed at a certain group. But when? The text does not yet say. Cannot the 'visit' signify that God himself will be present not only as judge but also as executioner? But how? Could the mention of the other 'families' of the earth somehow hint at some participation by other nations? If, therefore, 3.1-2 are to be taken as the introduction to chs. 3–6, then this strophe serves as one of a certain kind: it raises the issues (national judgment to be effected by Yahweh), but just as importantly the questions. Much is left unanswered.

The next sub-unit, 3.3-8, is best conceived as continuing the 'introduction', for these verses explore some of the queries that surfaced there. Verse 3 is a hinge verse that links 3.1-2 with 3.3-8 and

the text, and (3) how the allusion itself relates to the text (*Pleasures of Reading*, ch. 4). In 3.2 the allusion to the Exodus would be in 'ironic dissonance' with what is to be described later: divine judgment on the one hand, oppressive behavior by the Israelites on the other. An ironic use of the Exodus appears elsewhere as well in the chapters of Amos under discussion; it is no longer a source of national security (e.g. 3.9; 4.10; 5.17). This turning of tradition on its head is evident elsewhere as well— for example, 4.11 and the reference to Sodom and Gomorrah.

1. The relationship of 3.2a and 9.7 has proved problematic to commentators. Some have tried to tie 'know' and/or all of 3.1-2 to covenant ideas—see particularly H.B. Huffmon, 'The Treaty Background of Hebrew YADA', *BASOR* 181 (1966), pp. 31-37; L.A. Sinclair, 'The Courtroom Motif in the Book of Amos', *JBL* 85 (1966), pp. 351-53; Neher, *Amos*, pp. 34-48; M. O'Rourke Boyle, 'The Covenant Lawsuit of the Prophet Amos: III 1-IV 3', *VT* 21 (1971), pp. 338-62 (3.1-2 would form part of the 'call to witness'); Mays, *Amos*; Stuart, *Hosea–Jonah*. Would not the best approach in Amos be to allow the text itself to define its own terms? (Cf. Andersen and Freedman, *Amos*, pp. 91-93 and *ad loc*.)

heads the list of questions that follow.[1] This verse, however, is different from the others—it lacks a corresponding question and, at first
glance, can appear a bit innocuous.[2] Who are the two? As this verse
follows immediately after 3.1-2, the most natural assumption is that
they are Yahweh and the 'sons of Israel', but the text itself offers no
identification.[3] This seeming vagueness in tone and referent, however,
is quickly shattered by the series beginning in v. 4.

There is a growing ominousness as the questions move from references to animals alone (v. 4), to animals and man-made traps (v. 5),

1. Some have suggested that v. 3 belongs to 3.1-2 (e.g. W.R. Harper, *A
Critical and Exegetical Commentary in Amos and Hosea* [International Critical
Commentary; Edinburgh: T. & T. Clark, 1979]), a view apparently shared by the
LXX, which by metathesis reads *yd'* in 3.3 in parallel with 3.2b (followed by Cripps,
Amos). De Waard disagrees, however, and holds that 'to become acquainted with
one another' and 'to meet each other' belong within the same semantic domain, in
'Translation Techniques Used by the Greek Translators of Amos', *Bib* 59 (1978),
pp. 345-46. Other critics, noting both the similarities and differences between 3.3
and 3.4-6, say that the verse is an addition: H. Gese, 'Kleine Beiträge zum
Verständnis des Amosbuches', *VT* 12 (1962), p. 425; Schmidt, 'Die deuteronomische Redaktion', pp. 183-84; Vermeylen, 'Les relectures deutéronomistes', p. 526;
B. Renaud, 'Genèse et théologie d'Amos 3, 3-8', in *Mélanges bibliques et orientaux
en l'honneur de M. Henri Cazelles* (ed. A. Caquot and M. Delcor; AOAT, 212;
Neukirchen–Vluyn: Verlag Butzen & Berker Kevelaer, 1981), pp. 357-58, 368. See
the reply to these sorts of arguments by Wolff, *Amos*, p. 180 n. b, and the
structural arguments presented in my discussion.

2. The meaning of the niphal of *y'd* is disputed. Some would say that the term
implies meeting by appointment or agreement (e.g. Mays, *Amos*; Andersen and
Freedman, *Amos*; BDB 416 and KB 388; Waltke–O'Conner, *Introduction*, 234e;
most translations in Eng. and Sp.). R. Gordis ('Studies in the Book of Amos',
Proceedings of the American Academy for Jewish Research 42–47 [1979-1980],
pp. 218-19) has recently suggested that the nuance here is of 'sharing a common
purpose or intent' (cf. Gen. 22.8; Ps. 133.1). Others would argue that the verb con-
notes only a chance meeting or encounter (e.g. Wolff, *Amos*; S.M. Paul, 'Amos 3.3-
8: The Irresistible Sequence of Cause and Effect', *HAR* 7 [1983], pp. 210-11). Still
others think that the verb can mean either meeting by agreement or chance (e.g.
Soggin, *Amos*).

3. For Yahweh and Israel, see Harper, *Amos*; Cripps, *Amos*; Smith, *Amos*;
Hayes, *Amos* (cf. use of *hlk* in Lev. 26). Most other commentators take the verse to
refer to any two persons who talk together, usually taking the line as strictly proverbial. Andersen and Freedman would make the idea more abstract: two things go
together; although vague in v. 3, relationships, they claim, are specified in the
following verses.

to a human scene (v. 6). The lion's prey is caught,[1] the bird trapped.[2] The parallelism, not only in the identical opening of each questions (*h*-interrogative + imperfect) but also in the alternating endings beginning in v. 3 (*blty 'm\'yn lw\blty 'm\'yn lh*), structurally links the entire series (3.3-5a) together and seems to move this staccato sequence of death inexorably forward. The alternating series is abruptly broken by the emphatic construction of the last bicola of v. 5: infinitive absolute + negative + imperfect (also note the assonance and alliteration). Surely the victim has been snagged.

Commentators have noticed the shift from 'effect to cause' to 'cause to effect' with the change from the *h*-interrogative to '*m* in v. 6.[3] The sharpness of 3.5bB is compounded by this modification in 3.6a. The alteration, however, is more than structural; it also involves subject matter. Disaster now comes to the 'city'. Now human beings must respond to the trumpet blast. Although trumpets sounded primarily to warn of enemy attack,[4] the danger is left unspecified. Is it now a human prey that, like the other helpless victims, is facing certain death? The cause of the 'evil' is Yahweh, a climactic theological statement highlighted by thematic chiasm embedded in structurally equivalent lines:

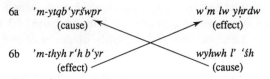

6a '*m-ytqb'yrs̆wpr*   *w'm lw yhrdw*
    (cause)   (effect)

6b '*m-thyh r'h b'yr*   *wyhwh l' 's̆h*
    (effect)   (cause)

1. Some would envisage two stages here: first the capture and killing of the prey, then its being taken to the lair (e.g. Wolff, *Amos*; De Waard and Smalley, *Amos*; Paul, 'Amos 3.3-8', pp. 211-12; Hayes, *Amos*). Andersen and Freedman cite verses to show that roaring can occur before, during, and after the kill. This observation would add an element of uncertainty (yet maintain an element of danger) and would underscore even more the movement to increasing ominousness in the passage.

2. For a helpful discussion of the textual and lexical problems in v. 5 see Paul, 'Amos 3.3-8', pp. 212-13; Andersen and Freedman, *Amos*.

3. Besides the commentaries, note Markert, *Struktur*, p. 92; Renaud, 'Gènese et théologie', p. 359; Paul, 'Amos 3.3-8', p. 214; F. Lindström, *God and the Origin of Evil: A Contextual Analysis of Alleged Monistic Evidence in the Old Testament* (trans. F.H. Cryer; ConBOT, 21; Lund: Gleerup, 1983), p. 204.

4. For the various uses of the trumpet, see BDB 1051; Harper, *Amos*; Cripps, *Amos*.

What is more, a contrast surfaces by comparing the second bicola of each line: the people appear powerless and in panic; Yahweh is sovereign. The imagery of the whole sequence (3.3-6) is vivid. The scenes that follow one upon the other are full of tumultous sound, and violent vignettes imprint themselves forcefully on the mind's eye.

Such literary artistry gives pause. Are these rhetorical questions just an example of primitive pastoral logic,[1] whose order is irrelevant to their impact?[2] In addition, do they all receive the same answer? One expects a negative to each, one by one, until the last (v. 6b). Can one be sure of the nation's reply (one must distinguish the reader's response from the characters')? Would those in this textual world readily agree with that line's point, that Yahweh would be behind the trumpeted calamity? Would this notion fit into their understanding of the nation's narrative (cf. 3.2)?

Several scholars have held that these words refer to a common belief in divine causality.[3] But a careful reading of *Amos* casts doubt on that assumption. For the moment, however, the answer is ambiguous; later Yahweh will unmask the nation's blindness to his ways (e.g. 4.6-11) and its pretentious self-confidence (e.g. 5.18-20; 6.1-3, 13-14).

Verse 6 can leave such an impression that some consider it the climax of an original pericope. For these commentators, what follows in the next two verses would then alter the initial purpose of 3.1-6 by focusing on the inescapability and authority of the prophetic call.[4]

---

1. Note the references to 'non-Western' logic in Mays, *Amos*; Martin-Achard, *Amos*, p. 36. Contrast A. Schenker's discussion on signs and perception, 'Zur Interpretation von Amos 3, 3-8', *BZ* ns 30 (1986), pp. 250-56.

2. Cf. Stuart's surprising statement: 'The particular structure of each question, including the order in which the related circumstances are mentioned is irrelevant to the impact' (*Hosea–Jonah*, p. 324).

3. See the discussion and authors cited in Lindström, *God and the Origin of Evil*, pp. 199-202. More recently, Smith has espoused this view (*Amos*).

4. The most detailed discussions appear in Schmidt, 'Die deuteronomische Redaktion', pp. 184-88; Markert, *Struktur*, pp. 86-94; Vermeylen, 'Les relectures deutéronomistes', pp. 526-28; Renaud, 'Genèse et théologie'; Lindström, *God and the Origin of Evil*, pp. 203-205. Most of the authors would claim that the list of seven rhetorical questions ends at a climax in v. 6. Wolff (*Amos*) would see a preliminary climax in 3.6b, but takes 3.3-6, 8, however, as a literary unit (cf. Mays, *Amos*; Rudolph, *Amos*; Soggin, *Amos*; W. Eichrodt, 'Die Vollmacht des Amos. Zu einer schwierigen Stelle im Amosbuch', in *Beiträge zum alttestamentlichen Theologie—Festschrift für Walter Zimmerli zum 70. Geburstag* [ed. H. Donner, R.

Verse 7 is said to be an insertion which, although tied to the previous verse by repeating (with some expansion) the final phrase, serves as a transition to the new theme of v. 8 (note the repetition of the divine name and the root *dbr*).[1]

Yet the interlocking of the whole unit is more complex than this. The introductory *ky* of 3.7 is part of a triple question series (*h...'m... ky*; cf. 6.12) and is therefore grammatically linked to 3.3-6.[2] If one follows a graduated ascending number scheme (N[7]+1), the climax is ultimately after the transitional 3.7 at v. 8. How can this stylistic observation be woven into the flow of the text?

Several comments are in order. First, the passage in no way speaks of the prophet Amos or his commissioning.[3] The prophet appears only in the book's title and later only briefly in the vision cycles and in the

---

Hanhart and R. Smend; Göttingen: Vandenhoeck & Ruprecht, 1977], pp. 124-31. Eichrodt finds a parallel in Mt. 16.2-4, Lk. 12.54-56.) Although Andersen and Freedman (*Amos*) do not follow other critics' lead in regards to authenticity or redaction, they do see the focus as the prophet's 'apologia'. As with other commentators, reference is made to 2.11-12; 7.10-17.

1. Most commentators consider v. 7 a late insertion. Those who would defend its authenticity would include Harper, *Amos*; Stuart, *Hosea–Jonah*; Smith, *Amos*; Hayes, *Amos*; Andersen and Freedman, *Amos*; Paul, 'Amos 3.3-8', pp. 206-207, 215-16; Y. Gitay, 'A Study of Amos's Art of Speech: A Rhetorical Analysis of Amos 3.1-15', *CBQ* 42 (1980), pp. 298-99, 304-305. On the criterion of the change from poetry (3.6) to prose (3.7) as proof of insertion, note the following methodological comment by Alter:

> I don't think we can confidently explain in all instances why a prophet made the crossover into prose, and in a good many cases the move may have been dictated chiefly by individual sensibility and gifts of expression. If there are more general reasons, they must be sought not primarily in chronology but in consideration of genre and discursive situation (*Art of Biblical Poetry*, p. 137).

Andersen and Freedman claim that the mixture of prose and poetry is common and intrinsic to the prophetic style (*Amos*, pp. 144-49, 391-92).

2. Paul, 'Amos 3.3-8', pp. 206-207; Limburg, 'Sevenfold Structures', p. 220. Auld also mentions the question series, but only considers 3.3-6, 8, and tries to apply the conclusion to a general statement on the nature of prophecy (*Amos*, pp. 34-35).

3. In light of their claim that the plural 'prophets' refers to the succession of prophets and that only one could appear at any one time in the celestial assembly, Andersen and Freedman understand 3.7 (and the visions of ch. 7) to refer to Amos's call (*Amos*).

biographical pericope (7.10-17). Even there he is overwhelmed; the divine word is more important and pressing than the prophet's person.

In 3.7, moreover, it is 'the prophets' who are mentioned, those anonymous servants of Yahweh alluded to in 2.11-12. To recognize this point is to discover their role in the passage: unlike the rebellious 'sons of Israel', they are approvingly 'known' (cf. 3.2a) as Yahweh's servants; what is more, they are 'in the know', as they accompany him (cf. 3.3) in the divine council. There is no hint of judgment or chastisement for these 'sons'—rather, revelation because of obedience. In other words, they serve more as contrastive foils than as the focus of 3.3-8.

In light of the preceding verses, the climax at v. 8 is strange, yet at once menacing. The lion has roared, but with 1.2 in mind and the juxtaposition with 'Lord Yahweh' in the next line, God himself must be this lion.[1] If that roar of 1.2 was followed by a list of irrevocable judgments, surely this one must be as well. That the roar in v. 4 signalled the capture of the prey only pushes that sense still further: the nation is already in the divine lion's grasp. Could not, then, the trumpet blast be that roar? Can not the 'evil', then, even now be at hand, or has the nation already suffered his judgment in some way? Can there be any doubt about whether it is the work of Yahweh? Could not also the 'secret' (*swd*) of 3.7 be the message of the imminent 'evil' from Yahweh's hand?

Questions keep welling up. If the 'evil' is apparently the chastisement of God, is it really 'evil' and for whom? In context, the judgment at hand is born within the celestial spheres (3.7). The ambiguity, however, may be intentional, because the reading will show that what is 'good' in the divine sight is of little significance within the national set of values (3.10), and that what is 'good' for the people's religiosity is but evil in Yahweh's view (5.18-27).

---

1. There is no need to say with Stuart regarding the voice of Yahweh: 'It may even have actually sounded that way to the prophets, sometimes or always. Old Testament descriptions of the sound of Yahweh's speaking audibly imply a loud, roaring sound' (*Hosea–Jonah*, p. 325). The focus here is on the lion as a predator whose roar is public and a warning to all to hear. Lion imagery was common for deities in the ancient Near East and in the OT is used of Yahweh (G.J. Botterweck, ''ry', *TDOT*, I, pp. 374-84. Note especially Hos. 5.14-15 and 11.10-11. In the latter the verb *hrd* also appears.) Cf. P.J. King, *Amos, Hosea, Micah—An Archaeological Commentary* (Philadelphia: Westminster Press, 1988), pp. 128-30.

He is roaring, who will fear? Who will hear (3.1a)? Certainly the prophets, but the people? Is there any hope of escape from the mouth of the lion if the nation responds to the clarion call? As this initial and very sketchy picture of the textual world begins to fill out and as the characters become more defined, the answer will be all too clear.

The *inclusio* with *dbr* (3.1, 8) marks the closure of this introductory section and focuses its purpose.[1] The word of Yahweh goes out against his people for all their sins, and his judgment is already at hand. That judgment could come as an enemy attack (3.6a). The prophet(s) are mentioned only in passing, and any 'messenger formula' in 3.1 is quickly overwhelmed by direct divine discourse. Just as the chastisement must come, the prophesying must go out (3.8b). This is a terrible word, a word with the stench of death, an announcement of unavoidable disaster. If the passage begins with the proclamation of chastisement, it ends with the revelation of its inexorable imminence.

3.1-8, therefore, is the introduction to 3.9–4.3 and to chs. 3–6 as well. These verses highlight the centrality of the word from Yahweh and its nature as certain, inescapable, judging. The characters on stage, however, are more obscure and just begin to take shape. The prophets remain nameless channels and merit only brief notice and little definition. In actuality, their service to Yahweh textually is to underscore, by way of contrast, the negative qualities of the nation, and to set the word of judgment in motion. The 'sons of Israel' are not yet explicitly described (unless, of course, one returns to 2.6-16); their chastisement, however, has been forcefully pushed to the foreground. A portrait of Yahweh, however, does start to emerge: violated, absolutely sovereign, decisive and outraged.

This introduction also begins to hint at what will become central and be developed in the rest of this reading. On the one hand, Yahweh is hitting at a very different view of the world than his own, a view he will unmask and overturn in judgment. Different conceptions of faith and of the deity and his people are at odds, and the disparity will prove fatal to Israel. On the other, the people as a people are guilty. The problem is more than theoretical, more than the issue of an erroneous world-view and religious practice; it is personal, Yahweh versus the nation.

---

1. Also note the suggestion in Andersen and Freedman that the total number of lines of ten with an imbedded seven pattern points to completeness (*Amos*, p. 393).

The target of his wrath will become clearer through the description of the nation's activity, the mention of its values and ideas, and the quoting of its leadership. Throughout these chapters there are also certain features of national life and belief that must be gleaned through implication—that is, by looking at how things are said and by being attentive to what is not said. In this opening passage the divine perspective begins to claim and command absolute sway on the text's stage. Yahweh's point of view apparently is not only unassailable, but also irrevocable. Chapters 3–6 will artistically develop the divine view and highlight its transcendent sovereignty. The 'rhetoric of entrapment' is already being put in place.

The introduction (3.1-8) emphasizes the divine word and initiates other character and point of view features, but also leaves much unsaid. The setting is still a bit unclear. Who more specifically are the guilty, and why are they deserving of punishment? How will Yahweh punish? What will be destroyed and how is the 'city' involved? With 3.9–4.3 the curtain rises yet further, and the scene becomes more clear and coherent.

Amos 3.9–4.3. Verse 9 clearly marks a new subsection with the change from the interrogative to the imperative. The nature of the imagery also changes dramatically. From the scenes drawn primarily from the animal world, ringing with alarming sounds and startling savagery, the setting now will concentrate on the 'city'; only now it will be named and described. Here a legal tone is developed, as witnesses are called and judgment passed.

3.9-11 is neatly arranged as a call to gather the witnesses (3.9a), the detailing of transgressions (3.9b-10), and the announcement of judgment (3.11). Messengers are apparently to be sent to other nations (*hšmyʻw*). But who are the messengers? Perhaps there is an allusion here to the prophets of v. 7, but, once again, if this is so, the envoys themselves are of no consequence.[1] They are kept faceless and nameless in order to advance the movement of the text; the central concerns are the depiction of life within Samaria and Yahweh's evaluation.

---

1. The proposed identifications of the messengers include Amos, the prophets (of the divine council), foreign nations, the people of Samaria. A number of commentators understand the imperative as simply a rhetorical device (e.g. Mays, *Amos*; Smith, *Amos*).

What is surprising is that Yahweh appeals to other nations to gather around the city to observe its sin. Rhetorically, this call can serve several functions. On the one hand, the gesture might reinforce the idea of some general moral consensus in that part of the world, an idea communicated through the structure of the first two chapters.[1] Yet, that point is taken much further here. In those first chapters any assumed consensus was in the matter of international warfare; now internal matters are the issue, and the verse implies that these pagan nations would be horrified at the state of affairs within Samaria and so concur with the divine verdict. The first nation, Ashdod,[2] is one of the very nations already indicted and under divine judgment (1.8), the second the oppressor nation from which Israel had been redeemed (2.10a; 3.1b). Why these two nations in particular? Perhaps Ashdod serves as a word play: *'šdwd* will witness the *šd* (3.10) in Samaria.[3] The already condemned neighbor, who trafficked in human lives (1.6; perhaps Israelites themselves), is now summoned to be present at Israel's condemnation for oppression; Egypt, as Israel's greatest (and paradigmatic) oppressor, would now ironically observe and be astonished at the oppression among the 'liberated' sons of Israel. To use Sicre's picture: traditional enemies of Israel are called to the amphitheatre of the mountains around Samaria to view the evidence and witness the verdict.[4]

But they, too, like the anonymous messengers, are mentioned and then passed over. There is no recording of their response to the invitation or their reaction to the scene. The rhetorical point made,

---

1. Barton, *Amos' Oracles against the Nations*, especially chs. 1, 6, 7, and the Appendix. Indeed, there are also lexical links with those chapters: the mention of strongholds (*'rmnwt* in 1.4, 7, 10, 12, 14; 2.2) and of a capital city.

2. LXX reads Assyria, perhaps to serve as a fitting imperial parallel to Egypt. This reading has been followed recently by Chávez, *Modelo*; Stuart, *Hosea–Jonah*; Andersen and Freedman, *Amos*; among the translations—Eng.: JB, RSV; Sp.: BLA.

3. Harper's (*Amos*) suggestion. For possible reasons for choosing these two nations see Wolff, *Amos*, and Smith, *Amos*. Hayes (*Amos*) says that the call for two is more important than their identity in that two witnesses are required by the law for capital cases (cf. Num. 35.30; Deut. 17.6; 19.5).

4. Sicre: 'Samaria, la rica y lujosa capital de Jeroboán II, aparece como un gigantesco anfiteatro en cuyo escenario se representa la tragedia del terror y la opresión. Una obra a la que se invita a un público entendido en la materia: egipcios y filisteos, opresores tradicionales del pueblo de Israel' (*'Con los pobres'*, p. 117).

the text now concentrates on the place of interest, Samaria. What is evident in the capital city is first 'tumult' (underscored by *rbwt*). The term *mhwmh* can be used of the panic that Yahweh sends.[1] Is this the 'fear' and 'evil' to which 3.6 referred, the calamity sent by God? The parallel term in 3.9, however, defines its thrust: the oppression ('*šwqym*)[2] is of the people and against the people; the terror is thus of their own making and not from God. Once more the scene, as in 3.3-8, is full of sound; but here it is the din of social confusion, not the roar of divine chastisement.

Verse 10 continues the depiction of violations. The description, however, is still a bit general, for the perpetrators are simply 'they' and their crime is signified indistinctly as 'they do not know to do the right'. This vagueness, however, will begin to disappear at closer inspection. On the one hand, 'they' will start to be defined by the second half of the verse. On the other, these are presented in sharp contrast to Yahweh through the different uses of the verbs *yd'* (he knows them [3.2a]; they do not know how to do the right) and '*śh* (he must do 'evil' as their judge [3.6]; they practice evil as a way of life). One is left wondering, nevertheless, if they know the right, but just refuse to do it.[3] 'Oracle of Yahweh' (*n'm yhwh*) sets off this phrase from the following as if to underline even further the perversity within Israel described in the rest of the line. The formula affirms both the seriousness of the charges as well as the authority of the accuser.[4]

---

1. BDB 223, KB 499. The term, as here, occurs elsewhere with *rb*. Even so Markert omits *rb* for supposed metric reasons, thereby missing its rhetorical value (*Struktur*).

2. For this term see J. Pons, *L'Oppression dans l'Ancien Testament* (Paris: Letouzey & Ané, 1981), pp. 69-83.

3. Andersen and Freedman (*Amos*) suggest, on the basis of Isa. 30.10, that the term alludes to the prophetic message. Though this idea might fit well into the context (3.1-8; cf. 2.11-12; 7.10-17), it perhaps is better to grant a broader meaning in order to include also the ethico-religious demands of Yahweh and maybe even the moral consensus of chs. 1 and 2.

4. Many scholars eliminate *n'm yhwh*. Note particularly the excursus by Wolff (*Amos*, p. 143) and Koch's discussion (*Amos*, pp. 113-15). These commentators want to limit its use to the conclusion of oracles. The fact that 8 of the 21 occurrences in the book (38 per cent) do not follow this pattern should indicate the inadequacy of the theory. Wolff admits that the formula opens sayings elsewhere (Num. 24.3-4, 15-16; 2 Sam. 23.1; Prov. 30.1), but precludes that possibility in Amos.

Not doing the 'right' is clarified by its opposite, through the terms that follow. These are in participial form and so characterize the behavior: 'those who store up *ḥms wšd*'.[1] These words are a hendiadys (note, e.g., Ezek. 45.9), and perhaps stand in antithesis to the book's other hendiadys, *mšpṭ wṣdqh* (5.7, 24; 6.12; cf. 5.11, 12).[2] If so, then maybe the 'good' can be contextually specified within Amos. These general terms will begin to take shape (indeed, they already have—cf. 2.6-8) as the reading progresses.

The place of hoarding also gives a clue as to the identity of 'them'. The fruit of violence and robbery[3] is stored in the *'rmnwt*, the 'palaces' or 'fortresses'.[4] These would represent royal buildings, as evident also in the oracles of chs. 1 and 2. The guilty, therefore, cannot be defined here simply as the upper classes, but rather those in power within the monarchy. The one responsible is not simply *a social stratum*, but *the sociopolitical system* itself.[5] The state, in other words,

1. For the terms and the hendiadys see Pons, *L'Oppression*, pp. 27-66. Wolff (*Amos*) tries to locate *nkḥh* within wisdom circles and is followed by Soggin (*Amos*), yet see the comments by J.L. Crenshaw, 'The Influence of the Wise on Amos', *ZAW* 79 (1967), p. 46. In any case, it is best to define this broad term contextually within Amos. For the use of participles in Amos to describe the activity of Israel, see Koch, *Amos*, pp. 129-30; Wolff, *Amos*, pp. 96-97.

2. Suggested by Wolff, *Amos*; Vesco, 'Amos de Teqoa', p. 495.

3. Taking the terms as a metonymy as do many commentators in contrast to those who understand the terms to be the perverse treasure ('murder and robbery') hoarded in the fortresses (e.g. C.F. Keil, *Commentary on the Old Testament*. X. *Minor Prophets* [Grand Rapids: Eerdmans, 1977]; Wolff, *Amos*), although the latter view would have a rhetorical effect as well.

4. For my understanding of this term, see especially King, *Amos*, p. 67; Dearman, *Property Rights*, pp. 25-27. If the term refers to 'defense works'/ 'battlements on defensive walls', as Andersen and Freedman propose (*Amos*, pp. 240-44), then the reference would not be limited to a social station, though still to the system in a broader sense. As Amos chs. 5 and 6 especially make clear (yet also note 3.11; 4.3, 10), the military establishment is brought into the purview of divine judgment, too.

5. Several commentators, for example, attribute the injustice to Canaanite influence (e.g. Wolff, *Amos*; Stuart, *Hosea–Jonah*; yet note the comments by Soggin, *Amos*; Smith, *Amos*). Dearman argues against this theory throughout his book and suggests instead that Israel adopted measures more akin to Assyrian bureaucracy (*Property Rights*, chs. 3–5). Fleischer argues against both the Canaanite theory as well as Dearman's hypothesis and then offers his own suggestions (*Menschenverkäufern*, pp. 284-90, 355-58, 364). Cf. the previous discussion in

is abusive and exploitative. This verse then reveals that the government is culpable, and as the reading progresses its ideology and mechanisms will begin to come to light. Yet no functionaries are named;
only their representative activity is described. Who they are is not as
crucial as what they do and symbolize.

Verse 11 declares the judgment through the divine word (the same
title used in 3.8b: the lion that roars, Lord Yahweh, now gives the
sentence). An enemy will surround the land and bring down its
'strength' (defeat the armies? destroy the strongholds?);[1] the places of
plunder will be plundered. The notice of invasion gains impact
through various stylistic devices: the enemy will 'surround' the land,
so implying no escape, and take the strength 'from you' (*mmk*), thus
emphasizing the directedness of the chastisement; the explicit mention
of *'rmnwt* links therefore the guilty and the destroyed (the term helps
tie 3.9-11 together, appearing four times). Nevertheless, the enemy is
not specified.[2] As with several other characters (the prophets, Ashdod,
Egypt) that surface in the text, the identity is not as important as the
instrumentality.

Verse 12 also begins with 'thus says the Lord' and provides a
metaphorical description of the judgment announced in the preceding

Chapter 2 above.

1. With most commentators and translations I read with the Peshitta the po'el
imperfect of *sbb*. Others propose an exclamation with an emendation to *msbyb*:
H.S. Pelser, 'Amos 3.11—A Communication', *OTWSA* 7–8 (1966), pp. 153-56
(cf. Chávez, *Modelo*); others maintain the MT form, 'and all about the land' (Keil,
Minor Prophets; Hayes, *Amos*; Andersen and Freedman, *Amos*). I maintain the
hiphil of *yrd* with the MT, instead of the hophal. Among the translations—Eng.: RSV,
NIV; Sp.: FC, RVA. Note that here, as in 3.14-15, a verb(s) indicating the judgment is
followed by a verb(s) describing the consequences. Translating *'z* as 'strength', not
'fortresses'. See BDB 739, KB 692. Among the translations—Eng.: JB; Sp.: FC,
BLA.

2. Many commentators hold that the reference is to Assyria. For a discussion of
the Assyrian army's organization and tactics, see H.W.F. Saggs, *The Might That
Was Assyria* (London: Sidgwick & Jackson, 1984), ch. 16; for how the Assyrians
structured their war accounts, see Younger, *Ancient Conquest Accounts*, ch. 2. Note
Hayes's view regarding the invader that follows his own particular historical reconstruction: the regional, anti-Assyrian coalition. Both Hayes (*Amos*, ch. 1) and
Rosenbaum (*Amos*, ch. 2, especially pp. 24-25) point out, though for different
reasons in line with their respective reconstructions, that the Jehu dynasty was pro-
Assyrian in order to discount the possibility that the reference is to Assyria.

verse. This verse functions, as v. 3 had earlier, like a hinge between 3.9-11 and 3.13-15, connecting the destruction of the palace-fortresses with that of the various 'houses' (also note that 3.12 itself mentions furniture).[1] Read in light of 1.2 and 3.4, 8, the initial impression might be that Yahweh is the lion. The juxtaposition with 3.11 would then equate God in some way with the enemy (cf. 3.6). But perhaps he is the shepherd who 'saves' through judgment, not from it. Irony surfaces in the ambiguity.[2] In either case, the attack that will come will only leave tatters, only bits and pieces as evidence of a sheep (a people) destroyed (Exod. 22.10-13 [Heb. 22.9-12]).

The last line of v. 12 is an interpretive crux.[3] The line specifies the

1. Most form critics will isolate this verse: Willi-Plein, *Vorformen*, p. 23; Mays, *Amos*; Wolff, *Amos*; Markert, *Struktur*. Melugin would agree, but explain its placement here by a redactor precisely because of its connections with 3.9-11 and 3.13-15 ('The Formation of Amos', pp. 379, 382).

2. R.B. Chisolm, Jr, 'Wordplay in the Eighth Century Prophets', *BSac* 144 (1987), pp. 47-48. Cf. Mays, *Amos*; Wolff, *Amos*; Smith, *Amos*. Andersen and Freedman say that, because of the ambiguity, the identification with Yahweh 'seems to break down' (*Amos*, p. 373); what they miss is the power of irony, which would be especially effective if one were to assume their scheme that Amos's early messages did offer hope to the people if they repented. The lion was also a symbol utilized by the Assyrians—see P. Machinist, 'Assyria and its Image in the First Isaiah', *JAOS* 103 (1983), especially pp. 728, 731; Rosenbaum specifically identifies Assyria as the lion in 5.19 (*Amos*, p. 19). For Assyrian art, see J. Reade, *Assyrian Sculpture* (London: British Museum Publications, 1983). Most commentators hold that this empire was the invader that fulfilled the predictions of doom of the historical prophet's oracles. Could this be an ironic use of the symbol, the identity of Yahweh the lion and his instrument of judgment?

3. The first issue is deciding whether 3.12e is an integral part of v. 12 (the view taken here) or if it provides the addressee for 3.13 (*BHS*; Amsler, *Amos*). Secondly, there is the problem of comparison: between the shepherd and Israel, who are able to save something from the devastation, or the notion that only insignificant pieces themselves are saved. Most understand the latter. Thirdly, the translation of the last line: for good surveys see especially Harper (*Amos*) for earlier views; Wolff, *Amos* (who follows Gese, 'Kleine Beiträge', pp. 424-27; cf. Markert, *Struktur*); Rudolph, *Amos*; De Waard and Smalley, *Amos*, pp. 71-73. Rosenbaum has recently proposed that the line exhibits an alternative northern spelling of 'Damascus' (*Amos*, p. 90). I follow the proposal of I. Rabinowitz, 'The Crux at Amos 3.12', *VT* 11 (1961), pp. 228-31. He offers the simplest solution with no emendation, just a separation of *wbdmśq* into *wbd mśq* to read the last two phrases as: 'in the form of a corner of a couch, and of a piece out of the leg of a bed'. He is followed by De Waard and Smalley, *Amos*; Smith, *Amos* (cf. the translations—Eng.: RSV, NEB).

'sons of Israel' who are singled out by Yahweh as those in power (cf.
the use of *yšb* in 1.5)[1] who enjoy a comfortable lifestyle. These words
reinforce the lion–sheep metaphor of the first part of the verse: only
scraps remain to testify to their destruction.

A pause is incumbent here. I have tried to let the text open up bit-
by-bit its picture of sin and judgment. Like a puzzle the pieces begin
to fall into place, although more details will be forthcoming: the capital is that 'city', a center of oppression to be destroyed; the 'trumpet'
will sound to announce an inescapable and devastating invasion by a
foreign force; a principle target of Yahweh's wrath is the governmental system and the nation's elite. But there is still an element of ambiguity that emerges, a tension that will be constant throughout these
chapters. If the reigning order is culpable, then why are all of the sons
of Israel to be visited and the entire land made to suffer? Is the rest of
the populace outside the circle of the powerful simply a victim, both
of internal oppression and attack from the outside—that is, always
suffering, whether to feed the sin of those who rule or to bear
unfairly the tragic consequences? Or, are they somehow willful participants in the condemned system? If so, how and why? At this point in
our reading, the purpose is simply to raise the issue. Just as the profile
of the system will become clearer, so will the role of the people.

The next strophe, 3.13-15, also begins with an imperatival form of
šm', but unlike 3.9 is a call not to observe but rather to testify against
Israel. Who is addressed? The text does not say, but, in light of 3.9,
perhaps Ashdod and Egypt are meant.[2] If so, the irony of pagan

For interesting archaeological evidence see the evidence and suggestion by
S. Mittmann, 'Amos 3, 12-15 und das Bett der Samarier', *ZDPV* 92 (1976),
pp. 149-67. J.F.A. Sawyer proposes that the LXX rendering is a deliberate polemic
against other sects and should be studied in its own right, not as simply a misreading
of the Hebrew, in '"Those Priests in Damascus": A Possible Example of Anti-
Sectarian Polemic in the Septuagint Version of Amos 3.12', *ASTI* 8 (1970–1971),
pp. 123-30.

1. On *yšb* see Gottwald, *Tribes of Yahweh*, pp. 512-34. In accordance with
their theory, Andersen and Freedman take *bny yśr'l* to refer to both North and South,
with the prophet limiting the reference in the last line of verse 12 (*Amos*, pp. 102-
103). Yet, it is better to let the context determine meaning: Israel, in particular her
rulers, is in view, not Judah (note the mention of Samaria in 3.9, 12 and 4.1, and of
Bethel in 3.14).

2. Options besides these two nations include the prophets, foreigners in
Samaria, the citizens of Israel, Amos. Again, many commentators view the impera-

powers being used in a court scene against the nation is heightened. As has been the style up to this point, the identity is ignored in order to emphasize the divine judgment against Israel (here called the 'house of Jacob'; cf. 6.8; 7.2, 5; 8.7; 9.8).[1] The move to the pronouncement, however, is interrupted by a speech formula with a long divine name and title. The indubitability of judgment, as earlier, continues to be underscored by the repeated references to the divine word (3.1, 8), speech (3.11, 12), and oracle (3.10). In light of the coming invasion to be raised up by Yahweh (3.11), the title *'lhy hṣb'wt* is not surprising; even less so since the following lines (3.14b-15) suggest that he himself will attack Israel. The placement of this long phrase here, therefore, is rhetorically appropriate and compelling.[2]

Verse 14 twice repeats the verb *pqd* and thereby further develops, although in a different way than previous strophes, the initial announcement of the divine visitation for Israel's sins (3.2a; note the different term for sin, *pš'*; cf. 2.6). This verse also introduces the concept of 'the day'. This term will gain in importance in later chapters. 3.14a begins with an asseverative *ky* to underscore the certainty of judgment. 3.14b-15 exhibit a structural parallelism of two pairs of lines in which the first begins with a *waw*-consecutive perfect first person singular, depicting the involvement of Yahweh; the second contains a pair of verbs (note the lexical variety) detailing the concrete consequences of his activity.

The scene of judgment presents a complex picture. For the first

tive more as a rhetorical device to gain attention instead of as directed at some person or group in particular.

1. Andersen and Freedman, however, take the phrase to refer to both North and South (*Amos*, pp. 99, 103-104).

2. For arguments for eliminating all or part of 3.13b see Willi-Plein, *Vorformen*, p. 24; Wolff, *Amos* (followed by Markert, *Struktur*), and his excursus on pp. 287-88; Rudolph, *Amos*. See the responses by Soggin, *Amos*, and Smith, *Amos*. The title 'God of hosts' appears another eight times in Amos (4.13; 5.14, 15, 16, 27; 6.8, 14; 9.5) and is important to its message. Note that all but the last reference appear in chs. 3-6. Cf. the extensive note regarding this phrase at 6.8 later in this chapter. For Polley the name is part of the national religious ideology of Judah. Interestingly, he does not develop the implications that this idea might have for his hypothesis in light of its repeated use in Amos (*Amos*, ch. 3, especially pp. 41-44; cf. T.N.D. Mettinger, 'YHWH SABAOTH—The Heavenly King on the Cherubim Throne', in *Studies in the Period of David and Solomon, and Other Essays* [ed. T. Ishida; Winona Lake, IN: Eisenbrauns, 1982], pp. 109-38).

time Bethel is mentioned, and its destruction is emphasized with the repetition of the removal of its altars.[1] What follows is the tearing down of the seasonal homes of the monarchy (3.15a),[2] and the luxurious and large (*rbym*) houses of those in power (3.14b),[3] of those who are perhaps behind the 'great (*rbwt*) tumults' of v. 9.

Because of 3.11 the demolition of the abodes of those who rule is not a complete shock, although the shift from royal buildings to personal property does work to narrow the focus of punishment. But what of Bethel? If the role of Bethel, however, as a shrine utilized to legitimate the northern regime is kept in mind (cf. 1 Kgs 12.25-33), a missing piece of our puzzle could fall into place.[4] The religious center forms part of the system and would play a key role in providing and propagating the divine seal of approval on the government and the public administration. The literary fact of the intertwining and constant juxtaposition throughout Amos of the sacred and the structural underscores that the book is describing a social construction of reality, a set of institutions, a religio-political 'world' within the textual world that is a fundamental object of Yahweh's punishment. Perhaps this observation can begin to explain the mention in 3.13 of the 'house of Jacob', a term which might point to broad participation in and an allegiance to the national ideology. More will become clearer later.

Yahweh singles out the horns of the altar (3.14c), for they are a

1. Several commentations wish to delete 3.14b, c and take the reference to Bethel as an intrusion into an oracle against Samaria (e.g. Willi-Plein, *Vorformen*, pp. 24-25; Wolff, *Amos*; Coote, *Amos*). For the change from the plural in v. 14b to the singular in v. 14c, see the comments by Soggin, *Amos*; Hayes, *Amos*.

2. S.M. Paul, 'Amos III 15—Winter and Summer Mansions', *VT* 28 (1978), pp. 358-60; King, *Amos*, pp. 64-65. The reference here is to the homes of the king, as the archaeological evidence shows, and does not extend to the rich class. Chávez understands the reference to be to different levels within the same house, so that in a merism the total destruction of the home is portrayed (*Modelo*, p. 70; cf. Harper, *Amos*).

3. Taking *rbym* as 'great' (cf. 3.10) not as 'many' (LXX). Among the translations that take this option—Eng.: RSV, NEB, NIV; Sp.: BLA. For archaeological data, see H.K. Beebe, 'Ancient Palestinian Dwellings', *BA* 32 (1968), pp. 38-58; King, *Amos*, pp. 61-64, 65-67.

4. An allusion to the Northern ideological system would make Polley's argument that the prophet is attacking more than ethical abuses more telling (Polley, *Amos*, ch. 5), yet he sees the Bethel reference as secondary (p. 96).

symbol of strength (cf. 1 Kgs 22.11) and could serve as a refuge for those guilty of violent crimes (cf. Exod. 21.14; 1 Kgs 2.28). But the nation's strength will be taken away (3.11b), and for the violence perpetrated by the system (3.10) there is now no escape and no hiding behind religion. This Yahweh—in contradistinction to the domesticated deity of the nation's version of ancient traditions (3.1-2) and of the sanctuary—will not be manipulated, nor be put at the service of the state. How is the destruction to be effected? By earthquake (considered by some to be the reference in 1.2; 4.11; 6.9-10; 9.1) or by invasion (3.6, 11)? Perhaps in context the latter is more likely. The *inclusio* with *n'm yhwh* (3.13, 15) once again gives an air of finality to the judgment. Yahweh has spoken.

The last strophe (4.1-3) continues to zero in on those in power in the capital city who live off of the nation's misery. The addressees of the imperative of *šm'* are specified, and the punishment moves from the destruction of the palaces/fortresses (3.11) and homes (3.15) to their very persons. These women, wives of officials, are called 'cows of Bashan' (4.1a), but again they are left nameless and attention is focused on their activity.[1] Even their characteristic oppressive behavior (note use of participles) in 4.1b is expressed in general t erms although the vocabulary echoes earlier verses that could fill in details (*dlym*, 2.7a; *'bywnym*, 2.6b; *'šq*, 3.9b). 4.1c is more explicit, and points to a system of values which longs to fulfill fleshly desires (cf. 6.6a; 2.8b): the juxtaposition of the mention of their sin (4.1b) and the call for drink (4.1c) signals the reader that enjoyment is grounded in extortion and that satiation ignores suffering. In a biting sarcastic description the leaders of Israel are seen to be at the beck

---

1. For *rṣṣ*, see Pons, *L'oppression*, pp. 91-94. For a good summary of suggestions as to the identity of the 'cows', see Hayes, *Amos*; Andersen and Freedman, *Amos* (cf. P.D. Miller, Jr, 'Animal Names as Designations in Ugaritic and Hebrew', *UF* 2 [1970], pp. 177-86). Calvin thought that the reference was to the judges, who were not worthy to be called men (J. Calvin, *A Commentary on the Twelve Minor Prophets*. II. *Joel, Amos & Obadiah* [Edinburgh: The Banner of Truth Trust, 1986]). Recently some have seen allusions here to the Baal cult: Neher, *Amos*, pp. 82-85; A.J. Williams, 'A Further Suggestion about Amos IV: 1-3', *VT* 29 (1979), pp. 206-11; H.M. Barstad, *The Religious Polemics of Amos: Studies in the Preaching of Am. 2, 7B-8; 4, 1-13; 5, 1-27; 6, 4-7; 8, 14* (VTSup, 34; Leiden: Brill, 1984), pp. 37-47; P.F. Jacobs, '"Cows of Bashan"—A Note on the Interpretation of Amos 4.1', *JBL* 104 (1985), pp. 109-10.

and call of their women; they are 'lords' who serve the appetites of their spouses.

For the first time in Amos, someone of the nation is directly quoted. This petition of indolent women is introduced, in line with the earlier verbs of 4.1b, by a participle.[1] This, therefore, is not an isolated request, but a constant one that marks their nature and lifestyle. This quote also sets the pattern for the rest of the book, for whenever others beside the prophet speak in this textual world they condemn themselves with their own words. Those who break into the steady condemnatory oracles of Yahweh only confirm their perversity and empty pretensions.

In sharp contrast to the 'lords' who bow to immoral requests sounds the 'Lord Yahweh'—the one who roars (3.8b) now swears in his holiness.[2] He communicates by the oath that his very person is offended by this corrupt world (4.2a). Therefore, he announces the days (cf. the 'day', 3.14a) of destructive invasion when the enemy will take these pampered women,[3] every last one,[4] like so many caught fish, into exile (4.2b-3).[5] The last verse paints a picture of city walls pierced and knocked down. The women march out single file through

---

1. For a discussion on how quotes are introduced in Amos, see Koch, *Amos*, pp. 130-31; Wolff, *Amos*, p. 97. On the switch to the use of the masculine suffix (*l'dnyhm*), see GKC 145p and R.J. Williams, *Hebrew Syntax: An Outline* (Toronto: University of Toronto Press, 2nd edn, 1976), p. 234. I suggest that this might be an instance of rhyming to maintain the *wt-ym* pattern of the previous line (cf. Watson, *Hebrew Poetry*, pp. 231-32).

2. Some commentators suggest eliminating *'dny* (e.g. Wolff, *Amos*; Markert, *Struktur*), yet stylistically the contrast between the 'lords' of 4.1 and the 'Lord God' of 4.2 is heightened by its inclusion. For oaths, see M.R. Lehmann, 'Biblical Oaths', *ZAW* 81 (1969), pp. 74-92. The introduction of an oath by *hnh* may signal emphasis (cf. Waltke–O'Conner, *Introduction*, 40.2.2b).

3. Understanding *nś'* as a piel. Among the translations that take this option— Eng.: RSV, NEB; Sp.: FC, BLA.

4. Taking *'ḥrytkn* as remnant or what is left (cf. Wolff, *La hora de Amoś*, pp. 112-15; Rudolph, *Amos*).

5. I follow the suggestion of some sort of fish imagery, although the lexical details are difficult (cf. S.M. Paul, 'Fishing Imagery in Amos 4.2', *JBL* 97 [1978], pp. 183-90). For good summaries of the options see Paul's article and Andersen and Freedman, *Amos*; for other summaries and views, see Soggin, *Amos*; Hayes, *Amos*. For the unique features of the LXX translation, see Wolff, *Amos*; and De Waard, 'Translation Techniques', p. 344.

the breaches to somewhere beyond the nation's borders.[1] Their world has collapsed: its palaces, their homes, their lives.

Conclusion and summary. This rather long sub-section (3.9–4.3), with its several strophes (3.9-11; 3.13-15; 4.1-3) and hinge verse (3.12), is not a loosely connected segment of independent pieces. It is a well-knit unit, but the integration is dynamic not static. Throughout the subsection the movement is to greater definition and more precision.

Coherence is evident, on the one hand, through structural markers and common vocabulary. Each strophe begins with an imperatival form of *šm'*, but whereas the first two (3.9, 13) are vague in their address, the last (4.1) strikes at the wives of those in power. The first two have parallel intent—indictment—but the last speaks most directly to the guilty.

The divine word appears in various forms throughout these verses, stressing the surety of judgment by interrupting verses (3.10), opening announcements (3.11, 12, 13), or marking finality through closure by *inclusio* (3.15; 4.3). Climactic movement is visible as the passage moves from an oracle tied to the deity's name and title (3.13) to an oath by his very person (4.2a). The day(s) which Yahweh proclaims (3.14a; 4.2a) will be one(s) of total devastation.

There is also a vocabulary of abuse that is repeated. Though at first those who commit the oppression (*'šq*) are not specified (3.9b), later they are revealed. The variety of terms describing the sins of the system and its rulers (3.9, 10; 4.1) is matched by the breadth of vocabulary depicting the devastation of the fortresses (3.11) and homes (3.12e, 15), as well as personal loss (4.2, 3).

Besides these more formal links, there are also powerful contrasts

---

1. Reading with the versions and most commentators, hophal of *šlk* (cf. Jer. 22.28). For good surveys of the possible meanings of *hhrmwnh*, see Harper, *Amos*; De Waard and Smalley, *Amos*; Hayes, *Amos* (although his suggestion to understand 'garbage heap' [N.H. Snaith, *Notes on the Hebrew Text of Amos* (2 vols.; London: Epworth Press, 1945; NEB] is precluded by De Waard and Smalley as poor translation technique (*Amos*, p. 234 n. 69). I prefer to understand the reference to be some place name. Because of its uncertain identity we are left with as vague a reference as in 5.27.

As some take the enemy to be Assyria, for Assyrian tactics in the breaching of walls, see Saggs, *The Might That Was Assyria*, pp. 260-61, and E. Bleibtren, 'Five Ways to Conquer a City', *BARev* 16.3 (1990), pp. 37-44.

by way of imagery that tie 3.9–4.3 together. This is a passage full of all kinds of sounds, all of them violent: the noise of oppression within the city (3.9-10) and of invading armies (3.11), the crashing of buildings and city walls (3.11, 14, 15; 4.3), the desolate silence of the march of the devastated into exile (4.3). Finally, there is the contrast between the marauding lion (3.12) and the satisfied cows of Bashan (4.1), who can only look forward to the slaughter.

The portrait that these verses present is, as the title to this whole section (3.1-4.3) suggested, two tales of one city. On one side, there is the perception of those who both run and profit from the system, a view which is communicated implicitly in the descriptions of behavior (3.9b-10; 4.1b) and by the quote of 4.1c. This is a capital of strong edifices and prosperity, with its supportive administrative and religious institutions. But this point of view is overturned and satirized: the palaces will be plundered, the cultic center destroyed, the homes demolished, and the guilty made to pay. Theirs is but the pretense of strength (3.11b) and the delusion of security (3.14b–4.3).

This 'natural order of things' stands not only condemned before the divine tribunal, as the passage's legal tone implies, but exposed in all of its sinful weakness before Yahweh (3.10, 12, 15; 4.3), Lord Yahweh (3.11; 4.2), Lord Yahweh God of Hosts (3.13)—the transcendent yet immanent deity. This is the vocabulary of what Sternberg labels the 'rhetoric of omnipotence and omniscience'.[1] Although the actors of the city remain nameless and their characteristic behavior is represented by participles, God's name comes in various forms and his activity is marked not by vague and iterative verbal forms, but by the decisive action of commanding and swearing, visiting and smiting. Even his agents (the prophets, the nations and the enemy) are not given much space. They are but instruments in his sovereign hands. This Yahweh offers, therefore, the other tale of this city; this is an irresistible point of view which those who inhabit the textual world and govern it must face at their peril.

3.9–4.3, however, is also connected in a number of ways with the introductory section, 3.1-8. Again, to begin with more formal markers, there is an overlap in vocabulary. 3.1 opens with an imperatival form of *šmʿ* addressed to the whole nation (and perhaps Judah). There is a progression then that indicts the people in

1. Sternberg, *Poetics of Biblical Narrative*, ch. 3 and *passim*.

general (3.1, 13, 14a) and the ruling elite in particular (3.12d; 4.1). In some way all are guilty, yet some are held more responsible, a tension which this reading will return to time and time again.

Mention has already been made of the importance of the divine word in 3.9–4.3. This is a key theme also in 3.1-8. The finality of Yahweh's announcement of judgment is increasingly emphasized, therefore, from 3.1 to 4.3. The object of punishment is also more defined: the trumpet sounds in the city (3.6, 9a), for it and all the land will be under attack (3.11a), but the particular targets are the palaces and homes of those that govern (3.11b, 15), the temple that legitimizes the oppressive system (3.14b, c), and the walls that protect this 'sinful' 'world' (4.3). In other words, the divine visitation (*pqd*, 3.2a) is specified more clearly, not only by the repetition of *pqd* in 3.14a but by the concatenation of oracles in 3.9–4.3.[1]

Finally the lion metaphor employed in 3.4 and again in 3.8 surfaces once more in 3.12. Although Yahweh is not explicitly mentioned in 3.12, the context leaves little doubt as to the lion's identity. But here, too, the imagery becomes more vivid. In 3.4(8) the lion signals its catching of the prey; in 3.12 the scene offers only the remains. Judgment will be terrible, but the rhetoric does not permit questioning whether it is deserved.

In sum, 3.1-8 raises the issues of conflicting understandings of Yahweh, the divine word, the city, imminent and total judgment, foreign invasion and national pretension, but does not present much detail. Rather that opening section serves to bring these items to the fore and to set the tone for the information of 3.9–4.3 that will begin to fill in the gaps. Stylistically, the main protagonists are set on the textual stage, and its world begins to take shape. The structure can be graphically portrayed then in the following manner:

---

1. In contrast to Gitay who takes this verb as an *inclusio* to mark the limits of the unit as 3.1-15, in 'A Study of Amos's Art of Speech', p. 295. His work claims that ch. 3 reflects an oral performance, but ignores that whatever the origin of the passage, it now forms part of the texture of a literary text.

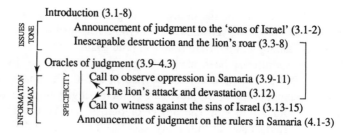

Introduction (3.1-8)

ISSUES TONE
    Announcement of judgment to the 'sons of Israel' (3.1-2)
    Inescapable destruction and the lion's roar (3.3-8)

Oracles of judgment (3.9–4.3)

INFORMATION CLIMAX   SPECIFICITY
    Call to observe oppression in Samaria (3.9-11)
    The lion's attack and devastation (3.12)
    Call to witness against the sins of Israel (3.13-15)
    Announcement of judgment on the rulers in Samaria (4.1-3)

b. *Love Can Be Blind* (4.4-13)

From the capital city, Samaria, attention now turns to two cult centers, Bethel and Gilgal. If read continuously after the preceding section, several connections are readily apparent through the technique of contrast. First, there are differences in time and place: the last strophe had predicted that those in power (in particular their wives) would be taken out to exile in the future (4.2, 3), while here there is the command to visit the cult places in the present; are those addressed the same? The women had earlier ordered their husbands to go get them drink (4.1c; *hby'h*); here sounds the divine directive to go (*b'w*) to the sanctuaries (4.4a) and bring (*hby'w*) their offerings (4.4b). In 3.14a Yahweh had visited Israel for its sins (*pš'*);here is an order to sin (repeated twice in 4.4a). Lastly, Bethel itself had been mentioned as a place to be destroyed along with the rulers' homes (3.14b-15); will the nuance of this wedding of interests be developed in these verses?

This passage will elaborate on the religious life of the Israel of this textual world in some detail. Sometimes the revelation will be direct and obvious, but there are also sides that surface by implication. The result will be more complexity for the reality within Amos.

Amos 4.4-5. At first glance, the imperatives of these verses are directed at those commanded last, the cows of Bashan (4.1). The directives in 4.4a are full of irony, as the addressees are ordered to go Bethel to sin and to Gilgal to multiply transgression. The repetition of the verb (*pš'*) and the addition of *hrbw* in the second colon serve to emphasize the true nature of the cultic activity. Religiosity is actually rebellion against God.[1]

1. For *bw'* as going to feasts see BDB 97. For *hrbw* see GKC 114n, n. 2. Note Coote's surprising unawareness of the poetics of 4.4: 'The call to worship at Bethel

Why are Bethel and Gilgal singled out? Each in its own way had been an important sanctuary in the canonical history.[1] Although Bethel reaches back into the patriarchal narratives (Gen. 28.10-22; 35.1-15), both had had significant roles to play in the national traditions. Gilgal was associated with the victorious conquest under Joshua (Josh. 3, 4) and was the place of the anointing of Saul, the first monarch of the twelve tribes (1 Sam. 11.15). Bethel was designated the principal national cultic center by Israel's first monarch, Jeroboam I. Both, in other words, symbolized divine promise and royal legitimacy.

The series of commands continues in 4.4b and instructs the pilgrims to go to the three great annual festivals[2] to offer the sacrifices on the

repeats the vague "transgress" with the colorless "transgress greatly"' (*Amos*, p. 77). A number of commentators take 4.4-5 to be a parody of a priestly call to worship on the basis of passages such as Ps. 95.1, 6; 100.1, 2, 4. Although that might be the case, the notion is not explicit in the text. This proposal, however, would add to the irony of my suggestion of the cultic personnel's stock in maintaining and fomenting religious activity.

1. For the biblical and archaeological data see Barstad, *Religious Polemics*, pp. 49-54; King, *Amos*, pp. 40-41. That the text is aware of and alludes to the patriarchal traditions is evident in the use of patriarchal names (e.g. Isaac, 7.9; Jacob, 3.13; 6.8; 7.2, 5; 8.7; Joseph, 5.6, 15; 6.6) and the mention of Sodom and Gomorrah (4.11). Other traditions alluded to include the exodus (2.10; 3.1; 4.10; 9.7), the wilderness (2.10; 5.26), and the conquest (2.9). No claims are made here, however, as to authorship, simply that these traditions form part of the theological world of the text. For the various theories regarding the traditions in Amos see Appendix 1. Note these recent ideas regarding the shrines' mention here: Hayes's historical reconstruction (*Amos*, p. 143)—competing national shrines (Bethel: Jeroboam II; Gilgal: Pekah); Polley (*Amos*, ch. 5)—only Jerusalem stands as a legitimate shrine over against those in the North; Andersen and Freedman (*Amos*, pp. 431-43)—Gilgal at this time may have been a shrine common to both Judah and Israel.

2. Several scholars have tried to relate 4.4-5 specifically to the autumn Feast of Booths in which the kingship of Yahweh is said to have been celebrated. Apparently Jeroboam I established a rival festival at Bethel in the eighth month to legitimate the new regime and win popular support (1 Kgs 12.25-33). His would have been an attempt to wed the royal coronation with the enthronement of Yahweh feast. For this view, yet with differing historical reconstructions, see J.D.W. Watts, *Vision and Prophecy in Amos* (Leiden: Brill, 1958), pp. 60-63; J. Gray, *The Biblical Doctrine of the Reign of God* (Edinburgh: T. & T. Clark, 1979), pp. 7-38, 134-39; Coote, *Amos*, pp. 53-58 (for 4.4-13); Hayes, *Amos* (also at 5.26). If this is the specific

morning of arrival and the tithes on the third day.[1] The kind of sacrifice is not specified,[2] but in light of the next verse the reference here is probably to the peace-offering, a sacrifice providing a banquet for the worshipper and the priest (cf. Lev. 3.1-17; 7.11-18, 28-36). This offering supposedly was to be a response to the peace and blessing sent by Yahweh. Yet, in light of 3.1–4.3 and the disapproving opening verse of this strophe (and the sufferings to be detailed in 4.6–11), there is no peace, there can be no blessing; indeed, the sword is about to fall. But not only is the worshipper involved in this pious delusion, the cult personnel are as well. Both benefit from the charade: the offerer confirms his 'reality' through ritual; the priest for his part receives his share, and so it behooves him to maintain the cultic fervor. The annual feasts were national events, and the private meals of communion before God and the public celebrations of his provision according to immemorial traditions would ratify the 'reality' of this world's making. Its natural goodness and divine necessity would thus settle into the national consciousness.

Verse 5 pushes the irony still further. The addressees are told to burn a thank-offering of leavened bread, which might be considered a direct countermand to cultic law (Lev. 2.11), whose mention could either reflect the loose fulfillment of regulations by the participants because of self-gratification or caprice, or sarcastically underscore the

festival in mind, then the notion that the text is attacking a national ideology sanctified by religion would thereby be strengthened. The vocabulary in 4.4-5, however, is too general to be dogmatic, but maybe is thus even more supportive, as then not only one feast alone but the whole cultic system would be involved in maintaining an erroneous social construction of reality. Andersen and Freedman suggest that there might be a connection between this passage and the celebration of military victory in 6.13. Although this again would make the critique of a religiously sanctioned national ideology more explicit and pointed, the wording is too vague. Polley would understand that behind the prophet's denunciation lies the conviction that only Jerusalem and the Davidic monarchy are legitimate (*Amos*, chs. 3, 5).

1.   Not reading the time annotations in a distributive sense (*contra* Williams, *Hebrew Syntax*, p. 103), which would require a different form. Cf. Wolff, *Amos*; Hayes, *Amos*; GKC 123c, 134q; Waltke–O'Conner, *Introduction*, 7.2.3b, 11.2.10c.

2.   For a good discussion of the various items mentioned in these two verses see H.H. Rowley, *Worship in Ancient Israel: Its Form and Meaning* (London: SPCK, 1967), ch. 4; H. Jagersma, 'The Tithes in the Old Testament', *OTS* 21 (1981), pp. 116-28.

inherent contradictions of the whole religious display itself.[1]

The last colon of 4.5a, however, begins to reveal more clearly the very heart of all the activity. The goal is the honoring of the worshippers, the publishing of piety. The travesty is unmasked both lexically and stylistically. On the one hand, they are to make known 'free-will offerings' (*ndbwt*), which were designed to reflect devotion to Yahweh (cf. Lev. 7.16; 22.18; Deut. 12.6-7), yet Yahweh ridicules their faithfulness to ritual. On the other hand, two different but parallel verbs envelope the term, overriding its true significance and thus reveal the worshipper's intent. What is yet more contradictory is that the worshippers are commanded to 'proclaim' (*hšmy'w*) their devotion to Yahweh while he calls for them to hear of their destruction (*šm'w*, 3.1; 4.1) and has their demise 'proclaimed' on the roof tops of surrounding nations (the same form as here, *hšmy'w*, 3.9), who are called to testify against Israel (*šm'w*, 3.13). In this list of religious activity no sacrifice for sin appears (even though the very act of worship was sin). There is no reflection or repentance, only good news and cheer.

The second line, however, reveals with yet more clarity the fundamental motivation: the love of liturgy (*ky kn 'hbtm*). The startling revelation is that the accused are the 'sons of Israel', the entire people and not just the rulers.[2] The religious institution thus has national

---

1. According to Lev. 7.11-14, the thank-offering (*zbḥ htwdh*) was to also include leavened bread, but apparently this would be for the meal and not to be burned (cf. *Mishnayoth* [ed. P. Blackman; Gateshead; Judaica Press, 1977], V: order *Kodashim*, tractate *Menachoth* 5.1, 2 and 7.1, 2 (pp. 121-22, 131-32, respectively). Some understand Lev. 7.13 as allowing the burning of leavened bread, so that no cultic violation is referred to. In either case, in context a thank-offering by sinful Israel is condemnable before God. Some commentators have suggested that the burning with leaven would be in imitation of Canaanite practices—therefore, another example of syncretism (e.g. S.R. Driver, *The Books of Joel and Amos* [The Cambridge Bible for Schools and Colleges; Cambridge: Cambridge University Press, 1907]; Harper, *Amos*; Cripps, *Amos*; Barstad, *Religious Polemics*, p. 55). To remove the reference to leavened bread on the basis of a privative *mn* (Snaith, *Notes*; among the translations—Eng.: NEB; Sp.: BLA) is to miss the force of the phrase.

2. Again, Andersen and Freedman consider 'sons of Israel' as a reference to both Israel and Judah, even in a context which continues to focus on the North. They do, however, admit the problem that the context creates for the theory (*Amos*, pp. 104-105).

commitment, its feasts national participation. Patronage is willful: *'hbtm* is the eighth verb after the seven commands and stands as their climax (7 + 1).[1] The object of divine sarcasm, therefore, is not only the addressees of 3.12 and 4.1, but the nation. This datum forces the reader to return to earlier passages and reconsider their possible import. Are the sins (*pš'*, 3.14a; 4.4a) which had been enumerated earlier—that is, the oppression and adherence to the national ideology—common to all the society of this textual world then, even though those in power are particularly responsible? Perhaps the second verse of our reading signalled this fact (*kl-'wntykm*, 3.2b). Could not the horns of the altar at the sanctuary at Bethel (3.14b, c) also symbolize as a consequence popular security and consensus, and not only the self-serving ideology of the social institutions? 3.9–4.3 had hinted that Yahweh was attacking the governmental system, but maybe this passage will broaden the target. The social and religiopolitical picture is becoming more complex.

Amos 4.6-13. The contrast between the description of 4.4-5 and the following verses could not be greater. The former strophe closes with an oracle formula with a longer name of God (*'dny yhwh*; cf. 3.8, 11; 4.2), marking the seriousness of the guilt and affront, and is succeeded by a *waw* adversative, *gm* intensive, and the first personal pronoun: 'But yet/indeed I...'[2] At the same time, a shortened form of the oracle of 4.5b will become the refrain of the next verses. There is both contrast, therefore, and continuity.

4.6-11 is a very artistically arranged piece. Five times the refrain *wl'-šbtm 'dy n'm yhwh* is repeated, and there are seven first person verbs with *km*-suffix forms.[3] This literary art highlights the dif-

---

1. Limburg, 'Sevenfold Structures', p. 220.

2. For intensive *gm* see GKC 153; Williams, *Hebrew Syntax*, p. 379; Waltke–O'Conner, *Introduction*, 39.3.4d. Note especially the following translations—Eng.: NEB ('It was I'), Sp.: RVA ('Por mi parte, yo'). A number of critics, however, remove *wgm 'ny* (e.g. Willi-Plein, *Vorformen*; Wolff, *Amos*; Markert, *Struktur*) as simply a redactional addition to tie 4.4-5 and 4.6-11 together. Note Rosenbaum's explanation of the usage of the first person pronouns in Amos according to dialect tendencies (*Amos*, pp. 92-93).

3. Note especially Gese, 'Komposition', pp. 85-86; Limburg, 'Sevenfold Structures', p. 220. Gordis also mentions the number seven, but of the kinds of disasters in 4.6-11, not verbal forms ('Studies', pp. 221-22). Note the observations on

ference and distance between Yahweh ('I') and the nation ('you'). It is a litany of disasters and failed perception, of divine intervention and human refusal to respond.[1] In the movement through the verses there is a building of intensity that is expressed in regard to content and style with the climax at the personal encounter with the Creator (4.12-13).[2]

Verse 6, in addition to the emphatic *wgm-'ny*, underlines the disparity between Yahweh's and Israel's activity by opposing ideas: he

---

the plays of sound in 4.6-11 that also tie the passage together by J.L. Crenshaw, 'A Liturgy of Wasted Opportunity (Am. 4.6-12; Isa. 9.7-10.4, 5.25-29)', *Semitics* 1 (1970), p. 32.

1. There have been several hypotheses regarding some sort of liturgical background to 4.4-13 or 4.6-13. Besides the view of an autumn Feast of Booths festival noted above at 4.4-5, these would include the following: (1) J.L. Crenshaw, 'A Liturgy' (cf. Soggin); (2) some sort of covenant renewal: H.G. Reventlow, *Das Amt des Propheten bei Amos* (FRLANT, 80; Göttingen: Vandenhoeck & Ruprecht, 1962), pp. 75-90; W. Brueggemann, 'Amos IV 4-13 and Israel's Covenant Worship', *VT* 15 (1965), pp. 1-15; (3) covenant lawsuit: Boyle, 'The Covenant Lawsuit', and G.W. Ramsey, 'Amos 4.12—A New Perspective', *JBL* 89 (1970), pp. 187-91; (4) unspecified: Mays, *Amos*; (5) Josiah's destruction of the Bethel altar (2 Kgs 23.15-20): Wolff, *Amos* (yet note Rudolph's criticisms in 'Amos 4, 6-13', in *Wort-Gebot-Glaube: Beiträge zur Theologie des Alten Testaments. Walther Eichrodt zum 80. Geburtstag* [ed. J. Stamm, E. Jenni and H.J. Stoebe; ATANT, 59; Zürich: Zwingli Verlag, 1970], pp. 27-38; and Markert, *Struktur*, p. 124). My discussion here, however, looks at the literary connections instead of possible backgrounds, which would be very hard to reconstruct.

Several attempts are made to pinpoint the references of 4.6-11: (1) specific historical events: e.g. Harper, *Amos*; (2) covenant curses: e.g. Reventlow, *Das Amt*; Brueggemann, 'Amos IV 4-13'; Wolff, *Amos*; Coote, *Amos*, p. 79; Stuart, *Hosea–Jonah*; (3) typical disasters of the region: e.g. Vollmer, *Rückblicke*, pp. 15-20; Rudolph, 'Amos 4, 6-13'; Mays, *Amos*. The last position is taken here. Although Andersen and Freedman also take these disasters as typical, they specifically try to find a correspondence with the visions of Amos, chs. 7–9 (*Amos*, pp. 445-47).

2. Several authors deny any building of intensity. For instance, Reventlow: 'In dem Abschnitt V. 6-11 herrscht dagegen das vollkommene Gleichmass, fast die Monotonie' (*Das Amt*, p. 84) Mays: 'There is no perceptible development in the sections, no heightening of the disasters' intensity. Each is terrible in its own right, no worse than the previous one. The sequence gains its effect from repetition, the recollection of one disaster after another as though the narrative meant to exhaust the catalogue of human misery' (*Amos*, p. 78). Most commentators, however, do see a heightening. My reading suggests that the increase is reflected not only in the kind of disaster, but also in the poetics of the passage.

'gave' (*ntty*) them hunger, they bring him sacrifices (4.5a—peace offerings: communal banquets); they come in pilgrimages to the sanctuaries (4.4a), but never 'return' to him; the nation as a whole gathers to celebrate its blessings at the public festivals, while he gave them want in 'all' (*kl*) their cities and 'all' (*kl*) their places (cf. the multiple use of *kl* in the announcement of judgment in 3.1-2). The hunger that the nation had to have experienced is stressed not only by the repetition of *kl*, but also by the double description, the first a powerful metaphor ('cleanness of teeth').[1]

Verse 7 repeats the *wgm* but changes the form of the personal pronoun, thus repeating the contrastive technique of 4.6 but with a stylistic variation.[2] The descriptions of vv. 7 and 8 emphasize the completeness of the new disaster but in a different way than the previous verse. Here the impact on the entire country is communicated by the alternation between field and city:

4.7a	field:	rain withheld before the harvest (disaster)
b	city:	uneven rainfall among the cities (disaster)
a′	field:	uneven rainfall, crops withered (disaster + result)
4.8b′	city:	people wandered, were not satisfied (result)

For some critics the length of these lines has been problematic,[3] but the wordiness can actually be a signal of rhetorical effect. Note the second half of v. 7:

city:	verb + (prep. +) object	(prep. +) object + verb [chiasm]
field:	subject + verb	subject + relative clause + verb

The tidy staccato sequence is broken by the relative clause, and the first result of the lack of rain appears. Verse 8 also is long; before the refrain appears a two member subject, two finite verbs, and an

---

1. Rudolph's comment is interesting: 'Der Ausdruck bittern Galgenhumors' (*Amos*, p. 32). For a comment on the LXX translation ('toothaches') see De Waard, 'Translation Techniques', p. 349.

2. Again, as in 4.6, some scholars would omit *wgm* + pronoun: e.g. Willi-Plein, *Vorformen*, p. 27; Wolff, *Amos*; Markert, *Struktur*.

3. For arguments to remove parts of vv. 7, 8 (although these scholars do not agree on exactly which) see Amsler, *Amos*; Willi-Plein, *Vorformen*, pp. 27-28; Vollmer, *Rückblicke*, p. 10; Rudolph, *Amos*; Markert, *Struktur*. On the other hand, note Andersen and Freedman's defense of the passage's authenticity (*Amos*, pp. 438-39). Regarding the interpretation of the imperfects in 4.7-8, see especially Waltke–O'Conner, *Introduction*, 32.2.3e.

infinitive construct. The verb sequence is also marked by assonance: *l štwt mym wlw yśb'w*. 4.7c-8 stylistically stretch out the consequences of the divine action. Not only is the harvest ruined, the sons of Israel are forced into a suffering quest for water. What had been captured in 4.6 by *kl* is expressed in 4.7-8 by artistic expansion.

Verse 9 demonstrates the divine emphasis in still a different manner. As in the previous verses, 4.9 begins with a first person singular verb form but then follows with a series of four affected areas, the first headed by *hrbwt*. The irony should not be lost either: they multiply sin (*hrbw*, 4.4a), even as their multiple gardens were devoured.[1] Surprisingly, the sequence ends with another agent, the locust. Emphasis, then, is communicated by repetition and an *inclusio* of destructive agents, as it were (Yahweh smote, the locust devoured). Once more, the stylistics effects completeness.

The next verse offers yet another way of underscoring the breadth of the divine visitation. Whereas 4.6-9 speaks of extreme want, 4.10 describes violent death. Three first person verbs are used in series. The first could likely allude to the final plague in Egypt, the death of all the firstborn (Exod. 11.4-7; 12.29-30).[2] Once more Egypt surfaces: no longer to serve the redemptive exodus tradition (2.10; 3.1), or even to function as Yahweh's witnesses (3.9, 13), but rather as a paradigm of judgment.

A connection between the death of the Egyptian firstborn and Israel's young fighting men is afforded by a possible wordplay (*bhwr* and *bkwr*).[3] Defeat is total, encompassing the army and its chariots (cf. 2.15; 6.12),[4] and the impression is heightened by the assonance

1. Most commentators and translations emend the hiphil infinitive construct (*hrbwt* from *rbh*) of the MT to the hiphil perfect first person singular *hḥrbty* (from *ḥrb*). Our discussion maintains the MT. One option has been to take the form as equivalent to the infinitive absolute of *rbh* (*hrbh*) and thus adverbially ('I smote you. . . repeatedly' or 'repeatedly. . . devoured'). Others take the form as a substantive to refer to the 'increase', i.e., harvest (Keil, *Minor Prophets*; Stuart, *Hosea–Jonah*; Hayes, *Amos*), or as an adjective to the 'many' gardens (Smith, *Amos*; Sp. translations: BLA, RVA).

2. Other options include a general reference to the plagues of Egypt or to the fifth in particular. It should be noted that a number of scholars consider the phrase an addition—e.g. Cripps, *Amos*; Willi-Plein, *Vorformen*, p. 28; Markert, *Struktur*.

3. Suggested by Rudolph in 'Amos 4, 6-13' (p. 33) and in his commentary.

4. The phrase *'m šby swsykm* has been understood or emended in several ways (see Rudolph, *Amos*; De Waard and Smalley, *Amos*) and has been considered a

(*hrgty bḥrb bḥwrykm*). The visual imagery is powerful in the last line, where dead men rot in the battlefield. Yahweh himself causes the stench to rise and emphatically says 'even to your nostrils'.[1] Completeness, therefore, in 4.10 is articulated by the chain of verbs, the nature of the final plague, and the violence of the war scene. The last of the series appears in 4.11. In this verse a verb important to chs. 5 and 6 makes its initial appearance. The root *hpk* is utilized twice here, initially in the first person to parallel the forms in the preceding verses and then in quick sequence in substantival form in a proverbial expression describing the destruction of Sodom and Gomorrah (cf. Gen. 19.21, 25, 29; Deut. 29.23 [Heb. 29.22]; Isa. 13.19; Jer. 49.18; 50.40).[2] The repetition of the root with the comparative *k* connects that tradition with Yahweh's activity within Israel's recent history and implies a correspondence not only of miraculous judgment but also of sinful character. Emphasis in this final item is more thematic, echoing as it does the total annihilation of the cities of the plain. Some were saved (an allusion to Lot and his

gloss by many (see especially the list of reasons by Willi-Plein, *Vorformen*, pp. 28-29). My reading understands the Hebrew to read 'along with the capture of your horses' and to refer to the giving of the horses as booty to the enemy. According to Stephanie Dalley, Israel was famous for its chariots, and in fact Israelite mercenaries later served in the chariot corps of Sargon II ('Foreign Chariotry and Calvary in the Armies of Tiglat-Pileser III and Sargon II', *Iran* 47 [1985], pp. 31-48). Cf. King, *Amos*, pp. 83-87; Saggs, *The Might That Was Assyria*, p. 244.

1. Understanding the *waw* on *b'pkm* as *waw explicativum* (GKC 154a, n. 1; Waltke–O'Conner, *Introduction*, 39.2.1b.). Note Moshe Weinfeld's exposition of ancient Near Eastern and biblical vocabulary used to describe God's help in war; in the chapters of Amos under study, however, all this is turned on its head as Yahweh fights against Israel ('Divine Intervention in War in Ancient Israel and in the Ancient Near East', in *History, Historiography and Interpretation: Studies in Biblical and Cuneiform Literature* [ed. H. Tadmor and M. Weinfeld; Jerusalem; Magnes Press, 1986], pp. 121-47). For plagues (4.10), p. 129; fire (5.6), pp. 131-36; torrents of water (5.8), p. 137. Cf. Younger, *Ancient Conquest Accounts*.

2. Some scholars suggest an emendation (note *BHS*) or that something has fallen out (e.g. Vollmer, *Rückblicke*, p. 12; Rudolph, *Amos*; Soggin, *Amos*). Stylistically, the present arrangement leaves the kind of 'overthrowing' vague and focuses rather on the parallel between Israel and Sodom and Gomorrah and on the fact of the totality of judgment. Some suggest an earthquake here, which is of course possible, but not explicit in the text. Gen. 19 speaks of fire from heaven (19.24-25)—fire sent by Yahweh is a judgment theme in Amos (e.g. 1.4, 7, 10, 12, 14; 2.2, 5, 6; 7.4).

family?), but as in 3.12 *nṣl* is used for expressing those few who are 'rescued' only after passing through terrible destruction.

The entire sequence moves to a climax in 4.12. Although some might consider the wording of the first line cumbersome,[1] stylistically the effect can be compelling. *Lkn kh*, as elsewhere in the chapters under consideration, points forward to an announcement of judgment or disaster (cf. 3.11; 5.16). The second half of this line, instead of specifying the punishment, however, repeats the same verb and preposition + personal suffix combination, changing only the introductory preposition phrase (*'qb ky-zwt*). The repetition of the verb and its object ('you') with 'Israel' placed in the middle of the two cola of 4.12a focuses attention on the two protagonists: Yahweh versus Israel.[2] What is more, 'Because I will do this to you' is ambiguous. Although reinforcing that the issue rests between the two principal characters (as indeed throughout 4.6-11), the colon develops suspense by postponing definition. What is 'this'? Will it be more of the same suffered in 4.6-11? The reader must push on.

Israel (note the repetition in 4.12b of the second person suffix and 'Israel' for even more emphasis) is told to prepare to meet its God. Yet the ambivalence apparently continues. *Hkwn lqr't*, on the one hand, echoes the language of the Sinai tradition and has led several scholars to propose that this is a call to covenant renewal;[3] but this is also vocabulary that speaks of war preparations.[4] Which will it be— renewed communion or hostile confrontation? The passage does not say explicitly, but the answer is implied: (a) this is a summons to meet

1. For good recent surveys regarding how the first line in 4.12 has been taken by scholars, see P. Carny, 'Doxologies—A Scientific Myth', *HebSt* 18 (1977), pp. 150-52; A.V. Hunter, *Seek the Lord! A Study of the Meaning and Function of the Exhortation in Amos, Hosea, Isaiah, Micah, and Zephaniah* (Baltimore: St Mary's Seminary and University, 1982), pp. 115-18; Polley, *Amos*, pp. 145-47. Andersen and Freedman take the verbs as preterites and, on the basis of the observation that of the seven uses of the term *z't* in Amos all but one refer back to a previous statement, contend that in 4.12a the judgments of 4.6-11 are meant (*Amos*, pp. 450-52).

2. A stylistic explanation of the repetitiveness for rhetorical impact seems a better explanation than the idea of scribal conflation of variant readings (Gordis, 'Studies', pp. 222-24; Hayes, *Amos*).

3. E.g. Brueggeman, 'Amos IV 4-13'; Crenshaw, 'A Liturgy'.

4. See Carny, 'Doxologies'; Hunter, *Seek the Lord!*, pp. 118-21; and among recent commentaries, especially Hayes, *Amos*; Smith, *Amos*.

the same *'lhym* who overturned Sodom and Gomorrah in the preceding verse (is the repetition of the divine name mere coincidence?); (b) the nation has continually refused to return to him in the past (4.6-11); (c) their understanding of what it means to meet him at the festivals is only so much sin (4.4-5); and (d) the first section of this reading (3.1–4.3) left little doubt that the meeting with Yahweh the lion would be a terrifying encounter. But still, the possibility of a change in the character of the nation and thus some chance of a stay of execution might remain open. Perhaps the key lies, therefore, in v. 13.

In an interesting twist the *ky hnh* that opens 4.13 is not the beginning of an announcement of judgment as in 4.2a, but rather a phrase that dramatically focuses the attention on the God whom Israel must meet.[1] As in 4.12a an introductory formula usually utilized for a declaration of judgment instead serves to turn attention to the deity. Once more the poetics generate impact. First, five participles (once again the number five—a play on the refrain?) are used to depict the activity of Yahweh. There are two pairs of participles describing the transcendent power of Yahweh that ring a single one that speaks of man— or better, of Yahweh's relation to man. The structure, therefore, centers the interest there. Indeed, the whole passage of 4.6-11 has concentrated on the people, while nature has been but the instrument used in Yahweh's hands to force their return to him.

The content of this central colon actually parallels the intent of 4.6-11, even as its location emphasizes its importance. Yahweh has revealed more than his own 'thought' to man;[2] he has communicated

---

1. 4.13 is usually considered as a hymn or hymn fragment. As Hayes says, the three key issues are: (1) its relationship to the other hymnic passages (5.8-9; 9.5-6); (2) the authenticity of these verses; and (3) the function of these verses in their present context. For good surveys of the literature see Watts, *Vision*, ch. 3 (who also offers his own unique reworking of the passages); the excursus in Mays (*Amos*, pp. 83-84); Wolff (*Amos*, pp. 215-17); Smith (*Amos*, pp. 140-41). For a recent defense of the authenticity of these passages, see T.E. McComiskey, 'The Hymnic Elements of the Prophecy of Amos: A Study of Form-Critical Methodology', in *A Tribute to Gleason Archer* (ed. W.C. Kaiser and R. Youngblood; Chicago: Moody Press, 1986), pp. 105-28. McComiskey interacts extensively with the conclusions of J.L. Crenshaw, '*YHWH ṣᵉbā'ôt šᵉmô*: A Form-Critical Analysis', *ZAW* 81 (1969), pp. 156-75. The interest of my reading lies in (3), the present literary function of the material.

2. Some commentators understand the suffix *w* ('his') to refer to man: Keil,

his 'complaint',[1] his dissatisfaction at Israel's stubborn rebellion (contrast 3.7). The participle (hiphil, *ngd*) rounds out the picture of God offered by the other four of this verse: sovereign and incomparably powerful, yet immanent and ever-visible in his creation. The nation has been constant in their refusal (fivefold refrain); Yahweh in his self-revelation (five participles).

The participle pairs that surround this colon show movement, and Yahweh's complaint serves as a hinge. The first two participles of the verse begin by describing his might as creator of the mountains and wind,[2] but, after the words regarding man, the last two depict the ominous potential of this power. There is the overturning of light to darkness. Even though the verb used here is '*sh* and not *hpk* as in 4.11 (*hpk* will be used, however, in 5.8), the nature of the reversal bodes ill. In addition, his 'treading on the high places of the earth' perhaps signals the coming of the divine judge to the encounter with his people (cf. Mic. 1.3-6). Indeed, he has already come to them in destructive power in the past! The contrast in context between Yahweh's decisive movement with the nation's staggering (4.8) and stubbornness (the refrain: 'did not return') underlines his absolute sovereignty.

Verse 13 closes with *yhwh 'lhy-ṣb'wt šmw*. Several observations are in order. First, the deity's names have been repeated throughout the entire passage: *yhwh* in the refrain (six times if 4.5b is included), *'lhym* three times in 4.11, 12; here another fuller name and title stand as a climax to the section. Secondly, as in 3.1–4.3, the guilty of Israel are nameless and the focus is on their sinful behavior. In contradistinction, here, too, multiple divine names and titles appear, and now even the 'name' is highlighted as key. Lastly, a bit longer formulation of the name and title were utilized in 3.13 in the introduction to a judgment oracle, so the repetition at this point most likely is not mere

---

Minor Prophets; Driver, *Amos*; Cripps, *Amos*; Rudolph, *Amos*; Smith, *Amos*; Sp. translation: FC. For the LXX translation 'his Messiah' and its impact among the Church Fathers, see Martin-Achard, *Amos*, pp. 202-206.

1. A hapax legomenon *śh* for *śyḥ*. For my translation as 'complaint' see, e.g., the use in 1 Sam. 1.16; Job 7.13; 9.27; 10.1; 21.4; 23.2.

2. Translating 'wind' for *rwḥ* not (human) 'breath', *contra* Wolff, *Amos*; Stuart, *Hosea–Jonah*; Carny, 'Doxologies', p. 155. There might be rhetorical impact, however, in the ambiguity: the One who creates the wind/man's spirit has revealed his complaint to man (again, the transcendence–immanence interplay). The ambiguity could serve as a transition to the following colon.

coincidence, but rather a purposeful reminder.

This final verse brings 4.4-13 to a dramatic close and underlines the fact that Yahweh himself is the issue at stake. The passage conveys in various ways his ubiquitous presence in Israel's *Unheilsgeschichte*. He was to have been encountered in their history time and time again, but the sons of Israel refused to return to him. Instead, they came and sought Yahweh in sanctuaries and feasts, in the liturgical calendar and not in the fabric of national life and existence. Seemingly in the nation's mind, Yahweh had made his appearance (redemptive, to be sure—3.1) in the past. But Yahweh is not now present in their brand of yahwism, and so now he calls them to a face-to-face encounter. All of the religious activity has neither realized Yahweh's approbation nor prepared them to meet him. Each of the disasters in 4.6-11 expresses completeness in its own fashion, and the movement from widespread hunger and thirst (4.6-8), to the total destruction of property (4.9), to horrendous loss on the battlefield (4.10), to the allusion to fire from heaven (4.11), forces the reader to fear an even more violent meeting with God.

Summary and conclusion. How can the world described in 4.4-13 complement that of 3.9–4.3? Whereas 3.9–4.3 had emphasized in detail the destruction of edifices and the fate of the powerful in the future, this section speaks of national disasters in the past and refers to a future encounter with Yahweh only in vague, although impressive, terms. Each, in other words, appears to offer not a different version of Israel's history, but instead focuses on different slots on the time line. At the same time, however, the descriptions of the present are dissimilar, though not disparate. 3.9–4.3 pictured in particular the injustice within Samaria with only a brief mention (3.14b, c) of Bethel; 4.4-5 picks up the allusion and provides a fuller depiction of the sphere of religious activity.

On the one hand, this entire passage undermines the religious realm. In 4.4-5 the festivals and offerings are said to be sin and to be motivated by conceit and self-gratification. The sacrifices that are mentioned are those that express gratitude for divine blessing and protection, yet 4.6-11 put the lie to that misconception of Yahweh's involvement in the national history by recounting a different story of a series of comprehensive disasters from his hand. If the exodus tradition is turned against Israel in 3.2, here the nation is made one with Sodom and Gomorrah. If 4.11c does refer to Lot, even in an oblique manner, the patriarchal tradition as well is turned on its head. To use the language of 4.13, their light he turns into darkness. If in 3.9–4.3 the reality constructed by Israel is to be destroyed, here it is held up to satiric ridicule; if in 4.1 the words placed on the lips of the women are self-condemning and inappropriate, here the religious discourse is revealed as thoroughly inadequate. Yahweh will not respond to all the noise and bustle of the feasts. He, however, speaks continually and forcefully in condemnation (*n'm yhwh*), as the delusion of communion must give way to the ominousness of confrontation.

In addition, 4.4-13 adds new dimensions to the religious world of Amos. To begin with, these verses do not allow the simple equation popular religion = the religion of only the masses. There is overlap, as both those who are in power (3.9–4.3) and the broader populace use and need Bethel (and Gilgal). These are sanctuaries common to the breadth of the society. Secondly, the passage would undercut the tidy notion of organized religion = the official religion sponsored by the state. Again there is overlap, because the cult centers can have a number of functions that once more cut across class lines. In the reading thus far, religion can apparently serve to support the regnant ideology as well as nurture a broader misconception of God and faith that embraces more than the state: the government can no longer claim divine help on the battlefield (4.10), it is true; but neither can the common man hold to a Yahweh of never-ending provision (4.6-9). National faith is more than politics. In other words, this is a world of religious complexity, where different interests interweave and can feed on an organized cult in any number of ways.

But the religious labyrinth perhaps can contain yet still another aspect. Why do these verses hit so hard at the issue of rain and fertility (4.6-8)? Why does v. 13 use the phrase 'on the heights of the earth', words that can refer to other sanctuaries (cf. 7.9)?[1] Is there another religious realm that lurks in the background that also constrains Yahweh to stress his nature and name?

Many scholars hold that Amos, in contrast to Hosea, denounces

---

1. J.L. Crenshaw, '*W^{e}dōrēk 'al-bām^{o}tê 'āreṣ*', *CBQ* 34 (1972), pp. 42-44. Cf. Watts, *Vision*, pp. 60-64; Wolff, *Amos*; Rudolph, *Amos*. Most uses of *bmh* do refer to cultic high places (BDB 119, KB 132).

injustice and an inadequate worship of Yahweh, but not pagan ritual.[1]
In its final form, nevertheless, the datum is there, however vague the
references and difficult the exegesis (cf. 5.26; 8.14).[2] Certainly other
gods are not the prime target of these verses as some have claimed.[3]
But the allusions do give the impression that there is a dark underside
to Israel's faith that contributes to its distorted views on God, life, and
history; that a Yahwistic monotheism must do battle against popular
monolatry. Indeed, later 8.11-14 will describe another kind of
wandering (cf. 4.8), more profound, when still the nation will refuse
to return to Yahweh and instead turn to other gods.[4] In a manner
similar to the structure of the passage here, the vision (9.1-4) that
follows that oracle describes a more terrible judgment and is also
followed by a 'hymn' to the one whose 'name' is Yahweh (9.5-6). In
8.11–9.6 there is no sustained suspense as here in 4.12-13, just
devastating finality.

Amos describes a 'world' within its world, only to destroy it. Piece
by piece, the picture of the nation's world takes shape and then the
divine word dismantles its pretension and delusion. Each of the sections (3.1–4.3; 4.4-13) contributes to a portrait of a reality condemned, of a socially constructed world under severe indictment.
Verses 12 and 13 do leave open, however, perhaps some glimmer of
hope, although another encounter, more terrible than those in the past,
seems imminent. Yahweh has rejected the religion Israel loves, for
this love is blind.

1.   Koch's comment can be taken as typical: 'What Amos attacks are not idola-
trous cultic practices, or the number of altars everywhere in the country—as his
contemporary Hosea does. The objects of his polemic are practices which, in the
opinion of his listeners, were absolutely enjoined by Yahweh on every Israelite. . . '
(*The Prophets*. I. *The Assyrian Period* [trans. M. Kohl; Philadelphia: Fortress Press,
1983], p. 52). Others, such as Wolff (*Amos*), allow for references to pagan rituals
in the text but will date them later.

2.   See the references and discussion in the section entitled 'Moral Life in
Ancient Israel and the Problem of the Text' in Chapter 3.

3.   For 4.4-13 see especially Barstad, *Religious Polemics*, pp. 54-75. On 4.12
see Ramsey, 'Amos 4.12'; R. Youngblood, '*lqr't* in Amos 4.12', *JBL* 90 (1971),
p. 98.

4.   See especially Barstad, *Religious Polemics*, ch. 6. Most recent commentators
see a reference to pagan gods in 8.14 (although some hold the verse to be an addition). Hayes is more of an exception, but he understands the verse in a way congruous with his historical reconstruction (*Amos*).

The point of view of 4.4-13 has been consistent and exclusive. Yahweh presents his case in such a way as to leave no doubt as to the nation's guilt. There is no response by Israel except that of the sequence in 4.6-11 ('but you did not return to me') and no expression of personal feeling beyond the phrase 'for so you love to do' in 4.5b. As in 3.1–4.3, therefore, the text allows only a rhetoric of divine omniscience and omnipotence that works to develop a rhetoric of entrapment. Israel both stands guilty and convicts itself. In contrast to that earlier piece, however, the description of characteristic behavior is handled differently: Israel's constant activity is expressed not through participles but by repetition (the series of verbs in 4.4-5, the refrain sequence of 4.6-11), whereas Yahweh's is through both repetition and participles.

This section can be outlined in the following way:

Divine parody of Israel's religiosity (4.4-5)	Delusion
Divine explosure of Israel's obduracy (4.6-11)	
Divine encounter with Israel (4.12-13)	Direct

c. *What Is in a Name? (5.1-17)*

This next section will provide a definitive answer to the touch of ambiguity that remained with 4.12-13. What the encounter with Yahweh will signify for the nation will be developed in very graphic terms. This piece will also continue to clarify the reality and characters denounced by God.

5.1-17 has been the object of several structural studies. My reading will follow the suggestion initially made by De Waard and seconded and expanded by Tromp that this passage forms a chiasm with its center at 5.8d, 'Yahweh is his name' (*yhwh šmw*).[1] The placement of

---

1. De Waard, 'The Chiastic Structure of Amos V 1-17', *VT* 27 (1977), pp. 170-77 (cf. De Waard and Smalley, *Amos*, pp. 189-92); Tromp, 'Amos V 1-17'. Tromp elaborates on what he considers the evidence for redactional work in the finished piece. Mention should be made of Donald W. Wicke, who juxtaposes the structural effort by De Waard and the form-critical method of Mays and Wolff, in 'Two Perspectives (Amos 5.1-17)', *CurTM* 13 (1986), pp. 89-96. Cf. Coote, *Amos*, pp. 79-82. Others who see a chiasm in 5.1-17, but who would eliminate 5.8, 13 in order to place the theme of justice in the center, include Coulot, 'Propositions pour une structuration', pp. 179-80 (center at 5.10); Sicre, *'Con los pobres'*, pp. 122-23 (at 5.7, 10-12). J. Lust tries to demonstrate a chiasm extending over 4.1–6.7, whose center is 5.7, 10-12 ('Remarks on the Redaction of Amos V 4-6,

this 'hymn' at this juncture seems illogical to many commentators and so has fostered several theories as to the order of the strophes,[1] but this chiasm proposal reveals its present literary sense. This section of Amos reflects not only this overall chiastic shape, but also numerous other internal connections which contribute to its impressive poetics. Up until this point the schematic outlines have come at the close of the discussions. Due to the chiastic structure of the passage, however, the diagram will come first and will be developed in the exposition.

> a (1-3) Lament for Israel
>   b (4-6) Seek Yahweh and live
>   c (7) Warning to Israel
>   d (8a, b, c) The power of Yahweh to create
>   e (8d) 'Yahweh is his name'
>   d′ (9) The power of Yahweh to destroy
>   c′ (10-13) Warning to the powerful
>   b′ (14-15) Seek Yahweh and live
> a′ (16-17) Lament for Israel

a: Amos 5.1-3. The opening verse begins just as 3.1, 'Hear this word' + relative clause, but the words that follow form a sharp change in tone. Yahweh now lifts a lament over the nation, the 'house of Israel'.[2] What is interesting is that this fact is expressed by the par-

14-15', *OTS* 21 [1981], pp. 153-54 n. 103).

   1. For an overview of other theories of composition, see Hunter, *Seek The Lord!*, pp. 56-60; Sicre, '*Con los pobres*', pp. 122-23. Studies not mentioned in those surveys would include the proposals by Gese, 'Kleine Beiträge', pp. 432-36; Vermeylen, 'Les relectures deutéronomistes', pp. 548-54; Spreafico, 'Amos: Struttura Formales', pp. 156-59. More recently, Andersen and Freedman do not even mention the chiasm proposal and also are a bit perplexed as to the placement of the 'hymn' here (*Amos*).

   2. For information on mourning in the Old Testament, see G. Stahlin, '*Kopetos*', *TDNT*, III, pp. 836-41. My reading understands the lament as Yahweh's not as the prophet's. Verse 3 with its opening formula is just the second movement of these opening words (cf., e.g., Mays, *Amos*). This is clearly the position of the LXX as evident in the addition *Kuriou*. In addition, as was mentioned earlier, the prophet(s) are absent from view after 3.7 until the visions of chs. 7–9. Lastly, comparison with 3.1 (*šm'w 't-dbr hzh 'šr dbr yhwh 'lykm bny yśr'l*) might suggest that the verb announcing chastisement has been turned here into a lament. Thus understood, the text maintains the confrontation as directly between Yahweh and Israel. Tromp would also claim that the lament is intensified by the rhythm and sound of 5.2. For this observation and similar ones about possible assonance

ticiple (*nś'*). The immediately preceding verse 4.13, as might be recalled, contained five participles depicting Yahweh, his power and his activity. Could this lament then be related to his characteristic activity (note also the personal pronoun as here in 4.6, 7), or at least as not only raised because of some future disaster, but as reaching back as well into the past and including the present? 4.6-11 (cf. 3.12; 4.2) had in fact mentioned death several times, and now the inescapable impression is that what awaits Israel is more loss of life. The threatening vein of 4.12-13 is thus confirmed, and any suspense in those lines is apparently ended.

5.2 forcefully underlines that the nation is already dead in several ways. To begin with, the meter is the 3 + 2 of laments, but other stylistics also come into play. The first line says that Israel has fallen (*nplh*) and cannot rise (*l'-twsyp qwm*). The second repeats the initial idea with a different verb (*nṭšh*) but makes it more graphic by adding 'on her ground'. What is more, the line, instead of a designation to parallel 'virgin Israel', expands the debacle by a colon communicating not only that Israel cannot rise, but that no one will lift the nation up (repetition of the root *qwm* of 5.2aA: *mqymh*). The virgin lies helpless and forsaken (cf. 7.2, 5). Yahweh, who once had brought Israel up out of Egypt ('*lh*, 2.10; 3.1; cf. '*qym*, 9.11), excludes even himself from lifting the nation up now.

'Virgin Israel' is a curious epitaph in light of the earlier descriptions of the sons of Israel.[1] The text has conveyed no sense of loss of innocence or tragic violation, rather willful rebellion. Perhaps the title is purposely ironic, alluding to what Israel should have been

throughout this section, see 'Amos V 1-17', pp. 74-80.

1. Some scholars would limit the reference of 'the virgin Israel' to Samaria and the reigning house: see especially J.H. Schmitt, 'The Gender of Ancient Israel', *JSOT* 26 (1983), pp. 115-25 (followed by Hayes, *Amos*). Schmitt's article does not adequately deal with passages that undermine his view (Jer. 31.4, 21; 48.13), and the textual data here would argue against its applicability to Amos. Andersen and Freedman postulate, on the other hand, that the various qualifiers on *yśr'l* and the 'virgin' in 5.1-6 point to all of Israel, North and South (*Amos*, pp. 106-109). They do, however, admit in their discussion that a good case can be made for a narrower reference to the northern kingdom. Besides the reading offered here, which takes the term to refer to the northern nation, see D.I. Block, 'Israel's House: Reflections on the Use of *byt yśr'l* in the Old Testament in the Light of its Ancient Near Eastern Background', *JETS* 28 (1985), pp. 257-75.

(pure and undefiled) or to what it could have been had it reached the hoped for maturity.

How has the nation fallen? The vocabulary in v. 2 hints at death by the sword in battle (cf. 2 Sam. 1.19, 25, 27; Lam. 2.21). The 'on her ground/land' might imply invasion (3.1; 4.3), and the forsaken body could recall 4.10c. Verse 3 continues the imagery. Beginning with a divine speech formula, these lines also describe terrible military decimation.[1] The cities simply can no longer provide the men necessary for Israel's war efforts.[2] These words reinforce 4.10: Israel's recent past is marked by defeat and not just victory (cf. 6.13). This implied barb at military pretensions will be developed to a greater extent later in the passage. The strophe closes with *byt yśr'l*, which forms an *inclusio* with verse one.

b: Amos 5.4-6. This strophe is connected with the previous one by the repetition of the same formula, but its content differs. These lines do not express a falling in the past, but move on through the imperatives in the present to warn of a disaster in the future. There is also geographic progression (from the cities to the sanctuaries) and the linking of the titles (*byt yśr'l*: 5.1, 3, 4) and themes (*w'yn mkbh*, 5.6b; *'yn mqymh*, 5.2). All of these conjunctive features stress that the entire nation is still in view. They also suggest that perhaps the juxtaposition of military language and cultic activity is not mere accident. The sanctuaries and the feasts, the settings for national celebration of blessing and triumph, would be visible symbols of divine election and pro-

---

1. Several items demonstrate the military tenor of the verse: (1) the decimal figures suggest military units (cf. 1 Sam. 10.19; 22.7; 2 Sam. 18.1, 4); (2) the verb *yṣ'* can signify going out to war (e.g. Num. 1.3, 20-46; Deut. 20.1; 1 Sam. 8.20; 18.30). Andersen and Freedman point out that, if the reference is to what happens in one city in particular, then the decimation is of 99 per cent .

2. Following Hayes's (*Amos*) discussion of *tš'yr* (although not agreeing with his historical reconstruction), the hiphil is read in an active sense. With 'the city' as subject, the verse would then refer to what it can 'spare'. The nuance of 'left over' is usually expressed in the niphal. Proposing that the men are 'for Israel' (i.e. her army) could also answer the problem some feel arises with the location of *lbyt yśr'l* at the end of 5.3c. Some scholars would transfer the phrase to the end of 5.3a (e.g. *BHS*; Mays, *Amos*; Wolff, *Amos*; translations—Eng.: JB; Sp.: BLA, RVA); or elsewhere (e.g. Harper [*Amos*]: end of 5.3b; Eng. translation NIV to end of 5.3bA); others eliminate it altogether (e.g. Rudolph, *Amos*; Markert, *Struktur*). Hayes's translation: (*Amos*) 'shall spare ten, for the house of Israel'.

tection. The lexical connections between the strophes point, however, to a common sad fate for both the military and religious institutions.

There is no need to rehearse here the observation made by others concerning the chiasm within these verses,[1] but several comments as to its import are in order. The apex of the chiasm falls at 'and do not cross over to Beersheba' (5.5b; note the colon's alliteration). The mention of a southern sanctuary has led some scholars to consider the colon a late addition.[2] The neat chiasm stands as a stylistic reply to that critical notion, but what could be the referent's rhetorical value? At this juncture, it is important to recall the discussion of 3.13-15. In that strophe the juxtaposition of the cult center Bethel and the homes of the king and powerful suggested the wedding of religion and state ideology. Here in 5.6 the topic returns. Bethel had been established as the principle sanctuary of Israel in order to discourage pilgrimages to centers in Judah, and a feast was inaugurated to give divine validity and to foster loyalty to the new government (cf. 1 Kgs 12.27-29). Obviously, the ploy succeeds as the people crowd the cult centers and avoid Jerusalem, yet to some degree the policy has failed, as the text strongly implies that the veneration at cult centers in the South continues. This observation, on the one hand, undercuts the regnant ideology, but also substantiates the earlier claim that the popular religious world can both include and transcend state interests. Both overlapping socioreligious constructions and their activity are undermined, and the sanctuaries are condemned with well-known wordplays.[3]

---

1. E.g. De Waard, 'The Chiastic Structure', pp. 171-72; De Waard and Smalley, *Amos*, pp. 195-98; Tromp, 'Amos V 1-17', pp. 65-66; Spreafico, 'Amos: Struttura Formale', pp. 156-57.

2. Those considering the colon a secondary addition include Willi-Plein, *Vorformen*, p. 32; Markert, *Struktur*; Wolff, *Amos*. For the cultic importance of Beersheba in Israel in general and in Amos in particular, see Barstad, *Religious Polemics*, pp. 191-201; King, *Amos*, pp. 47-48, 102-104. See the evidence for the influence of the North on a Southern shrine (Kuntillet 'Ajrûd) in Chapter 3 above, in the discussion entitled 'Moral Life in Ancient Israel and the Problem of the Text'. Andersen and Freedman, in contrast, hold that the mention of a southern shrine is evidence that both North and South are being referred to (*Amos*, pp. 108-109). Yet, in response, one would ask why the principal northern shrines are mentioned but not Judah's (i.e. Jerusalem) and why the verb *'br* is used, as it can speak of crossing boundaries (cf. 6.2 and BDB 717); here the idea would be that of Israelites are crossing over into Judah.

3. Gilgal: *hglgl glh yglh*. Syntactically the exile is emphasized by the construc-

The phrase 'seek me and live' (5.4b) has occasioned much debate on three fronts. First, what does the term 'seek' mean? Secondly, what is the life that is offered? Thirdly, in light of the constant emphasis on imminent disaster, is this a legitimate offer of hope, and for whom? The text in 5.4 does not define 'seek'.[1] The phrases that follow, however, certainly underline what it does not mean (a negative particle appears three times in 5.5a, b): looking for Yahweh at the sanctuaries during the feasts. This point, of course, has its parallel in 4.4-5 (also note the verb *bw'* in 5.5b; 4.4a, b). The focus is on 'me' and in 5.6a on 'Yahweh'—that is, on personal encounter, the theme stressed to such great effect in 4.6-13. The seeking, however, will be defined positively in the matching member of the chiasm, b' (5.14-15).

The offer of life seems so out of place in this litany of death. Could it refer to a quality of life—that is, blessing and prosperity (4.6-9; cf. Deut. 30.15-19)? In context the nuance is better taken as more drastic:

tion infinitive absolute + imperfect of the same root. Note these attempts to transmit the alliteration in translation: 'nomen ist omen' (Rudolph, *Amos*, p. 191); 'Gilgal wird zum Galgen gehn' (Wellhausen, cited by Rudolph, *Amos*, p. 189); 'it's going to be your gate into exile!' (De Waard and Smalley, *Amos*, pp. 100-102). Mention should be made of Lust's suggestion that *hglgl* is an appellative and not a proper name. The meaning would then be 'stone circle' and would refer to the shrine at Bethel. He believes that this explains its non-mention in 5.6 ('Remarks on the Redaction', pp. 142-45). For a general introduction to the concept of exile in Israel, see D.E. Gowan, 'The Beginnings of Exile-Theology and the Root *glh*', *ZAW* 87 (1975), pp. 204-207. It is possible that the colon that 'Bethel will become *'wn*' is a pun on *byt-'wn* (cf. Hos. 4.15; 5.8; 10.5). Cf. Chávez, *Modelo*, pp. 107-11. The fact that an explicit fate is not mentioned for Beersheba has been given several explanations by those who hold to the authenticity of its inclusion in 5.5: (1) its doom is left to the imagination of the hearers (Cripps, *Amos*); (2) the progression of the number of cities through vv. 5-6 is 3-2-1, so that Beersheba is left out at the end (Stuart, *Hosea–Jonah*); (3) Polley, in accordance with his hypothesis, says that it is not the southern shrine but the northern pilgrims who are condemned (*Amos*, pp. 101-11); (4) the shrine is not mentioned again because the judgment focuses on the North (Keil, *Minor Prophets*; Rudolph, *Amos*; Stuart, *Hosea–Jonah*). The last option would be the most congruous with my reading.

1. For surveys see S. Wagner, '*drš*', *TDOT*, III, pp. 298, 302-303; J.M. Berridge, 'Zur Intention der Botschaft des Amos. Exegetische Uberlegungen zu Am. 5', *TZ* 32 (1976), pp. 326-27; Lust, 'Remarks on the Redaction', pp. 138-40; Hunter, *Seek the Lord!*, pp. 72-79. The main options are: (1) consult Yahweh through a prophet; (2) visit the temple; (3) priestly torah language; (4) lament liturgy language; (5) a moral attitude of conversion and obedience.

this is an option of life or death; although it would of course involve prosperity, the focus is on escape or survival from the coming judgment versus complete destruction. But can this notion make any sense at all within the framework of the divine perspective of inevitable disaster that the text has been developing? In addition, is this a suggestion of hope for the entire nation or only for a remnant that might respond to the warnings in a way that Yahweh would approve? Is this a hope to be spared disaster or simply to be able to survive it?[1] The passage will make the meaning clear as it unfolds.

One initial indicator is the last half of v. 6. These words stand outside the chiasm and so bring attention to themselves.[2] The vocabulary has much in common with the oracles against the nations in chs. 1 and 2 (*' š, 'kl*), but at the same contains important differences. Yahweh speaks no longer of sending fire; he compares himself to fire.[3] Even more terrifying, this fire will be inextinguishable; no more as a brand plucked from the fire (4.11c), the victim will be annihilated. The tone of this concluding part of the strophe highlights the starkness of the option, and the repetition of *byt-'l* (5.5a, c; 5.6b) re-emphasizes that the 'house of Joseph (that is, the 'house of Israel', 5.4a) which trusts in

1. For surveys concerning whether the message (either in the final form or hypothetical redactional stages) in Amos offers any possibility of hope, see G.F. Hasel, *The Remnant: The History and Theology of the Remnant Idea from Genesis to Isaiah* (Berrien Springs: Andrews University Press, 3rd edn, 1980), pp. 173-215; Hunter, *Seek the Lord!*, pp. 61-67; Martin-Achard, *Amos*, pp. 143-59; Smith, *Amos*, pp. 153-54; Polley, *Amos*, ch. 7. The main options are: (1) there is no real offer of hope; (2) the announcement of judgment is irreversible, but there is a last chance for a remnant to respond; (3) the warnings are hyperbolic and designed to lead the nation to repentance; (4) the announcement of inevitable judgment is actually only directed at certain groups within the nation (i.e. the wealthy and powerful); (5) the chapter reflects redaction and different messages delivered in other epochs and contexts. The position taken here is a particular nuance of option (2).

2. De Waard would say that this fact 'confirms the secondary character of the *pen* clause of verse 6' ('The Chiastic Structure', p. 172). But chiasms can be partial (see Watson, *Classical Hebrew Poetry*, pp. 203-204), so the point is moot. In addition, the *pn* clauses serve as the motivation to the exhortation of 5.6a, as the clauses introduced by *ky* clauses (5.5c) do for the exhortations of 5.4b-5b. For the argumentation of other critics who would eliminate the second half of v. 6, see especially Wolff, *Amos*, and Markert, *Struktur*.

3. For the lexical discussion regarding *yṣlḥ k's*, see especially De Waard and Smalley's extended note (*Amos*, pp. 240-41 n. 7) and Soggin, *Amos*. My reading maintains the MT (cf. Jer. 4.4; 21.12), as do most translations in Eng. and Sp.

Bethel (taking the sanctuary name here as a metonymy, cp. 5.5cA—
Gilgal) cannot find protection in the national shrine (cf. 3.14c).[1]

c: Amos 5.7. As in 3.12, a participial expression seems out of place.
But like there, this verse describes the entity mentioned in the
preceding line—in this case, the nation.[2]

The poetics are revealing. The verse exhibits a chiastic structure,
with *mšpṭ* and *ṣdqh* at the center. These twin themes will be developed
extensively in the matching strophe, c' (5.10-13).[3] The phrase *l'rṣ* also
echoes *l'dmth* (5.2): the people that cast righteousness to the ground
are themselves cast down. But who is referred to here? Usually v. 7
has been read in light of 5.10-13, thus limiting the condemned to the
rich and powerful. My reading disagrees. The first 6 verses of this
chapter are aimed at the nation. Verse 7 continues in that line and says
that Israel as a whole is characterized by injustice. This in no way
excuses those who rule, for they stand under special condemnation, as
3.9–4.3 and verses later in this section clearly point out. The various
tensions in this textual world must be respected: official religion–
variegated popular faith, particular guilt–national blame.

Verse 7, therefore, signals that the chance of such a nation seeking
Yahweh is slim. The opportunity to choose life is foreclosed by the

---

1. Some scholars eliminate *byt-'l* (e.g. Amsler, *Amos*; Mays, *Amos*; Rudolph,
Amos; Markert, *Struktur*) or change to *byt yśr'l* in conformity with the LXX (Cripps,
Amos). De Waard would explain the LXX as assuming a synecdoche (a part for the
whole) and not as evidence of a different Hebrew *Vorlage* ('Translation Techniques',
p. 348). If the phrase is understood as a synecdoche or as a metonymy, then the
notion that the judgment is too limited is thereby eliminated. In the parallelism of the
two lines the fact that *byt-'l* is matched by *byt ywsp* demonstrates that a figure of
speech is being used. Andersen and Freedman do hold that 'house of Joseph' refers
to the northern kingdom, but do not permit that this term force a change in their
position that 'house of Israel' (5.4) is a broader term; they recognize the tension, but
only allow a shift from the wider reference to the narrower (*Amos*, p. 109).

2. Most scholars have proposed that *hwy* be inserted (having dropped out by
haplography) or assumed. Some would take the opening article as a vocative (Stuart,
Hosea–Jonah; Hayes, *Amos*; cf. GKC 126-27; Waltke–O'Conner, *Introduction*,
13.5.2).

3. For good discussions of these terms see especially Mays (*Amos*, pp. 91-93)
and Sicre ('*Con los pobres*', pp. 124-25). Koch's point of view is unique, as he
understands them as referring to spheres of power (Koch, *The Prophets*, I, pp. 56-
62; note the comments in Auld, *Amos*, p. 70).

very character of its people. The connections with the earlier strophe imply that the portrait of the cult can be further filled out: the cult neither leads to Yahweh (5.4-6) nor inculcates justice (5.7). These twin concerns are inseparable—a basic truth to be re-emphasized again in this section and the next (5.18-27). In this Israel of Amos, the 'natural order of things' is to overturn (*hpk*) Yahweh's foundations for society: what is their 'given', their 'natural morality', is a reversal of his demands.

d: Amos 5.8a, b, c. These lines begin the second 'hymnic' passage of Amos.[1] The passage exhibits several stylistic features: when v. 9 is considered with 5.8, there is a total of seven verbal forms; 5.8b is also a chiasm.

The absolute sovereignty of Yahweh is communicated in at least three ways. First, there is a progression through the spheres, from the stars in the heavens (cf. Job 9.9; 38.31),[2] to the daily rhythm of day and night (cf. 4.13c), to the earth itself. Secondly, his holy majesty is underscored by the repetition of terms from the previous verse (*hpk*, *h'rṣ*), which highlight the deep contrast with Israel: justice turned into poison (v. 7), here darkness into morning; righteousness cast to the ground (v. 7), now waters poured over the earth. Last, there is a progression in tone. Moving on from the initial words of descriptive praise of his power, the last line says that Yahweh gathers the waters and pours them out 'upon the face of the earth', likely an allusion to a destructive flood of judgment (cf. 9.5, 6).[3]

Yahweh establishes and maintains his own 'natural order of things' in every realm of the creation, and his might preserves this world order as well as punishing its violators. This part of the 'hymn' reinforces the direction of 5.1-7 which invalidates the 'world' of Israel's creation by focusing on God's power in nature.

---

1. For suggestions of emendation and omission, see Watts, *Visions*, pp. 54-57; Wolff, *Amos*, p. 216.

2. Different hypotheses have been proposed as to why these constellations were chosen (cf. Calvin, *Amos*; Driver, *Amos*; Wolff, *Amos*; Limburg, 'Sevenfold Structures', p. 219 n. 6).

3. Cf. Waltke–O'Conner, *Introduction*, 33.3.5. Others pick up a note of gloom in the preceding reference to day and night, understanding the line to refer to the darkness of death (Keil, *Minor Prophets*; Wolff, *Amos*; cf. LXX).

e: Amos 5.8d. The focal point of this entire passage is the phrase *yhwh šmw*. This fact develops the tendency observed in the two previous sections (3.1–4.3; 4.4-13) to concentrate on the divine names. On the one hand, this textual datum helps stress the profound contrasts between Yahweh and the nation and its leaders. Their activity is usually described in general terms (participles, iterative imperfects, characteristic perfects), and the actors remain nameless. They are type characters. In contradistinction to this generic casting stands Yahweh, whose names appear in numerous combinations and whose descriptions are couched in a multitude of forms (participles and finite verb forms; note the causative stems, e.g., 4.7b, 10c; 5.8bB) which all stress his individuality and absolute sovereignty. Yahweh, therefore, is truly the only full-fledged character.

On the other hand, the stress placed on Yahweh and his name(s) suggests that the crucial point within the textual world of Amos is Yahweh himself. As has been mentioned already at several junctures, these chapters depict the confrontation between the deity and a socio-religious construction of reality that pretends to exist and live in his name. The reading has been trying, and will continue, to allow the text to unfold step-by-step this 'world' that stands condemned. Each level or group within the complex fabric of this society claims to believe in Yahweh and busies itself in yahwistic worship. But he will not be manipulated or mocked. This emphatic appearance of *yhwh šmw* is strategically placed before the next verse.

d´: Amos 5.9. This other half of the 'hymn' split by 5.8d continues the progression of 5.8a-c, although now the attention reaches down to Israel itself. The suggestion to maintain references to constellations is ingenious,[1] but misses the climactic movement of 5.8-9: two protagonists are at odds, two realities in confrontation.

Yahweh causes destruction to flash against the strong, and destruction comes against the fortress.[2] The repetition of *šd*, rather than

---

1. For textual details and interaction with the many proposals, see especially L. Zalcman, 'Astronomical Allusions in Amos', *JBL* 100 (1981), pp. 53-58.
2. For the various hypotheses regarding *hmblyg*, see Wolff, *Amos*; Soggin, *Amos*; J.J. Glück, 'Three Notes on the Book of Amos', *OTWSA* 7-8 (1966); Gordis, 'Studies', pp. 230-31. Whatever the lexical decision the meaning is basically the same. Most would translate *'z* as 'stronghold'. For my translation as 'the strong' see BDB 738, KB 692. Because of the decision to maintain the qal in the

being a violation of the 'law of variation within *parallelismus membrorum*',[1] demonstrates that the same fate awaits both man and his fortifications. Yahweh in his incomparable power dismantles the military machine and pretense with biting language: before him, the strong are as nothing (4.10; 5.2, 3; cf. 2.14-16), and the nation's fortresses will be so much rubble (cf. 3.11; 4.3).

The term used here (*mbṣr*) is not '*rmnwt*, the word used in 3.9-11. The reference then is not to Samaria's palaces in which the spoil of oppression is stored, but rather to Israel's fortifications. These would be the defenses that would protect the nation against invasion. All would have a stake in that which would preserve their 'world' and their lives. But Yahweh can and will remove the walls and defeat the armies that maintain a false social universe. Neither the cult centers nor the defenses can offer Israel security. Both symbols of national identity and confidence will come crashing down.

c': Amos 5.10-13. These verses pick up the vocabulary of v. 7 and specify a certain realm of injustice and a particular group to be held responsible by God. Certain terms (*lqḥ*, 5.11aB, 12bA; *š'r*, 5.10, 12bB; terms for the poor, 5.10, 12b) weave this strophe into a unit, as does the alternation of crime (*y'n*, 5.11a; *ky*, 5.12a) and punishment (*lkn*, 5.11a, 13).

Verse 10 expresses in a chiasm the injustice (cf. 5.7) perpetrated at the city gates. The targets of the vituperation stand at the center of the structure: those who try to speak truth. Who are they? In the context of the strophe they appear to be not only the exploited who might stand up for their legitimate rights, but perhaps also others of integrity who might try courageously to defend them even at personal expense (2.11-12; 7.10-17).[2]

---

second colon, there is less pressure to seek an exact parallel with *mbṣr*. Opting for the qal *ybw'* of the MT instead of the suggestion by many to emend to hiphil, Zalcman would take the colon as a quotation or as a proverb (cf. Isa. 13.6; Joel 1.15; Job 5.21—'Astronomical Allusions', p. 57).

1. Wolff, *Amos*, p. 230 n. W. Yet Gordis points out that the repetition of the same root in parallel lines is not that uncommon ('Studies', pp. 231-32). For the LXX as stylistic variation and not as representing another Hebrew *Vorlage*, see Zalcman, 'Astronomical Allusions', pp. 56-57; De Waard, 'Translation Techniques', p. 347; Andersen and Freedman, *Amos*.

2. Several scholars would try to define *mwkyḥ* as 'judge' (Wolff, *Amos*;

But what is the sphere of activity (*bš'r*) referred to here? Most obviously, the reference is to at least the legal process. The needy are abused because justice is for sale (5.12b).[1] But the scope could be wider, and thus condemnation even more penetrating. The gate was indeed the arena for legal decisions, but also for business transactions. As 5.11 points out, the evil at the gate extends beyond the purely legal realm. If this observation is valid, then the object of criticism is more inclusive: a corrupt public administration.

The ones who hate integrity in the legal proceedings (5.10, 12b) are included in the group who trample upon the weaker members of society (5.11).[2] The victims in 5.11 cannot be the abject poor, but probably small landowners, as it is assumed that they have that with

Soggin, *Amos*), but most take the reference to be general. Some understand the term to refer to Amos himself (Wicke, 'Two Perspectives', p. 94; cf. L.J. Rector, 'Israel's Rejected Worship: An Exegesis of Amos 5', *RestQ* 21 [1978], p. 167; Andersen and Freedman, *Amos*).

1. For background regarding the legal process at the gate, see H.J. Boecker, *Law and the Administration of Justice in the Old Testament and Ancient East* (trans. J. Moiser; Minneapolis, MN: Augsburg, 1980), ch. 1. For a discussion on how justice could be manipulated, see Davies, *Prophecy and Ethics*, chs. 3, 4. Polley suggests that Amos speaks from the perspective that only the judicial system established under the Davidic monarchy was legitimate (*Amos*, ch. 6).

2. Reading a more general term *bwskm* 'trample' (*BHS*; BDB 100, 143; KB 114; cf. Isa. 63.12; Jer. 12.10) with Harper (*Amos*), De Waard and Smalley (*Amos*), and Smith (*Amos*) instead of a root unknown elsewhere in the MT (po'el of *bšs*). Most commentators look to an Akkadian cognate in order to have a neat parallel with the next colon. That reading also requires a metathesis. Rudolph, for his part, suggests that the MT reflects a conflation of an original erroneous word with its correction (*Amos*). The position taken in the reading follows a principle of dynamic parallelism, in which the first colon is specified in the second.

mš't: although some take the meaning to be some sort of extortion, whether by rent or unfair interest rates (e.g. Mays, *Amos*; Smith, *Amos*), the term is taken in the reading to refer to government taxes (see esp. Dearman, *Property Rights*, pp. 28-31, 115-31; Fendler, 'Zur Sozialkritik des Amos', pp. 37-38; Vesco, 'Amos de Teqoa', pp. 498-99; Harper, *Amos*). Andersen and Freedman understand the term to refer to the 'residue of grain' from the gleaning allowed for the poor, thus making the reference allude to the cruel demanding back by the powerful of the basic necessities required for the poor's survival (*Amos*).

The change in focus from the legal to the economic does not require that 5.11 be a redactional addition (Wolff, *Amos*; Markert, *Struktur*), once it is understood that the broader system is in view.

which to pay. Those of influence and power, who take advantage of others in the gate to build splendid homes (cf. 3.15) and enjoy a sumptuous lifestyle (cf. 5.1; 6.4-6), could very well be government officials, whether appointed judges or tax collectors.[1]

Thus the vocabulary of oppression becomes more complicated: the guilty cannot be simplistically said to be the 'rich'. In these verses those singled out could comprehend certain elders and state officials of various types, as well as landowners or businessmen (cf. 2.6, 8.4-6). Other passages suggest that smaller merchants (2.8a) and the priests (4.4-5; 7.12-13) also benefitted from the system. The afflicted would include the poorest of the urban and rural poor, peasant farmers, lesser landowners, and others who speak out in vain on their behalf.[2]

The result in v. 13 is that the prosperous[3] will be silent. In Amos silence is associated with that brought by death from divine judgment (cf. 6.9-10; 8.3).[4] But what is the significance of the silence? Is it

---

1. See especially the discussion by Dearman cited in the preceding note.

2. For a balanced view of the social complexity see Sicre, who compares and contrasts the positions of Koch and Fendler ('*Con los pobres*', pp. 145-56). Cf. the discussion of the prophetic critique of society in Chapter 2 above.

3. *hmśkyl* is usually translated as 'wise, prudent'. For the hiphil participle as 'the prosperous' see the references in BDB 968, KB 922, and especially J.F. Jackson, 'Amos 5, 13 Contextually Understood', *ZAW* 98 (1986), pp. 434-35; G.V. Smith, 'Amos 5.13: The Deadly Silence of the Prosperous', *JBL* 107 (1988), pp. 289-91. In this way the verse can fit neatly into the context, *contra* scholars who view it as a late addition from wisdom circles (Cripps, *Amos*; Mays, *Amos*; Willi-Plein, *Vorformen*; Wolff, *Amos*; Rudolph, *Amos*; Markert, *Struktur*). Duane A. Garrett discovers a chiasm in 5.10-13 which he feels would demonstrate the verse's authenticity, in 'The Structure of Amos as a Testimony to its Integrity', *JETS* 27 (1984), pp. 275-76.

4. The verb *dmm* means 'be/grow silent'. If one follows the translation 'prudent', then the reasons to remain silent could include: (1) because of the corruption in the courts, to speak out will only bring problems (Driver, *Amos*; Harper, *Amos*; Mays, *Amos*; De Waard and Smalley, *Amos*; Andersen and Freedman, *Amos*); (2) it is better not to resist the word of judgment (Wolff, *Amos*; Sicre, '*Con los pobres*', p. 128; Gordis, 'Studies', pp. 232-33); (3) in a context of civil war, it is best not to choose sides (Hayes, *Amos*); (4) Amos abandons the sinful nation to its corruption (Keil, *Minor Prophets*; Amsler, *Amos*). In the context and in light of my translation of *hmśkyl* as 'prosperous' the best option is to understand the silence in connection with the divine epiphany in judgment (cf. A. Baumann, '*dmh*', *TDOT*, III, pp. 263-65). Jackson ('Amos 5, 13') and Stuart (*Hosea–Jonah*) translate 'wail' on the basis of a supposed second root *dmm* (BDB 199, not recognized in KB, yet

because of grief? fright? repentance? anger? The text does not say, but
the nature of this response will be explored further in Chapter 6 after
a closer look at the lifestyle of those in power. In any case, the coming
of the wrath of Yahweh is the 'evil time' which those who manage the
social structures with unprincipled cruelty must face.

This strophe develops the general–particular judgment tension in
several ways. To begin with, the vocabulary of 5.7 is applied to a
certain segment of Israel. Secondly, 5.12 picks up earlier generalized
vocabulary with the same goal of particularizing it: *yd'ty* (3.2a) and
pš' (3.14a; 4.4a); 5.13 (*'t r'h*) echoes 3.6 (*r'h b'yr*). At the same time,
this group's responsibility is deepened in the second half of 5.12a by a
parallel colon which also mentions, although with different vocabulary, the multitude of their transgressions (cf. 4.4a—*wpš'w, hrbw
lpš'*); and, while all the nation had and would suffer loss (4.6-11), for
the second time the possessions and way of life of those in command
are singled out (cf. 3.15–4.3). In sum, although Israel as a people
stands under judgment, the nation's legal, administrative and economic
system and those who run it, or at least who are able to utilize it for
personal gain, are special objects of Yahweh's condemnation.

b': Amos 5.14-15. This strophe elaborates on the exhortation of *b*
(5.4-6). 'Seek' (*dršw*) and 'in order that you may live' (although in
5.14a the conjunction *lm'n* is used) is repeated, but new elements are
also added. The command is not to seek Yahweh, but to seek 'good
and not evil'.[1] These are vague terms. Nevertheless, 5.10-12 already
hints at what the moral content of the 'evil' is. The generality of the
line is also reminiscent of 3.10 (*wl'-yd'w 'swt-nkhh*). In that case, as
here, there was some specification after the broad term. The impression that arises is of a 'world' of perverse values which are incarnated
in social life and structures, and never questioned by (and perhaps are
even perpetuated by) the nation's religion.

The second line of v. 14 is thus full of irony. The mention of the
'God of hosts' up until this point has been in the context of divine
judgment (3.13; 4.13). To ask that he be with them would be a

mentioned in the *Supplementum*, p. 147; cf. Isa. 23.1-2).
    1. Andersen and Freedman (*Amos*) suggest that these terms, *ṭb* and *r'*, might be
personifications referring to deities—to the true God of Israel and a false pagan god,
respectively (cf. Hos. 7.15; 8.3; Isa. 5.20; Mic. 3.2).

terrifying experience indeed, but this is what people say (*k'šr 'mrtm*; cf. 4.5, *ky kn 'hbtm*). In context, this could be a belief arising within war contexts (cf. 5.3, 9), or the cult (cf. 5.4-6).[1] In light of earlier verses, both can be true as the cult reinforced national confidence in Israel's strength. The idea then is that the sovereign God is not to be found in the ritual at the sanctuaries either for blessing or victory, but that his presence is inseparable from the fulfillment of his moral demands. The repetition of 'Yahweh, God of hosts' in the next verse will return to the threatening tone of that title.

Who, however, is being addressed in this strophe? Because of the corresponding strophe of the chiasm with its common vocabulary and the parallels with other passages directed at the nation (4.5, *'hb*; 5.7, *m špt*), the initial answer could be Israel. Yet a careful reading indicates that they are those described in 5.10-13. This identification is more obvious once v. 15 is taken into account: the mention of *śn'w* (5.10) and *bš'r* (5.10, 12bA); the repetition of *r'* in 5.14, 15 (cf. *r'h*, 5.13). Once more the general–particular tension surfaces.

5.14-15 is tightly interconnected by a chiasm, but the changes in the parallel members in 5.15 signal further development of the exhortation. In the first colon of the parallel lines the repetition is at the level of objects not verbs, as *drš* is replaced by *śn'* and *'hb*. If the meaning of *r'* is suggested by 5.10-12, then *twb* is defined in the second colon of 5.15a: the establishment of justice at the gate. This mandate would entail a complete reversal of the values and the procedures in the public administration in every sphere. Instead of 'loving' a cult (4.5) that legitimates their self-gratifying and self-congratulating perspective on life, they are to 'love' what Yahweh demands and holds dear—justice. In short, the 'world'—its ideals, mores, and the system itself—must be changed.

The defining of the 'good' replaces the purpose clause regarding life in 5.14a. 5.15b parallels 5.14b, with admonitory particle and the repetition of the divine name and title. Can *yḥnn* be thought of as picking up the theme of life. Any security is removed by the

---

1. Regarding the possible background to 'Yahweh is with you', the main options are: (1) holy war, (2) salvation oracles in the cult, (3) the divine guidance of the patriarchs. For surveys see Lust, 'Remarks on the Redaction', pp. 131-32; Hunter, *Seek the Lord!*, pp. 82-83. Note the importance of the idea in prophets associated with the eighth century: Isa. 7-8; Mic. 3.11; Hos. 8.2.

conditional *'wly*.[1] The repetition of 'Yahweh, God of hosts'[2] coupled
with the 'remnant of Joseph' implies that, as earlier passages had
indicated, he would be 'with' them in destructive judgment. Any
ambiguity associated with the presence of God is removed. Only a few
are to be left alive, and even for them grace is qualified. The confident
'house of Joseph' (5.6) will become the 'remnant of Joseph'.[3] The
absolute divine demand of justice must be obeyed, but its fulfillment is
no guarantee of survival—survival for those who might endure the
judgment, because escape is precluded (cf. 3.11; 4.2-3; 5.2-3).

This revelation would be a radical critique of the popular reliosity,
but the fact that these verses are directed at those who run the system
also forces our reading to consider its impact on the ideology of the
state in Amos. Yahweh will not sustain the nation, despite the belief in
divine election, the accounts of miraculous victories in the historical
traditions, and the activities at the official shrines. Any idea of
'manifest destiny' is dismantled: the nation is to be invaded (3.11), the
capital with its palaces and the national defenses destroyed (3.15–4.3;
5.9), personal wealth plundered (3.11; 5.11), and the sanctuaries
demolished (3.14; 5.5-6). The larger 'world' of Israel will collapse,
yes, but also the comfortable 'reality' of those who prosper from and
pervert the mechanisms of power—whether social, economic,
military, political, or religious.

If this concept is pushed still further, this strophe would communicate that what little hope of the grace of God that remains depends on
those in positions of influence: if they establish justice in the gate—

1. Cf. Hunter, *Seek the Lord!*, pp. 94-95.
2. Some scholars would want to remove all or part of 'Yahweh, God of hosts'
in 5.14-15 (see references in Hunter, *Seek the Lord!*, pp. 83-84), but, as the reading
shows, the name and title have important rhetorical value in the context. It will also
be picked up (and expanded) in 5.16.
3. For discussions regarding the possible origin of 'the remnant of Joseph' see
Hasel, *The Remnant*, pp. 199-207; Hunter, *Seek the Lord!*, pp. 85-94. The former
connects the term to popular eschatological hopes, the latter to a popular confidence
in divine blessing for the nation in the present. Any formulation of the popular theology depends on drawing implications from the text. Both options could find support
in Amos, but actually within my reading no technical status needs to be given to the
term, as it may be nothing more than a play on *byt ywsp* (5.6; cf. 6.6). Andersen and
Freedman consider the referents of 'remnant' to change in the different parts of the
book (1.8; 5.15; 9.12) in accordance with the particular point of the prophet's
ministry (*Amos*).

that is, if they remake the system according to Yahweh's demands—
only then might there be a chance for some of Israel to survive the
holocaust that must come.[1]

a': Amos 5.16-17. This concluding strophe rounds out the chiasm by
returning to the theme of lament. The most striking difference
between these verses and the matching member (5.1-3) is that this
mourning is taken up by the nation itself; it is no longer Yahweh who
lifts up the dirge.

In addition to the formal structural location of the strophe, there
are several other connections with the preceding verses. The particle
lkn that opens v. 16 is the last and climax of a chain of three after the
'hymn' (5.8-9.) that declare the judgment of Yahweh (5.11, 13). The
divine name and title (*yhwh 'lhy-ṣb'wt*) from 5.14-15 is repeated (and
even expanded) in 5.16 and reinforces the revelation that the deity's
dealing with Israel will bring terrible loss of life. Those who survive
as the 'remnant of Joseph' will remain to mourn.

The wailing will reverberate throughout the country. On the one
hand, the generalized grieving is expressed by repetition: *bkl* + locative is utilized three times[2] to include both urban and rural areas.
mspd also appears three times and is intensified by the structure: in
5.16b the term is paralleled in the second colon by sound imagery
(*hw-hw*); at the center of a chiasm[3] in 5.16c it stands opposite *'bl*,
which highlights the visual imagery because of its more explicit
connection with funeral customs.[4]

1. Andersen and Freedman understand these verses to stand literally at the center
of the book (*Amos*, pp. 53-55, 465, 506-509). The verses are said to summarize the
prophet's message, while the demand for repentance and the note of possible hope is
an indicator that these words belong to what they call Phase One of Amos's ministry.
2. *Contra* Gese (followed by Mays, *Amos*), who suggests that *krmym* in 5.17
be translated as 'vinedressers' not 'vineyards' ('Kleine Beiträge', pp. 433-34). The
parallel construction in 5.16b, however, points to the locative (cf. LXX).
3. Following most commentators in the transposition of *'l* to before *mspd* in the
second colon (Driver says the unusual original word order is a stylistic variant
[*Amos*]). In contrast see Rudolph (*Amos*, who also takes *'kr* as the subject, not as
the object) and Tromp ('Amos V 1-17', pp. 79-80).
4. Cf. A. Baumann, "*bl*", *TDOT*, I, pp. 44-48; Neher on the vocabulary of
lament in ch. 5 (*Amos*, p. 102). Barstad believes that a public lament is in view with
a call to seek Yahweh as the only fertility god (*Religious Polemics*, pp. 76-88).
Such a setting is not all explicit in the text and remains a conjecture.

238

The extent of the national lament is also communicated by the breadth of those called to mourn in 5.16b. The mention of the peasant farmer does not, as some hold, suggest that in sharp irony the poor and oppressed are forced even to bury and lament the oppressors of 5.10-15.[1] Although the immediate context might imply as much, the line's meaning cannot be so limited.

To begin with, the chiastic structure of 5.1-17 would connect this strophe with 5.1-3, which focuses on the entire nation. But other echoes of that opening passage might also be in evidence: the formula *kh-'mr* + divine name appears in 5.16a and 5.3a, and *'mr* + divine name is again repeated at the close of 5.17; the divine name *'dny* is used only here and in 5.3 (though in a different order), and that only with the speech formula. In addition, the use of the singular pronominal suffix in 5.17, which stands in contrast to the plural verbals and suffix forms of 5.10-15, might be an indication that the nation as a whole ('Joseph') could be in view. Lastly, the use of *'bl* in other passages in Amos points to a more general referent: the roar of the divine lion in 1.2 which initiates this whole text of judgment speaks of a broad judgment and national mourning (note that in 1.2 shepherds are mentioned, here the farmer); the scene of national mourning reappears even more graphically in 8.8-10 (the threefold *'bl*, 8.8aA, 10aB, 10cA; and note *qynh*, 8.10aB; cf. 8.3).

To say this, however, is not to deny any link between the earlier indictments against those of influence and this strophe. In light of our reading, however, the connection should be formulated in a different way than others have thought. If those who run the country are those primarily responsible for the disaster which will leave only a remnant (5.15b), here their awful liability is underlined in stark imagery. They especially will be to blame for a quantity of dead so great that

---

1. For this meaning of *'kr* see especially Gese, who defines the term as the 'grundbesitzlose, dem Grundherren hörige Landbarbeiter, denen die Ackerbestellung obliegt'—that is, landless serfs (2 Chron. 26.10; Isa. 61.5; 'Kleine Beiträge', p. 433). He is followed by Amsler, *Amos*; Mays, *Amos*; Wolff, *Amos*; Markert *Struktur*; De Waard and Smalley, *Amos*. Glück (followed by Andor Szabó, 'Textual Problems in Amos and Hosea', *VT* [1975], p. 505) has suggested a different etymology in order to read 'gravedigger' ('Three Notes', pp. 116-19). See the response by Rudolph, *Amos*. Rather than being dogmatic as to social status, my reading translates 'peasant farmer'. Those holding to the interpretation of forced lament include Gese and those who follow his interpretation.

mourning will fill the country, both in and outside the city (or, alternatively, others will have to be called in as professional mourners will not suffice). A chorus of national wailing will be the final end of a perverse and unjust system perpetuated by those in power.

16b	*bkl* + locative *mspd*	\	*bkl* + locative sound imagery
16c	farmers to mourn (visual)	\	to *mspd* the mourners
		(chiasm)	
17	*bkl* + locative *mspd*	\	theophany, speech formula

The last colon of 5.17 breaks the neat symmetry, as where another *bkl* + locative would be expected instead comes the notice of divine visitation. The language of passing through Israel recalls the night of the passing of the angel of death (Exod. 11.4; 12.12) and a parallel scene of national wailing (Exod. 12.29-30). As later passages in the vision cycles attest, Yahweh will no longer pass by—that is, forgive the sin and stay the judgment (7.8; 8.2).[1] Once more, Egypt serves as a paradigm of chastisement, not deliverance in the meeting with Yahweh (cf. 3.9; 4.10; 8.8). Finally, the *inclusio* of the divine speech formula (*'mr yhwh*, 5.16a, 17) and the extra long divine name and title (cf. 3.13) add a note of finality to this encounter with the God of Israel (cf. 4.12-13). This closing strophe allows for nothing but death in the nation's future.

Summary and conclusion. The extended chiasm of this section continues to develop various features of earlier parts. The broad sweep of guilt and judgment is also manifest here in that before the 'hymn' Israel as a whole is highlighted (5.1-7), whereas afterward those of influence (5.10-15); both aspects are then combined in 5.16-17. This section, as others before, targets the various spheres of society that stand under judgment: the military (5.3, 9), the sanctuaries (5.4-6), and the public administration (legal, economic, governmental; 5.10-15). These several realms form a single 'reality', but also reflect interlocking 'worlds': all can march out to war to defend the country in nationalistic commitment, but those in command would have a particular stake in the campaigns and infrastructure; both the powerful and the poor go to the cult centers, yet the feasts do not legitimate the

1. See especially Crenshaw, 'Amos and the Theophanic Tradition', pp. 206-207, *contra* M.J. Havan, who says that the phrase refers to a call to covenant renewal ('The Background and Meaning of Amos 5.17B', *HTR* 79 [1986], pp. 337-48).

same exact understanding of life and the natural order; corruption is generalized, but those who control the mechanisms of the social structure can enjoy the fruits of oppression in ways that those of lower station and influence cannot.

This entire national social construction is condemned to ruin. The divine lament (5.1) begun for disasters of the past (4.6-11) will reach a horrifying crescendo of voices (5.16-17) because of the judgment to come. Herein lies the key to the difficult interplay between doom and hope. The 'hymn' of 4.13 had been a bit ambiguous about the divine encounter because of the vagueness of 'thus' and 'this' in 4.12. The chiasm of 5.1-17 dispels any false security, beginning and ending as it does with mourning: the divine encounter (5.17) brings death. The national yahwism must give way to Yahweh himself.

5.4, 6, 14, 15, then, cannot refer to a national escape from chastisement or the commuting of the certain sentence of destruction. The offer of life can only mean the possibility of survival for some, a chance to somehow form part of that 'remnant of Joseph'. But a terrible and cruel fate awaits even those who are able to endure (5.16, 17; 3.12; 4.2-3; cf. 9.1-4). Any amelioration of their suffering is ultimately contingent upon the grace of God (5.15b). The hope, therefore, depends, as does the judgment (5.8-9), on the sovereign decision of Yahweh. The absolute demand for justice and the building of a new society stands without conditions (5.14, 15).

In sum, this 'world' of Israel has no future; it will not last. Some sons of Israel might live through the holocaust, but the 'life after death' holds no guarantee. The earlier sections had stressed the divine–national confrontation by highlighting God's actions and his name. This section is no exception, as both the center of the chiasm (5.8d) and its climactic close (5.14-17) underline the cruciality of understanding Yahweh—his person, his demands, his relationship with the nation of his choosing.

d. *The Delusion of Religion (5.18-27)*

This section of Amos returns emphatically to expose even more of the unacceptable features of the religious life in Israel. Again, the religious beliefs and activity will not be able to be isolated from the country's nationalism and morality. The religious critique continues to be inseparable from the sociopolitical reality.

Analyses of the structure, of course, differ as some scholars prefer to understand the passage as made up of several units and not as a cohesive whole,[1] and there is debate over what several consider to be additions.[2] The poetic reading offered here, however, proposes a structural unity in which all the various elements play a role in a coherent argument.[3] The second unfolds in a chiasm in the following manner:

> a (5.18-20) the longing for the Day of the Lord
> b (21-23) the despised cult: rejection in the present
> c (24) the divine demand for justice
> b′ (25) the despised cult: comparison with the past
> a′ (5.26-27) the going into exile

As in the preceding discussion, the reading will follow the outline of the chiasm in order to reflect its logic and development.

a: Amos 5.18-20. Two new elements appear in this strophe that have occasioned many studies in Amos research. The first is what has been called the 'woe' oracle or cry (*hwy*). In the past several theories have been proposed as to the particle's original *Sitz im Leben*,[4] but newer

---

1. Many critics will divide the section into several units and develop the argument of each separately—e.g. Mays, *Amos* (5.18-20, 21-24, 25-27); Wolff, *Amos*; Rudolph, *Amos*; Markert, *Struktur*; Soggin, *Amos* (5.18-20, 21-27).
2. Here opinions can differ. Many critics regard at least 5.26 as secondary, while others would also include v. 25 and/or v. 27 as late. For full discussions from various viewpoints, see especially Schmidt, 'Die deuteronomische Redaktion', pp. 188-91; Vollmer, *Rückblicke*, pp. 37-43; Berridge, 'Zur Intention', pp. 336-39; Vermeylen, 'Les relectures deutéronomistes', pp. 555-59; Markert, *Struktur*.
3. Although some recent commentators defend the unity of the passage (e.g. Stuart, *Hosea–Jonah*; Hayes, *Amos*; Smith, *Amos*), the unity is portrayed as thematic (the problem of the cult) and is not developed structurally.
4. The three primary options, along with their seminal studies, include: (1) association with the covenant curses of Deut. 27—C. Westermann, *Basic Forms of Prophetic Speech* (trans. H. Clayton; London: Lutterworth Press, 1967), pp. 190-98; (2) roots in clan wisdom—E. Gerstenberger, 'The Woe Oracles of the Prophets', *JBL* 81 (1962), pp. 249-63; H.W. Wolff, *Amos the Prophet: The Man and his Background* (trans. F.R. McCurley; Philadelphia: Fortress Press, 1973), pp. 17-34, and his commentary, pp. 242-45; R.E. Clements, 'The Form and Character of Prophetic Woe Oracles', *Semitics* 8 (1982), pp. 17-29; (3) mourning contexts—R.J. Clifford, 'The Use of *Hôy* in the Prophets', *CBQ* 28 (1966), pp. 458-64; G. Wanke, ''*wy* und *hwy*', *ZAW* 78 (1966), pp. 215-18; J.G. Williams, 'The Alas—Oracles of the Eighth Century Prophets', *HUCA* 38 (1967), pp. 75-92;

Contexts for Amos

developments have shown that it is best to take *hwy* as an exclamation ('Ho!') which seeks to gain attention. This position can explain the use of the second person forms that often accompany the particle and allows for more fluidity in its use.[1]

This move to an understanding of *hwy* as direct address fits well into the context of ch. 5 in several ways. To begin with, this interpretation permits a greater continuity with the preceding strophe and section: the nation continues to be reprimanded[2] and the theme of erroneous concepts of the encounter with Yahweh (5.14-17) developed. Secondly, the choice of a different vocative form (*hwy* instead of *šm'w*, 5.1) is stylistically powerful, as the participle is juxtaposed to the twice-repeated *hw* of 5.16b. In other words, *hwy* is not in and of itself a lament cry. Rather, by the wordplay caused by its proximity to the wailing, *hwy* strongly suggests that those addressed are those who are to be mourned. The pale of death remains.

The misconceived 'Day of the Lord' that is ridiculed in this strophe

---

W. Janzen, *Mourning Cry and Woe Oracle* (BZAW, 125; Berlin: de Gruyter, 1972).

Koch tries to develop the idea of *hwy* as a structural marker for chs. 5 and 6 and proposes that the particle originally appeared also in 5.9, and maybe 5.7 (*Amos*, pp. 109-10). Andersen and Freedman (*Amos*, pp. 462-65) propose that the woe particles are extended throughout the book for a total of 19 participial statements which, by eliminating those in 4.1 and 9.10, can be structured thus: a central core of 7 (6.1-6) flanked by two pairs (5.7, 18 and the two in 6.13) in the Book of Woes (chs. 5, 6), and these by one pair (2.7; 3.10) in the Book of Doom (chs. 1-4) and another (8.4, 14) in the Book of Visions. Although the linking device to help tie the prophetic book together is an interesting suggestion, the need to remove from consideration participles that disturb the pattern makes the structural technique itself a bit suspect.

1. J.J.M. Roberts, 'Form, Syntax, and Redaction in Isaiah 1.1-20', *PSB* ns 3 (1982), pp. 293-306, and 'Amos 6.1-7', in *Understanding the Word: Essays in Honour of Bernhard W. Andersen* (ed. J.T. Butler et al.; JSOTSup, 37; Sheffield: JSOT Press, 1985), pp. 155-56; D.R. Hillers, '*Hôy* and *Hôy*—Oracles: A Neglected Syntactic Aspect', in *The Word of the Lord Shall Go Forth: Essays in Honor of David Noel Freedman in Celebration of his Sixtieth Birthday* (ed. C.L. Meyers and M. O'Conner; Winona Lake, IN: Eisenbrauns/American Schools of Oriental Research, 1983), pp. 185-88; Waltke–O'Conner, *Introduction*, 40.2.4a. Rosenbaum would hint that the change in spelling might be due to dialect differences (*Amos*, p. 87).

2. K.A.D. Smelik has recently proposed that those addressed are false prophets who offer unfounded hopes to the nation, but this idea does not fit the context ('The Meaning of Amos V 18-20', *VT* 36 [1986], pp. 246-48).

then is literally a fatal mistake. Debate over this second new element's meaning and background has stretched over decades,[1] but the context can serve to clarify its import in Amos. In the sections studied thus far, *ywm* (3.14; cf. 2.16) and *ymym* (4.2) have been utilized to refer to a future visitation of Yahweh; in addition to these verses, a future theophany has been announced several times already (4.12-13; 5.14, 15, 17). These references reflect the divine perspective, but the fact that here the people desire the Day's coming (cf. 5.14) also points to it as a future event in the popular understanding. Yet, although its *chronological* element seems clear, its *content* within the popular theology does not.

When Yahweh describes his presence among the people in the past (3.1b; 4.6-11; cf. 2.9-10) at least two spheres are mentioned, the agricultural and the military. The 'thus' and 'this' of 4.12 imply that the future holds more of the same, yet on a greater scale. The impression, however, gained in the preceding sections is that Yahweh's coming in judgment will be probably in and through an invading army (3.6, 11, 14; 4.2-3; 5.2, 3, 5, 9, 11). By implication then the 'Day of the Lord' in Amos is a popular belief in a future victorious divine intervention, but the text leaves no room for dogmatism. One cannot discount either the possibility that within the world of Amos, the theme was ambiguous. It is best, therefore, to hear how Yahweh himself defines the nature and the meaning of that 'Day'. At least his point of view is perspicuous and consistent: it will be a time of divine wrath, of terrible destruction and loss of life.[2]

Because that 'Day' is to be a day of suffering, to long for it is suicidal. The verb *'wh* (*hmt'wym*, 5.18a) can refer to reckless and self-destructive wants,[3] and that is the case here. For that reason, the question is asked '*Why* would you have the day of the Lord?' (5.18b).[4]

1. For surveys see especially Watts, *Vision*, pp. 68-76; C. van Leeuwen, 'The Prophecy of the YOM YHWH in Amos V 18-20', *OTS* 19 (1974), pp. 113-34; Barstad, *Religious Polemics*, pp. 80-108; Polley, *Amos*, pp. 162-73. The principal theories regarding origins are: (1) ancient Near East myth of cosmic and earthly catastrophe; (2) the enthronement of Yahweh at the New Year festival; (3) the holy war tradition; (4) covenant renewal; (5) a general term for any occasion associated with Yahweh and specified in context; (6) a theophany.
2. Cf. Y. Hoffmann, 'The Day of the Lord as a Concept and as a Term in the Prophetic Literature', *ZAW* 93 (1981), pp. 37-50.
3. G. Mayer, "*'wh*", *TDOT*, I, pp. 134-37.
4. The *zh* on *lmh* can add emphasis to the interrogative, thus making the question more forceful (GKC 136c; BDB 554). Though it is taken in this reading as

The second colon of 5.18b answers the question metaphorically, describing that 'Day' as 'darkness, and not light'. These words recall the 'hymns' of 4.13 and 5.8-9 Both passages concentrate on Yahweh's absolute power: in the former, this power in contrast to the nation's inadequate view of God in a context of stubborn rebellion; in the latter, the sovereign ability to turn the rhythmic cycles of nature and tear down fortresses in contradistinction to both Israel's overturning of the divine moral order and its military pretense. In each case, as here, the divine power has a role to play in the discrediting and destroying of a condemned 'world' and the inappropriate theology of the society's creation.

That common thread surfaces in 5.18b as well. Now what is dismantled is a false hope of a theophany of blessing and/or victory. Unfounded delusion is confronted with terrifying truth. The answer to the initial question is clear: this theophany, his encounter (4.12, 13) and passing through (5.16, 17), signify death and lament, 'darkness, and not light'. The impossibility of escape from imminent judgment is underscored by the extended simile of v. 19.

This comparison's opening line (*k'šr...mpny h'ry*) is remarkably similar to the earlier simile at 3.12. In the earlier verse, however, 'the shepherd rescues' the remains from the lion attack; here, 'a man' flees that attack, only to be met by a bear and finally to be bitten by a snake (cf. 9.3b).[1] In ch. 3 (3.4, 8, 12; cf. 1.2) the lion is Yahweh, and the affinity in vocabulary hints strongly that he is in view here, too. If 3.12 communicates that only bits and pieces will survive the destruction, in 5.19 'a man' becomes 'everyman', the nation, that will not be able to hide from or elude that disaster (cf. 2.14-16; 9.1-4).[2]

'why' (translations—Eng.: RSV, NIV; Sp.: RVA), some translate as 'what' (Eng.: NEB, JB; Sp.: FC, BLA). If the latter, the effect could be to demonstrate and probe the ambiguity of the term (i.e. 'what does this concept/term mean to you?'), as well as define it in the context of an announcement ('what will it mean to you?'). My reading prefers to highlight the irrationality of the people's decision and not their possible lack of understanding.

1. Reading 5.19 as one continuous attempt to escape and not as two separate examples (cf. 'sorites' in Watson, *Classical Hebrew Poetry*, pp. 212-13). Among the translations—Eng.: JB; Sp.: RVA. (Note Wolff [*Amos*] on 5.19b: 'when he [finally] reaches home'.)

2. There is no need to interpret the simile allegorically, as does Wolff to represent 'a preceding history of repeated deliverance' that now ends in judgment (*Amos*,

Verse 20 reasserts and expands the declaration of 5.18b. This connection between the verses is expressed by an *inclusio* (*ḥšk/wl'-'wr*), which is intensified by the asseverative *hl'*,[1] the change in word order (*ywm yhwh* is now placed at the center of the two phrases as the focal point of the colon), and the addition of a parallel colon with stronger words (*'pl, ngh*) to highlight the light–darkness theme.[2] The powerful language of simile and metaphor undercut any hope of benefit or aid on the 'Day of the Lord'.[3]

b: Amos 5.21-23. This divine diatribe against Israel's religiosity is markedly different from earlier passages. Whereas 4.4-5 sarcastically ridicules the activity at the sanctuaries and 5.4-6 commands the nation to seek Yahweh and not the sanctuaries because of their imminent destruction, these verses vividly portray the deity's complete rejection of every aspect of Israel's religious observance.

The repudiation is voiced, to begin with, by the asyndetic juxtaposition of two verbs of rebuff, *śn'ty* and *m'sty*. This syntactic emphasis[4] is underscored by the choice of vocabulary. The people 'hate' truth and integrity (5.10) when they should 'hate' evil and

p. 256). Besides reading too much into the imagery, this view misses the fact that the focus is on an inescapable future. Rosenbaum offers that the lion is Assyria, the bear Syria, and the serpent Egypt and that the references are to Israel's foreign policy options at that time (*Amos*, pp. 18-19).

1. For asseverative *hl'* see GKC 150e (cf. Keil, *Minor Prophets*; Rudolph, *Amos*; Markert, *Struktur*; Soggin, *Amos*; Smith, *Amos*). Among the translations— Eng.: NEB; Sp.: BLA, Chávez, *Modelo*. This reading takes 5.20 as parallel to 5.18bB and thus as declarative, *contra* those who take the whole line (Eng.: RSV, NIV; Sp.: FC, RVA) or at least the first colon (Eng.: JB) as interrogative. Wolff would eliminate *hw'-ḥšk wl'-'wr* in 5.18 as a 'premature denouement' (*Amos*, p. 253), but thus misses the literary effect of the *inclusio*. Wolff is followed by Willi-Plein, *Vorformen*, p. 37; Markert, *Amos*.

2. Taking the initial *waw* in the second colon as *waw explicativum*. Rudolph observes the eightfold use of *o* in 5.20, an assonance which he feels echoes the *hw-hw* of 5.16b (*Amos*). If the observation is valid, the structural and tonal connections between the strophes are strengthened.

3. Here the meaning is metaphorical and does not refer to signs in the heavens in the 'Day of the Lord' (cf. Joel 2.1-2; Zeph. 1.15-16), although there may be such an allusion in 8.9. Note that in 8.9-14, as here, the 'dark day' is followed by a divine rejection of Israel's feasts.

4. This is the only place where these two verbs occur together in the Old Testament. For the asyndetic connection as emphatic see GKC 154a n. 1 (a).

embrace the good (5.15); Yahweh 'hates' their religion (note the interplay between 'I' and 'your' in this strophe). 'Despise' can occur, too, in reaction to having been despised first by man (e.g. 1 Sam. 15.23; Hos. 4.6); the previous sections attest to the nation's constant refusal to seek God where he might be found, so now he rejects their misconceived religion.

These verses mention the breadth of Israel's worship: the feasts (v. 21), a variety of offerings (v. 22), and the psalmody (v. 23). The total number of items spurned is seven—thus utilizing a key number pattern within Amos. The comprehensiveness of rejection is also expressed by the lexical variety: the emotions (v. 21: *śn'ty, m'sty*) and the senses (v. 21: smell, *l' ryḥ*; v. 22: sight, *l' 'byt*; v. 23: sound, *l' 'šm'*).

Each verse stylistically highlights the divine distaste in a different manner. Verse 21 matches the combination of two verbs of dislike in the first colon with a single verb + *l'* in the second. This last verb sets a pattern in two ways: each verse's second colon (or in the case of 5.22, second line) will contain *l'* + a sense, and the other two verses will also contain terms associated elsewhere with Yahweh's (or the cult functionary's) positive response to the cult.[1] In other words, rejection is at once reversal of customary ritual.

The breaking of the neat parallel structure of the strophe by the initial colon of verse 22 has been the source of much speculation.[2] A closer look at the received text, however, does demonstrate its part in the strong negation of the national religious activity. Whether *ky 'm* is understood concessively ('even if') or emphatically ('surely if'),[3] the

---

1. For the references see Mays, *Amos*, pp. 107-108; Hunter, *Seek the Lord!*, pp. 108-12.

2. Some scholars would eliminate 5.22a as a late gloss (e.g. Harper, *Amos*; Cripps, *Amos*; Wolff, *Amos* [although in the received text he would place the line with 5.21]; Willi-Plein, *Vorformen*, p. 37 [follows Wolff]; Markert, *Struktur*; O. Loretz, 'Ugaritische und hebräische Lexikographie (II)', *UF* 13 [1981], p. 129). Others would suggest some parallel colon (see Rudolph, *Amos*, for a survey). For a translation that opts for the latter, see Eng.: JB. Andersen and Freedman recognize the awkwardness of the line but justify its placement here as an anticipation of 5.25 (*Amos*).

3. For *ky 'm* as a concessive, see GKC 163c and those commentators cited in the preceding note, as well as those who take 5.22a as authentic (Stuart, *Hosea–Jonah*; Smith, *Amos*). For *ky 'm* as emphatic see GKC 163d (Hayes, *Amos*). Among the translations most opt for the former (Eng.: RSV, NEB, NW; Sp.: FC, RVA,

interruption by its length serves to underline the contrast between Israel's intent (note the alliteration: *t'lw-ly 'lwt*) and Yahweh's repulsion (*l' 'rṣh*). Disrupted patterns do not necessarily entail redaction or scribal error, but may be purposeful literary effect (cf. 5.6b).

The second colon of 5.22b initiates a sequence of three colons in which the objects are no longer single terms, but rather construct patterns. There is another change here, too, as the middle member has the infinitive absolute[1] instead of the first person form. Once more the result is to contrast the human and the divine, although in a different manner than in the previous two colons.

The peace-offering,[2] as the others mentioned in 5.22, is a voluntary offering. Like in 5.4-5, therefore, the nation brings no sacrifice for sin. What is more, the peace-offering is qualified (*mry'ykm*): this is a sacrifice of highest material quality. But quality control is obviously not Yahweh's criterion.

The irony of Israel's evaluation versus Yahweh's rejection continues into v. 23. The nation's festive songs of pilgrimage and worship are but 'noise' (*hmwn*)[3] before him (*'ly*); the melodies of the harps which praise Yahweh for his majesty and redemption (cf. Exod. 15.2; Ps. 118.14; Isa. 12.2) fall on deaf ears. This emphasis on singing did not appear either in 4.4-5 or 5.4-6. On the one hand, its mention rounds out the picture of Israel's worship; but, on the other, the line is ironic in the context of ch. 5: Yahweh lifts up his lament (5.1, *qynh*) even as Israel sings his praises, but in the future they will join the chorus of wailing (5.16-17; cf. 8.10 *whpkty... wkl-šyrykm lqynh*).

Chávez, *Modelo*; cf. LXX). In Sp. BLA appears to go with the second choice.

1. The infinitive absolute is to be taken as an imperative, so no emendation is necessary. In 5.23 the plural suffixes are replaced by the singular. There is no need for explanations such as 'festival musicians are a small class of people. "You" (pl) has been referring to all Israel.' (Smith, *Amos*, p. 342 n. 23a). Soggin notes that this kind of change is common in Western Semitic, and makes sense here as the entire nation is in view (*Amos*). Andersen and Freedman suggest that, if someone in particular is meant, the best options would be Amaziah and particularly Jeroboam (*Amos*).

2. This is the only case of its use in the singular. Cf. Loretz, 'Ugaritische und hebräische Lexikographic (II)', pp. 127-31.

3. Note the translations—Eng.: 'noise' (RSV, NIV), 'din' (JB); Sp.: 'el ruido' (FC), 'el barullo' (BLA), 'el bullicio' (RVA).

c: Amos 5.24. In conjunction with Yahweh's repeated rejection of the cult as practiced in Israel comes this divine demand for human justice.[1] Not only is this verse the center of the chiasm of this section, it itself is a chiasm, and the center of this chiasm is *mšpṭ wṣdqh.* This mandate, then, is the focal point of 5.18-27.

The importance of this statement is evident in several ways. To begin with, the *waw* + jussive clearly sets it off from the preceding verses: rejection gives way to requisition.[2] The imagery is vivid. The rolling down of the water in the first colon is intensified by *knḥl 'ytn* in the second: this is not to be water from an intermittent rainfall which might create a temporary wadi, but rather that from a continuous and inexhaustible source which brings never-ending justice and righteousness.

This line also picks up ideas and vocabulary from 5.1-17 and deepens their significance. The similes recall the 'hymn' of 5.8-9, where Yahweh gathers the waters of the sea (*my-hym*) and pours them out (*wyšpkm*) upon the earth. The language of praise has turned into a metaphor of moral demand. At the same time, it will be remembered that those words that described his power over the waters in 5.8 in context could very well allude to a flood of judgment. That implied threat should not be forgotten, and in fact such an image is picked up again later (8.8b; 9.6b).

m špṭ and *ṣdqh* also appeared in a chiasm in 5.7. That chiasm is now opposed by this one: instead of overturning justice and casting down righteousness, the nation is to let them flow in an eternal torrent. The divine injunction in 5.24 also parallels 5.15a (*whṣygw bš'r mšpṭ*) and vividly underlines the requirement of justice in the public realm within the legal, economic and governmental spheres.

The point made in 5.24 substantiates the position taken earlier regarding the offer of hope (5.4-6, 14-15). As in those verses, the divine moral demand is unconditional; obedience is required irrespective of the consequences. The hope was that of possible survival, and it was *the hope* that was conditioned on God's grace. There are no words of hope, however, in 5.24. *mšpṭ* and *ṣdqh* are not optional

---

1. *Contra* Keil (*Minor Prophets*) and J.P. Hyatt ('The Translation and Meaning of Amos 5.23-24', *ZAW* 68 [1956], pp. 17-24) who take the justice and righteousness as divine. For responses see especially Vesco, 'Amos de Teqoa', pp. 500-501; Hunter, *Seek the Lord!*, pp. 113; Sicre, '*Con los pobres*', pp. 130-32.
    2. Some translations do not render this verb as a jussive—Sp.: FC.

within Yahweh's moral order, and in light of past rebellion and sin in the present, at this stage of the history of Israel within Amos not even compliance can save the nation from ruin. Yahweh's command stands as absolute.[1]

The fact that this verse is both preceded and followed by cultic concerns points to the inseparableness of faith and ethics. National religious activity is discredited here, as in 5.4-6, 14-15, because of its lack of moral concern. The cult centers are not explicitly mentioned (although the cultic busyness is; cf. 4.4-5), yet there may be a word-play with *wygl*.[2] The nation is to let justice 'roll down'; Israel must not seek *hglgl* as it *glh yglh* (5.5), for Yahweh will send the nation beyond Damascus (*whglyty*, 5.27). In contrast to the sanctuary and the sin that leads to Israel's dismal future, the call for justice is affirmed as immovable and as consonant with Yahweh's holy character.

b': Amos 5.25. This verse has occasioned much controversy regarding prophetic attitudes toward the cult. An older generation held that this line demonstrated the wholesale prophetic rejection of the cult in favor of what was called 'ethical monotheism'. More recently, some scholars have proposed that, in contraposition to the Pentateuchal traditions, for the prophet Amos the cult was not fundamental to Israel's faith (cf. Jer. 7.21-22).[3] Others understand this verse pragmatically: because of the lack of proper materials, it was simply impossible to offer sacrifices in the wilderness.[4] Yet others see a comparative idea here: true worship, not mere sacrifices, was offered.[5]

1. Some would hold that there is still an element of hope for a stay of judgment in 5.24. See especially Berridge, 'Zur Intention der Botschaft', pp. 336-39 (he eliminates vv. 25-27 to substantiate his point). For this reading's point of view that the moral demand in 5.24 is unconditional and without a mention of hope, see especially Hunter, *Seek the Lord!*, pp. 110-14.
2. This observation is taken from Hayes, *Amos*, pp. 174-75
3. E.g. Driver, *Amos*; Snaith, *Notes*; Mays, *Amos*; Gordis, 'Studies', pp. 233-325. Cf. Cripps, *Amos*, pp. 338-40.
4. E.g. Rudolph, *Amos*; Wolff, *Amos*; Soggin, *Amos*; Stuart, *Hosea–Jonah*.
5. E.g. Harper, *Amos*; Smith, *Amos*; Andersen and Freedman, *Amos*; cf. Vollmer, *Rückblicke*, pp. 37-43. Calvin (*Amos*), who is followed by Keil (*Minor Prophets*) gives a different twist: he believes idolatry was extant in the wilderness as in the prophet's day and that the question refers to proper sacrifices not offerings in general.

What has been lacking thus far is a comprehension of 5.25 within the framework of Amos itself. Instead of trying to force this verse into being the definitive prophetic declaration on the cult, the goal should be to allow the text to unpack its own meaning within its own world. Once these words are read with earlier passages in Amos as background, several correlations begin to stand out: (1) *zbḥym* was mentioned in 4.4b, *byt yśr'l* in 5.4a and *mnḥh* in 5.22b. This line, in other words, alludes to the other three polemical passages in Amos against cultic activity in the present. In these other cases, the religiosity as practiced is an abomination to Yahweh. (2) This connection is substantiated by the repetition of *ly* from 5.22a.[1] (3) 5.25 must also be read through the filter of 5.21-23 and 5.24: the cult in the present as empty, immoral ritual. (4) As elsewhere in Amos the rhetorical question undermines the accepted view of things; thus, the chronological factor, which is so crucial to 5.25, must be a key element in the subversion of the actual national religious consensus. (5) The forty-year sojourn is cited by Yahweh himself as a time when he was at the nation's side (2.10b). On the basis of these textual connections, 5.25 could be paraphrased as follows: 'Did you bring to me (the kind of) sacrifices and offering (you do now) those forty years in the wilderness, O (religious yet rebellious) house of Israel?' The answer must be 'no'.

What is condemned in Amos is the cult as understood and exercised in its world. Verse 25 leaves very much open the possibility of the proper practice of religion, where cult and ethics do not stand opposed. An inference in that direction might also be gleaned in that in the list of rejected sacrifices nowhere do offerings for sin appear. What Yahweh finds repulsive is a religion of pure benefit—whether it be the official organized sanctuary sustained by the state or the broad, multi-colored national belief in divine protection, agricultural prosperity, and the deity's acceptance of the social and political system. This verse hits at Israel's religion not by a frontal attack of repudication as does its matching strophe in the chiasm (5.21-23), but by exposing its heresy in the light of history.

a': *Amos 5.26-27.* Verse 26 may be the most difficult passage to inter-

---

1. Andersen and Freedman see a chiastic relationship with 5.22—verb + *ly* noun + *mnḥh* // noun + *mnḥh* verb + *ly* (*Amos*).

pret in all of Amos. Syntactically 5.26 is best taken as a statement (and not as a continuation of the rhetorical question of 5.25) which refers to the future.[1] In addition, although the wording appears awkward, the verse can make sense as it stands.[2]

A major difficulty is lexical: to what (or whom) do the various terms refer? The references are probably to pagan astral deities, whose precise identification is somewhat hard to specify.[3] Once more,

1. Although a large number of scholars continue the question through v. 26, almost all translations do not (cf. LXX). *Contra* De Waard and Smalley (*Amos*, pp. 121-22), *et al.*, it is not linguistically better to take *wnś' tm* as past in parallel to v. 25. The verb should be taken as future and parallel to v. 27, as both begin with *waw* consecutive + perfect. To take the first form as past and the second as future would be syntactically hard to defend. In addition, the literary reading makes the claim that 'Yahweh's intervention always precedes the description of the consequences of such intervention' (Wolff, *Amos*, p. 265) lose much of its force. Andersen and Freedman point out that elsewhere in Amos a strict chronological order is not maintained (e.g. 2.9, 10; *Amos*). Wolff also makes the claim that a change from the qal to the niphal is necessary to link v. 26 with v. 27. The qal, however, can be maintained and v. 26 seen as part of the biting description of Israel's future exile. Among the translations who opt for the future—Eng.: RSV, JB, NEV; Sp.: FC.

2. Among the several emendations in the translations: delete either *kwkb* or *kwkb 'lhykm* (Eng.: NEB, JB; Sp.: BLA); transpose *ṣlmykm* and *'lhykm* (Eng.: JB, RSV; Sp.: BLA); move *ṣlmykm* in front of *mlkkm* (Sp.: RVA). For more details see especially Harper, *Amos*; Rudolph, *Amos*. Smith's proposal that the verb 'to be' between each noun pair might solve the translation problems founders on *kwkb*, which is pointed as in construct with *'lhykm* (he recognizes this in *Amos*, p. 189 n. 37).

3. The difficulty in identification is evident even in the ancient versions. The MT pointing has been explained as a vocalization according to *šiqquṣ*, 'detested thing' (BDB 1055, KB 1007), a possible indication of the term's interpretation by the Massoretes as a reference to idols. For discussions regarding the sometimes confusing evidence for the names of these deities, see Willi-Plein, *Vorformen*, pp. 37-38; Barstad, *Religious Polemics*, pp. 118-26; R. Borger, 'Amos 5, 26, Apostelgeschichte 7, 43 und Surpu II, 180', *ZAW* 100 (1988), pp. 70-81. For other creative suggestions see especially S. Gevirtz, 'A New Look at an Old Crux: Amos 5.26', *JBL* 87 (1968), pp. 267-76, and Hayes, *Amos*. Most commentaries contain discussions on other possibilities.

For many the existence of Mesopotamian gods in Israel during the time of the prophet Amos poses a historical problem (particularly in light of 2 Kgs 17.29-31). Those who hold to earlier Assyrian influence would include Snaith, *Notes*; Stuart;, *Hosea–Jonah*; Smith, *Amos*; Andersen and Freedman, *Amos*; Gordis 'Studies', pp. 236-37; Barstad, *Religious Polemics*, pp. 119-26 and ch. 6 (on 8.14).

a reference to pagan gods surfaces (cf. 4.13; 8.14), and again it is helpful to look at this verse through the lens of a literary reading to better grasp its function.

To start with, (1) the verb used is *nś'*, a term which can be used to refer to carrying objects in processions (e.g. Exod. 25.14; Isa. 45.20; 52.11; Jer. 10.5). The imagery fits well into this context of religious critique, although here the target switches to pagan ritual. But *nś'* has appeared before: in 4.2b *nś'* appears in connection with taking the 'cows of Bashan' into exile; the verb is utilized in an exile connection here as well, although now it is Israel who is to do the carrying. (2) The idea of a star/standard (*kwkb*)[1] in conjunction with *'śh* returns attention to 5.8a, where Yahweh *'śh* the constellations. This is an initial clue to the possibility that what is at stake is not just the phenomenon of pagan rites, but rather the person of God. Whereas he makes the stars in the heavens, the people make the star/standard of the gods which they carry. The idea of human creation is also evident with *ṣlmykm*.

Several other observations emphasize even more strongly the focus of the strophe. (3) In contradistinction to *'lhykm* (5.26) stands *'lhyṣb'wt* (5.27): 'your gods' versus 'the God of hosts'. (4) The impact of the name (*šmw*), or of the God of the name, can lie in its stunning mockery of the other gods who are alluded to: Yahweh brought Israel out of Egypt and led the people in the wilderness (2.10; 3.1b), but the nation must now lift up these gods of their own creation; Yahweh sovereignly sends Israel into exile (*whglyty*), yet these gods will helplessly accompany the people into exile; Yahweh speaks (*'mr yhwh*), whereas these are but dumb images. In addition to these contrasts, there is the hypocrisy of a people who in their festivals celebrate Yahweh's majesty and preeminence (5.21-23), but who in actuality have other divine kings (*mlkkm*).[2]

---

1. For *kwkb* as 'standard' see Hayes, *Amos*. If the term is so translated, then the transposition suggested by some critics is obviated.

2. According to Hayes's interpretation and historical reconstruction, 5.21-27 would allude to 'a procession made on the climactic day of the fall festival celebrating the re-enthronement of Yahweh and the anniversary and reaffirmation of the royal coronation' carried out within the context of a threatened civil war (*Amos*, pp. 178-79). Apart from the historical reconstruction, the proposal is especially attractive for this reading's interest in the relationship between cult and state. Nevertheless, the terms of 5.21-23 appear to be broader than references just to the Feast of Booths,

If this strophe is paired with its matching passage in the chiasm (5.18-20), it can also fill in some details. The day of darkness is here specified as going into exile. The 'Day of Yahweh' is the day in which Yahweh (*'mr yhwh*) sends the nation 'beyond Damascus' (cf. 3.14a; 4.3). No instrument of his wrath is mentioned and even the geography is vague, because the purpose is to leave no doubt that attention is to center on the confrontation, Yahweh versus Israel. Another small detail might show this as well: the earlier notice that he will pass through the nation is followed by *'mr yhwh* (5.17), as is this announcement of exile; the phrase could be considered an *inclusio* cutting across and connecting in still another way the larger sections (5.1-17; 5.18-27).

The further revelation concerning the 'Day of the Lord' serves more than just to clarify misunderstanding; it also contributes to the dismantling of the nationalistic religion by overturning Israel's confidence in a certain future. What is more, whereas 4.2-3 described the trek into exile by those in power, this passage foretells the dis-placement of the broad population. This textual datum points to the complexity of a nationalistic religion. Those in power can foster a convenient religious ideology for their own ends, and the people can respond to that religious construct. Yet our reading strongly implies that the religious situation in Amos is more complicated than this. Many still perform pilgrimages to shrines in the South (5.5), so the correspondence between official ideology and national belief and practice is not one-to-one. There are also hints at pagan undercurrents (4.13; 5.26; cf. 8.14) that suggest that Israel's yahwism was not exclusive but rather part of a very wide, perhaps quite confusing, theology. The possibility that the 'Day of the Lord' was maybe not a fixed doctrine, but instead a fluid and general hope also would speak against limiting that hope to just official dogma. Nationalism, in other words, could have adherents and defenders of various stripes—of different social strata and on the basis of diverse theological reason-ing. Yet, whatever its color and shape, Yahweh destroys verbally and will tear down militarily the nationalistic conviction of his unfailing protection and blessing.

Summary and conclusion. The religious world of Amos is elaborated

and the textual data of 5.26, although difficult, points more to foreign idols.

with some new details in 5.18-27. The 'Day of the Lord' is alluded to in more direct terms, in contrast to the earlier more general 'in that day(s)' passages. Other sacrifices than those of 4.4-5 are mentioned and singing for the first time. The pagan element is cited again, and Israel's brand of yahwism undercut once more.

One final structural and thematic observation needs to be made. The chiasms of 5.1-17 and 5.18-27 are interrelated as foundation-development. The former had its apex at 5.8d with *yhwh šmw* and closes with the repetition of *yhwh 'lhy-ṣb'wt* (5.14, 15, 16) + *'mr yhwh* (5.17). 5.18-27 closes with the combination *'mr yhwh 'lhy-ṣb'wt* + *šmw*. The primary concern to stress the 'name' and the person of Yahweh as opposed to the national theology/theologies continues.

Two key features of 5.1-17 were the demand for justice and the cry of lament. 5.18-27 picks up the first of these and places the ethical mandate at the center of its chiasm. It remains to be seen if 6.1-14 will expand on the second.

e. *The Delusion of Power (6.1-14)*

The target of divine denunciation shifts from the cult (5.18-27) to those in power. Nevertheless, religion will not be entirely lost from view. The structure of this chapter, as in 5.1-17 and 5.18-27, can be seen as chiastic. Its center, however, has a different, although related, focus to those earlier sections: death. As before, the reading will follow the development of the section's organizing framework.

a (1-3) misplaced complacency
  b (4-7) injustice
    c (8) divine oath + decree
      d (9-10) death
    c′ (11) divine command
  b′ (12) injustice
a′ (13-14) unfounded pride

a: *Amos 6.1-3*. This strophe begins with another interjection in the form of *hwy*[1] but now those who are addressed are not the nation as a whole (5.18-27), but those who feel secure in their leadership positions in the capitals of both Judah[2] and Israel. These leaders

1. For *hwy* as exclamation, see the earlier comments regarding the term in 5.18.
2. A number of scholars would either delete or emend *bṣywn* in order to remove any reference to Judah. For good surveys see Rudolph, *Amos*; Wolff, *Amos*;

consider themselves to be the pre-eminent among the nations.[1] Their arrogant self-confidence in their power is confirmed by the control and influence exercised over the rest of the nation (*byt yśr'l*).[2] The people come—perhaps they must—as in this society those in control abuse whom they wish, determine the outcome of court cases, and manage the public administration (3.9-10; 5.11-13). Nothing can function without their approval, and no 'justice' can be secured without their backing. And so the people come, but their going to the leaders is as mistaken as their going to the sanctuaries (also *bw'*, 4.4). Both those who govern and the cult are bankrupt before God.

6.2b has been the subject of many different interpretations. Several emendations have been proposed,[3] but once again placing a difficult

Vermeylen, 'Les relectures deutéronomistes', pp. 559-61. Quite a few, however, retain the MT (e.g. Harper, *Amos*; Cripps, *Amos*; Amsler, *Amos*; Stuart, *Hosea–Jonah*; Smith, *Amos*; Hayes, *Amos*; Andersen and Freedman, *Amos*). Stylistically, there is a neat parallelism between the colons, as well as rhyming assonance with the word endings (Chávez, *Modelo*, p. 102). For Andersen and Freedman, 6.1 is a key verse in their theory that *byt yśr'l* refers to both Israel and Judah (*Amos*, pp. 110-11). Rosenbaum, however, takes 'Zion' not as a reference to that southern capital, but as a general term representing the dwelling place of God (*Amos*, pp. 90-91).

1. Cf. Waltke–O'Conner, *Introduction*, 14.5e. Some are uncomfortable with this construct form. Suggested changes include those of Harper (*hnqbym*), *Amos*; Roberts (*nqbw*), 'Amos 6.1-7', pp. 157-58. Hayes would identify these 'notables' as Assyrian officials upon whom the pro-Assyrian Israelite monarchy depended (*Amos*). His historical reconstruction, however, goes against the very tenor of the passage.

2. 6.1bB has occasioned quite a few conjectures (cf. LXX), and some delete the colon. For the various options see Rudolph, *Amos*; Wolff, *Amos*; more recently, W.L. Holladay (*tb't lhm*), 'Amos VI 1BB: A Suggested Solution', *VT* 22 (1972), pp. 107-10; Roberts (*b'w* as imperative), 'Amos 6.1-7', pp. 157-58. Andersen and Freedman claim, on the one hand, that 6.1 is a key verse for proving that *byt yśr'l* refers to both North and South (*Amos*, pp. 110-11), yet, on the other, they understand the plural construct form of 6.1bA (which in turn, they say, would refer to those in Zion and Samaria in 6.1a) to be the subject of *wb'w* and *byt yśr'l* to mean the shrine at *byt-'l* (pp. 550-51, 560). These statements regarding *byt yśr'l*, however, appear contradictory.

3. In the first colon of 6.2b *hṭwbym* is often changed into a second person plural verbal form or '*tm* is assumed to have dropped out; in the second, the pronominal suffixes are reversed. These changes, of course, turn the MT's comparisons around and communicate the idea that Israel is not better than these states and has no basis for its sense of security. For a fuller discussion, see Rudolph, *Amos*.

passage within the context of a careful reading of Amos can help solve
many of the apparent problems of the received text. Taking this line
as it stands also does not require either that a negative particle be
assumed[1] or that the line be interpreted as a quote from the arrogant
leadership.[2]

Other passages imply that on the basis of traditions the common
belief was that Israel was unique among all the nations (3.1-2a; cf.
2.10). Military victories and the nationalistic ideology had in fact
corroborated this self-confidence (6.13b), and the extent of Israel's
borders (6.14) confirmed its might. It is interesting to note the verbs
of motion in 6.1-2: the people 'come', but now the nation's leaders are
told to 'cross over' (*'br*), 'go' (*hlk*), and 'go down' (*yrd*). The idea of
going to another country + *r'h* is reminiscent of 3.9, where Ashdod
and Egypt gather to see Israel's sin. The difference in purpose, however, could not be greater: the pagan nations come to bear witness to
the sin and observe the judgment, whereas Israel's leaders go to bol-
ster their pride and so confirm themselves in that sin. Therefore, the
expected answer to the rhetorical questions posed to Israel's leaders,
'Are they better than these [i.e. Judah and Israel]? Are their borders
larger than yours?', would be an emphatic 'No' (cf. the attitudes
expressed by Assyria, Isa. 10.5-11). Commentators founder when they
attempt to force the text to make a definitive statement on certain
historical events and miss its rhetorical intent. Whatever the exact
historical referent in 6.2,[3] the point is that this is what *Israel believed*

Among the translations which opt for some or all of the emendations—Eng.: NEB,
NIV; Sp.: BLA, RVA, Chávez, *Modelo*.

1. Gordis (followed by Hayes, *Amos*), 'Studies', pp. 237-42. Gordis originally proposed this in 'A Rhetorical Use', p. 216.

2. This is the position of Mays (*Amos*). Elsewhere in the book, however, quotations are always introduced. Cf. earlier comments on 3.2.

3. Many would hold that the comparison depends upon the defeat of these states
by Assyria. Because these were taken after the dates usually proposed for Amos's
ministry, 6.2 is therefore taken as a later addition (Coote goes so far as to date the
ministry of the prophet [Coote's A Stage] after the reign of Jeroboam II to a large
extent because of the references in this verse [*Amos*, pp. 19-24]). Other commentators would say that Assyria's incursions into the area had begun earlier and that what
could be in view is these nations' decline, not defeat; the warning note could then be
contemporary to the prophet and a late date not required. See, e.g., Soggin, *Amos*;
Smith, *Amos*; Hayes, *Amos*; Rosenbaum, *Amos*, pp. 25-26; Gordis, 'Studies',
pp. 237-39. For detailed discussions of the confusing historical data see H. Tadmor,

and proclaimed in its nationalistic pride. And, because of ancient traditions and recent military successes, apparently the nation did have some reason to feel confident and assured.

What follows throughout the rest of this chapter is the dismantling of this hubris, for even though Israel did have broad borders and military success, the text has already pointed out past defeats (4.10) and announced the future destruction of the country's military infrastructure (3.11; 4.2-3; 5.3, 9). The verses that follow will continue to unmask this delusion of power and invincibility.

The subverting of pretense begins within 6.2 itself. 'Are they better?' is the question. But what does this really mean? The nation's leaders would probably take *ṭwb mn* at least in a military sense, but perhaps also in a religious sense. Was not Israel Yahweh's chosen nation and did he not meet them at the sanctuaries? There is no need to rehearse here how Amos has put the lie to these misconceptions, but the issue can be pursued further. Possibly there might even have been the thought of moral superiority as well, but the text eloquently demolishes the credulity in any sort of ethical hegemony (3.9; cf. 1.3–2.3; 9.7). Belief in 'better' in any sense is fatefully wrong.

Verse 3 continues the targeting of the nation's leaders,[1] but its sarcastic twist at the second colon makes it a hinge verse with the next strophe. Because of Israel's defenses, the leaders up until now had been able to stave off invasion and defeat (*hmndym lywm r'*);[2] but

---

'Azriyau of Yaudi', *SH* 8 (1961), pp. 232-71; M. Haran, 'The Rise and Decline of the Empire of Jeroboam Ben Joash', *VT* (1967), pp. 266-97; S. Page, 'Joash and Samaria in a New Stela Excavated at Tell Al Rimah, Iraq', *VT* 19 (1969), pp. 483-84. If 2 Kgs 14.25-28 (the taking of Hamath by Jeroboam II) and 2 Chron. 26.6 (Uzziah's taking of Gath) can be brought into consideration as historically legitimate and relevant (not all scholars would agree on this point), then the verse would refer to two kingdoms which the people of God had taken. Their pride would, therefore, be justified! Yet, at the same time, this reading demonstrates how this pride is ridiculed and then the confidence destroyed. Calneh is not mentioned in the above passages, hence what is its significance? This question has puzzled many; Andersen and Freedman do make the interesting observation that these kingdoms would mark the direction that an invasion from the north would take (*Amos*). This would suggest powerful irony: a reversal of both direction and fortune.

1. Smith (*Amos*), however, takes the participle in the first colon as referring to the three nations in 6.2, thus forming a contrast with the second half of the verse (i.e. they have been able to put off the 'evil day', not so Israel).

2. Andersen and Freedman (*Amos*), however, understand the root to have the

those who rule, on the other hand, cause 'violence' to 'reign'.[1] To what do these words refer? Whereas the first colon alludes to foreign nations, the most probable reference in the second is to the violence within Israel's borders (cf. 3.10). Here the focus is on the state of affairs within the nation. 6.4-7 will go on to describe the licentious ceremonies with which the powerful entertain themselves at the expense of others. As a hinge verse, then, 6.3 shifts the gaze from foreign policy to internal affairs. To be sure, both are linked together, for those in power have put the country on the road to self-destruction.

Within the context of earlier passages the verse acquires substantial irony. 3.6b had spoken of an evil (*r'h*) brought by Yahweh coming upon a city; 3.13a and 4.2a (cf. 8.9, 11, 12) referred to a day(s) coming that would be a time of divine judgment; 5.13 mentioned Yahweh's wrath as an evil time (*'t r'h*) which will silence the prosperous; and 5.18, 20 had described the 'Day of Yahweh' as darkness, and not light. The nation then in one sense had put off the 'evil day' because of the stability guaranteed by its military forces. That 'day', however, was now not far off and would come by Yahweh's hand.

The verb *ngš* (hiphil) in the second colon appears three other times in Amos (5.25; 9.10, 13), two of which have an interesting connection with this verse. In 5.25 the question is whether Israel had brought the same sort of vacuous offerings to Yahweh in the wilderness. Vain sacrifice to God and violence to the people are all that is on offer. The verb is also used in 9.10 in a quotation in which 'all the sinners' of

---

same meaning as *nwd* and *ndd*, hence they read '[Woe to] you who rush along toward the day of calamity' as parallel to 6.3b (cf. 5.19).

1. For discussions on the various emendation proposals for 6.3b see Willi-Plein, *Vorformen*, pp. 41-42; Wolff, *Amos*; Rudolph, *Amos*. More recently, Auld would translate 6.3a as 'you who defer evil to the day', thus hastening 'the enthronement of violence' (*Amos*, p. 62); Stuart has proposed the translation for v. 3 as 'Those who are forecasting a bad day and divining a harmful week' (*Hosea–Jonah*); Andersen and Freedman hold that a simple waw with the imperfect (perhaps originally a qal, they say, because of the consonantal form in the Aleppo Codex) would be the more appropriate verbal form and suggest that the preposition of the first colon 'serves double duty' in order to read: 'and [who] draw ever nearer to the reign of violence' (*Amos*). For the understanding of *šbt* as related to 'reign', see that nuance of *yšb* in 1.5, 8 (cf. BDB 442, KB 409). For translations which also take the view of the reading—Eng.: RSV, JB, NEB, NIV; Sp.: RVA, Chávez, *Modelo*.

Israel say that Yahweh will not bring (*l' tgyš*) *hr'h*.[1] These words put on Israel's lips in 9.10 bring both colons of 6.3 together in a powerful way by exposing the nation's blindness to the ways of Yahweh (cf. 3.6; 9.4) and demonstrate once again that nationalistic pride had theological substantiation. An ideology, in other words, not simply bare political and economic tactics, is on trial and stands condemned.

b: Amos 6.4-7. If the second half of v. 3 is understood to function as a hinge verse, then its vocabulary situates the lifestyle that is to be described and reveals an evaluative judgment of the proceedings. 3.10 had said that the nation's leaders had stored up *ḥms* in the palaces. Although the violence is not specified, the mention later of the nice homes and the bacchanalian tastes of their wives (3.15–4.1) implies that those in power benefit directly from the oppression. This impression is solidified in 5.11-12. This strophe in ch. 6, however, takes the reader for the first time inside the palaces (and/or spacious homes) and adds another dimension to that depiction. The introduction with *ḥms* strongly suggests that what is enjoyed here is the fruit of the oppression. Other textual observations and the wordplay with 6.6b will confirm this initial suspicion.

Much recent research has illuminated the background to the scene pictured in 6.4-6a.[2] The data of the ancient Near East lead to the conviction that what is being celebrated is a *marzeaḥ* banquet. Quite a few of the elements of these feasts are listed here. The light shed from archeology testifies to the debauchery and incredible expense in these verses.

---

1. Reading the hiphil with the MT, *contra* many who emend to niphal. Keeping the hiphil makes the impact of the self-delusion greater, especially when read in light of 3.6 (cf. 4.6-13). Note that other links between ch. 6 and 9.9-10 would also include: *ky-hnh 'nky mṣwh* (cf. 6.11), *bkl-hgwym* (cf. 6.1b), *byt yśrl* (cf. 6.14), the theme of death (cf. 6.9-10), a quote (cf. 6.13).

2. For archaeological data see M.H. Pope, 'A Divine Banquet at Ugarit', in *The Use of the Old Testament in the New and Other Essays: Studies in Honor of William Franklin Stinespring* (ed. J.M. Efird; Durham, NC: Duke University Press, 1972), pp. 170-203; Coote, *Amos*, pp. 36-39; J.C. Greenfield, 'The *Marzeaḥ* as a Social Institution', *AA* 22 (1974), pp. 451-55; King, *Amos*, ch. 6, and 'The *Marzeaḥ* Amos Denounces', *BARev* 15.4 (1988), pp. 34-44; Barstad, *Religious Polemics*, ch. 5 (he would also suggest that the feast is alluded to in 2.8 [pp. 33-36] and 4.1 [pp. 42-44]).

What this information also does is question the idea that Amos (or at least the 'authentic' oracles) is not concerned with idolatry.[1] These were pagan ritual feasts, and this fact points to an idolatry among those in power, a paganism which only they could enjoy because of the high costs. As in previous passages, the allusion is there, but it is not emphasized.

Why is not the problem of syncretism developed in the text? Again, my reading suggests that Amos is committed to subverting the religion and society that grounded themselves in Yahweh. It is the yahwism and the institutions which utilize its traditions in the social construction of reality that are attacked. For that reason, this strophe highlights a lifestyle based on *ḥms*, and to expound 6.4-6a in light of this term and earlier passages is to expose this 'world' in all its ugliness.

Those in power are at ease on fine beds and sprawled out (6.4a; note the intensification in the parallelism from *škb* to *srḥ*), while those less fortunate find no just recompense for their labor and no justice in their cause (5.11). The feast is stocked with the best of meat (6.4b; note the intensification: one verb governs both colons and a double object; cf. 5.22bB),[2] while the rest of the nation has gone hungry from lack of food (4.6, 9).

Verses 5 and 6 contain several possible allusions to a religious setting. 6.5 refers to music and makes David the point of comparison.[3] Although their goal is to imitate him, in contrast to this national leader and king who in the tradition composed and sang in acceptable praise to Yahweh (e.g. 1 Sam. 16.16; 1 Chron. 23.5; 2 Chron. 7.6, 29.26-27), these invent music in their feasting.[4] A connection with the

1. Several recent commentators make reference to the *marzeaḥ* banquet but refuse to grant any religious connotation in 6.4-6—e.g. Coote, *Amos*; Soggin, *Amos*; Hayes, *Amos*. Mays mentions the suggestion of a cultic setting by earlier scholars, but then rejects it (*Amos*).

2. Rosenbaum suggests that *mš'n* might be a word-play on *bṣywn*, 6.1 (*Amos*, p. 76). If so, another link between the revelry of 6.4-7 and the national leadership would be stylistically established.

3. A number of scholars consider *kdwyd* a gloss or try to emend (cf. LXX). For a good survey of the various suggestions see Rudolph, *Amos*.

4. Several terms in 6.5 have been the subjects of much discussion: besides Rudolph (*Amos*), for *prṭ* see the survey in De Waard and Smalley, *Amos*, p. 250 n. 42; for *ḥšb* see Gordis, 'Studies', pp. 242-43; for *'l* as a double-duty proposition see D.N. Freedman, 'But Did King David Invent Musical Instruments?', *BRev* 1 (1985), pp. 48-51; Andersen and Freedman, *Amos*. The positioning of *kdwyd* in

religious is underscored by a comparison with 5.23, with which 6.5 demonstrates a distant inverted parallelism: *šryk/nblyk* (5.23), *hnbl/kly-šyr* (6.5). This verse reveals even more clearly how self-serving the psalmody is among the rulers (*lhm*), and the context of *ḥms* in 6.3-6 explains why Yahweh would totally reject such worship and demand justice (5.24).

6.6a points to the perverse extravagance of the banquet, too. The wine is drunk in bowls, but the people suffer from thirst (4.7, 8). Only the finest oil is used, as the proud demand the very best: the *nqby r'šyt hgwym* (6.1b) anoint themselves with *r'šyt šmnym*.[1] But a religious scene is again implied by the vocabulary. Every use of *mzrq* is ritualistic and the verb *mšḥ* is often used for a cultic act.[2] The data suggest once more some kind of syncretism, and so the question of discovering the textual concerns and perspective needs to be raised yet again.

6.6b, a line which some commentators consider secondary,[3] reinforces the observation made above that Amos is more concerned with the injustice that makes the *marzeaḥ* feast possible than in the idolatry associated with it, but also adds a sharply ironic element to this social criticism. As in other passages (e.g. 3.12; 5.6b, 22a), lines that seem to be mere appendages actually prove to be important in the development of thought and to exercise key functions in their structural 'misplacement'. The line breaks the series of seven verbal forms (five participles + two finite forms) describing the revelry of the well-to-do in a climatic way with *wl'*.[4] Far from being an unnecessary line, 6.6b

the center of the line could also be emphatic. The name could very well be a pivot word (cf. Watson, *Classical Hebrew Poetry*, pp. 214-21) that can serve both colons: David as composer and inventor. This possibility can be substantiated by the very fact that it seems to some to overload the meter (e.g., Harper, *Amos*; Wolff, *Amos*; Markert, *Struktur*), and by the attempt by others to place the word in the first colon instead of the second (e.g. Stuart, *Hosea–Jonah*; translations—Eng.: NIV).

1. For more background on the oil see L.E. Stager, 'The Finest Oil in Samaria', *JSS* 28 (1983), pp. 241-45.

2. For *mzrq* see BDB 284, KB 511; for *mšḥ*, BDB 603, KB 573; the discussion in King, *Amos*, pp. 157-59. More recently Ulrich Dahmen has proposed that 6.6a is not authentic precisely because of the cultic language ('Zur Text- und Literarkritik von Am 6, 6a', *BibNot* 31 [1986], pp. 7-10).

3. So Wolff, *Amos*; Markert, *Struktur*. Andersen and Freedman make the observation that a tricolon that interrupts a series of bicola appears elsewhere (e.g. Ps. 94.23) to indicate a climax or mark a conclusion (*Amos*, p. 545).

4. Cf. Limburg, 'Sevenfold Structures', p. 221.

highlights the depth of their sin and reiterates the foundational basis of
the divine judgment to be announced in 6.7. Paronomasia links *šbr* of
this colon with *šbt* of v. 3 and acts as an *inclusio* to mark off the
bounds of this portrait of callous oppression. The connection is more
than auditory, for it is the *šbt ḥms* that has brought the *šbr ywsp*.
What makes this line even more pathetic is that the house of Israel has
to 'come to' the very ones who bring them to their ruin (6.1).

The verb *nḥl* can also unveil irony in the line. The *marzeaḥ* could
be a funerary banquet (cf. Jer. 16.1-6), but here Israel's leaders feel
no remorse either for the brokenness of those who suffer the rampant
corruption or for the nation in general, which had not been so fortunate as to withstand easily the times of want brought by Yahweh's
hand. In light of ch. 5, however, the reader can easily add yet another
dimension to this line: these leaders are oblivious to the 'ruin' that will
come upon Israel because of their behavior, policies, and ideology.
Because of the coming judgment, Joseph will be destroyed (cf. 5.15b:
š'ryt ywsp); and although they do not lament now, soon the streets
and the countryside will be full of wailing (5.16-17). Those in charge,
more than anyone else, are morally responsible for the direction and
the future of Israel. Their gross insensitivity and unbridled selfishness
assure that the suffering will continue and reach an unimaginable level
when Yahweh will pass through his people. 6.6b, therefore, can refer
both to the present and the future within the context of Amos.[1]

6.7, in fact, emphatically announces the divine judgment. In contrast
to what those in power have been enjoying, *'th* (as a particle introducing announcement of judgment also note 7.16), they will be made to
undergo affliction. Each colon functions stylistically as an *inclusio*: the
nqby r'šyt hgwym will now *yglw br'š glym* (6.1-7), and *wsr mrzḥ
srwḥym* (6.4-7; note also the alliteration).[2] Both the larger passage
and the description of the feast are thus tied together. Those most
responsible will have their lifestyle terminated. Those who so
confidently go to other countries to prove their superiority (6.2) will

---

1. Most commentators opt for understanding the reference as to the future
calamity. Those who take it as alluding to the present condition of the nation include
Mays, *Amos*; Rudolph, *Amos*.

2. Several commentators have tried to communicate the word-plays in their
translations. Note, for instance, Rudolph ('da schwindet das Schwadronieren der
Schwelger'), who also quotes Duhm ('da verlernen das Larmen die Lummel', *Amos*,
p. 218); Wolff ('and suppressed is the spree of the sprawlers', *Amos*).

now lead in shame those who march into exile (cf. 4.1-3). The 'day of evil' will have arrived (6.3A).

c: Amos 6.8. Verse 8 opens with the divine oath (cf. 4.2; 8.7) that declares the irrevocability of the judgment that follows. The fulfillment depends, as it were, on his very person. Each instance of a divine oath in Amos has another colon juxtaposed for emphasis; here it is the certainty of the decree that is stressed. *n'm-yhwh 'lhy ṣb'wt* will also serve as an *inclusio* for 6.8-14, and this particular divine title hints at a context of an enemy invasion (6.14; cf. 3.13–4.3; 5.15-17, 27). The colon, therefore, which others would transpose or delete,[1]

1. Those who would move the colon to the end of 6.7 include Harper, *Amos*; Cripps, *Amos*; Amsler, *Amos*; Rudolph, *Amos*; Wolff, *Amos*; Markert, *Struktur*; De Waard and Smalley, *Amos*; Soggin, *Amos*. LXX omits as do Willi-Plein, *Vorformen*, pp. 43-44; Stuart, *Hosea–Jonah*; Hayes, *Amos* (or he would move it to the end of 6.8). Among the translations NEB deletes. In contrast to the artfulness evident in a careful reading of 6.8-14, note these words by Coote: 'The B editor is running out of good material that says by itself what he wants it to say. If he had composed this unit on the basis of a well-preserved oracle of Amos or from scratch it would, I think, show more coherence and design. There are mere traces of design. . . The result is his least effective composition. . .'(*Amos*, p. 86).

A word is in order regarding the omission of this colon in 6.8, 14 in LXX. Auld (*Amos*, pp. 57-58) has criticized Koch's use of formulae in his structuring of Amos when the LXX differs from MT and specifically mentions these two verses. In reply, the following observations could be offered: (1) LXX is inconsistent in its use of the formula 'Yahweh, Lord God of hosts'. The formula is added at 5.8 and 9.5, probably as an attempt to make all the 'hymnic' passages uniform. Some manuscripts and later versions do agree with MT at 6.8, 14 (cf. the evidence in Ziegler, *Duodecim prophetae*, pp. 196-97). LXX is also inconsistent in its handling of divine names— for example, deleting one on occasion (e.g. 4.2; 5.3; 6.8), but leaving it doubled elsewhere (e.g. 3.7, 8, 11, 13; 4.5). Moreover, LXX exhibits several stylistic changes in ch. 6: 'from Ephraim' is added at 6.7, possibly to parallel 'of Joseph' in 6.6; 'a remnant will be left' is added at 6.10 to explain the presence of the one who takes out the bodies; a syntactical change occurs at 6.1 so that the 'house of Israel' becomes the subject of 6.2. All of this data regarding the varied treatment of the divine names and the features of the translation in ch. 6 itself could be the result of stylistic decisions and not of a different *Vorlage*. On the stylistics of LXX Amos, see De Waard, 'Translation Techniques' and 'A Greek Translational-Technical Treatment of Amos 1.15', in *On Language, Culture, and Religion: In Honor of Eugene A. Nida* (ed. M. Black and W.A. Smalley; The Hague: Mouton, 1974), pp. 111-18; J.A. Arieti, 'The Vocabulary of Septuagint Amos', *JBL* 93 (1974), pp. 338-47; G. Howard, 'Revision Toward the Hebrew in the Septuagint Text of Amos', *EI* 16

has a triple stylistic function: emphasis, marking the limits of a sub-section, and introducing a theme.

6.8b is in the form of a chiasm which describes Yahweh's repudiation. What is meant, however, by 'the pride of Jacob'? In other words, what does Jacob value, in what does Israel take 'pride'? The parallelism provides the content for the term.[1] The second colon specifies what particularly is abhorred by Yahweh but prized by Israel's leaders: the palaces. This mention of palaces recalls 3.9-11 with its description of injustice associated with them and their plundering by the enemy. The thrust of the divine displeasure at opulence built on oppression (6.4-7) continues into this verse.

The depth of Yahweh's hatred is underlined once a distant inverse parallelism with the verbs of 5.10 is recognized.[2] The nation's leaders

---

(1982), pp. 125-33. (2) Koch (*Amos*, pp. 112-13) is concerned with reconstructing the redactional history of the received text as well as explaining its present shape. In that enterprise the LXX evidence does need to be factored in. My reading, however, does not take the formula in 6.8, 14 as a major structural marker, but rather as a stylistic feature for emphasis and *inclusio*. What is more, Koch is inconsistent, labelling the formula in 5.14 and 6.8 as inauthentic (and in the latter case on the basis of LXX), because there it does not fit his scheme. If it is granted that the formula in 6.8, 14 is a late editorial edition, the editor is marking off a section that is stylistically clear even without it. This would in and of itself be a testimony to the coherence of 6.8-14.

The formula 'Yahweh, Lord God of hosts' in its various forms is not considered authentic by some scholars. Wolff is a case in point (*Amos*, pp. 287-88). His argument is based on statistics (not stylistics), but his understanding of its redactional purpose does parallel the suggestion made in the reading (i.e. the context as military). One senses that the distribution of all of the occurrences (except for 9.5) in chs. 3–6 is a bit awkward for his textual construction.

1. For the term, see D. Kellermann, '*g'h*', *TDOT*, II, pp. 344-50. Methodologically it is better to allow the context to provide the term's meaning instead of defining 'pride' as inherently negative. In such a way, possible difficulty with the same phrase in 8.7 is eliminated. In that passage, Yahweh swears by what Israel should have gloried in—i.e. Yahweh. Thus 8.7 would parallel 4.2 and 6.8a; the irony there is heightened by the people's swearing in the name of other deities (8.14).

2. Reading with most commentators and translations *mt'b* for *mt'b*. Other recent proposals include those of Mitchell Dahood ('Amos 6.8: *meta' ab*', *Bib* 59 [1978], pp. 256-57), who would divide the term into two (he is followed by Spreafico, 'Amos: Struttura Formale', pp. 159-60); and Gordis, 'Studies', pp. 243-44, who considers the possibility of *addad*, 'a word of like and opposite meaning'.

hate those of integrity who speak up for justice and question their self-serving manipulation in the gate (5.10-13); Yahweh hates the very symbol (the palaces) of those leaders' unjust lifestyle. Two verbs of abhorrence also appear in 5.21 (*śn'* and *m's*). Yahweh then detests the whole of what is representative of this 'world'—the impressive structures and the celebrations at the sanctuaries.

6.8c foretells the turning over of a 'city'. Earlier verses lead to the impression that Samaria is in view (3.6, 9, 12; 4.1; 6.1). What is disturbing is the inclusiveness of *wml'h*. Once more, the text presents the general–particular tension in judgment. The reading has been developing two aspects of this datum: national guilt, on the one hand; national suffering because of those in charge (e.g. 6.6b), on the other. The latter must be the focus here.

d: Amos 6.9-10. The completeness of judgment announced in 6.8c is expressed by the hypothetical situation of this strophe, where the subject is a home instead of the palaces.[1] Only ten people[2] are left over after the disaster. In context, this is probably the invasion by the enemy raised up by Yahweh.[3] The extent of the death toll is stressed by *wmtw* in 6.9, which echoes the loss of life of 5.3 and corroborates the ubiquitous lamenting of 5.16-17.[4]

---

1. Rosenbaum suggests that the reference might be to a *marzeaḥ* 'clubhouse', thus continuing the scene of 6.4-7 (*Amos*, p. 66).

2. Translating *'nšym* as 'persons' not 'men'. Stuart (*Hosea–Jonah*) and Hayes (*Amos*) would propose that the reference is to a squad of soldiers (cf. 5.3). Smith (*Amos*) believes that 'a large palatial home' is in view because of the large number of men. Both interpretations are obviated by the translation 'people', and Smith's in particular by the concept of extended families living under one roof (cf. De Waard and Smalley, *Amos*, p. 252 n. 53). Still another more fanciful interpretation is that which sees a reference to the ten tribes and the kingdom of Judah in 6.9-10 (G.W. Ahlström, 'King Josiah and the DWD of Amos VI 10', *JSS* 26 [1981], pp. 7-9; Vermeylen, 'Les relectures deutéronomistes', pp. 564-65).

3. Many scholars believe that either a plague and/or an earthquake is also presupposed by the description in 6.9-11. These are possible scenarios, of course, but the text throughout speaks specifically of a terrible invasion that would involve loss of life, the destruction of the city walls, and the razing of homes (1.3–2.3 also mention the fire that would accompany the attacks). Of course, a plague could follow the invasion as a consequence of siege and military defeat.

4. For the added comment at the beginning of 6.10 by LXX, see De Waard, 'Translation Techniques', pp. 343-44.

The imagery of death continues into v. 10. This verse is full of interpretive problems, but the picture seems to be of a kinsman of the family of 6.9, who with another must pick up and burn the bodies.[1] This depiction picks up earlier vocabulary and scenes and adds to the graphic portrayal of future national loss because of the imminent divine judgment. Burning is cited in 2.1, but here it is not meant as an affront but is rather a necessity because of the quantity of corpses (4.10; 5.16-17; cf. 8.3b); Moab was to be judged for the crime of burning a corpse, but now it is to be Israel's lot as punishment (cf. 5.6). In contrast to 4.11 where the nation is snatched from the fire, here the bodies have to be thrown in. In 4.2-3 every last one of the ladies of leisure is taken (*nś'*) away into exile and goes out (*yṣ'*) through the holes in the city walls; here every last one of the dead is taken (*nś'*) in order to bring (*yṣ'*) their bones from out of the house.

The conversation between the kinsman and the other person sent in to see if anyone remains is revealing. The command to be quiet is not because of fear of provoking more wrath, whether out of terror of Yahweh's presence or some magical fear of his name; neither is it a note which despairs of any mercy from Yahweh.[2] Rather, this is a final note of defiance. The nation had never returned to Yahweh after earlier disasters (4.6-11), and everything in the present in every sphere of life indicates that the rebellion will continue. The contrast in imagery with 6.4-6 could not be greater: from the shouting and singing to silence. One thing remains constant: there is no grieving over the ruin of Joseph, no repentance before God.

The importance of the 'name' of Yahweh surfaces again. The 'name'

---

1. For good surveys of the several lexical problems in 6.10, see Rudolph, *Amos*; De Waard and Smalley, *Amos*; Soggin, *Amos*; Gordis, 'Studies', pp. 245-47. The options taken in this reading: *dwdw* as 'uncle', *wmśrpw* for *wmsrpw* (although the term is not taken in a technical sense; Rosenbaum attributes the change in spelling to dialect differences, *Amos*, p. 94). For the singular verbal suffix see GKC 145m.

2. For examples of the various options: fear of Yahweh's presence (Keil, *Minor Prophets*; Mays, *Amos*); magical fear of his name (Cripps, *Amos*; Wolff, *Amos*); no hope of mercy (Amsler, *Amos*; Smith, *Amos*). Cf. GKC 1141; Waltke–O'Conner, *Introduction*, 36.2.3-4.

In contrast to 6.11, *hs* in 8.3b is voiced by God. If taken as a separate exclamation, then there God could be demanding silence (cf. 5.23) as a response to his judgment; this instead of bodies being taken out in silence, because even 8.3a declares that there will be loud wailing (cf. 5.16-17)!

had been the climax of the divine encounter of 4.4-13, the center of
the chiasm in 5.1-17, and a sharp rebuke to the use of the names of other
gods in 5.26-27. In each case the 'name' is used to expose Israel's stubborn blindness of Yahweh's ways and demands—whether in history,
society, or the cult. Now that refusal to acknowledge him, even in the
face of terrible judgment, confirms the nation's profound guilt.

The intent of this strophe, therefore, is to sustain the responsibility
of Israel for its own destruction, as well as to highlight the awful
price to pay. As the apex of the chiasm of ch. 6, this strophe picks up
and develops these two themes from 5.1-17 through its imagery and
the dialogue. Although some consider these lines an insertion or out of
place,[1] the change to a more prosaic style and its location can point to
its purposeful literary function.

c': Amos 6.11. Those words of bitter defiance are framed by the
words of Yahweh: on one side, by the divine oath and a speech
formula + divine name and title (6.8a); on the other, by his command
(6.11). The divine voice drowns out the anger of the rebellious and
puts the sovereign plan of judgment into action.

ky-hnh introduces the divine command and will form an *inclusio*
with v. 14.[2] In the latter Yahweh raises up an enemy army to oppress
Israel. Because here the means of catastrophe are not stated, this
structural link can clarify the agent of the divine smiting in 6.11b as
the invader (cf. *swh* in 9.3, 4, 9).[3] The same imagery of the broad
devastation wrought by foreign armies is used in 3.11–4.3, where
Yahweh also smites (*nkh*) the abodes of the powerful and the Bethel
sanctuary (various constructs with *byt*). In this context, however, the
damage extends beyond these grander homes to even those of the less
fortunate.[4] The assonance of the line makes the imagery more striking

---

1. See in particular Harper, *Amos*; Rudolph, *Amos*; Wolff, *Amos*. For a recent
vigorous defense of the authenticity of 6.9-10, see McComiskey, 'The Hymnic
Elements of the Prophecy of Amos', pp. 110-13.

2. Several commentators consider 6.11a a gloss which functions simply to make
a connection with 6.9-10. See Harper, *Amos*; Wolff, *Amos*; Markert, *Struktur*.
Rudolph, (*Amos*) would place 6.11 after 6.8. Both options miss the poetics of the
received text.

3. Again, some commentators have also seen an earthquake in 6.11, but cf.
comments regarding 6.9-10.

4. Other suggestions include: the houses of 5.11 and the little ones of those

and poetically suggests similarity in judgment.[1] The extent of the ruin agrees with the scene of 6.9-10 and so once again stresses the dreadful fate secured for the nation by its leadership. The use of the participle can indicate that the command to destroy is close at hand or that it has just gone out.[2] The invasion is not far off.

b': Amos 6.12. The absurdity of this drive to self-destruction is exposed in this verse by a series of rhetorical questions. Commentators all recognize the insanity of the images of running horses on rocks or plowing the sea with oxen.[3] Nevertheless, what can be missed is the rhetorical impact of these two lines, because this foolishness is sinister and destructive.

These questions appear in the same sequence as those in 3.3-7 (*h, 'm, ky*), with the climax on the last.[4] 6.12b also has a different structure than 6.12a: the latter is a chiasm introduced by *ky* + verb. On the one hand, 6.12b echoes 5.7 and 5.24 (cf. 5.15), which are also chiasms—yet there are some changes. Instead of simply *ṣdqh*, this verse has *pry ṣdqh*, and here *ll'nh* is linked with *ṣdqh* and not *mšpṭ* (5.7). If *mšpṭ* is considered as the legal commands grounded in *ṣdqh*

vineyards (Wolff, *Amos*), different government buildings in Samaria (Hayes, *Amos*). Harper would take the great house to mean Israel, the small one Judah (*Amos*).

1. Mentioned by Wolff, *Amos*; De Waard and Smalley, *Amos*. Calvin finds significance in the kind of destruction assigned to each house, each appropriate to the size (*Amos*).

2. GKC 116p, Waltke–O'Conner, *Introduction*, 37.6-7.

3. Reading with most commentators *bbqr ym* in the second colon. Other recent suggestions include Szabó: *bqbrym*, 'among tombs' ('Textual Problems', pp. 506-507); M. Dahood: *b* as 'without' ('Can One Plow Without Oxen? [Amos 6.12] A Study of *BA* - and '*AL*', in *The Bible World: Essays in Honor of Cyrus H. Gordon* [ed. G. Rendsburg *et al.*; New York; Ktav, 1980], pp. 13-23); Stuart (*Hosea–Jonah*) and Hayes (*Amos*): *bsl'* can do double duty in the second colon; Alan Cooper identifies Sela and Beqa' as place names denoting the boundaries of Israel's territory and believes the verse anticipates 6.13-14 ('The Absurdity of Amos 6.12a', *JBL* 107 [1988], pp. 725-27). Although a reference to military campaigns would fit well in the context, a military metaphor is not absolutely essential here, especially if the focus of the series of questions is 6.12b. In addition, the references appear to be a bit cryptic. Among the translations who take the interpretation followed in this reading—Eng.: RSV, JB, NEB; Sp.: FC, BLA, RVA.

4. Cf. the references in the discussion of 3.7.

(*m špṭ* = *pry ṣdqh*), as some believe, then *ll'nh* might still be connected with *mšpṭ*, but through a synonymous phrase.

5.7 and 5.24, moreover, were an indictment of the nation as a whole, but other differences between the verses indicate that now the accusation is directed at a particular group.[1] In place of the participle of *hpk* of 5.7 or the jussive addressed to Israel, 6.12b uses the qal perfect, second person plural. The target, then, is possibly those addressed in 6.1-7, the nation's leaders. This suspicion might be confirmed by the wordplay occasioned by the homonym *r'š*: the 'first' among the nations (6.1b), who will be the 'first' to go into exile (6.7), are those who turn justice into 'poison'. They have enjoyed the fruit of violence and injustice, but the overturning of God's moral order (*hpk*) brings his overturning of this perverse 'world'. The dismantling of pretense in this section has already mentioned exile (6.7) and the destruction by invasion (6.8b-11). The final strophe will be even more explicit about the nation's future.

a': Amos 6.13-14. Like 3.12e and 5.7, 6.13 serves as a hinge verse, which further identifies through its participles those referred to in the previous line.[2] In this verse the participles point to the nation's leaders, who boast of their military success. The text, however, mocks them through its language. The folly of 6.12 continues, but in another realm.

They rejoice over Lo-debar (*ll'dbr*; 2 Sam. 9.4; 17.27; Josh. 13.26), very possibly a wordplay on 'nothing'. Their highly regarded victory is very insignificant.[3] They brag of taking Karnaim by their own strength, while 3.14c had announced the tearing down of the *qrnwt*, 'horns', which can be a symbol of strength and refuge.[4] Their pride is

---

1. Andersen and Freedman, in contrast, hold that 5.7 and 6.12 (as well as 5.18 and 6.13) are an *inclusio* structure and that, therefore, both verses refer to the same group of people—i.e. the nation's leadership (*Amos*, pp. 601-605).

2. E.g. Smith, *Amos*. In addition, De Waard and Smalley present a diagram that demonstrates the inter-connectedness of 6.12-14 (*Amos*, pp. 208, 210); the foolishness and sad consequences of injustice and military pride would thus be structurally linked. Some critics, however, consider this verse as fragmentary (e.g. Wolff, *Amos*, and Markert, *Struktur*).

3. So most commentaries. For the location of these two places, see especially Wolff, *Amos*; Soggin, *Amos*.

4. Rosenbaum would understand the term to refer to horns used in the *marzeaḥ* ritual (*Amos*, pp. 66-67).

emphasized in 6.13b, where they are quoted as saying *hlw' bḥzqnw lqḥnw lnw* (note the alliteration and assonance, especially the repetition of *-nw*). Earlier passages, however, declare that Israel's strength (3.11) will be lost, and that the mighty would be brought down (5.9). The quote, while containing an element of truth (cf. 6.1-2), at the same time ridicules the emptiness of the vainglory by the wordplays (e.g. the revelation of defeats in the past 4.10). The quote also exposes the hypocrisy of those in power: while at the cult the victories might be attributed solely to the deity and the nation led to believe in Yahweh's unfailing support of the ruling regime and system, much was actually claimed for the prowess of the military itself. Lastly, the quote proves yet once more the insatiable greed for wealth and power, as these victories were *lnw*.

6.14 begins with *ky hnny*, and the *inclusio* with Yahweh's command of smiting is joined to his raising up the adversary (as in 6.11, a participle is used). Throughout the reading divine action and human agency in judgment are combined, but here the synchronism perhaps is at its clearest (note especially 3.11; 4.2-3, 10; 5.9, 27). Also, *byt* ties together this strophe with the other descriptions of devastation (6.9, 10, 11; cf. 3.14-15). The verse, however, suspends the mention of his instrument until the very end of the line. The expectation is delayed by the speech formula + divine name and title. These words form an *inclusio* with 6.8 and so tie together the announcement of complete destruction with that of the agent, as well as emphasize the irreversibility of judgment through the association with the divine oath (even as does *ky hnny* in 6.14a by the *inclusio* with the divine command of 6.11a). Far from being an awkward interpolation,[1] the phrase is stylistically important because of its location at the center of a possible chiasm in v. 14.[2] The word of the God of hosts, therefore, testifies to the certainty of punishment by the hand of the Almighty.

The biting irony of the judgment is further underscored by several

---

1. The phrase is often either deleted (Cripps, *Amos*; Mays, *Amos*; Amsler, *Amos*; Willi-Plein, *Vorformen*, p. 44; Wolff, *Amos*; Markert, *Struktur*; cf. LXX) or moved to the end of the verse (Harper, *Amos*; Rudolph, *Amos*; Soggin, *Amos*). Among the translations which take the later option—Eng.: NEB; Sp.: RVA. NIV places the phrase at the beginning of 6.14.

2. Suggested by De Waard and Smalley, although they do not discount its secondary nature or original location at the end of 6.14 (*Amos*, pp. 139, 208, 210, 253 n. 71).

more features. First, Yahweh raises up a *gwy*. The *byt yśr'l* had come
to the leaders (6.1), but now the *byt yśr'l* must await the arrival of the
foreign invader. The leaders of the first of *hgwym* will now face a
divinely sponsored attack of a *gwy*. Secondly, the vacuity of the words
of 6.13 is put into relief when juxtaposed to the efficacious word of
the sovereign Lord. The true precariousness of the military will be
disclosed by the God of hosts. Finally, the allusion to boundaries in
6.14b returns the reader to the attitudes manifest in 6.2. The pride in
the military's power and in the extent of the national borders is to be
turned against Israel's leaders. This line, as several scholars have
observed, is similar to the notice of 2 Kgs 14.25.[1] In contrast to the
words of the historical tradition which attribute the expansion to
Yahweh, the leaders in Amos claim any victories as their own. The
same Yahweh who granted them the territory of promise, therefore,
now decrees oppression throughout the land. As with the patriarchal
accounts (4.11-12) and the exodus (3.1-2, 9; 4.10a; cf. 2.10; 9.7),
comforting allusions to national traditions of redemption or blessing
are turned on their head, and the canonical history reversed.

Summary and conclusion. Structurally, ch. 6 is a very artistically
constructed unit. Besides the chiasm that extends across the fourteen
verses, there are quite a number of *inclusios* that connect different
strophes (for example—*ky hnh*, 6.11 with 6.13-14), mark off the
two subsections (for 6.1-7, *r'š*; for 6.8-14, *n'm-yhwh 'lhy ṣb'wt*),
and bind the chapter together (6.1-14—*gwy*; *byt yśr'l*; *hmt*). In
addition, the center of the chiasm at 6.9-10 focuses attention on the
terrible consequences of the lifestyle and policies of those who rule
Israel. The end of each subsection contributes by specifying the

---

1. Among those who make reference to 2 Kgs 14.25, several suggest that this
verse mocks not only the national pride, but also the prophet of weal, Jonah (cf.
Rudolph, *Amos*; Wolff, *Amos*; Coote, *Amos*, pp. 129-34; Soggin, *Amos*). Gowan
claims that the text of 2 Kgs 14.25 is citing Amos, in 'The Beginnings of Exile-
Theology', pp. 206-207. According to the historical reconstruction of Andersen and
Freedman, chronologically 2 Kgs 14.25-28 is later than the events alluded to in this
verse and serves to contradict the prophet Amos's words (*Amos*, pp. 247-50, 585-
96). It should also be pointed out that in 6.14, Andersen and Freedman try to be
consistent with their hypothesis that *byt yśr'l* refers to both Israel and Judah; here as
elsewhere, however, their argumentation is a bit stretched (pp. 112-14). At least,
however, these authors do attempt to 'rate' these ideas (pp. 126-39).

cause of death: exile (6.7), invasion (6.14).

Consistent with the style of chs. 3–5, ch. 6 presents the guilty as type characters, faceless sinners known only by participles and finite verbal forms. The quote in 6.13 only confirms the self-serving arrogance witnessed in the opening scene of uncontrolled revelry.

In contradistinction to those so secure, so deluded, in their positions, stands Yahweh, the Lord God of hosts. He is not a type character; his name appears in a variety of forms and his sovereign actions stress his uniqueness. The striking shift in imagery between 6.1-7 and 6.8-14, with the change from feasting to death and destruction, is matched by this contrast in characters: instead of empty boasting. Yahweh swears (6.8), speaks (6.8, 14), and commands (6.11); instead of the dependence on a false sense of power in the national armies, he raises up an irresistible invader (6.14).

Chapter 6 thoroughly tears down the leaders' 'world' by putting a stop to its pagan banquets (6.7), by silencing the music (6.9-10), and by defeating its forces (6.7, 14). Those who live off violence (6.3) will bring horrible violence not only upon themselves, but also on the entire people (6.6b, 9-11, 14). There is no hope of peace for Israel, no chance of escaping the divine wrath. The nation's leaders have sealed its destiny.

This chapter is the second and last section (the other being 5.18-27) that expands on the themes of 5.1-17. 6.1-14 and 5.1-17 are linked together in various ways. The most obvious is the thematic connection of death and defeat. Not only is the stench of death everywhere (6.9-10; 5.16-17), the appeal to multiples of ten to emphasize the scope of the loss of life is used in both sections (6.9; 5.3). The nation's defeat is marked by the destruction of edifices, in particular the houses (6.11; 5.9-11). There is also irony in that the virgin has fallen never to rise (*qwm*, 5.2aA) and with no one to lift her up (*mqymh*, 5.2bB), but now Yahweh raises up (*mqym*) an invader to oppress Israel across the breadth of the land (6.14; 5.2bA).

Both sections also substantiate the general–particular judgment tension. On the one hand, *byt yśr'l* is in view (note the *inclusio*—5.1; 6.14), but, on the other, the prosperous and powerful are singled out as the most responsible (note especially the use of *mšpṭ* and *ṣdqh*— 5.15; 6.12) for the misery in the present and the suffering in the future. The lack of concern for the 'ruin of Joseph' (6.6b) will mean that the 'house of Joseph' (5.6) will be left (and that only perhaps)

with a 'remnant' (5.3, 15b; 6.8, 9). In spite of all the tribulation, however, those who govern remain unrepentant, in quiet yet stubborn
rebellion before the wrath of God (6.10; 5.13). Yahweh appears as the
Lord God of hosts (6.8, 14; 5.14-16), who effects his judgment with
an invading army.

2. *Religion and the Social Construction of Reality in Amos*

This reading of Amos has attempted to bring to light a textual world
in which religion plays an important role in the definition and maintenance of the social reality in Israel. The initial impression is one of a
phenomenon of some complexity. There exists an active yahwism of
national feasts celebrated at the sanctuaries (4.4-5; 5.4-5, 21-23), but
from time to time an allusion to paganism also surfaces. Indirect reference can perhaps be seen in the emphasis in 4.6-13 on rain and the
high places, and the difficult 5.26 (cf. 8.14) could point to the worship
of astral deities. 6.4-6 points to a paganism of the well-to-do, in which
participation is limited to those with the means to satisfy extravagant
tastes. The data of the text, therefore, suggests a syncretism able to
cross theological boundaries, as it were, and venerate several gods.

Still, this is a nation that claims to be Yahweh's own, and it is this
belief that magnetizes the concentration of the text. The complexity of
the religion of Israel is more than just beliefs in a number of different
gods. What Amos reveals to the reader is a socioreligious tapestry. It
will not do to separate neatly the social from the religious critique or to
oversimplify the problem of yahwism as that of empty ritual. The fabric
of this 'world' created by the nation within this textual world is too
complicated for that sort of approach.[1] The following summary of the

1. Many authors do not integrate the social and religious critiques in Amos (e.g.
Fendler, 'Zur Socialkritik des Amos'), or offer only very vague connections (e.g.,
Wolff, *La hora de Amós*, pp. 39-65; R.R. Wilson, *Prophecy and Society in Ancient
Israel* [Philadelphia: Fortress Press, 1980], pp. 266-69). Bernhard Lang ties in his
Yahweh-alone theory with (especially international) politics, but does not link
yahwism with his discussion of the socioeconomic problems in Amos *(Monotheism*,
chs. 1, 2, 4). More sensitive are the discussions of H.B. Huffmon, 'The Social Role
of Amos' Message', in *The Quest for the Kingdom of God: Studies in Honor of
George E. Mendenhall* (ed. H.B. Huffmon, F.A. Spina and A.R.W. Green; Winona
Lake, IN: Eisenbrauns, 1983), pp. 109-16; J.L. Sicre, *Los dioses olvidados. Poder
y riquezas en los profetas preexílicos* (Estudios de Antiquo Testamento, 1; Madrid:

nature of religion discovered in the reading of Amos chs. 3–6 will highlight some aspects of its identity and judgment. The discussion will look for the *inclusios* between the opening (3.1–4.3) and closing section (6.1-14) and will follow the trajectory of vocabulary and themes through these chapters.[1] In that way, the reading can be shown to demonstrate both textual coherence and movement.

The picture of yahwism that emerges from the text is one that is inexorably tied together with the history and fate of Israel, as well as with its present social make-up. First, there are the traditions of election as a nation unique among all others. Chapters 3 (3.1-2) and 6 (6.1-2) both begin by alluding to this special choosing. But this foundation of national security is satirized in both passages: special knowledge will require a personal visit of Yahweh (3.2b), and the foremost of the nations will be invaded by an enemy people (6.14). To trace the textual interplay with other traditions is to find that they also are turned on their head: Israel already has suffered the fate of Egypt and Sodom and Gomorrah (4.10-11); and the time in the wilderness now stands as an indictment of Israel's hypocritical worship (5.25).

It is not only these venerable traditions that are overturned, however, but the 'world' that uses them to legitimize its existence and shape. Throughout chs. 3–6 religious centers and ceremonies are juxtaposed to a variety of institutions. Bethel is mentioned amidst references to the homes of those in power (3.14-15), Bethel and Gilgal

Ediciones Cristiandad, 1979), esp. pp. 13-33, 101-16, 153-56, 173-79; Sicre, *'Con los pobres'*, pp. 152-59; Koch, *The Prophets*, I, pp. 44-76. Contrast D.L. Petersen's confusion in calling Amos a 'central morality prophet' who speaks 'on behalf of values central to the society and on behalf of the god who sanctions the moral structure of society' (*The Roles of Israel's Prophets* [JSOTSup, 17; Sheffield: JSOT Press, 1981], p. 68). Amos is attacking the moral structure on behalf of Yahweh and does so apparently from the periphery as a foreigner. For a good discussion of the relationship between religion and ideology in biblical studies, see Gottwald, *Tribes of Yahweh*, chs. 47–50.

For the mixture of state and religion in the ancient Near East, see, for example, J. Reade, 'Ideology and Propaganda in Assyrian Art', in *Power and Propaganda: A Symposium on Ancient Empires* (ed. M.T. Larsen; Mesopotamia; Copenhagen Studies in Assyriology, 7; Copenhagen: Akademisk Forlag, 1979), pp. 329-59. Machinist underscores the importance of political propaganda in prophetic texts in 'Assyria and its Image in the First Isaiah'.

   1. For some of the textual observations regarding *inclusio*, see Spreafico, 'Struttura Formale', pp. 161-65.

(and Beersheba) alongside references to city defenses (5.2-9). In addition, the confession of the divine presence (5.14b) is connected with the administration of justice, taxes and business in the gate (5.10-15). But this interweaving of religion and national life is evil, this 'world' created by Israel and sustained by its version of yahwism perverse.

ḥms appears first in 3.10 and then in 6.3: social violence reigns. These chapters move from the initial notice of oppression by those in power (3.9-10) to the mention of luxurious homes (3.15), debauchery (4.1), luxury bought of injustice (5.11-12), and lastly to unrefrained feasting (6.4-6). Those who rule live at the expense of others and are held most accountable for the nation's fateful course; yet Israel as a people are guilty. The initial word is spoken to all of Israel (3.1), as are the call to worship (4.4), the lament (5.1), the warning of false hopes (5.18), the threat of exile (5.26-27), and the final notice of invasion (6.14). Those who govern do manipulate justice (5.10, 15; 6.12), but unrighteousness is a national malady (5.7, 24). All have sinned (note the various terms for sin in 3.1, 14; 4.4; 5.12)—but there is no sacrifice of repentance (4.4-5; 5.21-23), only the praise to a god of blessing and victory, to a deity who never questions the social context in spite of the suffering of the weak and the true (3.9-10; 4.1; 5.10; 6.6).

But the religion which sanctifies this 'natural order of things' is not simply an opiate dictated by Israel's leaders. Of course, they have a hand in supporting the cult for their positions are at stake, but the religion of the people is broader than the official ideology. For one, they still go on pilgrimage to Judah (5.5), and other gods also beckon. The rhetorical questions in the text both at the beginning and close of the reading demonstrate general blindness (3.3-8; cf. 5.18, 25), as well as the unfounded pride of the powerful (6.13). But the blindness is not innocent; it is born of a refusal to return to Yahweh (4.6-11) or to seek him (5.4-5, 14-15; 6.10). They will have him as they will (4.5b; 5.14), and when and where they will (4.4-5; 5.5; 5.21-23). But this stubborn blindness is irrational (again note the structural *inclusio*, 3.3-6 and 6.12a) and suicidal, for now must come the wrath of a Yahweh who refuses to be manipulated.

This 'world' is to come crashing down. The stylistics of destruction can be traced in several ways. To begin with, the literal structures are destroyed. 3.13-15 and 6.8-14 ring most of the oracles and repeat *byt* a number of times: Bet-el (3.14), the homes of the leaders (3.15, four times; cf. 5.11), a house of death (6.9, 10), the big and small houses (6.11), the house of Jacob/Israel (3.13, 6.14). In 3.9-11 the focus is on the palace-fortresses (four times), a term picked up again in 6.8 as the object of divine hatred. Moving on to other sections: in 4.3 and 5.9 the defenses are singled out. The sanctuaries are also to be a target of demolition (3.14; 5.5-6). These passages include, then, a wide variety of structures upon which all of society would depend in one way or another.

Secondly, these chapters focus on the 'city'. Once more, a term appears at both extremes (3.6a; 6.8c); in this case the city is also named: Samaria, the capital of Israel (3.9, 12; 6.1). The vague 'evil' brought by Yahweh to the city (3.6a) is affirmed and intensified by his oath to deliver it up *wml'h* (6.8c). In addition, although the enemy remains nameless, his hand in the destruction is progressively developed: surrounding and attacking the land (3.11), destroying the walls (implied 4.3), taking the nation into exile (5.27), bringing death (5.3; 6.9-10) and oppressing Israel across the breadth of its territory (6.14).

Thirdly, there is a progression in tone, and this course is also marked by a structural pattern. The initial 'hear', which announces judgment (3.1; 4.1), gives way to a 'hear', which sounds out a lament (5.1). 5.1-17 closes with wailing (5.16-17), and then appears the exclamation *hwy*, a paronomastic play on *hw* (5.18; 6.1). All three sections of chs. 5 and 6 (5.1-17, 18-27; 6.1-14) are chiasms, and the latter two develop key themes of the first—the lack of justice and death, respectively. But the movement is impactful: from warning to wailing. Israel's doom and the death of a multitude are sealed.

The most important textual technique for dismantling the socioreligious 'world' of Israel is the concentration on Yahweh himself. Although Amos juxtaposes Yahweh and this yahwism in a number of ways, only three will be underscored here. On the one hand, these chapters contrast the power of Yahweh with the pretense of the nation and its leadership. His might is evident by the constant interplay between his direct intervention and his sovereign moving of instruments of his wrath. Note how his work is indistinguishable from or parallel to the enemy's (e.g. 3.14-15 with 3.11; 4.2-3, 10; 5.2-3, 5, 9, 27; 6.8, 11, 14), and how his omnipotence in nature has been and will be released against Israel (4.6-9, 13; 5.8-9).

Secondly, the contrast between Yahweh and Israel is marked by dissimilar, but ironic, characterization. For example, there are few quotes of the people and those in power, but in each case the words are self-condemnatory (4.1; 6.13; cf. 5.14). These chapters, however, repeatedly stress the efficacy and finality of the divine speech with a broad range of terms: *dbr*, *š'g*, *n'm*, *šb'*, *'mr*, *ṣwh*. The variety of forms and the constant hammering at the certainty of the message of judgment allow no room for doubt as to the future. This difference in the manner of speech goes hand in hand with this reading's repeated observation that Yahweh is the only full-fledged charter in Amos. All the others are either type characters who stand for certain groups and behavior, or agents who are but instruments in the sovereign hands of God.

The contrast is also drawn by the ironic use of the same terms. Three, in particular, stand out, and were developed in the reading: *yd'*, *hpk* and *śn'*. Each in their own way highlight the divine response: Yahweh knows all the sins of those who do not know how to do good (3.2, 10; 5.12); he will overturn the 'world' which has overturned his 'natural order of things' (4.11; 5.7-8; 6.12); and he hates those who hate justice and truth (5.10, 15, 21; 6.8).

Finally, the complicated yahwism of this 'world' is confronted personally by Yahweh. The encounter with the deity is expressed both by the variety of names and titles in the text, as well as by the structure. Not only are the names in the several combinations important, the 'name' (*šm*) is also crucial; observe its placement at the climax of the 'hymn' (4.4-13), the center of 5.1-17, and the climax of 5.18-27. One name and title that particularly stand out are Yahweh, Lord God of hosts, which appears to imply a context of invasion (3.13; 5.14-16, 27; 6.8, 14). In other words, the fateful encounter with Yahweh (4.13, 5.17) will be in that ('evil') 'day', the time of the awful destruction wrought by the enemy and the forced removal from the land.

Yahweh not only contends with the nation's yahwism, he orders the eradication of the 'world' that lives in his name. These chapters present the powerful announcement of the absoluteness of another kingdom, of a sovereign who brooks no rivals and who demands justice. He will not be mocked by a 'world' made of human hands. Amos depicts two conceptions of life and society in conflict in ancient Israel. What now remains to be seen is how this textual vision of the divine perspective might impact the social construction of reality in the modern world.

Chapter 6

FROM THE TEXT TO THE WORLD:
AMOS IN THE MODERN CONTEXT

The dialogue with the text from within a given context is a complex affair that involves a number of methodological decisions. This book has tried to offer a particular perspective, which necessarily entails a series of commitments: the option to begin from a consideration of the complexity of moral life in a cultural setting (Chapter 3) and the choice of a textual approach, poetics, that is sensitive to the power of the received text of the Bible (Chapter 4). The last chapter then explored the world represented in a section of Amos in order to explore the 'reality' so emphatically denounced in that prophetic book by the deity—in particular, the nature and role of religious life within Israel's society.

Whereas the previous theoretical discussion has centered on *how* to read, as it were, another difficult task remains. How is one now to move *from* that poetic reading *to* the modern world? Although the book's ultimate concern is to interact with and perhaps make some sort of contribution to the theological debates taking place within Latin America, the attempt to contextualize might, I hope, find resonance beyond those borders.

The discussion that follows can only be suggestive. As earlier chapters have tried to point out, a text within a context can 'do' so many things—legitimatize or challenge, confirm or revolutionize—from so many different angles, precisely because of the situatedness of the interpreter and his community and because of the various decisions in method (whether conscious or not) that must be made. This chapter will base its observations and proposals on that afore-developed theoretical framework and is divided into two major sections. The first indicates several ways in which Amos can draw its readers into its world and submits some ideas as to possible implications for a reading from within Latin America. The second turns more specifically to the issue of popular religion in that continent and to the work of several liberation theologians who see its potential as a vehicle for social transformation. Can Amos offer an insight into the religious world of that crucible of change that is Latin America?

1. *Participation in the Textual World*

Chapter 4 elaborated on the moral authority of the Scripture, an authority grounded in the Bible's privileged role as the shaper of the moral vision of the Christian church. The text can represent a world which offers a truthful understanding of God and his demands on those who claim to call on his name. How, though, can the reader and the believing community be brought into dialogue, even confrontation, with that text, and moral life be challenged and reshaped? At least three ways can be suggested.

a. *The Text as an Identity Document*
The argument based on the work of narrative theology which was presented in Chapter 4 mentioned that the biblical text can be taken as an 'identity document' that presents a picture of the community of faith in its relationship with God and the world.

In Amos that picture is very complex. Religious life is in no way monolithic in orientation or unitary in theology. Although shared symbols and common rituals can bind this religious world together, what is graphically depicted is a society with overlapping and intersecting religious activities and beliefs. There is an officially sponsored cult that enjoys broad participation that would foster nationalism and a confidence in a benevolent deity; but the yahwism of the Israel in Amos extends beyond that country's boundaries to pilgrimages to Beersheba in Judah. Apparently there is also a widespread pagan influence, but even that is not of one stripe, as the wealthy, for example, enjoy their own exclusive festive worship.

This religious life is intertwined with social realities: the cult can seek allegiance to the state and legitimacy for the crown, public ceremonies can give an appearance of social solidarity, other deities can handle areas beyond Yahweh's believed purview. But the solid and powerful verdict of this prophetic book is that this socioreligious construction is condemned and doomed: Yahweh will not be manipulated by those who govern, no religious activity can mask the injustice or replace the divine demand for righteousness, other gods are as nothing before Yahweh, God of hosts.

Chapter 3 of this book briefly described the cultural and religious life of Latin America. There, too, common symbols and ceremonies among Roman Catholics, for instance, can link social strata and span the continent, but there is much local flavor and variety. Also, among countries with strong Amerindian history and presence, charges of syncretism continually surface; but modern philosophical and sociopolitical influences must also come into play in any evaluation of belief and practice. Latin America, it is said, is a Christian continent—perhaps, but there are several gods and Jesus can have so many faces.[1]

The identity document that is the text will not permit that this montage be simply admired as culturally interesting, because the picture it paints is of total judgment. This divine chastisement gives pause and stimulates reflection, as in Latin America religion and society have historically been and continue to be interrelated in any number of ways, and because this religious continent has for so long been characterized by injustice. To read Amos from within Latin America is to face any number of penetrating questions. For example, how has religion both tied these societies together yet masked or ignored inequalities? What are the origins and functions of the myriad of expressions of Christian worship? How are they to be evaluated? If historically there have been mutual commitments and common interests between governments and religious institutions, what might be the contemporary manifestations? The list could go on, but the key is to remember that Amos dismantles a socioreligious construction of reality; it exposes it in all of its complexity and then judges the perversity and erroneous belief. Although the particular intricate shape of the modern 'world' differs from that of the text, and even though today's mechanisms of privilege and ways of religious self-delusion and self-gratification are not the same, the point stands.

But can this vision of ancient religion and monarchy truly be relevant to contemporary Latin America? Can this denunciation continue to speak? The growing clamor for a 'prophetic voice' that was briefly documented in Chapter 1 serves as an emphatic positive answer

---

1. This last phrase is a play on the work edited by liberationist J. Míguez Bonino, *Faces of Jesus: Latin American Christologies* (Maryknoll: Orbis Books, 1984).

to the latter query. The social injustice and systematic abuse decried in the prophetic books has become a powerful word in recent years. But what of the first question? There is no one-to-one correspondence between the world of Amos and the Latin American continent at the end of the twentieth century, no matter how hard some try to establish exact parallels. Whence then the impact?

I would claim, in contradistinction to those seeking sociopolitical and religious equivalents, that precisely because Amos presents a monarchy, a style of government not in existence in Latin America, its vision can transcend that structural form of another time and place. That is, its descriptions are vague enough to be able to move beyond that textual setting. It will be recalled that in Chapter 4, in the discussion of the text and history, allusion was made to Fernand Braudel's categories of history. There it was suggested that the vagueness of the prophetic text's handling of what Braudel calls *conjucture* and *longue durée* allows it to seem to function in some degree as a reflection of actual reality. I also proposed another category, *l'histoire constitutive*, because these broad elements (whether of evil or good) march across the centuries. What remains constant are the common sins of humanity and the eternal and uncompromising demand for justice.

Besides this fusing of horizons at the level of political and economic structural sin, there is contact and merging with regard to religion. Even though Baalism is not now celebrated nor a yahwistic cult practiced, religious ceremonies in Latin America continue to mark the calendars and enjoy extensive public participation. Difference there is, but echo as well. In fact, the dissimilarities are the basis of textual power, because no one religious expression, governmental form, or combination of these in any given society can be neatly tagged as the modern target of the text's moral critique. Both right and left, Protestant and Roman Catholic, indeed all of Latin America's Christian society and movements, must come under the scrutinizing light of the divine demand represented in the church's 'classic' text. The *discontinuities*, in other words, make a *continuity* of social imagination possible.

Amos unrelentingly and comprehensively condemns, and by so doing it can generate a constant effort to conform the modern world to the values of the textual world. More must be explored, but goes unsaid: how is the condemnation to be effectuated today? What is the shape of a more just society and a more proper cult? The means of fleshing out the ancient text's vision is the difficult challenge for today's people of God and requires further theological reflection and the discerning of an appropriate pastoral practice.

If Amos is an identity document that depicts the people of God in its world, it also offers a portrait of Yahweh as the all-powerful, holy sovereign in creation and history. Other issues arise here: how does Yahweh act in history now? Is there a sacred history separate from the secular? How does the particular history of God's community integrate into broader 'profane' currents?

Amos can provide a vision, but the ascertaining of the precise practical steps (both Yahweh's and ours) in this era requires further reflection beyond the scope of this book. But the issues are crucial and the hard questions unavoidable if there is to be any change towards a socioreligious reality in Latin America more attuned to God's ethical mandates.

b. *Archetypes and Textual Ambiguity*

Another manner by which readers are drawn into the textual world of Amos is through the generality of the characterizations and the anonymity of many of the actors in the textual representation. The 'everyman' that appears can generate several levels of archetypes. In his discussion of archetypes in the prophetic literature, Alter mentions certain tendencies, which my reading shows are also evident in Amos. His comments are worth citing in full:

> Now, the archetyping force of vocative poetry in the Prophets can move in two directions beyond the primary mode of accusation, where its general effect is to fix the particular vices within an authoritative, timeless scheme of moral judgment. If the speaker sarcastically invokes the viewpoint of his human objects of reproof, conjuring up the illusory pleasures or power to which they are addicted, he produces a satirical depiction of how the evil are self-deceived. Tonally, the satires tend to jeer where the accusations angrily expose and impugn; substantively, they tend to be evocations of the moral psychology of overweening wickedness. If, on the other hand, the speaker focuses on the cataclysmic consequences of the misdeeds he is stigmatizing, then he produces a vision of the terrible swift force of God in history, wreaking havoc among the nations. The outer limit of archetype is myth, and, for all that has been written about the demythologizing impulse of the Hebrew Bible, prophetic poetry

exhibits a certain predilection to mythologize its historical subjects, setting the here and now in cosmic perspectives.[1]

Because the wicked remain nameless and their ways are not specified in great detail, the bridge to modern society is facilitated and *people* and *structures* worthy of condemnation can be pointed to. Self-deception, self-destruction and divine judgment—Amos is eloquent in the portrayal of the pretensions and machinations of the wicked who run Israel's society in its various spheres, whether administrative, economic or religious. Some in that society live at the expense of others, and the scenes are those of ugly violation and hard calculations. The perversity is underscored because of the sanctioning that is found in the religious realm: not only does the cult celebrate national traditions and victories, the public ceremonies also help preserve this world and its evil structures and base morality as the 'natural order of things'. Yahweh mocks this distorted reality and decrees an enemy invasion to destroy it.

But the archetypes are not only of the evil ones, the broader textual *setting* itself also appears so lifelike and true to reality. In other words, its rebellious and misguided world can be archetypal, its mistakes and fate ours. Both modern leadership and modern life appear to find parallels within the textual world. In countries, such as in Latin America, where religion is still very prominent, nationalism a potent ideological force, and injustice open and rife, Amos can appear so very history-like. As Alter observes:

> In this fashion, a set of messages framed for a particular audience of the eighth century BCE is not just the transcription of a historical document but continues to speak age after age, inviting members of otherwise very different societies to read themselves into the text.[2]

The satirizing and denouncing of the wicked and of societal structures and mindsets that perpetuate injustice have always been prominent themes in some of the most powerful of Latin American poetry and novels. Latin American literature at its best is a literature of protest. The archetypal potential of the prophetic books permits this literary characteristic to find expression also in so much of the recent theology writing within that continent. But if this archetypal

1. Alter, *Art of Biblical Poetry*, pp. 146-47.
2. Alter, *Art of Biblical Poetry*, p. 146.

relating can move across the horizon of 'the evil and their evil', can it function as well in terms of the victims of oppression? If so, how?

Jauss's examination of 'interactional patterns of aesthetic identification with the hero' can help probe this important topic of ethical concern.[1] Jauss identifies five levels of identification, each of which can evoke either positive or negative moral responses from the reader. His discussion is involved, so only certain of the elements he discusses will be used here. The first level is 'associative' identification, where the reader can enjoy 'free existence' as he enters into roles within the textual world and where there is liberty to assume the posture of various characters. The serious and condemnatory tone of Amos, however, precludes this kind of playful option.

At the next level is 'admiring' identification, where a perfect hero can serve as a model. In the prophetic text under study only two candidates are available for this category. On the one hand stands Yahweh, but he is God, and his holy and majestic character elicits fear; there is no possibility of emulation, only the demand of obedience.

On the other hand, there is the prophet Amos or the prophets (2.11-12; 3.7; cf. 5.10; 7.1-17), who serve as Yahweh's mouthpieces. There is much talk within theological circles of being 'prophetic', but in Amos, at least, as the reading demonstrated, these characters are not very well developed as Yahweh himself commands center stage. Some, however, might turn to these as examples of truth and courage in the face of opposition worthy to be followed. But what of the oppressed?

The next two categories might prove more relevant here. Jauss speaks of 'sympathetic' identification with an imperfect hero in whom the reader can see himself and gain a new ethical perspective. There is both a sense of solidarity and empathy. At this level can enter that sociohermeneutic stance of a reading 'from below'. The complication that arises, however, is that Amos juxtaposes portraits of the 'poor masses', as it were, as victims and as willful participants in sin. Is it that only certain of the lower classes are really innocent? Or, is it that both pictures are true: they can be oppressed, while they themselves mistreat their own in accordance with the prevailing morality and share in a religion far from Yahweh's liking? The gaps and discontinuities of the poetical reading make tidy ethical compartmentalizing

1. H.R. Jauss, 'Levels of Identification of Hero and Audience', *NLH* 5 (1974), pp. 283-317, especially pp. 298-317.

impossible. There is coherence in the picture of the world of Amos, but intelligibility is not gained through strategies of simplification (whether, for example, by denying the complexity altogether or by redefining terms such as 'the sons of Israel') but by wrestling with the tensions. The text can force the reader to a new moral vision, a more realistic comprehension of moral life and social existence.[1]

The same can be said of the fourth level, 'cathartic' identification with the suffering hero, which moves the reader beyond the previous disposition to a powerful confrontation with the text. 'Tragic emotional upheaval' leads to 'critical reflection' and freely chosen moral options. Although here the interaction with the text is more profound, the problem of the 'poor' as hero remains. It must be stressed that these observations do not negate action on their behalf or trivialize the commitment to (even radical) change. They do, however, suggest that the text's tensions should be respected for a more true-to-life moral understanding.

Jauss's last category is that of 'ironic' identification, the level at which no hero exists and expectations of solidarity are frustrated and disappointed. Cannot Amos function in this way as well? If the prophets appear too removed from ordinary experience and the oppressed, at least in part, as sinful sufferers, then the reader is forced to acknowledge that Amos is holding out neither pure models for imitation nor an innocent social bloc to be liberated; it is rather demanding the dismantling of a world that claims Yahweh and the acceptance of his ethical principles. Amos seeks allegiance and obedience in a realistic assessment of the world. The Jewish scholar Samuel Sandmel says of this book:

> We must also wonder at the Hebrew mind. Why did the Hebrews preserve, and even cherish, this impressive record of unsavory actions and attitudes? Why should they not, in understandable national pride, have suppressed and destroyed it? Why did they keep alive this indictment of their infamy? We cannot readily explain this; we can only observe that they felt no shame in the shameful record of their past, and, far from concealing it, they glorified the literature which portrayed their shortcomings.[2]

---

1. See Sternberg, *Poetics of Biblical Narrative*, especially chs. 6–8.

2. Quoted in A. Preminger and E.L. Greenstein (eds.), *The Hebrew Bible in Literary Criticism* (A Library of Literary Criticism; New York: Ungar, 1986), p. 275.

In other words, the literature of protest also can gain power as literature of honest self-exposure.

In sum, the archetypal potential of Amos can operate in a wide variety of ways. The result of the textual data from this text is what some might consider moral ambiguity or compromise. I would say otherwise: the text challenges the readers of believing communities to uncompromising and honest self-appraisal and commitment to Yahweh's moral demands. The call for change is not thereby weakened or solidarity with the oppressed eliminated; rather, realism and responsibility gain their proper place.

Again, however, pragmatics raises questions. Once one moves beyond general *impact* and initial *impressions* to concrete social realities, what, if any, *implementation* for change can be gleaned from the text's archetypal reality? For instance, what are the modern means of dismantling systematic injustice? If in Amos the divine judgment entailed the raising up of an invasion for a violent destruction of that society, is a bloody revolution therefore justified today? The vagueness of the text, while allowing it to resonate within modern realities, pushes those who would hold the prophetic book as a moral resource to move beyond its limitations. Hence the need for other analytical tools and other guides to concretize the text's concerns; analysis eventually must turn to action, and here the text is mute. In other words, the textual description of a world of oppression, which is offered in general (and value-laden) terms, is not a prescription for social change, and so ideological and praxiological commitments come to the fore.[1] To say as much is to demand that theological reflection and pastoral action be responsible; that any talk of changes leave behind pious pronunciations of ideals and romantic motions of

---

1. Note John Goldingay's comment after his elaboration of the political world portrayed in the received text of Daniel:

> Yet the stories offer a *narrative* politics. The embodiment of such generalizations in a concrete portrayal is more vital than the principles we may extract from it. They invite us to set Daniel's experience and testimony alongside the stories which emerge from our political experience and to see what happens. They may help us to see what praxis we need to be committed to. The nature of narrative, however, is not to point directly to action but to invite reflection (a characteristic which may in the end make it more powerful because more subliminal). And a major theme of that reflection will likely concern not so much what we may do in politics, but what God may do ('The Stories in Daniel: A Narrative Politics', *JSOT* [1987], p. 115).

Christian communities and come to grips with life as it is really lived on the ground in Latin America with all its complexity and confusion; that the prophetic text be read and applied in context.

c. *Direct Address and the Modern Reader*
One final means by which readers of the believing community can be drawn into the prophetic text is by the presence of second personal plural commands directed at eighth-century Israel but which in the reading now address the people of God today. Fisch mentions in particular the verb *šm'*:

> the verb *šema'* implies not only hearing, perceiving, interpreting, but also *remembering*. Past occasions are linked by memory to present occasions—that is the true hermeneutic circle of interpretation. 'Hear O Israel' in fact says something about history: the word that has been heard validates itself in the historical present as it did in the past; it continues to resound. The words 'Hear O Israel' can thus be glossed, '*Continue* to hear, O Israel; a living word is carried into the future by a living people constituting an undying community of auditors. I declare myself to be part of that community'.[1]

This is a prominent verb in the chapters which were the focus of the poetic reading of Amos. The entire nation is addressed and accused in 3.1 (*bny yśr'l*) and then, beginning in ch. 5, sound the laments (5.1, *byt yśr'l*; cf. 5.18). The calls to 'hear' and other commands and descriptions in the second person plural are a challenge to self-examination.

To claim to be the people of God today means to listen to these words directed against the people of God of the text and to be willing to look at present moral conduct and attitudes from that perspective. As Fisch points out:

> The reading of the poem becomes a struggle for vindication. The notion of a trial or a court of law is not here a pleasing trope... but rather a *Gattung*, a way of structuring the relationship between the text and the reader, or more correctly, between the reader and the God who is seen to stand behind the words of the text.[2]

The sins of Israel can be seen as possible sins of the church: social abuse, nationalistic or ideological jingoism, empty ritual, erroneous

---

1. Fisch, *Poetry with a Purpose*, p. 50 (author's emphasis).
2. Fisch, *Poetry with a Purpose*, p. 53.

beliefs—all coming under (or hiding behind) the name of Yahweh, God or Jesus.

The textual artistry, however, could be even more intricate and penetrating in at least three ways not considered by Fisch. For example, some of the imperatives are directed at certain groups within Israel (e.g. 4.1, *prwt hbšn*; 6.1, *h š' nnym bṣywn whbṭḥym bhr šmrwn*). As the reading attempted to point out, though the whole nation is guilty, there are some who are held to be especially responsible by Yahweh for the abominable state of the society and the impending disaster. The audience, both today and in the text, can move between the general and the particular, from the universally condemned to the uniquely accountable.

Another feature is the participial constructions and third person verbal forms that describe the sinful actions and attitudes of both the general public and the leadership. In contrast to the second person forms, these verbs can create a distancing effect: the guilty are 'other'. But herein lies the impact, a poetics of 'entrapment'. Along with the deity and his prophet the reader justifiably condemns the wicked, yet in so doing the community of faith convicts itself. The distancing serves to entrap by inviting solidarity in sentencing, even as the second person forms create solidarity in guilt through direct address.

Finally, mention should be made of another category of second person imperative, the call to foreign peoples to come and witness (3.9; note the verb *šm'*, 3.13) the sins of Israel. The 'struggle for vindication', therefore, is not only before God or within the community of faith, but also before the world. How is the moral life of the people of God different from that of other communities (cf. 1.3–2.3; 9.7)? How should it be? The community of believers is not only *drawn into the text* to evaluate itself before the ethical tribunal of this history-like mirror; it is also will *draw unto itself* the searching gaze of the world in the inescapable and constant challenge to define and prove its moral uniqueness.

Difference, however, does not mean separation or isolation; Israel is but one of the nations within the textual reality of Amos, even if an elect people. Within Amos, however, Israel is not just in the world; not merely of the world, the nation is actually worse than the rest. In light of this textual datum it is interesting to note the struggles within Latin American theologies from across the spectrum to try to define the place of the church within the continent and to adjudge its performance as a moral force in the past, present and future. The self-appraisal is necessary, and on this very religious continent those outside Christian circles are watching and gaging the possible contributions of the church in these turbulent times.

In sum, the three means—the text as an identity document, the text's archetypal potential, and the text's addressing of the reader—work together as the 'art of persuasion' of Amos.[1] On the one hand, the tensions and ambiguities of the entry into the text both complicate modern moral vision and complement the complexity of the moral world of the text. Amos undercuts reductionistic understandings and works to reshape ethical world-views. At the same time, the three strategies cohere around a univocal posture: this is Yahweh's point of view. The interaction with the text, therefore, is stamped with a serious tone and the evaluations must be honestly pursued to avoid self-delusion.

The discussion up to this point has been of a general sort, and once more the focus has been on methodology. The next section turns to a specific concern, the role of popular religion in liberation movements, in order to apply the observations of this section and some of the insights of the poetic reading of the last chapter in a more concrete way.

2. *Popular Religion and the Revolutionary*
Proyecto Histórico

This section proposes to examine briefly how Latin American Liberation Theology has interacted with Roman Catholic popular religion in its desire to move the continent towards what it contends would be a more just sociopolitical life. Several caveats are in order. To begin with, we continue to seek dialogue with liberation theologians in order to seek clarifications and to establish possible contrasts in approach. To interact with these thinkers also has as a goal to warn of potential dangers in the theological enterprise and in the commitments of Christian mission. It is not the intent to single out this current for criticism as if to ignore other postures, which all naturally would have weaknesses, but rather to seek constructive dialogue. Anyone familiar with Latin America is aware of just how intricate has

---

1. Sternberg's term in *Poetics of Biblical Narrative*, chs. 12, 13.

been the relationship between church and society over the centuries, and analysis and debate must continue as the Christian church, both Roman Catholic and Protestant, tries to perceive how to have a moral impact in the present. Chapter 3 had mentioned that the church–state issue is an inheritance from the days of the conquest. Today there is a wide spectrum of postures and commitments, including the utilization of Christian symbols and beliefs by what liberationists would call the 'national security state', the ruling powers of the right.[1] This initial notice is necessary because of how highly charged the theological, pastoral and political reflection and decisions have been in recent years.

The following discussion is divided into three parts, which pick up key themes from the reading of Amos. The first looks at the problem of the identity and role of popular religion vis-à-vis a regnant ideology and socially constructed 'world' by presenting how certain liberationists have viewed the events in Nicaragua under the Sandinista regime. Here especially tensions can run high, but this opening discussion is not an attempt to evaluate that government, its ideology, its performance or its policies. Rather, the desire is to consider some of the theologizing done there. The situation in that Central American country is in a state of flux and development (especially in light of the electoral defeat of the Sandinista government in February, 1990), and the views of the authors cited here will probably not remain static. This is a methodological case study, so it might be helpful to consider these theologians' views as 'ideal types', so to speak, in order to see some of the options that have been taken. The second part looks at the reorientation of the nature and purpose of the cult in some liberation circles. What is its value? What should be its shape? Finally, this section closes with a brief mention and evaluation of a new approach to the concept of idolatry that attempts to elucidate the nature and work of God within the continent.

1. See, for example, Gutiérrez, *Power of the Poor*, pp. 83-90; Míguez Bonino, *Toward a Christian Political Ethics*, ch. 5; Segundo, *Faith and Ideologies*, pp. 289-301; Berryman, *Liberation Theology*, pp. 96-98, 118-22. Cf. for Africa, The Kairos Document, *Challenge to the Church*, pp. 17-24.

a. *Religion and a Particular* Proyecto:
The Case of Sandinista Nicaragua
Chapter 3 presented a semiotic approach to culture, a focus that tried to emphasize the systems of meaning that would be operative in defining cultural identity. This 'web of significances' is also influential in any discussion of cultural change. And change does and must come. In Latin America, where religion and ritual have been so much a part of the cultural landscape, the Christian church can have a substantial voice in the formulation of changes in socioeconomic and political structures and policies. But what is the proper place of a Christian contribution within these movements? How will traditional symbols and ceremonies be reoriented, or will they be substituted? How can a part be played in the dissemination of values commensurate with divine ethical demands?

For at least the last two decades the Roman Catholic Church has been wrestling as an ecclesiastical body with the church-culture problem. The Bishops Conference in Puebla in 1979, for example, spoke of the positive and negative elements in the popular culture and how it might be 'evangelized' on a continent in transition.[1] The case of Nicaragua since the fall of Somoza proved to be a particularly divisive issue, especially with the presence of several clergy in government posts.[2] For liberationists, the Sandinista regime afforded both an opportunity to experiment with, develop and mature their ideals, as well as serve as the motivation to further them elsewhere in Latin

---

1. CELAM, *Puebla. La evangelización en el presente y en el futuro de América Latina*, III Conferencia General del Episcopado Latinoamericano (Bogotá: Editorial L. Canal y Asociados, 3rd edn, 1979), paras. 385-469 (pp. 121-36). The bishops highlight the change from an agrarian to an urban-industrialized society and not so much the dependency paradigm of Liberation Theology. The Conference was not without its ideological controversy, however.

2. For the personal view of Ernesto Cardenal, who functioned for a time as Minister of Culture, see the interview in T. Cabestrero, *Ministros de Dios, ministros del pueblo. Testimonio de tres sacerdotes en el Gobierno Revolucionario de Nicaragua* (Managua: Ministerio de Cultura, 1983), pp. 19-51, and the account given in Beverley and Zimmerman, *Literature and Politics*, pp. 66-72, 82-87, 94-104, 109-10. Cf. 'Los cristianos en la revolución popular sandinista', a document released by 'La Dirección Nacional del FSLN', October 7 1980. For comments on this document by liberationists, see Berryman, *Religious Roots*, pp. 249-54; Girardi, *Sandinismo, marxismo, cristianismo*, pp. 257-61.

America. Pablo Richard testifies to this creative space in Sandinista Nicaragua:

> The Theology of Liberation (TL) which is being born in Nicaragua certainly has a Central American and Latin American horizon. Nicaragua, for its part, created a new climate for Latin American TL: for the first time in the history of our continent Christians participate massively and consciously—directly inspired by TL—in a triumphant revolutionary process.[1]

Giulio Girardi, an Italian theologian, came out strongly in favor of Christian participation in the *proyecto histórico* of the Sandinista government.[2] His is an enthusiasm to be involved in the battle for cultural hegemony, the implanting and nurturing of a new cultural identity to replace the old:

> For the Sandinista leadership, it is certainly not a question of only bringing the masses closer to the culture, which up until now had been denied them, but rather of developing in the movement itself a new culture; it is a question of both a new ideology and an art, a poetry, a literature, a science, a theology, in which to express the revolutionary event.[3]

---

1. P. Richard, 'Nicaragua en la Teología de la Liberación latinoamericana', in *Nicaragua, trinchera teológica. Para una Teología de la Liberación desde Nicaragua* (ed. G. Girardi, B. Forcano and J. Ma. Vigil; Managua: Centro Ecuménico Antonio Valdivieso, 1987), pp. 237-55 (237).

2. Girardi, *Sandinismo, marxismo, cristianismo*; idem, 'Revolución y toma del templo', in *Nicaragua, trinchera teológica*, pp. 221-35.

3. *Sandinismo, marxismo, cristianismo*, p. 170. Besides that discussion, see his 'Educación popular liberadora, segunda evangelización de América Latina', in *Nicaragua, trinchera teológica*, pp. 365-415. Cf. on cultural hegemony, A. Gramsci, *Selections from Cultural Writings* (ed. D. Forgacs and G. Nowell-Smith; trans. W. Boelhover; London: Lawrence & Wishart, 1985). Note, for example, the following quotes:

> The proletarian revolution cannot but be a total revolution. . . This revolution also presupposes the formation of a new set of standards, a new psychology, new ways of feeling, thinking and living that must be specific to the working class, that must be created by it, that will become 'dominant' when the working class becomes the 'dominant' class. . . Just as it has thought to organize itself politically and economically, it must also think about organizing itself culturally (p. 41).

> One must speak of a struggle for a new culture, that is, for a new moral life that cannot but be intimately connected to a new intuition of life, until it becomes a new way of feeling and seeing reality and, therefore, a world intimately ingrained in 'possible artists' and 'possible works of art'. . . A new social group that enters history with a hegemonic attitude, with a self-confidence which it initially did not have, cannot but

Speaking from within that period of time of the Sandinista regime, Girardi explains that the aim is to replace the culture of the 'democratic bourgeoisie' from within the framework of the revolutionary project:

> The rise of the people as a cultural subject is closely linked to their rise as a political subject. In other words, there is a strong relationship of interaction, interdependency and interpretation between popular power and culture. At both levels, it is a question of achieving a reversal of the historical tendency, of radically changing the tendency imposed for the first time in the country's history by the Spanish colonization, and afterward by American domination and the dictatorship.[1]

This cultural process of an extensive *concientización* will be long and arduous, he says, but the FSLN (Frente Sandinista de Liberación Nacional) needs more than political hegemony; cultural hegemony is necessary in order to create a new *pueblo*:

> In a certain sense, the hegemony is already actively present, just as it was more and more throughout the war. This is what has shaped the popular block. Nevertheless, it is necessary to remember here the difference between the two meanings of the term 'hegemony' which we have already pointed out: power over a social group based on consensus and power over a social group based on the interiorization of a vision of the world and of history.[2]

For his part, Ernesto Cardenal saw his post as Minister of Culture, as well as the role of other clergy in the government, as significant:

> Now that I have this other ministry, besides the priestly, that of Culture, I have been charged with promoting the culture of the country... It is the ideological Ministry of the Revolution. And it is significant that this ideological Ministry, which means so much to the Revolution, has been given to a priest. Just like the Ministry of Foreign Affairs, which in every country and even more so in a revolution is the most important of all the ministries, has been given to a priest [Miguel D'Escoto]. And the Literacy Campaign, which was not only a literacy campaign but also a political and ideological one, was given to a priest, to my brother Fernando. And now the development of the young people of the Sandinista Youth has been given to him... In regards to culture, there has been a great cultural

stir up from deep within itself personalities who would not previously have found sufficient strength to express themselves fully in a particular direction (p. 98).

1. Girardi, *Sandinismo, marxismo, cristianismo*, p. 191.
2. Girardi, *Sandinisimo, marxismo, cristianismo*, p. 197.

renaissance since the triumph of the revolution. And culture in this revolution is a priority. . . And just as Christ charged his disciples to share the bread and the fish, I feel that He has placed me here to share culture.[1]

These extensive quotes demonstrate that for many, Nicaragua was a ground-breaking case. Not only did some Christians actively participate in the defeat of Somoza, several were involved in the formulation of what was considered to be a new kind of Marxism, where there would be pluralism and space for a Christian contribution. The purpose of these citations is not to try to delineate the 'proper' roles of Christians and the church in the politico-cultural process nor to discuss what kind of government is needful. They can, however, serve to introduce a brief observation regarding what level of commitment might be appropriate in the light of the methodological decisions of this book.

One consequence that can arise when support seems whole-hearted and convergence appears total is that identities might be blurred. Girardi says: 'as part of the popular block, the revolutionary Church participates in the hegemony exercised by the vanguard of the block, the Sandinista Front. . . The leading role is exercised by the Sandinista Front', or 'Sandinismo, Marxism and Christianity characterize this hegemony, because the people have recognized in them, from different points of view, the expression of their own historical project'.[2] Not that liberationists do not make distinctions, but the danger is at least latent.

Opposition from any other sector of the Christian church, then, becomes considered by some as a conspiracy against the Revolution, as the wedding of interests with the bourgeoisie to regain lost privileges.[3] There can be no doubt that this might be the case in some instances or in some measure in a broad sense, but the motivations and intentions of opposition cannot be so neatly reduced.[4] Moral consid-

---

1. Cabestrero, *Ministros de Dios, ministros del pueblo*, pp. 25-26. Beverley and Zimmerman place Cardenal's views within a theoretical discussion of Gramsci's notion of 'cultural hegemony' and of the 'nation-popular' (*Literature and Politics*, pp. 9-25).

2. Girardi, *Sandinismo, marxismo, cristianismo*, pp. 415 and 434-35, respectively.

3. Girardi, *Sandinismo, marxismo, cristianismo*, pp. 299-329, 399-431; *idem*, 'Marxismo, Teología de la Liberación e "Iglesia popular"'.

4. Abelino Martínez offers more of a balanced point of view in *Las sectas en*

erations in context are more complex than this. The danger is that once religion embraces a particular political option as God's own, the *proyecto* can be made redemptive and the demand of allegiance absolute. Girardi approvingly quotes a poem that appears to reflect Micah 5.2.:

> And you, little Nica,you are not the least of my cities,
> says the Lord,
> because from you has been born
> my daughter Liberty,
> my son the New Man.
> Guerilla embroidered with tenderness,
> flower of liberation, champion,
> sacrament—guerrilla of the New America,
> Nicaragua![1]

Biblical themes and narratives can also become one with an ideological line. Saravia's article, 'Nicaragua en la Biblia', for example, sees Nicaragua as the widow of Nain and the Revolution as the son raised from the dead (Luke 7.11-17); Nehemiah now finds its parallel with the reconstruction of Nicaragua under the pressure of anti-Revolutionary ('Contra') forces.[2] Cardenal will describe a 'mystical vision' in which God identifies himself with the letters FSLN and so the Revolution.[3] Pixley can find similarities between Hosea and the revolutionary project, and even as the prophet returned to his sources in tradition so must Nicaragua go back and rescue its history from the

---

Nicaragua. Oferta y demanda de salvación (Colección Sociología de la Religión; Managua/San Jose, CR: Centro Ecuménico Antonio Valdivieso/DEI, 1989). His is a study of Protestant groups, in particular Pentecostals. The latter he would consider apolitical and separatist (cf. M.M. Poloma, 'Pentecostals and Politics in North and Central America', in *Prophetic Religions and Politics: Religion and the Political Order* [ed. J.K. Hadden and A. Shupe; New York: Paragon House, 1986], pp. 329-52). Even he, however, does not totally escape conspiracy theories concerning those who are in disagreement with the FSLN (see especially ch. 3 of his book). Note the discussion on Nicaragua in Stoll, *Is Latin America Turning Protestant?*, ch. 8.

1. Girardi, *Sandinismo, marxismo, cristianismo*, p. xvi.
2. J. Saravia, 'Nicaragua en la Biblia', *RIBLA* 1 (1988), pp. 100-106. The Nehemiah analogy has also been used by those of a very different persuasion: John Carrette utilized it to draw positive connections with the Rios Montt regime in Guatemala (*Guatemala: ¡milagro en marcha!* n.p., n.d.).
3. Cardenal, *Flights of Victory*, pp. 86-87.

perversions of the capitalist 'empire'.[1] To mention these authors is not to claim that they are representative of all liberation thinking or to dismiss their effort to read the Bible from their context; it is, however, to suggest that there exists a danger of sanctifying government and of idealizing a social experiment.[2] Uriel Molina, a fervent supporter of the regime, is a case in point: because of the identification of God with the Revolution, he is at a loss to explain the electoral defeat of the Sandinistas.[3]

Not all liberationists would be so unreservedly sanguine. Dussel in his recent book *Ethics and Community* points out weaknesses in contemporary socialism.[4] He also does allow a place for a voice to question a revolutionary project:

> The authentic theologian can never become the ideologue of a party, however authentically revolutionary the party. The theologian will always maintain an eschatological, prophetical reserve, which will announce its presence through a critique stemming from the *new* poor. Any revolutionary process, however just, will inevitably and necessarily produce new poor.[5]

To use Dussel's terminology, it is important that Jerusalem not become Babylon. Yet, other passages in this work put a question mark as to how such a criticism would actually be raised. On the one hand, stands the 'hero', the politically committed individual who creates a new, more just, social order. Among the heroes he would include

---

1. J. Pixley, 'Oseas: Una nueva propuesta de lectura desde América Latina', *RIBLA* 1 (1988), pp. 67-86. Note Girardi's effort to link Augusto Sandino's thought and life to Sandinista ideals: the regime then would offer both continuity and recovery of the national hero (*Sandinismo, marxismo, cristianismo*, pp. 17-58; with an evaluation of this effort in context, see Christian, *Nicaragua*, pp. 232-33). Cf. on history as a cultural and political instrument, B. Lewis, *History: Remembered, Recovered, Invented* (New York: Simon & Schuster, 1987).

2. See the testimonies of a number of theologians from around the world in J.M. Vigil (ed.), *Nicaragua y los teólogos* (Mexico: Siglo XXI, 1987). Girardi appears on pp. 141-57.

3. U. Molina, 'Dios, el proceso revolucionario y las elecciones del 25 de febrero de 1990', *RIBLA* 7 (1990), pp. 113-20. He does go on to list some lessons learned, to put his hope in the remnant who did vote for the Frente, and to wait for God to manifest himself once more. Cf. 'Elecciones en Nicaragua y lecciones para El Salvador', comment in *Estudios Centroamericanos* 45 (1990), pp. 73-76.

4. Dussel, *Ethics and Community*, ch. 17.

5. *Ethics and Community*, p. 95.

Carlos Fonseca (one of the founders of the FSLN) and the Sandinistas.
On the other hand, stands the 'prophet', the Christian dedicated to
building the utopian communities among the poor.[1] The prophet provides a model of orthopraxy for the people and inspires the theologian
in the liberation process.[2] Dussel never raises the possibility, however,
that the hero and the prophet, who are both central figures in a liberating project, might be wrong or in need of censure. Both kinds of
individual are charisms bestowed by God and appear to stand above
reproach.[3] Moreover, Dussel leaves the impression that the revolutionary project itself can hardly be scrutinized by anyone not deeply
committed to its success:

> Many who kept their counsel in Egypt, in Babylon, or under Somoza,
> suddenly recall, once the revolution has triumphed, that the prophet's role
> is to 'criticize'. And lo, the dumb speak. Now we have criticism in abun-
> dance, and from every direction. But there is criticism, and then again
> there is criticism. It is the Dragon and the Beast [i.e. capitalism] who are
> to be criticized. The New Jerusalem is not a legitimate object of criticism.
> In the New Jerusalem, the first priority is to *work*, to *produce* bread, for
> the table, for the eucharist.[4]

Although obviously also in favor of the Revolution in Nicaragua,
Berryman, by way of contrast, is more realistic regarding the opposition among Christians and is cognizant of the importance of criticism.
Discernment in difficult times, he says, is often no easy task. There
are no facile answers, and no perfect revolutions. On behalf of those
who do side with this specific process, he explains that,

> They do not intend to say, for instance, that God endorses the FSLN;
> rather, their reasoning is that God is on the side of the poor, and that, all
> things considered, this particular revolution (de facto with such-and-such
> characteristics) is a 'mediation' in history of the kingdom, since it is the
> concrete way by which the poor will be able to live more fully. This latter
> is a political judgment, provisional, subject to critical revision—but

---

1. *Ethics and Community*, ch. 9.
2. *Ethics and Community*, pp. 227-28.
3. For this and other critiques of Dussel's book, see E. Vijver, 'El éxodo: ¿un modelo para la ética social? Una crítica a la "Etica Comunitaria" de Enrique Dussel', *CuadTeol* 9 (1988), pp. 177-207.
4. Dussel, *Ethics and Community*, pp. 92-93 (author's emphasis). Cf. his comments in Vigil, *Nicaragua y los teólogos*, pp. 134-40.

nonetheless one on which a commitment can and must be made to something absolute—God's love for the poor.[1]

Berryman is also at pains to distinguish what he feels are the possible limitations and contributions of the church, the clergy and the hierarchy within the movements that are working for change in Latin America.[2]

In light of the comments by Girardi, Cardenal, Dussel and Berryman it is clear that there is diversity among liberation theologians. Among some there can be a tendency towards too quick and global an endorsement of the *proyecto histórico* of the Revolution. How would this book's approach respond? First, the discussion in Chapter 3 on the role of sociology in doing theology and the distinction between values and ideology would signify a more modest approval of any social experiment. The phenomenological fact of the social construction of reality and the commitment to meaning systems yields a more skeptic and relativistic posture and perhaps more realistic evaluations and commitments.

My position on popular religion would press for a more honest admission of moral complexity and political diversity among Christians. Simplistic and reductionist analyses make for good rhetoric, but too often fall short of coming to grips with actual religious life. Even some of those who strongly endorsed the Revolution as of 'the people' and Christian participation as 'massive', admitted that, among both Protestants and Catholics, this posture actually represented a minority group.[3] Both organized and popular religion's beliefs are much broader than the theologizing done by the 'advanced Christians', their ritual sometimes far removed from those liberation commitments. Some theologians, who are sympathetic in some measure to the ideals of those Christians committed to that *proyecto*, warn of the possibility of a new 'Constantinianism'—a sociopolitical

1. Berryman, *Religious Roots*, p. 359. For his fuller discussion, see pp. 354-63, and *Liberation Theology*, pp. 144-47.

2. *Religious Roots*, ch. 10.

3. 'Advanced Christians' is Martínez's term for those who support the Revolution and who claim to speak for the *pueblo*. He gives statistics among Protestants showing that they are a minority in *Las sectas en Nicaragua*, pp. 61-62, 136-38; for the Roman Catholic Church, see Berryman, *Religious Roots*, pp. 265-67. Note also the data mentioned earlier in the Excursus in Chapter 3 on base ecclesial communities.

hegemony with strong religious sanction—but now of the left. Yoder observes, despite assurances to the contrary, that,

> Pixley says this cannot happen because *poder popular* will not let it, Míguez [Bonino] because the world will not let it, Shaull (if I understand him) because the temptation of state power is less perverse if the church is not behind it and the poor are. These reassurances seem to me to contradict each other, and to fall short of realism about the power of sin and the nature of the principalities and powers, whether that realism be articulated in a Marxist, a biblical or a historical frame of reference.[1]

The poetic reading of Amos and the suggestions in this chapter on how readers are drawn into the textual world would bring a more critical appraisal of too great a convergence of church and state. The text would continually force the believing community, and especially the religious institutional bodies, to consider whether they can fall into the sins described there—for instance, the promotion of ritual and theology in line with state ideology and pretense, the enjoyment of privilege because of the relationship to the state, and the propagation of another 'yahwism'; whether this community can accept and listen to the prophet(s) who radically denounces the socioreligious world of human making—even if one is convinced that that world is in the right; whether it can admit the reality of religious complexity and commitments beyond its purview; and whether it realizes the terrible judgment that can await a 'reality' built in the name of Yahweh, yet which knows him not. These sort of probings cannot be limited, of course, to Liberation Theology, especially on a continent where religion and politics have historically gone hand in hand. The text is no respecter of persons or systems, and its 'drawing-in' strategies let none escape its penetrating discontents.

b. *The Proposal of a New Liturgy*
The re-thinking of theology 'from below' has also generated new perspectives on theological method and themes. Increasingly Liberation Theology is placing more and more emphasis on ecclesiology—the shape of believing communities, their relationship to existing hierarchies, pastoral practice and forms of liturgy.

---

1. J.H. Yoder, 'Orientation in Midstream: A Response to the Responses', in *Freedom and Discipleship: Liberation Theology in Anabaptist Perspective* (ed. D.S. Schipani; Maryknoll: Orbis Books, 1989), pp. 159-68 (163).

The re-evaluation and reorientation of the liturgy can take several forms. On the basis of biblical studies, some would hold that the original faith of Israel was not cultic or that the cult was a secondary issue, the principle focus of yahwistic faith being the demand for social justice. Amos 4.4-5 and 5.21-25 usually surface in these arguments.[1]

The task that occupies the attention of most, however, has not been the discovery of possible biblical origins, but instead the reorientation of popular piety according to what they feel are the biblical imperatives within the historical realities of the moment. In contrast to the traditional religiosity which can tend not to question the status quo or spur the people on to social change, new forms, it is felt, must be worked out for *concientización* and to celebrate God's commitment to the poor and to human liberation. This conviction goes beyond just the desire for a liturgy that is more 'Latin' than foreign in its vernacular and music, to the effort for a more 'liberating' cult.

This new push can be of a general sort which realigns the liturgy with liberation aspirations,[2] as well as particular in its basis in a specific revolutionary experience as in Nicaragua.[3] Thus arise transformations in the understanding and practice of, for instance, the Eucharist,[4] the Stations of the Cross[5] and prayers.[6] The Virgin, who is revered in national feasts and pilgrimages in many countries of Latin

---

1. E.g. Miranda, *Marx and the Bible*, pp. 53-67; R. Avila, *Worship and Politics* (trans. A. Neely; Maryknoll: Orbis Books, 1981), ch. 1; J.A. Díaz, 'Religión "versus" fe: Antiguo Testamento. Proyecto desde la praxis histórica de Israel', *Fe y Religión* 14 (1988), pp. 25-50; J. Pixley, '¿Exige el Dios Verdadero sacrificios cruentos?', *RIBLA* 2 (1988), pp. 109-31.

2. De Santa Ana, *Towards a Church of the Poor*, ch. 11; Avila, *Worship and Politics*, ch. 3; I. Ellacuría, 'Liturgia y liberación', in *Conversión de la Iglesia al reino de Dios. Para anunciarlo y realizarlo en la historia* (Colección Teología Latinoamericana, 5; San Salvador: UCA Editores, 1985), pp. 279-92.

3. D. Irarrázaval, 'Nicaragua: Una sorprendente religiosidad', in P. Richard and D. Irarrázaval, *Religión y política en América Central. Hacia una nueva interpretación de la religiosidad popular* (San José, CR: DEI, 1981), pp. 35-52.

4. Gutiérrez, *A Theology of Liberation*, pp. 262-65.

5. L. Boff, *El camino sagrado de la justicia. Meditación sobre la pasión de Cristo ayer y hoy* (trans. M. Agudelo and J.G. Ramírez G.; Colección Iglesia Nueva, 34; Bogotá: Indo-American Press Service, 1979).

6. J. Esquivel, *El Padre Nuestro desde Guatemala y otros poemas* (San José, CR: DEI, 1981).

America, is seen now not just as the compassionate Mother of the silent sufferers; she stands today beside the oppressed in their struggle. Indeed, the Virgin did play a part in earlier revolutions—such as those of Hidalgo and Zapata in Mexico.[1]

The design of the liturgy is to create a different kind of symbolic language for a new religious universe. And since Latin American culture is so very religious, this kind of popular religiosity can serve to reinforce and influence the process of *concientización* and commitment to praxis and the historical project.[2]

Amos also will not allow ethics to be separated from the cult; Yahweh demands justice unconditionally, and any cult that ignores this mandate or reworks traditions to avoid social obligation is anathema. This, too, is the cry of Liberation Theology. How the liturgy and this ethical demand are to be worked out practically is an area of debate and experiment beyond the limits of our discussion here. But in general terms, how can this liberationist effort to rework Christian liturgy be appraised?

The discussion of culture in Chapter 3 would again raise some questions—such as, does the new symbolic framework violate the present systems of meaning? If so, how? Is it a reorientation according to necessary but missing Christian ideals and demands, or an imposition of a particular ideological perspective in the struggle to attain comprehensive hegemony? Or, is the attempt tentative and exploratory, full of unforeseen pitfalls and occasional exaggerations? Liberation Theology is not unaware of the tensions and has moved from hostility to the staidness and apparent inertia of popular religiosity, to a recognition of its deep roots within Latin American consciousness and an appreciation of its potential contribution to the creation of another society.

On the one hand, an evaluation according to the poetic reading of Amos and the opening section of this chapter would focus on the relationship between the liturgy and a sociopolitical movement or project. Does the cult legitimize and sanction without reserve? How can the

---

1. V. Elizondo, 'La Virgen de Guadalupe como símbolo cultural', in *Raíces de la teología latinoamericana. Nuevos materiales para la historia de la teología* (ed. P. Richard; San José, CR: DEI, 2nd edn, 1987), pp. 393-401.

2. Besides the references already noted in this section on liturgy, see J.S. Croatto, 'Cultura popular y proyecto histórico', *Cuadernos Salmantinos de Filosofía* 3 (1977), pp. 367-78.

cult both celebrate and criticize? Does the cult center or functionaries gain from the connection with the ruling regime? How?

On the other hand, the representation of religious life within the textual world would also force an evaluation of the popular religion. What kind of god(s) is (are) worshipped by the people? How in tune are the popular theology and celebrations with the biblical picture of God and his demands? In what ways does the popular religion affect, through its world-view and ethos, the day-to-day life and experience of the nation? What needs preserving as a proper Christian-cultural expression, and what should be redirected or excised?

Again, the reading raises the questions, and the text pulls the reader in to force him to vindicate himself, his faith and the institutions (religious and secular) he holds dear before its accusations and to prove the innocence of a religion that might not know the guilt of the text's typologies. Divine condemnation, according to Amos, brings not only the dismantling of a world-view and the humiliation of the government, but also the destruction of the sanctuaries.

c. *The Nature of God and Idolatry*

In the last analysis, the evaluation of any liturgy rests on factors like the kind of community it represents and produces and on the God that is worshipped. One of the many significant contributions of Liberation Theology has been its criticism of theologies which (whether consciously or not) have sustained and reflected the unjust context in which they were elaborated; its hermeneutics of suspicion has done much to expose hidden influences and ignored interests in the understanding of God.

Recently, several liberationists have begun to develop the category of 'idolatry'. As Berryman rightly says of the Latin American situation:

> The problem of God, then, is seen not as a struggle between belief and unbelief but as a struggle between rival divinities, between the 'Living God' and idols. Central American (and Latin American) theologians are seeing idolatry as a *theological* category.[1]

The issue for them is not whether God exists, but how and for whom. This study of idolatry has taken the theoretical orientation of

---

1. Berryman, *Religious Roots*, p. 378. For a fuller discussion see ch. 11 in the same work, and his more recent effort, *Liberation Theology*, ch. 10.

the Marxist category of fetishism,[1] or sought more explicitly biblical foundations.[2] Richard defines the key issue:

> The principal problem is not the negation of God, but rather the perversion of the image of God or the substitution of God by other gods, which is accomplished by the dominant oppressor system. To discover God among the poor means at the same time to fight against the idols of oppression. A different God, the God of life, the God of the poor, who has nothing to do with the god of the Western system, with the god in whom the dictators and the oppressors of the people believe, began to reveal to us the faith of the poor. Evangelization has the task of *distinguishing* or *discerning* between this true God of Jesus Christ and the other gods of the system. Evangelization thus changed into a process of removing idols, of destroying all the dominating system's gods of death and of positive living of the presence of the God of Jesus Christ among the poor.[3]

Yet although many of the observations in these studies are insightful and timely, once more there is a lack of comprehensiveness. Theirs is a crusade to denounce the idolatry of the capitalist system. Well and good, but whither the voice of self-evaluation, the consideration of the possibility that new idols are being created? Will the biblical text, which repeatedly confronts its world and the reader with Yahweh, God of hosts be silenced and its means of implicating today's people of God be ignored? Could not God again be domesticated, even if in the name of what many hold to be a just cause?

A possible danger signal is the phenomenon of the 'loss of Christian faith' of those Christians involved in the Revolution. With such a convergence of commitment between the Theology of Liberation and the Sandinista experiment, some see no reason to maintain a distinctively

---

1. E. Dussel, 'El concepto de fetichismo en el pensamiento de Marx: Elementos para una teoría general marxista de la religión', *CrSoc* 85 (1985), pp. 7-59; *Ethics and Community*, chs. 2, 10, 12, 15.

2. J. Pixley, 'Antecedentes bíblicos a la lucha contra el fetichismo', *CrSoc* 84 (1985), pp. 91-101, and 'Dios enjuicia a los idólatras en la historia', in *La lucha de los dioses. Los ídolos de la opresión y la búsqueda del Dios Liberador* (ed. P. Richard *et al.*; Managua/San José, CR: Centro Ecuménico Antonio Valdivieso/DEI, 1980), pp. 57-78; P. Richard, 'Nuestra lucha es contra los ídolos. Teología bíblica', in *La lucha de los dioses*, pp. 9-32. J.S. Croatto, 'Los dioses de la opresión', in *La lucha de los dioses*, pp. 33-56.

3. Richard, 'Nicaragua en la Teología de la Liberación latinoamericana', pp. 241-42.

Christian confession. Girardi deals extensively with this problem and
suggests that what has been lost is simply the religious expression of
the Christian faith, and not its essence as service to the poor.[1]
Cardenal also reflects on this tendency and re-reads Jesus' words
recorded in Luke 18.8 in order to interpret this distancing from the
church and Christian belief:

> Finally I want to add that also the faith of the young people in the com-
> munity began to disappear, and only I was left holding on to it. Bit by bit
> they became less and less believers, some definitely atheists, others
> neither atheists nor non-atheists, not interested in the matter. I have
> thought of a verse in Saint Luke where Christ, speaking of prayer, when
> he gives the example of the widow and the judge, asks whether the Son of
> Man will find faith on the earth when he comes to establish the Kingdom.
> I begin to think: Christ says that he will come to establish the Kingdom,
> or in other words perfect justice, and that maybe there will not be faith on
> the earth. I get the impression that Jesus is not lamenting that. He is
> simply asking the question. . . and he supposes, apparently, that possibly
> there will be no faith; but the Kingdom will be established. . . Will it be
> that important whether there will be faith or not? One does not get the
> impression that it is a lament. . . Now we only talk about the loss of
> faith. . . I never hear that anyone loses hope, loses charity. And actually
> one cannot say concerning any of these young people that they have lost
> hope, and even less that they have lost love.[2]

By way of contrast, Amos chs. 3–6 highlights the person of
Yahweh: he is never lost from view. Israel's God is creator,
sovereign, transcendent yet immanent. His constant questioning of
how the nation understood and worshipped him is still obviously a
central issue for the modern community that claims him. Although
Yahweh demands an ethic of justice, he also desires a proper cult and
never loses himself within or behind history; he is surely there, and,
even if his presence and activity are hard to define, he never reduces

---

1. Girardi, *Sandinismo, marxismo, cristianismo*, pp. 354-62. For his part,
Alistair Kee makes the interesting observation that many will be lost to Liberation
Theology because of its failure to match its radical social stance with a thorough-
going application of Marx's critiques of religion to theology itself. Liberation
Theology in the last analysis, he says, is not radical enough (*Marx and the Failure of
Liberation Theology*, chs. 11, 12).

2. Cardenal, 'El Evangelio en Solentiname fue obra del pueblo', in *Nicaragua,
trinchera teológica*, pp. 342-43.

without remainder the revelation of his person to a righteous morality.

What is more, a further contribution can be made to Christian liturgy from narrative ethics. It will be remembered that Hauerwas offers an ethic of virtue to be nurtured in Christian communities.[1] This view stresses *the kind of people* sustained by certain traditions, not just *the kind of society* toward which the church is to move the world. Crucial are identity and character.

This perspective is a needed focus for Latin America. What is imperative is not only justice, but charity; not only the championing of certain human values, but the living out of Christian virtue. The call for justice without charity can lead to and legitimize violence, as effectiveness overwhelms the need for truthfulness to a vision for life. The goal from the view of an ethic of virtue is now not to attain just *un pueblo concientizado*, but rather to train up a transformed people capable of fleshing out a different qualitative existence on this violent continent. Difference does not signify isolation, but does warn of too easy an identification with the powers that be—whether of the left or the right.

Within this scheme of things the sacraments take on a new significance. For the church they would represent how it is to re-enact and enter into the story of Jesus. McClendon goes beyond Hauerwas in his discussion of the sacraments by utilizing MacIntyre's category of a 'practice'.[2] The community's sacraments would foster certain moral practices—that is, activities and intentions grounded in the virtues of the Christian narrative (in the inclusive sense described in Chapter 3). Practices have both internal and external goods, and if the former is linked to the virtues and the second identified with more equitable social interaction and structures, then from this point of view one is incomplete without the other. Worship, then, is to be suited to the kind of practices it is to generate and sustain.

Amos emphasizes moral demand, but what of virtue? Perhaps the mention of 'the right' (3.10), 'the good' (5.14), and the person of integrity (5.11) can point to a possible new dimension to explore in the text and within the religious life of Latin America. Hauerwas and

1. For what follows regarding Hauerwas, see 'The Politics of Charity', in *Truthfulness and Tragedy*, pp. 132-43; Hauerwas, *The Peaceable Kingdom*, chs. 5, 6, 8; Hauerwas and Willimon, *Resident Aliens*.

2. McClendon, *Systematic Theology*, I, pp. 160-77, 214-19, 255-59, 259-326. Cf. MacIntyre, *After Virtue*, ch. 14; Stout, *Ethics After Babel*, ch. 12.

McClendon see the narrative of Jesus, the primary narrative for the Christian, as one of charity, of courageous, selfless peace-making, and of service and not power. Within a continent of so much violated 'social ecology' (to use Segundo's term) this work cannot but second that vision. A community attuned and committed to the virtues perhaps can be more sensitive and open to the text, more willing to be drawn into its world and be implicated in the sin of that people of God, and so be more able to be shaped anew so as to speak with a greater moral authority.

3. A Final Word

This study has been an essay in theological reflection in context. Perhaps raising more questions (or to use the richer Spanish word, *inquietudes*) than answers, this work has tried to wrestle with how the Christian community can live responsibly in context. The discussion has moved back and forth between two concerns: *textual method* and *cultural realism*.

Chapters 2 and 4 proposed that a poetic reading of the prophetic text might be a more fruitful approach for ethics than the myriad of sociological reconstructions of so much recent scholarship. Chapter 5 then offered such a reading of several chapters of Amos. Chapter 3 explored the nature of moral life in community and context from the perspective of several disciplines before applying those insights to Latin America and the Old Testament. Finally, this last chapter attempted to bring both tracks together and briefly enter into dialogue with how some understand the nature and role of popular religion in Latin America today.

The driving motivation behind these chapters has been the desire to push the debates within Latin America into new areas, both biblical and contextual. The hope is that the suggestions and warnings might prove helpful for the Christian church in a continent in crisis.

APPENDIX 1
TRADITION AND HISTORY IN AMOS

The impossibility of any dogmatic and definitive identification of the ministry of the prophet is brought into even greater relief when the plethora of views regarding his theological sources and historical setting are brought to bear. The broad spectrum of positions serves to underscore the necessarily tentative nature of any ethical posture that might be grounded in a reconstruction effort, whether sociological as demonstrated in Chapter 2, or theological-historical as this appendix will show. Once again, the purpose of these observations is in no way to suggest that these studies are fruitless for understanding the prophetic text, but rather the aim is to question their functioning as the basis for elaborating an ethic.

Traditions

Much research over the last several decades has been dedicated to ascertaining the fundamental traditions behind the message of the prophet. Earlier studies attempted to demonstrate that, in one way or another, Amos was to be related to the cult.[1] Various posited Amos as a cult prophet,[2] but later research distanced itself from this position and turned to literary forms[3] or liturgical language[4] as the links with the cult. Another aspect of the interest in the cult would be the argument that the book pictures the

1. For evaluative surveys of the relationship of Amos to the cult, see Martin-Achard, *Amos*, pp. 77-78; Sicre, '*Con los pobres*', pp. 161-63; J.L. Crenshaw, 'Amos and the Theophanic Tradition', *ZAW* 80 (1968), pp. 203-15, especially pp. 203-206; J.J.M. Roberts, 'Recent Trends in the Study of Amos', *RestQ* 13 (1970), pp. 1-16. A full-length study not mentioned by several of these surveys is Watts, *Vision*. Although most of the works cited in these sources have been read by this writer, for the sake of brevity only those studies not mentioned therein will appear in the following footnotes concerned with the cult.

2. Watts, *Vision*, pp. 18-22. J. Lindblom would hold that Amos was part of the sanctuary staff at Bethel, but only for a short time (*Prophecy in Ancient Israel* [Philadelphia: Fortress Press, 1962], pp. 182-85, 202-10). A. Kapelrud has suggested that Amos might have furnished sheep for the sacrifices (*Central Ideas in Amos* [Oslo: Universitetsforlaget, 1971], p. 69).

3. E.g. J.M. Ward, *Amos & Isaiah: Prophets of the Word of God* (Nashville: Abingdon Press, 1969), ch. 3. Attention has usually focused on 4.4-13 and the 'hymnic' passages. See the discussion and references in Chapter 5 of this book.

4. J.L. Crenshaw, 'The Influence of the Wise Upon Amos: The "Doxologies of Amos" and Job 5:9-16, 9:5-10', *ZAW* 79 (1967), pp. 42-52, especially pp. 49-51; 'Amos and the Theophanic Tradition'. These two articles are mentioned by Martin-Achard, *Amos*, but in other contexts.

struggle against the popular religion so influenced by the cultural context, a confrontation in the fight to establish Yahwistic religion.[1]

Others have worked to demonstrate a covenant background.[2] Besides trying to point out the existence of what has been labelled covenant vocabulary,[3] these scholars would also mention the violations of covenant stipulations,[4] the use of covenant cursings and blessings,[5] and the prominence of the covenant lawsuit.[6]

The third major school of thought has claimed to have established the clan wisdom background of the prophetic experience and message.[7] Once again appeal is made to vocabulary, themes and literary forms. More recently, scholars have begun to take the view that the *geistige Heimat* of Amos cannot be limited to any singular tradition,

1. See, for example, Neher, *Amos*, pp. 214-24 and his comments on 4.1-3, but especially Barstad, *Religious Polemics*, pp. 1-10, and the references to Israelite popular religion in Chapter 3 of this book, in the section 'Moral Life in Ancient Israel and the Problem of the Text'. Earlier articles on prophetic ethics also entertained some connection (both positive and negative) with the Canaanite context: Porteous, 'The Basis of the Ethical Teaching of the Prophets', pp. 143-56; Hammershaimb, 'On the Ethics of the Old Testament Prophets', pp. 75-101.

2. For an evaluative survey, see Martin-Achard, *Amos*, pp. 75-77, 89-95 (only those sources not mentioned in that survey appear in the following footnotes dealing with the covenant), and the detailed study of terms and passages in J. Barton, 'The Relation of God to Ethics in the Eighth Century Prophets' (PhD thesis presented to the University of Oxford, 1974), ch. 4. For a particular focus on the book of Isaiah see Davies, *Prophecy and Ethics*, pp. 17-29, as well as his detailed discussion of various pericopes. Recent and enthusiastic defenses of the covenant perspective are found in the commentaries by Neher (*Amos*) and Stuart (*Hosea–Jonah*).

3. H. Huffmon, 'The Treaty Background of Hebrew *YADA* ', *BASOR* 181 (1966), pp. 131-77. Stuart (*Hosea–Jonah*) repeatedly points out what he feels are covenant terms.

4. P.E. Dion reviews the oft-claimed allusions to the legal corpus and classifies them as explicit, probable, possible, or those beyond its purview ('Le message du prophéte Amos s'inspirait-il de "droit de l'alliance"?', *ScEs* 27 [1975], pp. 5-34). Note Bright's confidence, however:

> That Amos' accusations presuppose some commonly known tradition of Yahweh's commandments seems certain, else they would have carried little weight. Whether or not this was the Book of the Covenant as we know it (Ex., chpts. 21 to 23) may be left an open question, though it is entirely likely that both Amos and his hearers knew of these laws (*Covenant and Promise: The Prophetic Understanding of the Future in Pre-exilic Israel* [Philadelphia: Westminster Press, 1976], p. 84 n. 6).

5. See especially Stuart, *Hosea–Jonah*, pp. xxxiii-xlii, where he catalogues 27 types of curses and 10 of blessings.

6. In the part of Amos handled in this book particular mention can be made, for example, of 3.1-2. See the references for these in Chapter 5 of this book, at that passage. Also note Stuart's observations throughout his commentary in the 'Form/Structure/Setting' sections.

7. For evaluative surveys see Martin-Achard, *Amos*, pp. 79-82; Sicre, '*Con los pobres*', pp. 163-65; Crenshaw, 'The Influence of the Wise Upon Amos'; Davies, *Prophecy and Ethics*, pp. 29-36. The key figure here, of course, is H.W. Wolff, who, as well as in the book cited by Crenshaw and Martin-Achard (*Amos the Prophet: The Man and his Background* [trans. F.R. McCurley; Philadelphia: Fortress Press, 1973]), elaborates his thesis throughout his commentary (see especially *Amos*, pp. 93-98). Mention should also be made of Wolff's distinction between 'clan' vs. 'court wisdom' (*Amos the Prophet*, pp. 78, 85), the latter a topic dealt with by W. McKane, *Prophets and Wise Men* (London: SCM Press, repr., 1983).

but rather that the rich variety of available traditional material was fully and creatively utilized to carry out the charge commissioned by Yahweh.[1]

Historical Background

The problem of any certainty of a precise sociological reconstruction is compounded by the confused and complicated state of affairs in recent scholarship regarding the historical context and nature of the prophet's calling and ministry.[2]

The book dates its contents during the reigns of Jeroboam II and Uzziah.[3] Key questions abound about conditions then extant in Israel: does the prophetic material reflect a generally prosperous reign, or is the wealth so bitterly denounced actually a description of affairs witnessed only during its closing years?[4] Other possibilities would include that, to the contrary, the last years of Jeroboam's reign were marked by defeat and Syrian pressure, or that his reign fits into a longer pattern of slow

---

1. See, for example, the conclusions of Martin-Achard, *Amos*, pp. 82, 95-97; Sicre, 'Con los pobres', pp. 165-66; Davies, *Prophecy and Ethics*, pp. 113-19.

2. Other critical problems would include:

   a. The relationship of Amos 7 to the material in 1 Kgs 13 and 2 Chron. 25. See Martin-Achard, *Amos*, pp. 30, 174-75; Auld, *Amos*, pp. 27-30; P.R. Ackroyd, 'A Judgement Narrative between Kings and Chronicles? An Approach to Amos 7:9-17', in *Canon and Authority: Essays in Old Testament Religion and Authority* (ed. G.W. Coats and B.O. Long; Philadelphia: Fortress Press, 1977), pp. 71-87.

   b. The non-mention of Amos in 2 Kings. Frank Crüsemann proffers that the prophet is omitted because of his radical claim of the end of Israel ('Kritik an Amos im Deuteronomischen Geschichtswerk: Erwägungen zu 2. Könige 14.27', in *Probleme biblischer Theologie: Gerhard von Rad zum 70. Geburtstag* [ed. H.W. Wolff; Munich: Kaiser Verlag, 1971], pp. 57-63). For Christopher Begg the lack of mention is due to the Deuteronomomist's objection to Amos's evaluation of Jehu's dynasty ('The Non-mention of Amos, Hosea and Micah in the Deuteronomistic History', *BibNot* 32 [1986], pp. 41-53). Cf. Andersen and Freedman, *Amos*, p. 588.

   c. Another issue is the importance the historical traditions had for the prophet. Vollmer, for example, holds that Amos only assumed the traditions for the sake of his arguments, which were designed to eliminate any confidence in election (*Rückblicke*, ch. 1). For a survey of views and analysis, see J.J. Collins, 'History and Tradition in the Prophet Amos', *IrTQ* 41 (1974), pp. 120-33.

3. For a recent survey of the literature, see Martin-Achard, *Amos*, pp. 38-45. Most scholars would date the ministry of the prophet somewhere around 760 BC, but there have been some recent exceptions. Coote would not date the ministry of Amos as early as the reign of Jeroboam II, but rather during the reign of his successors after the accession of Tiglat-pileser III (*Amos*, pp. 19-24; note Rosenbaum's reply, *Amos*, pp. 25-26). Hayes, for his part, dates the prophet's ministry a bit later than most (750 BC) in accordance with his historical reconstruction that would take some oracles to refer to the threat of Pekah to the throne (see his discussion, especially *Amos*, pp. 26-27, 38-39, 45-47, and at 1.5; Rosenbaum, however, claims that the textual data shows that Amos did not know of a split in the Northern Kingdom, *Amos*, pp. 26-27).

4. Among recent commentators, for example, apparently Coote, *Amos*; Sicre, 'Con los pobres'; King, *Amos*; Smith, *Amos*. Cf. M. Haran, 'The Rise and Decline of the Empire of Jeroboam Ben Joash', *VT* 17 (1967), pp. 266-97.

decline that had begun in the previous century.[1] Moreover, to what events do the oracles in the first two chapters refer, and what would be their relationship to the prophet's own context?[2]

Regarding the person of Amos himself, although most would hold him to be a Judean, some still opt for a northern origin.[3] In addition to the issue of provenance, questions arise concerning the place of ministry.[4] Besides these problems of geography, mention also can be made of those of chronology: for how long did Amos prophesy?[5]

Finally, for years there has been debate over defining the original activity of Amos. What had Amos done prior to his speaking out and what had been his social status?[6] A related crux is the interpretation of 7.14. Should this verbless sentence be

---

1. For the former, though with very different understandings of the context, see especially S. Cohen, 'The Political Background of the Words of Amos', *HUCA* 36 (1965), pp. 153-60, and Hayes, *Amos*, pp. 20-27. For the latter view, see J.K. de Geus, 'Die Gesellschaftskritik der Propheten und die Archäologie', *ZDPV* 98 (1982), pp. 50-57, who is cited with approval by Auld, *Amos, passim*.

2. For an overview of the various options, see Barton, *Amos's Oracles against the Nations*, ch. 4. More recently, Hayes (*Amos*) has suggested that the oracles allude to attacks by members of the anti-Assyrian coalition contemporary with his dating of Amos.

3. See the discussion in J.G. Trapiello, 'Situación histórica del profeta Amós', *EstBíb* 26 (1967), pp. 249-74, especially 251-55. The northern idea is usually dismissed without much discussion. Trapiello himself says, 'Todos estos esfuerzos por situar la patria de Amós fuera de Judá no merecen mucha atención' (p. 253). A recent defense, however, has been proposed by S.N. Rosenbaum, 'Northern Amos Revisited: Two Philological Suggestions', *HebSt* 18 (1977), pp. 132-48, and more recently in *Amos of Israel*. Klaus Koch also takes this position (*The Prophets*. I. *The Assyrian Period* [trans. M. Kohl; Philadelphia: Fortress Press, 1983], p. 70).

4. Was the ministry confined to Bethel or did it also include Samaria? Did it continue after the confrontation with Amaziah? Did the prophet return to Judah and continue to minister there? See Trapiello, 'Situación histórica del profeta Amós', pp. 255-57.

5. Trapiello, 'Situación histórica del profeta Amós', pp. 272-74. Most would hold that the prophet's ministry was short, but Morgenstern proposed the most precise dating of the time and extent of his activity:

> The entire incident transpired in one brief half hour, beginning shortly before dawn and concluding a few minutes after sunrise on the New Year's Day, the day after the fall equinox, 751 BC. And two years later, to the day and the hour, the great earthquake happened (J. Morgenstern, *Amos Studies—Parts I, II, III* [Cincinnati: Hebrew Union College Press, 1941], p. 177).

Morgenstern was followed by Cohen ('The Political Background of the Words of Amos', p. 153 n. 1). Hayes would hold that most likely 'Amos's preaching is best understood as occurring in conjunction with the fall festival in Marheshvan 750' (p. 47), but would not limit Amos to one speech or to one day. Note also Rosenbaum, *Amos*, pp. 24 n. 4, 80-84, 100.

6. For helpful summaries of the terms in 1.1 and 7.14, see Martin-Achard, *Amos*, pp. 17-23; Soggin, *Amos*, pp. 9-12; Trapiello, 'Situación histórica del profeta Amós', pp. 257-64; Hayes, *Amos, ad loc*. Although Trapiello believes Amos to be of humble background, most would give the prophet some degree of high social status. Sicre mentions both sides of the debate and its importance for appreciating the possibility of Amos's willingness not to defend his own social stratum, yet says that no firm decision can be made either way ('*Con los pobres*', p. 87). Helga Weippert says that it

translated in the present or the past tense?[1] If understood as a present tense, is Amos claiming to be an independent prophet as opposed to a professional one, or, is he denying any connection whatsoever with the prophets and the schools of the prophets and testifying rather to his specific and short-term call to prophesy?[2] Could the issue be sociological, so that Amos is saying that he has been called to prophesy but not to be a *nabi'* (a supposed northern designation)?[3] If, on the other hand, the time frame is taken as in the past he may be saying that he had not been but now is to be considered a prophet in virtue of his call.[4]

The uncertainty over exactly who Amos was and what he did can, and perhaps must, force the reader's attention elsewhere. Martin-Achard remarks:

> unfortunately for us, the texts are not very explicit about their subject; at the same time, by their silence they reveal to us that it is not the life of Amos with which they occupy us, but with his message; their reason for being is not biographical but theological, in the sense that they communicate a word of God to his people.[5]

Dating and historical-biographical reconstructions cannot be *determinative*, therefore, for ethical approaches to the text, only possibly *illuminative* of textual details. It is the text as text that should command primary attention.

---

does not really matter which is the case; the book, however, demonstrates throughout familiarity with rural life ('Amos. Seine Bilder und ihr Milieu', *OBO* 64 [1985], pp. 1-29; see her comment on p. 6). Rosenbaum presents Amos as a Northern government official (*Amos*, ch. 4).

1. For a survey of views, see Martin-Achard, *Amos*, pp. 24-30 (sources not mentioned there are noted in the following footnotes).

2. Among the translations—Eng.: NEB; Sp.: BLA, FC, RVA. The present tense option has been presented in a variety of ways:

   a. The initial *l'* is construed as a sharp denial to the designation of *hozeh* in order to affirm his status as a *nabi'*: 'No! I am a prophet, though I am not a professional prophet'. See Stuart (*Hosea–Jonah*), who follows Z. Zevit, 'A Misunderstanding at Bethel, Amos VII 12-17', *VT* 25 (1975), pp. 783-90; *idem*, 'Expressing Denial in Biblical Hebrew and Mishnaic Hebrew, and in Amos', *VT* 29 (1979), pp. 505-509. For a reply to Zevit see Y. Hoffmann, 'Did Amos Regard Himself as a *NABI'*?', *VT* 27 (1977), pp. 209-12.

   b. Alternatively, to affirm that Amos is claiming to be a prophet the negatives are taken as interrogatives: 'Am I not a prophet?'. See Ackroyd, 'A Judgment Narrative Between Kings and Chronicles?', p. 83.

   c. Recent commentators who understand that Amos is denying that he is a professional prophet include Gordis, 'Studies', p. 256; Auld, *Amos*, pp. 26-27; Smith, *Amos*.

   d. Wolff (*Amos*) and Hayes (*Amos*) focus on the act of prophesying instead of the office of prophet.

3. Wilson, *Prophecy and Society*, pp. 269-70; Petersen, *Israel's Prophets*, ch. 4.

4. Among the translations—Eng.: JB, RSV, NIV. Trapiello, 'Situación histórica del profeta Amós', pp. 264-68; Soggin, *Amos*, pp. 125-33.

5. Martin-Achard, *Amos*, p. 45. (Cf. the comments regarding the uncertainties of historical reconstruction and interpretation by Barton [*Amos's Oracles against the Nations*, p. 35] and Auld [*Amos*, chs. 2 and 3].)

APPENDIX 2

TEXTUAL METHOD IN LATIN AMERICAN LIBERATION THEOLOGY

This appendix is designed to present a brief overview of the variety of textual methods being used by some Latin American liberation theologians to study the prophetic literature.[1] Each of the authors mentioned, in addition to presenting a careful exegesis, is very method-conscious. Once again, the purpose of a discussion of the work of certain liberationists is to offer a contrast to the approach of this book—in this case, in regard to textual method. This discussion will not directly critique the fundamental philosophical basis of each method, but will point out possible shortcomings in how each approach is applied, particularly to Amos.

Three authors conspicuous by their absence in what follows are Gustavo Gutiérrez, Juan Luis Segundo, and Jorge Pixley. Gutiérrez is not taken into consideration as his work is primarily theological and not exegetical. His recent commentary on Job, for example, is more a wrestling with what should characterize theological reflection committed to the liberation of the poor than a careful study of the biblical text itself.[2]

For his part, Segundo has proposed an approach he has called 'deutero-learning',[3] which distinguishes the 'faith' present within a text from the 'ideology' of its time and place. The former is grounded in the process of liberation, but learns from the latter in the attempt to realize liberation within a particular context. Faith then is constant in its goal, yet dynamic in that it must always learn how to incarnate itself in each circumstance through ideologies. This learning process is evident within the pages of the Bible itself, Segundo claims, and stands as a challenge to modern theologizing. Today Christians must also 'learn to learn—that is, they should be involved in a 'process of learning in and through ideologies how to create the ideologies needed to handle new and unforeseen situations in history'. [4] Segundo, however, has not done any detailed work in the Old Testament, and has only given glimpses of his use of higher critical methods in certain texts in the move to discriminate his two basic elements.[5]

---

1. Rowland and Corner provide examples of biblical work, yet these are drawn from the New Testament (*Liberating Exegesis*).
2. G. Gutiérrez, *Hablar de Dios desde el sufrimiento del inocente. Una reflexión sobre el libro de Job* (Salamanca: Ediciones Sígueme, 2nd edn, 1988).
3. J.L. Segundo, *The Liberation of Theology*, ch. 4; *Faith and Ideologies*, ch. 6.
4. *Idem, The Liberation of Theology*, p. 120.
5. *The Liberation of Theology*, pp. 112-13 (Exodus); *Faith and Ideologies*, pp. 159-64

Pixley, however, has published two detailed commentaries, one on Exodus, the other on Job. In both cases he proposes a socioliterary reconstruction that emphasizes discerning the determining sociopolitical factors in the production of the text. The traditions within Exodus, for example, are said to reflect four levels: (a) the small group of workers (who came to be known as Levites) that actually experienced the liberation, (b) the various tribes that took that account as their own in the struggle against Canaanite monarchies, (c) the ideological production of the Israelite monarchy that eliminated the class struggle focus, and (d) the religious interpretation of the priestly redaction.[1]

Job, he says, while on the one hand demonstrating its origin within an elite wisdom group, does begin to question the accepted theology 'from above' (i.e. the idealist perspective of Job's friends) of retribution. What is more, the book points to a material solution (restoration): God restores Job, and Job begins to orient his friends to a more just world. The reader then is also called to work for a more just world.[2]

Pixley has recently published an article in which he develops the theme of prostitution within Hosea with regard to the religious, political and economic life of eighth-century Israel.[3] He once again demonstrates concern both for ancient Near Eastern backgrounds and the light they might shed on the text, as well as for the possible contexts in which pericopes of Hosea and other biblical material might have been produced. His is a sustained effort to seek parallels with modern Central America, where he says national sovereignty and identity have too easily been compromised for unjust gain. Citations from Amos are woven into the discussion, but, because that prophetic book is only peripheral to his study, this appendix will investigate four other authors.

Four Liberation Approaches to the Prophets

1. José Miranda: Source and Tradition Criticism
In *Marx and the Bible*, Miranda has as his stated target to seek out the basic message of the Bible, which he holds to be the unwavering demand for justice.[4] The biblical attacks on injustice are said to be directed especially at 'differentiating ownership', today institutionalized in and propagated by capitalism.[5] His textual method, he says,

(Ecclesiastes, the flood account, the Succession Narrative); *Theology and the Church: A Response to Cardinal Ratzinger and a Warning to the Whole Church* (trans. J.W. Diercksmeier; Minneapolis, MN: Seabury/Winston Press, 1985), pp. 43-55.

1. J.V. Pixley, *Exodo, una lectura evangélica y popular* (Mexico: CUPSA, 1983), pp. 10-15.

2. *Idem, El libro de Job* (Comentario bíblico latinoamericano; San José, CR: Ediciones SEBILA, 1982), pp. 11-15.

3. *Idem*, 'Oseas: Una propuesta de lectura desde América Latina', *RIBLA* 1 (1988), pp. 67-86. For his understanding of prophetism as the task of denouncing injustice in solidarity with the oppressed, see his 'Hacia una teoría de la profecía', in *Misión profética de la iglesia* (P.N. Rigol *et al.*; Buenos Aires: Tierra Nueva, 1981), pp. 15-31.

4. Miranda, *Marx and the Bible*.

5. *Marx and the Bible*, ch. 1.

follows 'the most rigorous and scientific exegesis'[1] and, indeed, his is a very detailed study aiming to reconstruct, through source and tradition criticism, the original biblical concerns.

Miranda presents at least three fundamental contributions of the prophets. First, several prophets (especially Jeremiah and Hosea) are said to clarify what it actually means to know Yahweh and thus provide the clue to understanding the strident prophetic criticism of the cult: first justice then cult, because God can only be found in the practice of inter-human justice.[2] Secondly, Miranda criticizes the various attempts to base the prophetic message on anything else but the moral imperative of justice. The covenant theology, he claims, is no earlier than the seventh century and is thus eliminated, whereas the 'authentic' laws and the nation's salvation history were originally grounded in the 'Exodus-liberation tradition'.[3] To resort to the notion that the prophets only appeal either to the law collections (Würthwein) or history (von Rad), therefore, is to misconstrue the prophet's anathema, whose content goes back to that original liberating conception.[4] Thirdly, the prophets offer a hope of universal justice.[5]

The question of the sharp criticism of the cult is taken up in the reading of Amos in Chapter 5 of this book, so just two comments will be made on Miranda's discussion regarding the possible sources of the prophetic denunciation. On the one hand, the picture that arises from within Amos studies is much more complex than he would have his readers believe (see Appendix 1). Many would contest, for example, the sweeping claims that 'in the eighth century the existence of the covenant was unknown' or that 'when the eighth-century prophets announced Yahweh's rejection of Israel (an announcement central to all of them), they never based their message on Israel's nonfulfillment of the covenant'.[6] He never does mention the wisdom strand; and, although Wolff's commentary on Amos is listed in the bibliography, it is never cited at all in any footnote (his commentary on Hosea, by way of contrast, is mentioned several times). Whereas in works on Amos some scholars have been reductionistic in eliminating all but one theological tradition, Miranda disregards all of the traditions in his own particular reduction of the entire biblical message to the demand for justice.

On the other hand, in light of the multitude of textual reconstruction theories (note the variety offered for Amos!), his bold affirmations can appear under-informed and over-confident. Of course, the deep prophetic concern for justice is not thereby eliminated or even mitigated; rather, Miranda's work can be said to be in need perhaps of a more careful re-examination of the textual data.

1. *Marx and the Bible*, p. xvii.
2. *Marx and the Bible*, pp. 44-67.
3. *Marx and the Bible*, pp. 137-60.
4. *Marx and the Bible*, pp. 160-69.
5. *Marx and the Bible, passim.*
6. *Marx and the Bible*, p. 141.

2. Elsa Tamez: Word Studies

In Tamez's own words, her aim in *Bible of the Oppressed* 'is to ascertain what the experience of oppression is *in the theology of the Bible*'.[1] Hers is an analysis of nine Hebrew roots related to oppression and an attempt to discover the connotations and nuances of each. The work organizes the biblical material on oppression into two levels (international and national; chs. 1, 2), two groups (the agents and objects of oppression; ch. 3), and two means (forms and methods of oppression; ch. 4). Her contribution lies in the highlighting of the breadth of the biblical unmasking and condemnation of oppression.

Tamez's method, however, has numerous theoretical problems. To begin with, to hope to develop theology on the basis of word studies is to attempt a precarious exercise and to fall into what Silva calls 'theological lexicography'.[2] Moreover, a more thorough study would investigate diachronic factors and not level out the entire Old Testament canon, which Tamez consciously does.[3] Her look at individual roots also can not only leave the impression that meanings are inherent in the roots (the problems of etymologies and denotation),[4] but also appear to simplify the differences and overlapping that a more careful examination of synonyms would bring to light.[5] Usage is often lumped together without due consideration of context.[6]

One of the terms discussed under 'oppression at the international level' is *lahats* (her transliteration), which appears in Amos 6.14 and can help serve as an example of her methodological shortcomings. This term, she says, demonstrates that 'oppression causes a people to cry out for liberation'.[7] In biblical usage this often occurs because of a foreign yoke: oppression leads to an outcry, and God responds:

> In the majority of instances the reason God takes the side of Israel is primarily because it is living under the rule of another and more powerful nation, in wretched conditions as compared with those of its conqueror. Correspondingly, when we see oppression gaining the upper hand in Israel, when this nation itself becomes an oppressor, God abandons the oppressor class and rescues the lowly and the poor. '"I will raise up

---

1. E. Tamez, *Bible of the Oppressed* (trans. M.J. O'Connell; Maryknoll: Orbis Books, 1982), pp. 4-5 (emphasis hers).

2. M. Silva, *Biblical Words & Their Meaning: An Introduction to Lexical Semantics* (Grand Rapids: Zondervan, 1983), pp. 22-28. Tamez is indebted to her former teacher Thomas Hanks (see her fn. 1, p. 6), who also grounded his work on word studies. She cites in several places the essay which formed the basis of his *Opresión, pobreza y liberación. Reflexiones bíblicas* (Miami: Editorial Caribe, 1982), especially ch. 1. In the expanded English version of that book (*God So Loved The Third World: The Bible, the Reformation, and Liberation Theologies* [Maryknoll: Orbis Books, 1983]) Hanks then cites Tamez's work. A more judicious study that does take into account linguistic studies is Pons, *L'oppression*.

3. Tamez, *Bible of the Oppressed*, p. 5; cf. Silva, *Biblical Words*, chs. 1-3.

4. Cf. Silva, *Biblical Words*, pp. 38-51, 103-108.

5. Tamez: 'All of them [i.e. the nine Hebrew roots] convey the idea of oppression' (*Bible of the Oppressed*, p. 9); cf. Silva, *Biblical Words*, ch. 5 and pp. 159-69. Contrast Pons, *L'oppression*, pp. 111-27.

6. Cf. Silva, *Biblical Words*, pp. 138-59.

7. Tamez, *Bible of the Oppressed*, p. 15.

against you a nation, O house of Israel', says the Lord, the God of hosts; 'and they shall oppress you [*lahats*]. . . "' (Amos 6.14).[1]

Several comments are in order. First, what Tamez does not mention is that in the instances when this verb appears in Judges, for example, the people as a whole (not just an oppressor class) are guilty and thus oppressed in divine judgment.[2] Secondly, her cataloguing of this term for oppression (i.e. it leads the people to cry out) is a case of an illegitimate totality transfer, because in Amos one problem from the prophetic point of view is that the people do *not* respond, let alone cry out, to Yahweh. Thirdly, in her citation of Amos 6.14 she confines the judgment to the 'oppressor class', whereas the verse is directed against 'the house of Israel';[3] destruction will also be total, ranging from Hamath to the brook of the Arabah (she does not quote that part of the line with the inclusive geographical description).[4] The judgment and prophetic denunciation is not as simple or as selective as she would suggest.

These observations are not meant to deny that oppressor classes and oppression exist in the world of Amos or that a particular judgment awaits the unjust. They are designed, however, to question facile distinctions and uncomplicated results that fit too easily into preset classifications of the biblical material, as well as in the analysis of Latin America.

3. *Pablo Rubén Andriñach: Structuralism*

Andriñach's study has several theoretical bases.[5] His view of the autonomy, power and surplus of meaning of a text looks primarily to Ricoeur. His structuralist method follows the work of Greimas.[6] The reading of the text of Amos develops from the fundamental binary opposition of oppression–justice (parts I, II), which also serves as the underpinning of the hermeneutical move to modern day Latin America in the areas of ideology, cult, praxis and *concientización* (parts III, IV).

---

1. *Bible of the Oppressed*, p. 17.
2. Judg. 2.18; 4.3; 10.12. For a more sensitive look at this book and a close textual rendering of the people's role, see B.G. Webb, *The Book of Judges: An Integrated Reading* (JSOTSup, 46; Sheffield: JSOT Press, 1987).
3. For my own view regarding the judgment as falling upon the nation as a whole, with a special focus on certain groups that have a greater responsibility and guilt before YHWH, see my literary reading of Amos in Chapter 5.
4. This verse admittedly does pose some problems as to the identification of place names, although it is generally agreed that the whole territory of Israel is in view (2 Kgs 14.25). For the various theories see especially Harper, *Amos*; Wolff, *Amos*; Hayes, *Amos*. For my reading of this verse see Chapter 5.
5. P.R. Andriñach, 'Amós: memoria y profecía. Análisis estructural y hermenéutica', *RevBib* [Argentina] 43.12 (1983), pp. 209-301.
6. For helpful introductions to structuralism in general and to Greimas in particular see T. Hawkes, *Structuralism and Semiotics* (Berkeley: University of California Press, 1977), ch. 3 and pp. 87-95, respectively. For a good introduction and application to biblical studies see D. Jobling, *The Sense of Biblical Narrative: Structural Analyses in the Hebrew Bible*, I (JSOTSup, 7; Sheffield: JSOT Press, 2nd edn, 1986).

Andriñach works through the book of Amos and offers helpful diagrams in his attempt to uncover the deep structures of the prophetic message. Yet, at times, one wonders whether the analysis adequately reflects the complexities of the text. One example is his actantial schema for chs. 3 and 4 of Amos. The observation he makes is that throughout this section there is always opposition between Yahweh and Israel. For 4.6-12 this can be pictured in the following manner:

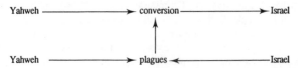

Yet he immediately follows this mention of 'Israel' with this interpretive move:

> This leads us to a more profound conclusion which has to do with all of reality in the sense that what is announced by Amos is that in *whatever* touchy situation there will be found this opposition between the desires of God and those of Israel. There is no possible connection between the project of the dominating classes and the will of Yahweh.[1]

Throughout his study any word of criticism or judgment is limited to the oppressor classes: Israel = rich. This sort of neat reductionism negates any possibility of considering textual ambiguities and sidesteps the problem of why inclusive language (e.g. 'Israel', 'house of Israel; see my reading of Amos in Chapter 5) is used alongside specific denunciations of the wealthy. Others have used structuralism to highlight textual tensions and multiple options;[2] Andriñach simply defines any complications away.

4. *J.S. Croatto: The Relectura of the Biblical Text*
In two major works[3] Croatto has outlined his philosophical framework, which is admittedly dependent in many ways on Ricoeur. Croatto is concerned to demonstrate the autonomy and potential of a text, especially the production of meaning that is generated by new readings in different contexts. These readings cannot be limited by authorial intent or canonical parameters.

In fact, Croatto claims, the process of re-reading (*relectura*) in light of new contexts is discernible in the redactional re-working of key themes in the course of textual transmission. With the delimitation of the canon there comes a moment of closure of meaning, in that this creative activity stops as the received traditions receive their final shape and placement within a set corpus. Yet the biblical text still

---

1. Andriñach, 'Amós: memoria y profecía', p. 230.

2. For example, Jobling's reading of the transition from judgeship to monarchy in *Sense of Biblical Narrative*, I, ch. 1, and in *The Sense of Biblical Narrative: Structural Analyses in the Hebrew Bible*, II (JSOTSup, 39; Sheffield; JSOT Press, 1986), ch. 2.

3. J.S. Croatto, *Exodus: A Hermeneutics of Freedom* (trans. S. Attanasio; Maryknoll: Orbis Books, 1981); *Hermenéutica bíblica. Para una teoría de la lectura como producción de sentido* (Buenos Aires: Ediciones La Aurora, 1984).

lives on in its ever-new appropriation as Scripture. The ability to discover and explore new understandings of the text, however, 'pertains to' and is 'pertinent for' the oppressed within the praxis of liberation.[1]

Croatto has applied this concept of *relectura* on various levels. On the one hand, he traces the successive interpretations of the 'foundational event' that is the Exodus throughout the Bible with the aim of demonstrating its 'reservoir of meaning' from the perspective of Latin America.[2] The ministry of prophets, both Old Testament and modern, is read in light of the effort to call the community back to fidelity to this central event.[3] Secondly, Croatto has also done careful study of the redactional stages and final structure of certain passages in Isaiah to point out the original prophetic denunciation, its re-interpretation in ancient times, and its relevancy for a *relectura* in light of today's sociopolitical situation.[4]

A third manner of applying this approach is his focus on larger blocks of biblical material. This Croatto has done with what he considers to be the canonical shaping of Amos, and it is to this effort that I bring brief attention here. He separates Amos 9.11-15 from the rest of the book as a postexilic reading that modifies the original condemnatory tone.[5] This reinterpretation in light of the new hope of liberation would demonstrate that the earlier text can indeed take on new significance.

Croatto applies this structure (judgment→ restoration) to the volatile situation in Argentina, where thousands disappeared under past military regimes: justice on the guilty generals must precede any pardon or move toward reconciliation.[6] The structuring of prophetic books, therefore, offers a clue to their contextualization.

What is at issue here is not the method *per se*, but how his study is presented. Regarding the two-part division of Amos, Croatto says, 'Obviously these final verses [i.e. 9.11-15] are later than Amos (the imagery, the content, the contrast with the rest [of the book], are proof enough)'.[7] Yet, is such a self-confident assertion really possible? On the contrary, many would not see the elimination of that concluding passage as self-evident.[8] How would its inclusion affect his stance? One might

1. *Idem, Hermenéutica bíblica*, pp. 43-56, 66-72, 78-83.

2. For the discussion of his method, see *Exodus*, chs. 1, 2. I have approached the subject of his treatment of the Exodus in 'Del éxodo a la liberación actual: Apuntes metodológicos sobre Croatto', *Kairos* [Guatemala] 2 (1988), pp. 23-27.

3. Croatto, *Exodus*, ch. 4; 'Palabra profética y no-conversión. La tematización del rechazo al profeta ', *Vox Evangelii* ns 1 (1984), pp. 9-20; 'Violencia y desmesura del poder', *RIBLA* 2 (1988), pp. 9-18.

4. *Idem*, 'Desmesura del poder y destino de los imperios. Exégesis de Isaías 10:5-27a', *CuadTeol* 8 (1987), pp. 147-51; 'Una liturgia fúnebre por la caída del tirano', *RIBLA* 2 (1988), pp. 59-67.

5. *Idem, Hermenéutica bíblica*, pp. 61-63; 'Del juicio a la reconciliación. Una lectura de textos proféticos', *CuadTeol* 8 (1987), pp. 7-16.

6. *Idem*, 'Del juicio a la reconciliación', pp. 8, 9, 16.

7. *Idem, Hermenéutica bíblica*, p. 62.

8. Although the following would hold to the authenticity of all or parts of Amos 9.11-15, they do not all agree on the interpretation: J. Mauchline, 'Implicit Signs of a Persistent Belief in the Davidic Empire', *VT* 20 (1970), pp. 287-303 (especially pp. 288-92); H.N. Richardson, 'SKT (Amos 9.11): "Booth" or "Succoth"?', *JBL* (1973), pp. 375-81; Hasel, *Remnant*, pp. 209-15;

also ask, why just these two stages? Why not Coote's three, or Wolff's six? Can contextualization be so easily linked to a hypothetical redaction history? Once more, the issues are oversimplified and other options not considered.

Conclusion

Liberation theologians have used a wide variety of exegetical approaches in their readings of the prophetic text. This spectrum of methods mirrors the phenomenon evident in Old Testament studies in general. Interestingly, these authors are not often very generous to methods other than their own. Miranda, in his focus on *the* message of the Bible says,

> some day we will have to give up completely the very common idea that to interpret the bible is a matter of the mind of the interpreter, since the Scripture has various 'meanings' and each adopts the one which 'moves' him or suits him best. Such a belief has been promulgated by conservatives to prevent the Bible from revealing *its* own subversive message.[1]

What are the implications of such a stance for those who hold to models dependent on Ricoeur's notion of a surplus of meaning? Andriñach and Croatto do, however, in their own ways opt for a closure of meaning by, respectively, maintaining a strict interpretation of the primary binary opposition in Amos or limiting an 'adequate' reading to a particular group or commitment.[2]

Croatto will criticize structuralists who abstract the text from history;[3] Andriñach disagrees with those who put emphasis on the original production of the text and thereby ignore the text's subsequent autonomy and trajectory.[4] Both authors find fault with more traditional historical-critical methods that look 'behind' the text and give no attention to the present structure.[5]

There are many ways to read the prophetic text, therefore, in Latin America. This book proposes yet another approach that I hope can also shed some light on how the Christian community might use Amos in that sociocultural context.

G. Henton Davies, 'Amos—The Prophet of Re-Union', *ExpTim* 92 (1980-81), pp. 196-200; Polley, *Amos*, pp. 70-74, 173-75; Rosenbaum, *Amos*, pp. 21, 73-75. For recent commentators who defend this passage's authenticity, see Stuart, *Hosea–Jonah*; Smith, *Amos*; Hayes, *Amos*; Andersen and Freedman, *Amos*.

1. Miranda, *Marx and the Bible*, p. 36.
2. Croatto, *Exodus*, pp. 6-11, 45-47, 81-82; *Hermenéutica bíblica*, pp. 66-72.
3. *Idem, Hermenéutica bíblica*, p. 16.
4. Andriñach, 'Amós: memoria y profecía', pp. 266-71.
5. Andriñach, 'Amós: memoria y profecía', pp. 209-16; Croatto, *Hemenéutica bíblica*, p. 14.

BIBLIOGRAPHY

Abercrombie, N., 'Knowledge, Order, and Human Autonomy', in *Making Sense of Modern Times: Peter L. Berger and the Vision of Interpretive Sociology* (ed. J.D. Hunter and S.C. Ainlay; London: Routledge & Kegan Paul, 1986), pp. 11-30.

Ackroyd, P.R., 'A Judgment Narrative between Kings and Chronicles? An Approach to Amos 7.9-17', in *Canon and Authority: Essays in Old Testament Religion and Authority* (ed. G.W. Coats and B.O. Long; Philadelphia: Fortress Press, 1977), pp. 71-87.

Aejmelaeus, A.,'Function and Interpretation of KY in Biblical Hebrew', *JBL* 105 (1986), pp. 193-209.

Ahlstrom, G.W., 'King Josiah and the DWD of Amos vi. 10', *JSS* 26 (1981), pp. 7-9.

Aiken, H.D., *Reason and Conduct: New Bearings in Moral Philosophy* (New York: Alfred A. Knopf, 1962).

Ainlay, S.C., 'The Encounter with Phenomenology', in *Making Sense of Modern Times: Peter L. Berger and the Vision of Interpretive Sociology* (ed. J.D. Hunter and S.C. Ainlay; London: Routledge & Kegan Paul, 1986), pp. 1-54.

Albrektson, B., 'Prophecy and Politics in the Old Testament', in *The Myth of the State* (ed. H. Biezais; Stockholm: Almqvist & Wiksell, 1972), pp. 45-56.

Alonso Díaz, J., 'Religión "versus" fe: Antiguo Testamento. Proyecto desde la praxis histórica de Israel', *Fe y Religión* 14 (1988), pp. 25-50.

Alonso Schökel, L., 'Die stilistische Analyse bei den Propheten', *VTSup* 7 (1959), pp. 154-64.

—*Hermenéutica de la Palabra*. I. *Hermenéutica bíblica* (Madrid: Ediciones Cristiandad, 1986–87).

—*Hermenéutica de la Palabra*. II. *Interpretación literaria de textos bíblicos* (Madrid: Ediciones Cristiandad, 1986–87).

Alter, R., *The Art of Biblical Narrative* (New York: Basic Books, 1981).

—*The Art of Biblical Poetry* (New York: Basic Books, 1985).

—*The Pleasures of Reading in an Ideological Age* (New York: Simon & Schuster, 1989).

Alves, R., *Protestantism and Repression* (trans. J. Drury; Maryknoll: Orbis Books, 1985).

Amsler, S., 'Amos, prophète de la onzième heure', *TZ* 21 (1965), pp. 318-28.

—*Amos* (Commentaire de l'Ancien Testament, 11a; ed. E. Jacob, K.-A. Keller and S. Amsler; Neuchâtel: Delachaux & Niestlé, 1965).

Andersen, F.I., and D.N. Freedman, *Amos* (AB, 24; Garden City, NY: Doubleday, 1980).

Andriñach, P.R., 'Amós: memoria y profecía. Análisis estructural y hermenéutica', *RevBib* [Argentina] 43 (1983), pp. 209-301.

Anfuso, J., and D. Sczepanski, *Efraín Rios Montt: siervo o dictador—la verdadera historia del controversial presidente de Guatemala* (Guatemala: Gospel Outreach, 1983).

Arciniegas, G., *The Green Continent: A Comprehensive View of Latin America by its*

Leading Writers (trans. H. de Onis *et al.*; New York: Alfred A. Knopf, 1972).

—'Nuestra América es un ensayo', in *Temas de filosofía latinoamericana* (ed. L.J. González Alvarez; Colección Antología, 6; Bogotá: Editorial El Buho, 1983), pp. 95-110.

Arieti, J.A., 'The Vocabulary of Septuagint Amos', *JBL* 93 (1974), pp. 338-47.

Asad, T., 'Anthropological Conceptions of Religion: Reflections on Geertz', *Man* ns 18 (1983), pp. 237-59.

Assman, H., *Theology for a Nomad Church* (trans. P. Burns; Maryknoll: Orbis Books, 1976).

—(ed.), *El juego de los reformismos frente a la revolución en Centroam érica* (San José, CR: DEI, 1981).

—*La iglesia electrónica y su impacto en América Latina* (San José, CR: DEI, 2nd edn, 1988).

Asturias, M.A., *Weekend en Guatemala* (Buenos Aires: Editorial Losada, SA, 1968).

—*Torotumbo, La audencia de los confines, Mensajes índios* (Barcelona: Plaza & Janes, SA, 1984).

Auerbach, E., *Mimesis: The Representation of Reality in Western Literature* (trans. W. Trask; Garden City, NY: Doubleday, 1957).

Auld, A.G., *Amos* (Old Testament Guides; Sheffield: JSOT Press, 1986).

Avila, R.,'La profecía en América Latina', in *Misión profética de la Iglesia* (P.N. Rigol *et al.*; Mexico: CUPSA, 1981), pp. 87-103.

—*Worship and Politics* (trans. A. Neely; Maryknoll: Orbis Books, 1981).

Barr, J., *The Scope and Authority of the Bible* (Philadelphia: Westminster Press, 1980).

Barstad, H.M., *The Religious Polemics of Amos: Studies in the Preaching of Am. 2, 7B-8; 4, 1-13; 5, 1-27; 6, 4-7; 8, 14* (VTSup, 34; Leiden: Brill, 1984).

Barton, J., 'The Relation of God to Ethics in the Eighth Century Prophets' (unpublished DPhil thesis, University of Oxford, 1974).

—'Understanding Old Testament Ethics', *JSOT* 9 (1978), pp. 44-64.

—'Natural Law and Poetic Justice in the Old Testament', *JTS* ns 30 (1979), pp. 1-14.

—*Amos's Oracles against the Nations: A Study of Amos 1.3-2.5* (SOTSMS, 6; Cambridge: Cambridge University Press, 1980).

—'Ethics in Isaiah of Jerusalem', *JTS* ns 32 (1981), pp. 1-18.

—'Approaches to Ethics in the Old Testament', in *Beginning Old Testament Study* (ed. J.W. Rogerson; London: SPCK, 1983), pp. 113-30.

—*Reading the Old Testament: Method in Biblical Study* (Philadelphia: Westminster Press, 1984).

—*Oracles of God: Perceptions of Ancient Prophecy in Israel after the Exile* (London: Darton, Longman & Todd, 1986).

—*People of the Book? The Authority of the Bible in Christianity* (Louisville: Westminster/John Knox Press, 1988).

Bastian, J.P., 'Para una aproximación teórica del fenómeno religioso protestante en América Central', *CrSoc* 85 (1985), pp. 61-68.

—*Breve historia del protestantismo en América Latina* (Mexico: CUPSA, 1986).

—'Religión popular protestante y comportamiento político en América Central, clientela religiosa y estado patrón en Guatemala y Nicaragua', *CrSoc* 88 (1986), pp. 41-56.

Beehler, R., *Moral Life* (Oxford: Basil Blackwell, 1978).

Begg, C., 'The Non-mention of Amos, Hosea and Micah in the Deuteronomistic History', *BibNot* 32 (1986), pp. 41-53.

Bellah, R.N., 'Biblical Religion and Social Science in the Modern World', *NICM Journal* 6 (1981), pp. 8-22.

—'Social Science as Practical Reason ', *The Hastings Center Report* 12 (1982), pp. 32-39.

Belli, H., *Breaking Faith: The Sandinista Revolution and its Impact on Freedom and Christian Faith in Nicaragua* (Garden City, NY: The Puebla Institute, 1985).

Bercovitch, S., *The American Jeremiad* (Madison: University of Wisconsin Press, 1978).

Berger, P.L. *Invitation to Sociology: A Humanistic Perspective* (Garden City, NY: Doubleday, 1963).

—'Charisma and Religious Innovation: The Social Location of Israelite Prophecy', *AmSocRev* 28 (1963), pp. 940-50.

—*The Sacred Canopy: Elements of a Sociological Theory of Religion* (Garden City, NY: Doubleday, 1967).

—'The Socialist Myth', *The Public Interest* 44 (1976), pp. 3-16.

—'In Praise of Particularity: The Concept of Mediating Structures', *RevPol* 38 (1976), pp. 399-410.

—*Pyramids of Sacrifice: Political Ethics and Social Change* (London: Allen Lane/Penguin Books, 1976).

—'Secular Theology and the Rejection of the Supernatural: Reflections on Recent Trends', *ThSt* 38 (1977), pp. 39-56.

—'On the Obsolescence of the Concept of Honor', in *Revisions: Changing Perspectives in Moral Philosophy* (ed. S. Hauerwas and A. MacIntyre; Revisions, 3; Notre Dame, IN: University of Notre Dame Press, 1983), pp. 172-81.

—*The Capitalist Revolution: Fifty Presuppositions about Prosperity, Equality, and Liberty* (New York: Basic Books, 1986).

—*A Rumor of Angels: Modern Society and the Rediscovery of the Supernatural* (New York: Anchor Books/Doubleday, rev. edn, 1990).

—'Capitalism and the Disorders of Modernity', *First Things* 9 (1990), pp. 14-19.

Berger, P.L., and H. Kellner, *Sociology Reinterpreted: An Essay on Method and Vocation* (Harmondsworth: Penguin Books, 1981).

Berger, P.L., and T. Luckmann, *The Social Construction of Reality: A Treatise in the Sociology of Knowledge* (Harmondsworth: Penguin Books, 1966).

Berlin, A., 'On the Bible as Literature', *Prooftexts* 2 (1982), pp. 323-332.

—*Poetics and Interpretation of Biblical Narrative* (Bible and Literature Series; Sheffield: Almond Press, 1983).

—'Narrative Poetics in the Bible', *Prooftexts* 6 (1986), pp. 273-84.

Bermúdez, F., *Death and Resurrection in Guatemala* (trans. R.R. Barr; Maryknoll: Orbis Books, 1986).

Berridge, J.M., 'Zur Intention der Botschaft des Amos: exegetische Uberlegungen zu Am. 5', *TZ* 32 (1976), pp. 321-40.

Berryman, P., *The Religious Roots of Rebellion: Christians in Central American Revolutions* (Maryknoll: Orbis Books, 1984).

—'El Salvador: From Evangelization to Insurrection', in *Religion and Political Conflict in Latin America* (ed. D. Levine; Chapel Hill: University of North Carolina Press, 1986), pp. 58-78.

—*Liberation Theology: Essential Facts about the Revolutionary Movement in Latin America and Beyond* (Bloomington, IN: Meyer Stone Books, 1987).

Beverley, J., and M. Zimmerman, *Literature and Politics in the Central American*

Revolutions (New Interpretations of Latin America Series; Austin, TX: University of Texas Press, 1990).

Bierstedt, R., *The Social Order* (New York: McGraw–Hill, 4th edn, 1974).

Birch, B.C., and L.L. Rasmussen, *Bible & Ethics in the Christian Life* (Minneapolis, MN: Augsburg/Fortress Press, rev. edn, 1989).

Blackman, P. (ed.), *Mishnayoth* (7 vols.; Gateshead: Judaica Press, 1977).

Blank, S.H., 'Irony by Way of Attribution', *Semitics* 1 (1970), pp. 1-6.

Bleibtren, E., 'Five Ways to Conquer a City', *BARev* 16.3 (1990), pp. 37-44.

Blenkinsopp, J., *A History of Prophecy in Ancient Israel—From the Settlement in the Land to the Hellenistic Period* (Philadelphia: Westminster Press, 1983).

Block, D.I., ' "Israel's House" Reflections on the Use of *Byt Yśr'l* in the Old Testament in the Light of its Ancient Near Eastern Background', *JETS* 28 (1985), pp. 257-75.

Boecker, H.J., *Law and the Administration of Justice in the Old Testament and Ancient East* (trans. J. Moiser; Minneapolis, MN: Augsburg, 1980).

Boer, W. den, *Private Morality in Greece and Rome: Some Historical Aspects* (Leiden: Brill, 1979).

Boff, L., *El camino sagrado de la justicia. Meditación sobre la pasión de Cristo ayer y hoy* (trans. M. Agudelo and J.G. Ramírez G.; Colección Iglesia Nueva, 34; Bogotá: Indo-American Press Service, 1979).

—*Church: Charism and Power—Liberation Theology and the Institutional Church* (trans. J.W. Diercksmeier; London: SCM Press, 1985).

Borger, R. von, 'Amos 5, 26, Apostelgeschichte 7,43 und Surpu II, 1980', *ZAW* 100 (1988), pp. 70-81.

Botterweck, G.J., and H. Ringgren (eds.), *Theological Dictionary of the Old Testament* (6 vols.; trans. J.T. Willis *et al.*; Grand Rapids: Eerdmans, 1974–).

Bottomore, T., *Sociology and Socialism* (Brighton: Wheatsheaf Books, 1984).

Braudel, F., *On History* (trans. S. Matthews; Chicago: University of Chicago Press, 1980).

Bright, J., *Covenant and Promise: The Prophetic Understanding of the Future in Pre-Exilic Israel* (Philadelphia: Westminster Press, 1976).

Brown, F., S.R. Driver and C.S. Briggs (eds.), *A Hebrew and English Lexicon of the Old Testament* (Oxford: Clarendon Press, 1907; repr. 1977).

Brown, R.McA., *Theology in a New Key: Responding to Liberation Themes* (Philadelphia: Westminster Press, 1978).

—'My Story and "The Story" ', *TTod* 32 (1975), pp. 166-73.

Bruce, F.F., *History of the Bible in English* (London: Lutterworth, 3rd edn, 1979).

Brueggemann, W., 'Amos IV 4-13 and Israel's Covenant Worship', *VT* 15 (1965), pp. 1-15.

—'Jeremiah's Use of Rhetorical Questions', *JBL* 92 (1973), pp. 358-74.

—*The Prophetic Imagination* (Philadelphia: Fortress Press, 1978).

—'Trajectories in Old Testament Literature and the Sociology of Ancient Israel', *JBL* 98 (1979), pp. 161-85.

—*The Creative Word: Canon as a Model for Biblical Education* (Philadelphia: Fortress Press, 1982).

—'Imagination as a Mode of Fidelity', in *Understanding the Word: Essays in Honour of Bernhard W. Anderson* (ed. J.T. Butler, E.W. Conrad and B.C. Ollenburger; JSOTSup, 37; Sheffield: JSOT Press, 1985), pp. 13-36.

—*Hopeful Imagination: Prophetic Voices in Exile* (Philadelphia: Fortress Press, 1986).

—*Revelation and Violence: A Study in Contextualization* (Milwaukee: Marquette University Press, 1986).

—'Prophetic Ministry: A Sustainable Alternative Community', *HorBT* 11 (1989), pp. 1-33.

Brunelli, D., *Profetas del Reino. Grandes lineas de la actual Teología de la Vida Religiosa en América Latina* (CLAR, 58; Bogotá: Secretariado General de la CLAR, 1987).

Bruns, G.L., 'What is Tradition?', *NLH* 22 (1991), pp. 1-21.

Buss, M.J., 'The Social Psychology of Prophecy', in *Prophecy: Essays Presented to Georg Fohrer on his Sixty-fifth Birthday* (ed. J. Emerton; BZAW, 150; Berlin: de Gruyter, 1980), pp. 1-11.

Calvin, J., *A Commentary on the Twelve Minor Prophets. II. Joel, Amos & Obadiah* (Edinburgh: The Banner of Truth Trust, 1986).

Camic, C., 'Weber and the Judaic Economic Ethic: A Comment on Fahey', *AmJSoc* 89 (1983), pp. 1410-16.

Cabestrero, T. (ed.), *Ministros de Dios, ministros del pueblo. Testimonio de tres sacerdotes en el gobierno revolucionario de Nicaragua* (Managua: Ministerio de Cultura, 1983).

Camara, H., *Spiral of Violence* (London: Sheed & Ward, 1971).

Cardenal, E., *The Gospel in Solentiname* (4 vols.; trans. D.D. Walsh; Maryknoll: Orbis Books, 1976-1982).

—'El Evangelio en Solentiname fue obra del pueblo', in *Nicaragua, trinchera teológica. Para una Teología de la Liberación desde Nicaragua* (ed. G. Girardi, B. Forcano and J.Ma. Vigil; Managua/Madrid: Centro Ecuménico Antonio Valdivieso/Lóguez Ediciones, 1987), pp. 339-43.

—*Flights of Victory/Vuelos de Victoria* (ed. and trans. M. Zimmerman *et al.*; Willimantic, CT: Curbstone Press, 1988).

Carney, P., 'Doxologies—A Scientific Myth', *HebSt* 18 (1977), pp. 149-59.

Carrera, M.A., *Costumbres de Guatemala. Cuadros de costumbres* (Guatemala: Edinter, 1986).

Carrette, J., *Guatemala ¡milagro en marcha!* (Guatemala: n.p., n.d.).

Carroll R., M.D., 'The Relevance of Cultural Conditioning for Social Ethics', *JETS* 29 (1986), pp. 307-15.

—' "Liberation Theology Come of Age": Clarifying an Assessment', *ExpTim* 98 (1987), p. 170.

—'Del éxodo a la liberación actual. Apuntes metodológicos sobre Croatto', *KAIROS* [Guatemala] 2 (1988), pp. 23-27.

Carroll R., M.D., and G.W. Méndez L., 'Another Voice from Latin America: Concerned Evangelicals and a Continent in Crisis. An Introductory and Bibliographic Essay', *ModChm* 30.4 (1989), pp. 42-46.

Cazelles, H., 'Bible, histoire et sociologie du prophétisme', *CahRRRel* 3 (1973), pp. 7-15.

CELAM, *Puebla. La evangelización en el presente y en el futuro de América Latina*, III Conferencia General del Episcopado Latinamericano (Bogotá: Editora L. Canal y Asociados, 3rd edn, 1979).

Chaliand, G, *Revolution in the Third World* (trans. D. Johnstone; New York: Penguin Books, 1978).

Chávez, M., *Modelo de oratoria. Obra basada en el análisis estilístico del texto hebreo del libro de Amós* (Miami: Editorial Caribe, 1979).

Chea, J.L., *Guatemala. La cruz fragmentada* (San José, CR: DEI, 1988).

Childs, B.S., *Introduction to the Old Testament as Scripture* (Philadelphia: Fortress Press, 1979).

Chisolm, R.B., Jr, 'Wordplay in the Eighth-Century Prophets', *BSac* 144 (1987), pp. 44-52.

Christian, S., *Nicaragua: Revolution in the Family* (New York: Random House, 1985).

Claasen, W.T., 'Speaker-Orientated Functions of KI in Biblical Hebrew', *JNWS* 11 (1983), pp. 29-46.

Clements, R.E., 'The Form and Character of Prophetic Woe Oracles', *Semitics* 8 (1982), pp. 17-29.

—'History and Theology in Biblical Narrative', *HorBT* 4–5 (1983), pp. 45-60.

Clifford, R.J., 'The Use of *Hôy* in the Prophets', *CBQ* 28 (1966), pp. 458-64.

Clines, D.J.A., *I, He, We, & They: A Literary Approach to Isaiah 53* (JSOTSup, 1; Sheffield: JSOT Press, 1976).

—*The Theme of the Pentateuch* (JSOTSup, 10; Sheffield: JSOT Press, 1978).

—'Story and Poem: The Old Testament as Literature and Scripture', *Int* 34 (1980), pp. 115-27.

Coggins, R.J., 'History and Story in Old Testament Study', *JSOT* 11 (1979), pp. 36-46.

Cohen, M.A., 'The Prophets as Revolutionaries: A Sociopolitical Analysis', *BARev* 5 (1979), pp. 12-19.

Cohen, S., 'The Political Background of the Words of Amos', *HUCA* 36 (1965), pp. 153-60.

Collins, J.J., 'History and Tradition in the Prophet Amos', *IrTQ* 51 (1974), pp. 120-33.

—'The "Historical Character" of the Old Testament in Recent Biblical Theology', *CBQ* 41 (1979), pp. 185-204.

Cook, G., 'La espiritualidad en las comunidades de base', *BolTeol* 24 (1986), pp. 227-52.

Cooper, A., 'The Absurdity of Amos 6.12a', *JBL* 107 (1988), pp. 725-27.

Coote, R.B., *Amos among the Prophets: Composition and Theology* (Philadelphia: Fortress Press, 1981).

Costas, O.E., *El protestantismo en América Latina hoy. Ensayos del camino (1972–1974)* (San José, CR: Publicaciones INDEF, 1975).

—*Christ outside the Gate: Mission beyond Christendom* (Maryknoll: Orbis Books, 1982).

Coulot, C., 'Propositions pour une structuration du livre d'Amos au nivel rédactionnel', *RSR* 51 (1977), pp. 169-86.

Craghan, J.F., 'The Prophet Amos in Recent Literature', *BTB* 2 (1972), pp. 242-61.

Craig, H., 'The Geneva Bible as a Political Document', *The Pacific Historical Review* 7 (1938), pp. 40-49.

Crenshaw, J.L., 'The Influence of the Wise upon Amos: The "Doxologies of Amos" and Job 5.9-16; 9.5-10', *ZAW* 79 (1967), pp. 42-52.

—'Amos and the Theophanic Tradition', *ZAW* 80 (1968), pp. 203-15.

—'YHWH *ṣᵉbaʾôt šᵉmô*: A Form-Critical Analysis', *ZAW* 81 (1969), pp. 156-75.

—'A Liturgy of Wasted Opportunity (Am. 4.6-12; Isa. 9.7–10.4; 5.25-29)', *Semitics* 1 (1970), pp. 27-37.

—'Wᵉdārēk ʿal-bāmᵒtê ʾāreṣ', *CBQ* 34 (1972), pp. 39-53.

Cripps, R.S., *A Commentary on the Book of Amos* (n.p.: Klock & Klock, 2nd edn, repr., 1981).

Crites, S., 'The Narrative Quality of Experience', *JAAR* 39 (1971), pp. 291-311.

Croatto, J.S., 'Cultura popular y proyecto histórico', *Cuadernos Salmantinos de Filosofía* 3 (1977), pp. 367-78.

—'Los dioses de la opresión', in *La lucha de los dioses. Los ídolos de la opresión y la búsqueda del Dios Liberador* (ed. P. Richard; San José, CR/Managua: DEI/Centro Antonio Valdivieso, 1980), pp. 33-56.

—*Exodus: A Hermeneutics of Freedom* (trans. S. Attanasio; Maryknoll: Orbis Press, 1981).

—*Hermenéutica bíblica. Para una teoría de la lectura como producción de sentido* (Buenos Aires: Ediciones La Aurora, 1984).

—'Palabra profética y no-conversión', *Vox Evangelii* ns 1 (1984), pp. 9-20.

—'Del juicio a la reconciliación. Una lectura de textos proféticos', *CuadTeol* 8 (1987), pp. 7-16.

—'Desmesura del poder y destino de los imperios. Exégesis de Isaías 10.5-7a', *CuadTeol* 8 (1987), pp. 147-51.

—'Violencia y desmesura del poder', *RIBLA* 2 (1988), pp. 9-18.

—'Una liturgia fúnebre por la caída del tirano (Isaías 14.4b-23)', *RIBLA* 2 (1988), pp. 59-67.

Crüsemann, F., 'Kritik an Amos im Deuteronomischen Geschichtswerk: Erwägungen zu 2 Könige 14,27', in *Probleme biblischer Theologie: Gerhard von Rad Zum 70. Geburtstag* (ed. H.W. Wolff; Munich: Kaiser Verlag, 1971), pp. 57-63.

Cussianovich, A., *Religious Life and the Poor: Liberation Theology Perspectives* (trans. J. Drury; Maryknoll: Orbis Books, 1979).

Dahmen, U., 'Zur Text- und Literarkritik von Am 6, 6a', *BibNot* 31 (1986), pp. 7-10.

Dahood, M., 'Amos 6, 8 *meta'eb*', *Bib* 59 (1978), pp. 265-67.

—'Can One Plow without Oxen? (Amos 6.12) A Study of *BA*- and '*Al*'', in *The Bible World: Essays in Honor of Cyrus H. Gordon* (ed. G. Rendsburg, R. Adler, M. Arfa and N.H. Winter; New York: Ktav/The Institute of Hebrew Culture and Education of New York University, 1980), pp. 13-23.

Dalley, S., 'Foreign Chariotry and Calvary in the Armies of Tiglath-Pileser III and Sargon II', *Iraq* 47 (1985), pp. 31-48.

Dallmayr, F.R., 'Phenomenology and Marxism: A Salute to Enzo Paci', in *Phenomenological Sociology: Issues and Applications* (ed. G. Psathas; New York: John Wiley & Sons, 1973), pp. 305-56.

Dalton, G., 'Peasantries in Anthropology and History', *CurrAnth* 13 (1972), pp. 385-415.

Davies, E.W., *Prophecy and Ethics: Isaiah and the Ethical Tradition of Israel* (JSOTSup, 16; Sheffield: JSOT Press, 1981).

Davies, G.H., 'Amos—The Prophet of Reunion', *ExpTim* 92 (1980–81), pp. 196-200.

Davies, P.R., and D.M. Gunn (eds.), '*A History of Ancient Israel and Judah*: A Discussion of Miller–Hayes (1986)', *JSOT* 39 (1987), pp. 3-63.

Dearman, J.A., 'Hebrew Prophecy and Social Criticism: Some Observations for Perspective', *PerspRelSt* 9 (1982), pp. 131-43.

—*Property Rights in the Eighth-Century Prophets: The Conflict and its Background* (SBLDS, 106; Atlanta: Scholars Press, 1988).

de Geus, J.K., 'Die Gesellschaftskritik der Propheten und die Archäologie', *ZDPV* 98 (1982), pp. 50-57.

De Santa Ana, J. (ed.), *Towards a Church of the Poor: The Work of an Ecumenical Group on the Church and the Poor* (Maryknoll: Orbis Books, 1979).

Dever, W.G., 'Recent Archaeological Confirmation of the Cult of Asherah in Ancient Israel', *HebSt* 23 (1982), pp. 37-43.

—'Asherah, Consort of Yahweh? New Evidence from Kuntillet 'Ajrûd', *BASOR* 255 (1984), pp. 21-37.

De Waard, J., 'A Greek Translation-Technical Treatment of Amos 1.15', in *On Language, Culture, and Religion: In Honor of Eugene A. Nida* (ed. M. Black and W.A. Smalley; The Hague: Mouton, 1974), pp. 111-18.

—'Chiastic Structure of Amos V 1-17', *VT* 27 (1977), pp. 170-77.

—'Translation Techniques Used by the Greek Translators on Amos', *Bib* 59 (1978), pp. 339-50.

De Waard, J., and W.A. Smalley, *A Translator's Handbook of Amos: Helps for Translators* (New York: United Bible Societies, 1979).

Dijkema, J., 'Le fond des prophéties d'Amos', *OTS* 2 (1943), pp. 18-34.

Dion, P.E., 'Le message moral du prophète Amos s'inspirait-il du droit de l'alliance?', *ScEsp* 27 (1975), pp. 5-34.

Dirección Nacional del FSLN (Frente Sandinista de Liberación Nacional), 'Los cristianos en la Revolución Popular Sandinista' (Comunicado Oficial de la Direcci ón Nacional del FSLN sobre la religión, Managua, October 7, 1980).

Dorfman, A., and A. Mattelart, *Para leer al pato donald. Comunicaci ón de masa y colonialismo* (Mexico: Siglo XXI Editores, 1972).

Douglas, J.D. (ed.), *Understanding Everyday Life: Toward The Reconstruction of Sociological Knowledge* (London: Routledge & Kegan Paul, 1970).

Douglas, M. (ed.), *Rules and Meanings: The Anthropology of Everyday Knowledge* (Harmondsworth: Penguin Books, 1973).

—*Implicit Meanings* (London: Routledge & Kegan Paul, 1975).

—'Morality and Culture', *Ethics* 93 (1983), pp. 786-91.

Dover, K.J., *Greek Popular Morality in the Time of Plato and Aristotle* (Oxford: Basil Blackwell, 1974).

Driver, G.R., 'A Hebrew Burial Custom', *ZAW* 66 (1954), pp. 314-15.

Driver, S.R., *The Books of Joel and Amos* (The Cambridge Bible for Schools and Colleges; Cambridge: Cambridge University Press, 1907).

Dunkerley, J., *Power in the Isthmus: A Political History of Central America* (London: Verso, 1988).

Dussel, E., *Filosofía ética latinoamericana. 6/III. De la erótica a la pedagoía de la liberaci ón* (Filosofía y liberación latinoamericana; Mexico: Editorial EDICOL, 1977).

—*A History of the Church in Latin America: Colonialism to Liberation (1492–1979)* (trans. rev. A. Neely; Grand Rapids: Eerdmans, 1981).

—'La iglesia latinoamericana en la actual coyuntura (1972-1980)', in *Teología de liberación y comunidades cristianas de base* (ed. S. Torres; Salamanca: Ediciones Sígueme, 1982), pp. 93-122.

—'La "Cuestión popular" ', *CrSoc* 84 (1985), pp. 81-90.

—'El concepto de fetichismo en el pensamiento de Marx: Elementos para una teoría general marxista de la religión', *CrSoc* 85 (1985), pp. 7-59.

—'Cuatro temas en torno a la teología y economía', *CrSoc* 87 (1986), pp. 67-91.

—'Religiosidad popular latinoamericana (hipótesis fundamentales)', *CrSoc* 88 (1986), pp. 103-12.

—'El factor religioso en el proceso revolucionario latinoamericano', *Cr Soc* (1987), pp. 41-55.

—*Ethics and Community* (trans. R.R. Barr; Liberation and Theology Series, 3; Tunbridge Wells: Burns & Oates, 1988).

—'¿Descubrimiento o invasión de América? Visión histórico-teológica', *Conc* 220 (1988), pp. 481-88.

—'Teología de la Liberación y Marxismo', *CrSoc* 98 (1988), pp. 37-60.

Eagleton, T., *The Function of Criticism: From 'The Spectator' to Post-Structuralism* (London: Verso Editions and NLB, 1984).

Ebeling, G., *Word and Faith* (trans. J.W. Leitch; The Preacher's Library; London: SCM Press, 1963).

Ehlers, T.B., 'Central America in the 1980s: Political Crisis and the Social Responsibility of the Anthropologist ', *LARR* 25.3 (1990), pp. 141-55.

Eichrodt, W., *Theology of the Old Testament* (trans. J.A. Baker; Philadelphia: Westminster Press, 1967).

—'Die Vollmacht des Amos. Zu einer schwierigen Stelle im Amosbuch', in *Beiträge zur alttestamentlichen Theologie—Festschrift für Walter Zimmerli zum 70. Geburtstag* (ed. H. Donner, R. Hanhart and R. Smend; Göttingen: Vandenhoeck & Ruprecht, 1977), pp. 124-31.

Eisenstadt, S.N. (ed.), *Max Weber on Charisma and Institution: Selected Papers* (The Heritage of Sociology; Chicago: University of Chicago Press, 1968).

'Elecciones en Nicaragua y lecciones para El Salvador', Comment in *Estudios Centroamericanos* 45 (1990), pp. 3-76.

Elizondo, V., 'La Virgen de Guadalupe como símbolo cultural', in *Raíces de la teología latinoamericana. Nuevos materiales para la historia de la teología* (ed. P. Richard; San José, CR: DEI, 2nd edn, 1987), pp. 393-401.

Ellacuría, I., *Conversión de la Iglesia al reino de Dios. Para anunciarlo y realizarlo en la historia* (Colección Teología Latinoamericana, 5; San Salvador: UCA Editores, 1985).

—'Quinto centenario de América Latina ¿Descubrimiento o encubrimiento?', *RLT* 21 (1990), pp. 271-82.

Emmett, D., 'Prophets and their Societies', *JRoyAnthI* 86.1 (1956), pp. 13-23.

—*The Moral Prism* (London: Macmillan, 1979).

Epsztein, L., *Social Justice in the Ancient Near East and the People of the Bible* (trans. J. Bowden; London: SCM Press, 1986).

Equipo CLAR, *Tendencias proféticas de la Vida Religiosa en America Latina* (CLAR, 24; Bogota: Secretariado General de la CLAR, 1975).

Escobar, S., *La fe evangélica y las teologías de la liberación* (El Paso: Casa Bautista de Publicaciones, 1987).

Esquivel, J., *El Padre Nuestro desde Guatemala y otros poemas* (San José, CR: DEI, 1981).

Estess, T.L., 'The Inenarrable Contraption: Reflections on the Metaphor of Story', *JAAR* 42 (1974), pp. 415-34.

Fackre, G., 'Narrative Theology: An Overview', *Int* 37 (1983), pp. 340-52.

Fahey, T., 'Max Weber's Ancient Judaism', *AmJSoc* 88 (1982), pp. 62-87.

—'Text and Context in Interpreting a Text: Reply to Camic', *AmJSoc* 89 (1983), pp. 1417-20.

Farr, G., 'The Language of Amos, Popular or Cultic', *VT* 16 (1966), pp. 312-24.

Fendler, M., 'Zur Socialkritik des Amos: Versuch einer wirschaft- und sozialgeschichtlichen Interpretation alttestamentlicher Texte', *EvT* 33 (1973), pp. 32-53.

Fiensy, D., 'Using the Nuer Culture of Africa in Understanding the Old Testament: An Evaluation', *JSOT* 38 (1987), pp. 73-83.

Fisch, H., *Poetry with a Purpose: Biblical Poetics and Interpretation* (Indiana Studies in Biblical Literature; Bloomington, IN: Indiana University Press, 1988).

Fleischer, G., *Von Menschenverkäufern, Baschankühen und Rechtsverkehrern. Die Sozialkritik des Amosbuches in historisch-kritischer, sozialgeschichtlicher und archäologischer Perspektive* (BBB, 74; Frankfurt am Main: Athenäum Verlag, 1989).

Fogel, D., *Revolution in Central America* (San Francisco: Ism Press, 1985).

Fox, M.V., 'Identification of Quotations in Biblical Literature', *ZAW* 90 (1980), pp. 416-31.

Franco, J., 'What's in a Name? Popular Culture Theories and their Limitations', *Studies in Latin American Popular Culture* 1 (1982), pp. 5-14.

Frankena, W.K., 'Conversations with Carney and Hauerwas', *JRelEth* 3 (1975), pp. 45-62.

—'MacIntyre and Modern Morality', *Ethics* 93 (1983), pp. 579-87.

Freedman, D.N., 'But Did King David Invent Musical Instruments?', *BRev* 1 (1985), pp. 48-51.

Freedman, D.N., and F.I. Anderson, 'Harmon in Amos 4.3', *BASOR* 198 (1970), p. 41.

Frei, H.W., *The Eclipse of Biblical Narrative: A Study in Eighteenth and Nineteenth Century Hermeneutics* (New Haven: Yale University Press, 1974).

Freire, P., *Pedagogy of the Oppressed* (trans. M.B. Ramos; New York: Seabury Press, 1970).

Fuentes, C., *Myself with Others: Selected Essays* (New York: Farrar, Straus & Giroux, 1988).

Gadamer, H.G., *Truth and Method* (ed. and trans. G. Barden and J. Cumming; New York: Continuum, 1975).

Garcia Márquez, G., *El olor de la guayaba. Conversaciones con Pino Apuleyo Mendoza* (Barcelona: Editorial Bruguera, 1982).

—*The General in his Labyrinth* (trans. E. Grossman; New York: Alfred A. Knopf, 1990).

García Trapiello, J., 'Situación histórica del profeta Amós', *EstBíb* 26 (1967), pp. 249-74.

Garrad Burnett, V., 'Protestantism in Rural Guatemala, 1872-1954', *LARR* 24.2 (1989), pp. 127-42.

Garrett, D.A., 'The Structure of Amos as a Testimony to its Integrity', *JETS* 27 (1984), pp. 275-76.

Geertz, C., *The Interpretation of Cultures: Selected Essays* (New York: Basic Books, 1973).

—*Local Knowledge: Further Essays in Interpretive Anthropology* (New York: Basic Books, 1983).

—'Culture and Social Change: The Indonesian Case', *Man* ns 19 (1984), pp. 511-32.

—*Words and Lives: The Anthropologist as Author* (Stanford: Stanford University Press, 1988).

—'History and Anthropology', *NLH* 21 (1990), pp. 321-35.

Gerstenberger, E., 'The Woe Oracles of the Prophets', *JBL* 81 (1962), pp. 249-63.

Gese, H., 'Kleine Beiträge zum Verständnis des Amosbuches', *VTSup* 12 (1962), pp. 417-38.

—'Komposition bei Amos', *VTSup* 32 (Leiden: Brill, 1980), pp. 74-95.

Gesenius, W., *Gesenius' Hebrew Grammar* (ed. E. Kautzsch; trans. A.E. Cowley; London: Oxford University Press, 2nd edn, repr. 1976).

Gevirtz, S., 'A New Look at an Old Crux: Amos 5.26', *JBL* 87 (1968), pp. 267-76.

Geyer, G.A., *The New Latins: Fateful Change in South and Central America* (Garden City, NY: Doubleday, 1970).

Gibbons, R., 'Political Poetry and the Example of Ernesto Cardenal', *CritInq* 13 (1987), pp. 648-71.

Gill, R., *Prophecy and Praxis: The Social Function of the Churches* (Contemporary Christian Studies; London: Marshall, Morgan & Scott, 1981).

—'Berger's Plausibility Structures: A Response to Professor Cairns', *SJT* 27 (1974), pp. 198-207.

Girardi, G., *Sandinismo, marxismo, cristianismo; la confluencia* (Managua: Centro Ecuménico Antonio Valdivieso, 1986).

—'Revolución popular y toma del templo', in *Nicaragua, trinchera teológica. Para una Teología de la Liberación desde Nicaragua* (ed. G. Girardi, B. Forcano and J.Ma. Vigil; Managua/Madrid: Centro Ecuménico Antonio Valdivieso/Lóguez Ediciones, 1987), pp. 221-35.

—'Educación popular liberadora, segunda evangelización de América Latina', in *Nicaragua, trinchera teológica. Para una Teología de la Liberación desde Nicaragua* (ed. G. Girardi, B. Forcano and J.Ma. Vigil; Managua/Madrid: Centro Ecuménico Antonio Valdivieso/Lóguez Ediciones, 1987), pp. 365-415.

—'La revolución cubana en la historia de la esperanza', *CrSoc* 98 (1988), pp. 23-36.

—'Marxismo, Teología de la Liberación e "Iglesia popular" en la lucha ideológica actual', *CrSoc* 100 (1989), pp. 19-42.

Gitay, Y., 'A Study of Amos's Art of Speech: A Rhetorical Analysis of Amos 3.1-15', *CBQ* 42 (1980), pp. 293-309.

Glück, J.J., 'Three Notes on the Book of Amos', *OTWSA* 7-8 (1966), pp. 115-21.

Godelier, M., *Perspectives in Marxist Anthropology* (trans. R. Brain; Cambridge Studies in Social Anthropology, 18; Cambridge: Cambridge University Press, 1977).

Goldberg, M., *Theology and Narrative: A Critical Introduction* (Nashville: Abingdon Press, 1981).

Goldingay, J., 'The Stories in Daniel: A Narrative Politics', *JSOT* 37 (1987), pp. 99-116.

Gómez H., J.F., 'El intelectual orgánico según Gramsci y el teólogo de la liberación en América Latina', *CrSoc* 91 (1987), pp. 95-109.

González Echeverría, R., *The Voice of the Masters: Writing and Authority in Modern Latin American Literature* (Austin, TX: University of Texas Press, 1985).

Gordis, R., 'A Rhetorical Use of Interrogative Sentences in Biblical Hebrew', *AJSL* 49 (1933), pp. 212-17.

—'The Composition and Structure of Amos', *HTR* 33 (1940), pp. 239-51.

—'Studies in the Book of Amos', *Proceedings of the American Academy for Jewish Research* 46-47 (1979-80), pp. 201-64.

Gotay, S.S., 'Las condiciones históricas y teóricas que hicieron posible la incorporación del materialismo histórico en el pensamiento cristiano en América Latina', *CrSoc* 84 (1985), pp. 25-48.

Gottwald, N.K., *All the Kingdoms of the Earth: Israelite Prophecy and International Relations in the Ancient Near East* (New York: Harper & Row, 1964).

—*The Tribes of Yahweh: A Sociology of the Religion of Liberated Israel 1250–150 BCE* (Maryknoll: Orbis Books, 1979).

—(ed.), *The Bible and Liberation: Political and Social Hermeneutics* (Maryknoll: Orbis Books, rev. edn, 1983).

—*The Hebrew Bible: A Socio-Literary Introduction* (Philadelphia: Fortress Press, 1985).

Gouldner, A.W., *Renewal and Critique in Sociology Today* (London: Allen Lane, 1973).

Gowan, D.E., 'The Beginnings of Exile-Theology and the Root *glh*', *ZAW* 87 (1975), pp. 204-207.

Gramsci, A., *Selections from the Prison Notebooks* (ed. and trans. Q. Hoare and G. Nowell-Smith; London: Lawrence &Wishart, 1971).

—*Selections from Cultural Writings* (ed. D. Forgacs and G. Nowell-Smith; trans. W. Boelhower; London: Lawrence & Wishart, 1985).

Gray, J., *The Biblical Doctrine of the Reign of God* (Edinburgh: T. & T. Clark, 1979).

Greenfield, J.C., 'The *Marzeah* as a Social Institution', *AA* 22 (1974), pp. 451-55.

Greenhouse, C.J., 'Looking at Culture, Looking for Rules', *Man* ns 17 (1982), pp. 58-73.

Gros Louis, K.R.R., 'Some Methodological Considerations', in *Literary Interpretations of Biblical Narrative*, II (ed. K.R.R. Gros Louis and J.S. Ackerman; Nashville: Abingdon Press, 1982), pp. 13-24.

Gunn, D.M., 'New Directions in the Study of Biblical Hebrew Narrative', *JSOT* 39 (1987), pp. 65-75.

Gunn, G., 'The Semiotics of Culture and the Interpretation of Life', *Studies in the Literary Imagination* 12 (1977), pp. 109-28.

Gustafson, J.M., *Can Ethics Be Christian?* (Chicago: University of Chicago Press, 1975).

—*Christian Ethics and the Community* (New York: Pilgrim Press, 1979).

Gutiérrez, G., *A Theology of Liberation: History, Politics and Salvation* (trans. C. Inda and J. Eagleson; Maryknoll: Orbis Books, 1973).

—*The Power of the Poor in History* (trans. R.R. Barr; Maryknoll: Orbis Press, 1983).

—'Teología y ciencias sociales', *CrSoc* 84 (1985), pp. 49-67.

—*Hablar de Dios desde el sufrimiento del inocente. Una reflexión sobre el libro de Job* (Salamanca: Ediciones Sígueme, 1988).

Hadley, J.M., 'The Khirbet El-Qom Inscription', *VT* 37 (1987), pp. 50-62.

Hahn, H.H., *The Old Testament in Modern Research* (Philadelphia: Fortress Press, 1966).

Hall, B., *The Geneva Version of the English Bible* (London: The Presbyterian Historical Society of England, 1957).

Hamilton, P., *Knowledge and Social Structure: An Introduction to the Classical Argument in the Sociology of Knowledge* (London: Routledge & Kegan Paul, 1974).

Hammerschaimb, E., 'On the Ethics of the Old Testament Prophets', *VTSup* 7 (Leiden: Brill, 1959), pp. 75-101.

Hammond, P.E., 'Religion in the Modern World', in *Making Sense of Modern Times: Peter L. Berger and the Vision of Interpretive Sociology* (ed. J.D. Hunter and S.C. Ainlay; London: Routledge & Kegan Paul, 1986), pp. 143-58.

Hampshire, S., *Morality and Conflict* (Oxford: Basil Blackwell, 1983).

Hanks, T.D., *Opresión, pobreza y liberación. Reflexiones bíblicas* (Miami: Editorial Caribe, 1982).

—*God So Loved the Third World: The Bible, the Reformation and Liberation Theologies* (trans. J.C. Dekker; Maryknoll: Orbis Books, 1983).

Haran, M., 'The Rise and Decline of the Empire of Jeroboam Ben Joash', *VT* 17 (1967), pp. 266-97.

Harper, W.R., *A Critical and Exegetical Commentary on Amos and Hosea* (International Critical Commentary; Edinburgh: T. & T. Clark, repr. 1979).

Harris, M., 'Why a Perfect Knowledge of All the Rules One Must Know to Act Like a Native Cannot Lead to the Knowledge of How Natives Act', *JAnthRes* 30 (1974), pp. 240-51.

—'History and Significance of the Emic/Etic Distinction', *AnnRevAnth* 5 (1976), pp. 329-50.

—*Cultural Materialism: The Struggle for a Science of Culture* (New York: Vintage Books, 1979).

—*The Sacred Cow and the Abominable Pig: Riddles of Food and Culture* (New York: Simon & Schuster, 1985).

Harrison, L.E., *Underdevelopment is a State of Mind: The Latin American Case* (Lanham, MD: The Center for International Affairs, Harvard University and University Press of America, 1985).

Hartt, J., 'Theological Investments in Story: Some Comments on Recent Developments and Some Proposals', *JAAR* 52 (1983), pp. 117-30.

Hastrup, K., and P. Elsass, 'Anthropological Advocacy: A Contradiction in Terms?', *CurrAnth* 31 (1990), pp. 301-11; 32 (1990), pp. 387-90.

Hauerwas, S., *Character and the Christian Life: A Study in Theological Ethics* (San Antonio, TX: Trinity University Press, 1975).

—'Natural Law, Tragedy, and Theological Ethics', *American Journal of Jurisprudence* 20 (1975), pp. 1-19.

—'Learning to See Red Wheelbarrows: On Visions and Relativism', *JAAR* 45 Supp. 1 (1977), pp. 643-55.

—'The Moral Authority of Scripture: The Politics and Ethics of Remembering', *Int* 34 (1980), pp. 356-70.

—'Reply to R.J. Neuhaus', *Center Journal* 1 (1982), pp. 42-51.

—*The Peaceable Kingdom: A Primer in Christian Ethics* (London: SCM Press, 1983).

—'The Church as God's New Language', in *Scriptural Authority: A Narrative Interpretation* (ed. G. Green; Philadelphia: Fortress Press, 1987), pp. 179-98.

Hauerwas, S., with R. Bonti and D.B. Burrell, *Truthfulness and Tragedy: Further Investigation in Christian Ethics* (Notre Dame, IN: University of Notre Dame Press, 1977).

Hauerwas, S., and A. MacIntyre (eds.), *Revisions: Changing Perspectives in Moral Philosophy* (Revisions, 3; Notre Dame, IN: University of Notre Dame Press, 1983).

Hauerwas, S., and P. Wadell, Review of A. MacIntyre's *After Virtue*, *The Thomist* 46 (1982), pp. 313-22.

Hauerwas, S., and W.H. Willimon, *Resident Aliens: Life in the Christian Colony* (Nashville: Abingdon Press, 1989).

Havan, M.J., 'The Background and Meaning of Amos 5.17B', *HTR* 79 (1986), pp. 337-48.

Hawkes, T., *Structuralism and Semiotics* (Berkeley: University of California Press, 1977).

Hawkins, J., *Inverse Images: The Meaning of Culture, Ethnicity and Family in Postcolonial Guatemala* (Albuquerque: University of New Mexico Press, 1984).

Hayes, J.H., *Amos the Eighth-Century Prophet: His Times and his Preaching* (Nashville: Abingdon Press, 1988).

Heinen, H.D., 'On Cultural Materialism, Marx, and the "Hegelian Monkey"', *CurrAnth* 16 (1975), pp. 450-56.

Herion, G.A., 'The Impact of Modern and Social Science Assumptions on the Reconstruction of Israelite History', *JSOT* 34 (1986), pp. 3-33.

Hillers, D.R., '*Hôy* and *Hôy*-Oracles: A Neglected Syntactic Aspect', in *The Word of the Lord Shall Go Forth: Essays in Honor of David Noel Freedman in Celebration of his Sixtieth Birthday* (ed. C.L. Meyers and M. O'Conner; Winona Lake, IN: Eisenbrauns/American Schools of Oriental Research, 1983), pp. 185-88.

Hirsch, E.D., Jr, *Cultural Literacy: What Every American Needs to Know* (Boston: Houghton Mifflin, 1987).

Hobbs, T.R., 'Amos 3.1b and 2.10', *ZAW* 81 (1969), pp. 384-87.

Hoffmann, Y., 'The Day of the Lord as a Concept and a Term in the Prophetic Literature', *ZAW* 93 (1981), pp. 7-50.

Holladay, J.S., Jr, 'Assyrian Statecraft and the Prophets of Israel', *HTR* 63 (1970), pp. 29-51.

Holladay, W.L., 'Amos VI 1B: A Suggested Solution', *VT* 22 (1972), pp. 107-110.

Holm-Nielsen, S., 'Die Social Kritik der Propheten', in *Denkender Glaube: Festschrift Carl Heinz Ratschow* (ed. O. Kaiser; Berlin: de Gruyter, 1976), pp. 7-23.

Holstein, J.A., 'Max Weber and Biblical Scholarship', *HUCA* 46 (1975), pp. 159-79.

Howard, G., 'Some Notes on the Septuagint of Amos', *VT* 20 (1970), pp. 108-12.

—'Revision toward the Hebrew in the Septuagint Text of Amos', *EI* 16 (1982), pp. 125-33.

Huffmon, H.B., 'The Treaty Background of Hebrew YADA', *BASOR* 181 (1966), pp. 31-37.

—'The Social Role of Amos' Message', in *The Quest for the Kingdom of God: Studies in Honor of George E. Mendenhall* (ed. H.B. Huffmon, F.A. Spina and A.R.W. Green; Winona Lake, IN: Eisenbrauns, 1983), pp. 109-16.

Hunter, A.V., *Seek the Lord! A Study of the Meaning and Function of the Exhortations in Amos, Hosea, Isaiah, Micah, and Zephaniah* (Baltimore: St Mary's Seminary and University, 1982).

Hunter, J.D., 'The Modern Malaise', in *Making Sense of Modern Times: Peter L. Berger and the Vision of Interpretative Sociology* (ed. J.D. Hunter and S.C. Ainlay; London: Routledge & Kegan Paul, 1986), pp. 76-100.

Hyatt, J.P., 'The Translation and Meaning of Amos 5.23-24', *ZAW* 68 (1956), pp. 17-24.

Irarrázaval, D., 'Nicaragua: una soprendiente religiosidad', in *Religión y política en América Central. Hacia una nueva interpretación de la religiosidad popular* (P. Richard and D. Irarrázaval; San José, CR: DEI, 1981), pp. 35-52.

Jackson, J.F., 'Amos 5,13 Contextually Understood', *ZAW* 98 (1986), pp. 434-435.

Jacobs, P.F., '"Cows of Bashan"—A Note on the Interpretation of Amos 4.1', *JBL* 104 (1985), pp. 109-10.

Jagersma, H., 'The Tithes in the Old Testament', *OTS* 21 (1981), pp. 116-28.

Jameson, F., *The Political Unconscious: Narrative as a Socially Symbolic Act* (London: Methuen, 1981).

Janzen, W., *Mourning Cry and Woe Oracle* (BZAW, 125; Berlin: de Gruyter, 1972).

Jauss, H.R., 'Levels of Identification of Hero and Audience', *NLH* 5 (1974), pp. 283-317.

—*Toward an Aesthetic of Reception* (trans. T. Bahti; Theory and History of Literature, 2; Minneapolis, MN: University of Minnesota Press, 1982).

Jeremias, J., 'Amos 3–6. Beobachtungen zur Entstehungsgeschichte eines Prophetenbuches', *ZAW* 100 (1988), pp. 123-38.

Jobling, D., *The Sense of Biblical Narrative: Structural Analyses in the Hebrew Bible*, I (JSOTSup, 7; Sheffield: JSOT Press, 2nd edn, 1986).

—*The Sense of Biblical Narrative: Structural Analyses in the Hebrew Bible*, II (JSOTSup, 39; Sheffield: JSOT Press, 1986).

Jones, L.G., 'Alasdair MacIntyre on Narrative, Community, and the Moral Life', *ModTh* 4 (1987), pp. 53-69.

Kairos Document, The, *Challenge to the Church: A Theological Comment on the Political Crisis in South Africa* (Grand Rapids: Eerdmans, 1986).

Kapelrud, A.S., 'New Ideas in Amos', *VTSup* 15 (Leiden: Brill, 1966), pp. 193-206.

—*Central Ideas in Amos* (Oslo: Universitetsforlaget, 1971).

Kee, A., *Marx and the Failure of Liberation Theology* (London/Philadelphia: SCM Press/Trinity Press International, 1990).

Keesing, R.M., 'Theories of Culture', *AnnRevAnth* 3 (1974), pp. 73-97.

—'Anthropology as Interpretative Quest', *CurrAnth* 28 (1987), pp. 161-69, 174-76.

—'Models, "Folk" and "Cultural": Paradigms Regained', in *Cultural Models in Language and Thought* (ed. D. Holland and N. Quinn; Cambridge: Cambridge University Press, 1987), pp. 369-93.

Keil, C.F., *Commentary on the Old Testament. X. Minor Prophets* (Grand Rapids: Eerdmans, 1977).

Kelsey, D.H., *The Uses of Scripture in Recent Theology* (Philadelphia: Fortress Press, 1975).

Kessler, M., 'Inclusio in the Hebrew Bible', *Semitics* 6 (1978), pp. 44-49.

—'An Introduction to Rhetorical Criticism of the Bible: Prolegomena', *Semitics* 7 (1980), pp. 1-27.

—'A Methodological Setting for Rhetorical Criticism', in *Art and Meaning: Rhetoric in Biblical Literature* (ed. D.J.A. Clines, D.M. Gunn and A.J. Hauser; JSOTSup, 19; Sheffield: JSOT Press, 1982).

Kimbrough, S.T., Jr, *Israelite Religion in Sociological Perspective: The Work of Antonin Causse* (Wiesbaden: Otto Harrasowitz, 1978).

King, P.J., *Amos, Hosea, Micah—An Archaeological Commentary* (Philadelphia: Westminster Press, 1988).

—'The *Marzeaḥ* Amos Denounces', *BARev* 15.4 (1988), pp. 34-44.

Kittel, G., and C. Friedrich (eds.), *Theological Dictionary of the New Testament* (10 vols.; ed. and trans. G.W. Bromiley; Grand Rapids: Eerdmans, 1965–1974).

Klor de Alva, J.J., 'Spiritual Conflict and Accommodation in New Spain: Toward a Typology of Aztec Responses to Christianity', in *The Inca and Aztec States 1400–1800: Anthropology and History* (ed. G.A. Collier, R.I. Rosaldo and J.D. Wirth; Studies in Anthropology; New York: Academic Press, 1982), pp. 345-66.

Knight, D.A., 'Jeremiah and the Dimensions of the Moral Life', in *The Divine Helmsman: Studies on God's Control of Human Events, Presented to Lou H. Silberman* (ed. J.L. Crenshaw and S. Sandmel; New York: Ktav, 1980), pp. 87-105.

Knox, J., *The First Blast of the Trumpet Against the Monstrous Regiment of Women—1558* (ed. E. Arber; London: n.p., 1878).

Koch, K., *et al.*, *Amos: Untersucht mit den Methoden einer strukturalen Formgeschichte* (AOAT, 30; Neukirchen–Vluyn: Neukirchener Verlag, 1976).

—*The Prophets*. I. *The Assyrian Period* (trans. M. Kohl; Philadelphia: Fortress Press, 1983).

Kselman, T.A., 'Ambivalence and Assumption in the Concept of Popular Religion', in *Religion and Political Conflict in Latin America* (ed. D.H. Levine; Chapel Hill: University of North Carolina Press, 1986), pp. 24-41.

Kuhn, T., *The Structure of Scientific Revolutions* (International Encyclopedia of United Science, 2.2; Chicago: University of Chicago Press, 2nd edn, 1970).

Labuschagne, C.J., 'Amos' Conception of God and the Popular Theology of his Time', *OTWSA* 7-8 (1966), pp. 122-33.

Lafferty, W.M., 'Externalization and Dialectics: Taking the Brackets Off Berger and Luchmann's Sociology of Knowledge', *CultHerm* 4 (1977), pp. 139-61.

Lang, B., 'Sklaven und Unfreie im Buch Amos (II 6, VIII 6)', *VT* 31 (1981), pp. 482-88.

—*Monotheism and the Prophetic Minority: An Essay in Biblical History and Sociology* (SWBAS, 1; Sheffield: Almond Press, 1983).

—(ed.), *Anthropological Approaches to the Old Testament* (Philadelphia/London: Fortress Press/SPCK, 1985).

Lategan, B.C., 'Reference: Reception, Redescription, and Reality', in *Text and Reality: Aspects of Reference in Biblical Texts* (SBL Semeia Studies; Atlanta: Society of Biblical Literature, 1985), pp. 67-93.

Lehman, M.R., 'Biblical Oaths', *ZAW* 81 (1969), pp. 74-92.

Lemaire, A., 'Who or What Was Yahweh's Asherah', *BARev* 10 (Nov.–Dec. 1984), pp. 42-51.

Levine, D.H. (ed.), *Religion and Political Conflict in Latin America* (Chapel Hill: University of North Carolina Press, 1986).

Lewis, B., *History: Remembered, Recovered, Invented* (New York: Simon & Schuster, 1987).

Lewis, C.S., *Christian Reflections* (ed. W. Hooper; Grand Rapids: Eerdmans, 1967).

Lichtenstein, M.H., 'The Poetry of Poetic Justice: A Comparative Study in Biblical Imagery', *JANESCU* 5 (1973), pp. 255-65.

Limburg, J., 'Sevenfold Structures in the Book of Amos', *JBL* 106 (1987), pp. 217-22.

Linbeck, G.A., *The Nature of Doctrine: Religion and Theology in a Postliberal Age* (Philadelphia: Westminster Press, 1984).

Lindblom, J., *Prophecy in Ancient Israel* (Philadelphia: Fortress Press, 1962).

Lindström, F., *God and the Origin of Evil: A Contextual Analysis of Alleged Monistic Evidence in the Old Testament* (trans. F.H. Cryer; ConBOT, 21; Lund: Gleerup, 1983).

Liss, S.B., *Marxist Thought in Latin America* (Berkeley: University of California Press, 1984).

Long, B.O., 'The Social Setting for Prophetic Miracle Stories', *Semeia* 3 (1975), pp. 46-63.

Long, T.E., 'Prophecy, Charisma, and Politics: Reinterpreting the Weberian Thesis', in *Religion and the Political Order*. I. *Prophetic Religions and Politics* (ed. J.K. Hadden and A. Shupe; New York: Paragon House, 1986), pp. 3-17.

—'A Theory of Prophetic Religion and Politics', in *Religion and the Political Order*. II. *The Politics of Religion and Social Change* (ed. J.K. Hadden and A. Shupe; New York: Paragon House, 1983), pp. 3-16.

Longwood, M., 'How Ethics Should Be Done', *Int* 49 (1986), pp. 75-77.

Lorctz, O., 'Die prophetische Kritik des Rentcapitalismus. Grundlagen-Probleme der Prophetenforschung', *UF* 7 (1975), pp. 271-78.

—'Vergleich und Kommentar in Amos 3, 12', *BZ* ns 20 (1976), pp. 122-25.

—'Ugaritische und hebräische Lexikographie (II)', *UF* 13 (1981), pp. 127-35.

Lotman, J.W., 'Point of View in a Text', *NLH* 6 (1975), pp. 339-52.

Lowance, M.I., *The Language of Canaan: Metaphor and Symbol in New England from the Puritans to the Transcendentalists* (Cambridge, MA: Harvard University Press, 1980).

Lubetski, M., 'SM as Deity', *Rel* 17 (1987), pp. 1-14.

Lukács, G., *History and Class Consciousness: Studies in Marxist Dialectics* (trans. R. Livingstone; London: Merlin Press, 1971).

Lupton, L., *A History of the Geneva Bible* (London: Compton Press, 1972).

Lust, J., 'Remarks on the Redaction of Amos V 4-6, 14-15', *OTS* 21 (1981), pp. 129-54.

Machinist, P., 'Assyria and its Image in the First Isaiah', *JAOS* 103 (1983), pp. 719-37.

MacIntyre, A., 'Epistemological Crises, Dramatic Narrative and the Philosophy of Science'. *The Monist* 60 (1977), pp. 453-72.

—'Does Applied Ethics Rest on a Mistake?', *The Monist* 67 (1984), pp. 498-513.

—*After Virtue* (Notre Dame, IN: University of Notre Dame Press, 2nd edn, 1984).

—*Whose Justice? Which Rationality?* (Notre Dame, IN: University of Notre Dame Press, 1988).

Mackay, J.A., *The Other Spanish Christ: A Study in the Spiritual History of Spain and South America* (New York: Macmillan, 1932).

Magnarella, P.J., 'Cultural Materialism and the Problem of Probabilities', *AmAnth* 84 (1982), pp. 138-46.

Maldonado, L., *Introducción a la religiosidad popular* (Colección Presencia Teología, 21; Santander: Editorial Sal Terrae, 1985).

Mandelkern, S., *Veteris Testamenti Concordantiae Hebraicae atque Chaldaicae* (Tel Aviv: Schocken Books, 1971).

Mansilla, H.C.F., 'La herencia ibérica y la persistencia del autoritarismo en América Latina', *CrSoc* 100 (1989), pp. 81-94.

Marcus, G.E., and D. Cushman, 'Ethnographies as Texts', *AnnRevAnth* 11 (1982), pp. 25-69.

Marcus, G.E., and M.M.J. Fischer, *Anthropology as Cultural Critique: An Experimental Moment in the Human Sciences* (Chicago: University of Chicago Press, 1986).

Mardones, J.M., 'La razón económica capitalista y la teología política neoconservadora', *RLT* 21 (1990), pp. 283-306.

Margalit, B., 'Some Observations on the Inscription and Drawing from Khirbet El-Qôm', *VT* 39 (1989), pp. 371-78.

—'The Meaning and Significance of the Asherah', *VT* 40 (1990), pp. 264-97.

Markert, L., *Struktur und Bezeichnung des Scheltworts: Eine gattungskritische Studie anhand des Amosbuches* (BZAW, 140; Berlin: de Gruyter, 1977).

Martin, D., *Tongues of Fire: The Explosion of Protestantism in Latin America* (Cambridge, MA: Basil Blackwell, 1990).

Martin-Achard, R., *Amos: l'homme, le message, l'influence* (Geneva: Labor et Fides, 1984).

Martínez, A., *Las sectas en Nicaragua. Oferta y demanda de salvación* (San José, CR/Managua: DEI/Centro Ecuménico Antonio Valdivieso, 1989).

Martínez Peláez, S., *La patria del criollo. Ensayo de interpretación de la realidad colonial guatemalteca* (San José, CR: EDUCA, 8th edn, 1981).

Mayer, A.C. (ed.), *Culture and Morality: Essays in Honour of Christoph von Furer-Haimendorf* (Delhi: Oxford University Press, 1981).

Mayers, M.K., *A Look at Latin American Lifestyles* (SIL Museum of Anthropology, 2; Dallas: SIL Museum of Anthropology, 1976).

Mays, J.L., 'Words about the Words of Amos', *Int* 13 (1959), pp. 259-72.

—*Amos: A Commentary* (Old Testament Library; Philadelphia: Westminster Press, 1969).

—'Justice: Perspectives from the Prophetic Tradition', *Int* 37 (1983), pp. 5-17.

McClendon, J.W., Jr, *Systematic Theology. I. Ethics* (Nashville: Abingdon Press, 1986).

McComiskey, T.E., 'The Hymnic Elements of the Prophecy of Amos: A Study of Form-Critical Methodology', in *A Tribute to Gleason Archer* (ed. W.C. Kaiser, Jr, and R. Youngblood; Chicago: Moody Press, 1986), pp. 105-28.

McFadyen, J.E., *A Cry for Justice: A Study in Amos* (Edinburgh: T. & T. Clark, 1912).

McKane, W., *Prophets and Wise Men* (London: SCM Press, repr. 1983).

McKeating, H., 'Sanctions Against Adultery in Ancient Israelite Society, with Some Reflections on Methodology in the Study of Old Testament Ethics', *JSOT* 11 (1979), pp. 57-72.

Mechling, J., 'Myth and Mediation: Peter Berger's and John Neuhaus's Theodicy for Modern America', *Soundings* 62 (1979), pp. 338-68.

Meilander, G., 'Virtue in Contemporary Religious Thought', in *Virtue—Public & Private* (ed. R.J. Neuhaus; Encounter Series; Grand Rapids: Eerdmans, 1986), pp. 7-29.

Meléndez, G., 'La iglesia católica centroamericana en la década de los ochenta', *CrSoc* 103 (1990), pp. 19-40.

Melugin, R.F., 'The Formation of Amos: An Analysis of Exegetical Method', in *Society of Biblical Literature Seminar Papers 1978* (Missoula, MT: Scholars Press, 1978), pp. 369-91.

Mendenhall, G.E., 'The Monarchy', *Int* 29 (1975), pp. 155-70.

Meshel, Z., 'Did Yahweh Have a Consort? The New Religious Inscriptions from the Sinai', *BARev* 5 (March–April 1979), pp. 24-34.

Mesters, D., 'The Use of the Bible in Christian Communities of the Common People', in *The Bible and Liberation: Political and Social Hermeneutics* (ed. N.K. Gottwald; Maryknoll: Orbis Books, 1983), pp. 119-33.

Mettinger, T.N.D., 'YHWH SABAOTH—The Heavenly King on the Cherubim Throne', in *Studies in the Period of David and Solomon and Other Essays* (ed. T. Ishida; Winona Lake, IN: Eisenbrauns, 1982), pp. 109-38.

Miguez, N.O., 'Profecía y proyecto histórico', in *Misión profética de la Iglesia* (P.N. Rigol, et al.; Mexico: CUPSA, 1981), pp. 69-33.

Míguez Bonino, J., 'Popular Piety in Latin America', in *The Mystical and Political Dimension of the Christian Faith* (ed. C. Geffré and G. Gutiérrez; New York: Herder & Herder, 1974), pp. 148-57.

—*Doing Theology in a Revolutionary Situation* (Philadelphia: Fortress Press, 1975).

—*Christians and Marxists: The Mutual Challenge to Revolution* (Grand Rapids: Eerdmans, 1976).

—*Toward a Christian Political Ethics* (Philadelphia: Fortress Press, 1983).

—(ed.), *Faces of Jesus: Latin American Christologies* (Maryknoll: Orbis Books, 1984).

Miller, P.D., Jr, 'Animal Names as Designations in Ugaritic and Hebrew', *UF* 2 (1970), pp. 77-86.

Miranda, J.P., *Marx and the Bible: A Critique of the Philosophy of Oppression* (trans. J. Eagleson; Maryknoll: Orbis Books, 1974).

—*Communism in the Bible* (trans. R.R. Barr; Maryknoll: Orbis Books, 1982).

Mires, F., *En nombre de la cruz. Discusiones teológicas y políticas frente al holocausto de los indios (período de conquista)* (San José, CR: DEI, 1986).

—*La colonización de las almas. Misión y conquista en Hispanoamérica* (San José, CR: DEI, 1987).

Mitchell, B., *Morality: Religious and Secular—The Dilemma of the Traditional Conscience* (Oxford: Clarendon Press, 1980).

Mittmann, S., 'Amos 3, 12-15 und das Bett der Samarier', *ZDPV* 92 (1976), pp. 149-67.

Molina, U., 'Dios, el proceso revolucionario y las elecciones del 25 de febrero de 1990', *RIBLA* 7 (1990), pp. 113-20.

Momigliano, A., 'A Note on Max Weber's Definition of Judaism as a Pariah-Religion', *History and Theory* 19 (1980), pp. 313-18.

Monloubou, L., 'Prophètes. Amos', in *Dictionnaire de la Bible* (ed. L. Pirot, A. Robert, H. Cazelles and A. Feuillet; Paris: Letouzey & Ané, 1972), Supplément 8, cols. 706-724.

Morgan, E. (ed.), *Puritan Political Ideas 1558-1794* (Indianapolis, IN: Bobbs–Merrill, 1965).

Morgenstern, J., *Amos Studies—Parts I, II, III*, I (Cincinnati: Hebrew Union College Press, 1941).

Mouw, R.J., 'Alasdair MacIntyre on Reformation Ethics', *JRelEth* 13 (1985), pp. 243-57.

Muilenburg, J., 'A Study in Hebrew Rhetoric: Repetition and Style', *VTSup* 1 (Leiden: Brill, 1953), pp. 97-111.

—'Form Criticism and Beyond', *JBL* 88 (1969), pp. 1-18.

—'The Linguistic and Rhetorical Usages of the Particle KY in the Old Testament', *HUCA* 32 (1961), pp. 135-60.

Nash, D., and R. Wintrob, 'The Emergence of Self-Consciousness in Ethnography', *CurrAnth* 13 (1972), pp. 527-42.

Ndiokwere, N.I., *Prophecy and Revolution: The Role of Prophets in the Independent African Churches and in Biblical Tradition* (London: SPCK, 1981).

Neher, A., *Amos. Contribution a l'étude du prophétisme* (Bibliothèque d'Histoire de la Philosophie; Paris: Libraire Philosophique J. Vrin, 2nd rev. edn, 1981).

Neruda, P., *Odas elementales* (Letras Hispánicas; Madrid: Ediciones Cátedra SA, 2nd edn, 1985).

Nesti, A., 'Gramsci et la religion populaire', *SocComp* 22 (1975), pp. 343-54.

Neufeld, E., 'The Emergence of a Royal Urban Society in Ancient Israel', *HUCA* 31 (1960), pp. 31-53.

Neuhaus, R.J., *The Naked Public Square: Religion and Democracy in America* (Grand Rapids: Eerdmans, 1984).

Nida, E.A., *Understanding Latin Americans: With Special Reference to Religious Values and Movements* (South Pasadena: William Carey Library, 1974).

Novak, M., *The Spirit of Democratic Capitalism* (New York: American Enterprise Institute/Simon & Schuster, 1982).

—*Will it Liberate? Questions about Liberation Theology* (New York: Paulist Press, 1986).

Núñez, E.A., *Liberation Theology* (trans. P.E. Sywulka; Chicago: Moody Press, 1985).

Núñez, E.A., and W.D. Taylor, *Latin America in Crisis: An Evangelical Perspective* (Chicago: Moody Press, 1989).

Ogletree, T.W., 'Character and Narrative: Stanley Hauerwas' Studies of the Christian Life', *RelStR* 6 (1980), pp. 25-30.

—*The Use of the Bible in Christian Ethics* (Philadelphia: Fortress Press, 1983).

O'Laughlin, B., 'Marxist Approaches in Anthropology', *AnnRevAnth* 4 (1975), pp. 341-70.

O'Meara, J.T., 'Anthropology as Empirical Science', *AmAnth* 91 (1989), pp. 354-69.

O'Rourke Boyle, M., 'The Covenant Lawsuit of the Prophet Amos: III 1-IV 3', *VT* 21 (1971), pp. 338-62.

Outka, G., 'Character, Vision and Narrative', *RelStR* 6 (1980), pp. 110-18.

Overholt, T.W., 'Commanding the Prophets: Amos and the Problem of Prophetic Authority', *CBQ* 41 (1979), pp. 517-32.

—'Prophecy: The Problem of Cross-Cultural Comparison', *Semeia* 21 (1982), pp. 55-78.

—'Seeing is Believing: The Social Setting of Prophetic Acts of Power', *JSOT* 23 (1982), pp. 3-31.

—*Channels of Prophecy: The Social Dynamics of Prophetic Activity* (Minneapolis, MN: Fortress Press, 1989).

Padilla, C.R., *Mission between the Times: Essays on the Kingdom* (Grand Rapids: Eerdmans, 1985).

—'La nueva eclesiología en América Latina', *BolTeol* 24 (1986), pp. 201-26.

Page, S., 'Joash and Samaria in a New Stela Excavated at Tell Al Rimah, Iraq', *VT* 19 (1969), pp. 483-84.

Parunak, H.V.D., 'Oral Typesetting: Some Uses of Biblical Structure', *Bib* 62 (1981), pp. 153-68.

—'Some Axioms for Literary Structure', *Semitics* 8 (1982), pp. 1-16.

—'Transitional Techniques in the Bible', *JBL* 102 (1983), pp. 525-48.

Paul, S.M., 'Amos III 15—Winter and Summer Mansions', *VT* 28 (1978), pp. 358-60.

—'Fishing Imagery in Amos 4.2', *JBL* 97 (1978), pp. 183-90.

—'Amos 3.3-8: The Irresistible Sequence of Cause and Effect', *HAR* 7 (1983), pp. 203-20.

Paz, O., *The Bow and the Lyre: The Poem, the Poetic Revelation, Poetry and History* (trans. R.L.C. Simms; The Texas Pan American Series: Austin, TX: University of Texas Press, 1973).

—*El ogro filantrópico. Historia y política (1971-1978)* (Mexico: Editorial Joaquín Mortiz, 1979).

—*One Earth, Four or Five Worlds: Reflections on Contemporary History* (trans. H.R. Lane; San Diego: Harcourt Brace Jovanovich, 1985).

—*Convergences: Essays on Art and Literature* (trans. H. Lane; San Diego: Harcourt Brace Jovanovich, 1987).

Pearson, L., *Popular Ethics in Ancient Greece* (Stanford: Stanford University Press, 1962).

Pelser, H.S., 'Amos 3.11—A Communication', *OTWSA* 7–8 (1966), pp. 153-56.

Perera, V., *Rites: A Guatemalan Boyhood* (London: André Deutsch, 1986).

Petersen, D.L., *The Role of Israel's Prophets* (JSOTSup, 17; Sheffield: JSOT Press, 1981).

Phillip, N., and V. Neuberg (eds.), *Charles Dickens: A December Vision and Other Thoughtful Writings* (New York: Continuum, 1987).

Piedra S., A., 'Evaluación crítica de la actual coyuntura evangélica centroamericana', *VPens* 4 (1984), pp. 3-20.

—'Protestantismo y sociedad en América Central', *CrSoc* 103 (1990), pp. 87-106.

Piñón G., F., 'Antonio Gramsci y el análisis del fenómeno religioso', *CrSoc* 91 (1987), pp. 63-79.

Pixley, J., 'Dios enjuicia a los idólatras en la historia', in *La lucha de los dioses. Los ídolos de la opresión y la búsqueda del Dios Liberador* (ed. P. Richard; San José, CR/Managua: DEI/Centro Antonio Valdivieso, 1980), pp. 57-78.

—'Hacia una teoría de la profecía', in *Misión profética de la iglesia* (P.N. Rigol *et al.*; Mexico: CUPSA, 1981), pp. 15-31.

—*El libro de Job* (Comentario bíblico latinoamericano; San José, CR: Ediciones SEBILA, 1982).

—*Exodo, una lectura evangélica y popular* (Mexico: CUPSA, 1983).

—'Antecedentes bíblicos a la lucha contra el fetichismo', *CrSoc* 84 (1985), pp. 91-101.

—'Oseas: una propuesta de lectura desde América Latina', *RIBLA* 1 (1988), pp. 67-86.

—'¿Exige el dios verdadero sacrificios cruentos?', *RIBLA* 2 (1988), pp. 109-31.

Polan, G.J., *In the Ways of Justice toward Salvation: A Rhetorical Analysis of Isaiah 56-59* (American University Studies, Series VII: Theology and Religion, 13; New York: Peter Lang, 1986).

Polley, M.E., *Amos and the Davidic Empire: A Socio-Historical Approach* (New York: Oxford University Press, 1989).

Poloma, M.M., 'Pentecostals and Politics in North and Central America', in *Religion and the Political Order. I. Prophetic Religions and Politics* (ed. J.K. Hadden and A. Shupe; New York: Paragon House, 1986), pp. 329-52.

Pons, J., *L'oppression dans l'Ancien Testament* (Paris: Letouzey & Ané, 1981).

Pope, M.H., 'A Divine Banquet at Ugarit', in *The Use of the OT in the New & Other Essays: Studies in Honor of William Franklin Stinespring* (ed. J.M. Efird; Durham, NC: Duke University Press, 1972).

Porteous, N.W., *Living the Mystery: Collected Essays* (Oxford: Basil Blackwell, 1967).

Preminger, A., and E.L. Greenstein (eds.), *The Hebrew Bible in Literary Criticism* (New York: Ungar, 1986).

Rabinowitz, I., 'The Crux at Amos III 12', *VT* 11 (1961), pp. 228-31.

Radday, T., 'Chiasmus in Hebrew Biblical Narrative', in *Chiasmus in Antiquity: Structures, Analyses, Exegesis* (ed. J.Welch; Hildesheim: Gerstenberg Verlag, 1981), pp. 50-115.

Ramsey, G.W., 'Amos 4.12—A New Perspective', *JBL* 89 (1970), pp. 187-91.

Rangel, C., *Del buen salvaje al buen revolucionario. Mitos y realidades de América Latina* (San José, CR: Kosmos Editorial SA, 1986).

Raphaël, F., 'Max Weber et le judaïsme antique', *ArEurSoc* 11 (1970), pp. 297-336.

Reade, J., 'Ideology and Propaganda in Assyrian Art', in *Power and Propaganda: A Symposium on Ancient Empire* (ed. M.T. Larsen; Copenhagen Studies in Assyriology, 7; Copenhagen: Akademisk Forlag, 1979), pp. 329-59.

—*Assyrian Sculpture* (London: British Museum Publications, 1983).

Rector, L.J., 'Israel's Rejected Worship: An Exegesis of Amos 5', *RestQ* 21 (1978), pp. 161-75.

Redfield, R., *Peasant Society and Culture: An Anthropological Approach to Civilization* (Chicago: University of Chicago Press, 1956).

Redfoot, D.L., 'The Problem of Freedom', in *Making Sense of Modern Times: Peter L. Berger and the Vision of Interpretive Sociology* (ed. J.D. Hunter and S.C. Ainlay; London: Routledge & Kegan Paul, 1986), pp. 101-18.

Reich, R.B., *Tales of a New America* (New York: Times Books, 1987).

Renaud, B., 'Gènese et théologie d'Amos 3, 3-8', in *Mélanges bibliques et orientaux en l'honneur de M. Henri Cazelles* (ed. A. Caquot and M. Delcor; AOAT, 212; Neukirchen–Vluyn: Verlag Butzen & Berker Kexelaer, 1981), pp. 353-72.

Reventlow, H.G., *Das Amt des Propheten bei Amos* (FRLANT, 80; Göttingen: Vandenhoeck & Ruprecht, 1962).

— *The Authority of the Bible and the Rise of the Modern World* (trans. J. Bowden; London: SCM Press, 1984).

Rice, K.A., *Geertz and Culture* (Anthropology Series: Studies in Cultural Analysis; Ann Arbor: University of Michigan Press, 1980).

Richard, P., 'Nuestra lucha es contra los ídolos. Teología bíblica', in *La lucha de los dioses. Los ídolos de la opresión y la búsqueda del Dios Liberador* (ed. P. Richard; San José, CR/Managua: DEI/Centro Antonio Valdivieso, 1980), pp. 9-32.

—'Religiosidad popular en Centroamérica', in *Religión y política en America Central. Hacia una neuva interpretación de la religiosidad popular* (P. Richard and D. Irarrázabal; San José, CR: DEI, 1981).

—'Nicaragua en la Teología de la Liberación latinoamericana', in *Nicaragua, trinchera teológica. Para una Teología de la Liberación desde Nicaragua* (ed. G. Girardi, B. Forcano and J.Ma. Vigil; Managua/Madrid: Centro Ecuménico Antonio Valdivieso/Lóguez Ediciones, 1987), pp. 237-55.

Richard, P., and G. Meléndez (eds.), *La iglesia de los pobres en América Central. Un análisis socio-político y teológico de la iglesia centroamericana (1960–1982)* (San José, CR: DEI, 1982).

Ricoeur, P., *Essays on Biblical Interpretation* (ed. L.S. Mudge; Philadelphia: Fortress Press, 1980).

Robbins, J.W., 'On the Role of Vision in Morality', *JAAR* 45 Supp. 1 (1977), pp. 623-42.

—'Narrative, Morality and Religion', *JRelEth* 8 (1980), pp. 161-76.

Roberts, J.J.M., 'Recent Trends in the Study of Amos', *RestQ* 13 (1970), pp. 1-16.

—'Form, Syntax, and Redaction in Isaiah 1.2-20', *PSB* ns 3 (1982), pp. 293-306.

—'Amos 6.1-7', in *Understanding the Word: Essays in Honour of Bernhard W. Anderson* (ed. J.T. Butler et al.; JSOTSup, 37; Sheffield: JSOT Press, 1985), pp. 155-66.

Rodó, J.E., *Ariel* (trans. M.S. Peden; Austin, TX: University of Texas Press, 1988).

Rodd, C.S., 'On Applying a Sociological Theory to Biblical Studies', *JSOT* 19 (1981), pp. 95-106.

Rogerson, J.W., *Myth and Old Testament Interpretation* (BZAW, 134; Berlin: de Gruyter, 1974).

—*The Supernatural in the Old Testament* (London: Lutterworth, 1976).

—'The Old Testament View of Nature: Some Preliminary Questions', *OTS* 20 (1977), pp. 67-84.

—'The Old Testament and Social and Moral Questions', *ModChm* ns 25 (1982), pp. 28-35.

—(ed.), *Beginning Old Testament Study* (London: SPCK, 1983).

—*Anthropology and the Old Testament* (Sheffield: JSOT Press, 1984).

—'The Use of Sociology in Old Testament Studies', *VTSup* 36 (Leiden: Brill, 1985), pp. 245-56.

Rosales Nelson, S., 'Bolivia: Continuity and Conflict in Religious Discourse', in *Religion and Political Conflict in Latin America* (ed. D.H. Levine; Chapel Hill: University of North Carolina Press, 1986), pp. 218-35.

Roseberry, W., 'Balinese Cockfights and the Seduction of Anthropology', *SocRes* 49 (1982), pp. 1013-28.

Rosenbaum, S.M., 'Northern Amos Revisited: Two Philological Suggestions', *HebSt* 18 (1977), pp. 132-48.

—*Amos of Israel: A New Interpretation* (Macon, GA: Mercer University Press, 1990).

Rowland, C., and M. Corner, *Liberating Exegesis: The Challenge of Liberation Theology to Biblical Studies* (Biblical Foundations in Theology; London: SPCK, 1990).

Rowley, H.H., *Worship in Ancient Israel: Its Form and Meaning* (London: SPCK, 1967).

Rudolph, W., 'Amos 4, 6-13', in *Wort–Gebot–Glaube: Beiträge zur Theologie des Alten Testaments—Walter Eichrodt zum 80. Geburtstag* (ed. J.J. Stamm, E. Jenni and H.J. Stoebe; ATANT, 59; Zürich: Zwingli Verlag, 1970), pp. 27-38.

—*Joel–Amos–Obadja–Jona* (KAT, XIII.12; Gütersloh: Gerd Mohn, 1971).

Runciman, W.G., *A Treatise on Social Theory*. I. *The Methodology of Social Theory* (Cambridge: Cambridge University Press, 1983).

Ryken, L., 'Literary Criticism of the Bible: Some Fallacies', in *Literary Interpretations of Biblical Narrative* (ed. K.R.R. Gros Louis, J.S. Ackerman and T.S. Warshaw; Nashville: Abingdon Press, 1974), pp. 24-40.

—*Words of Delight: A Literary Introduction to the Bible* (Grand Rapids: Baker Book House, 1987).

Saggs, H.W.F., *The Might That Was Assyria* (London: Sidgwick & Jackson, 1984).

Said, E.W., 'Opponents, Audiences, Constituencies, and Community', *CritInq* 9 (1982), pp. 1-26.

—*The World, the Text, and the Critic* (Cambridge, MA: Harvard University Press, 1983).

Sandeen, E.R. (ed.), *The Bible and Social Reform* (Philadelphia/Chico, CA: Fortress Press/Scholars Press, 1982).

Saravia, J., 'Nicaragua en la Biblia', *RIBLA* 1 (1988), pp. 100-106.

Sasson, J.M., 'On Choosing Models for Recreating Israelite Pre-Monarchic History', *JSOT* 21 (1981), pp. 3-24.

Sawyer, J.F.A., ' "Those Priests in Damascus": A Possible Example of Anti-Sectarian Polemic in the Septuagint Version of Amos 3, 12', *ASTI* 8 (1970–71), pp. 123-30.

—'A Change of Emphasis in the Study of the Prophets', in *Israel's Prophetic Tradition: Essays in Honour of Peter R. Ackroyd* (ed. R. Coggins, A. Phillips and M. Knibb; Cambridge: Cambridge University Press, 1982), pp. 233-49.

Saydon, P.P., 'Assonance in Hebrew as a Means of Expressing Emphasis', *Bib* 36 (1955), pp. 36-50, 287-304.

Scannone, J.C., 'Evangelization of Culture; Liberation, and "Popular Culture": The New Theological-Pastoral Synthesis in Latin America', in *The Church & Culture since Vatican II: The Experience of North and Latin America* (ed. J. Gremillion; Notre Dame, IN: University of Notre Dame Press, 1985), pp. 74-89.

Schenker, A., 'Zur Interpretation von Amos 3, 3-8', *BZ* ns 30 (1986), pp. 250-56.

Schipani, D.S. (ed.), *Freedom and Discipleship: Liberation Theology in an Anabaptist Perspective* (Maryknoll: Orbis Books, 1989).

Schlesinger, S., and S. Kinzer, *Bitter Fruit: The Untold Story of the American Coup in Guatemala* (Garden City, NY: Doubleday, 1983).

Schmidt, W.H., 'Die deuteronomistische Redaktion des Amosbuches', *ZAW* 77 (1965), pp. 165-93.

Schmitt, J.H., 'The Gender of Ancient Israel', *JSOT* 26 (1983), pp. 115-25.

Scholes, R., *Semiotics and Interpretation* (New Haven: Yale University Press, 1982).

—*Textual Power: Literary Theory and the Teaching of English* (New Haven: Yale University Press, 1985).

—*Protocols of Reading* (New Haven: Yale University Press, 1989).

Scholte, B., 'Cultural Anthropology and the Paradigm-Concept: A Brief History of their Recent Convergence', in *Functions and Uses of Disciplinary Studies* (ed. L. Graham, W. Lepenies and Peter Weingart; n.p.: Reidel, 1983), pp. 229-78.

Schoors, A. ,'The Particle KY', *OTS* 21 (1981), pp. 240-76.

Schreiter, R.J., *Constructing Local Theologies* (Maryknoll: Orbis Books, 1985).

Seed, P., ' "Failing to Marvel": Atahualpa's Encounter with the Word', *LARR* 26.1 (1991), pp. 7-32.

Segundo, J.L., 'Capitalism–Socialism: A Theological Crux', in *The Mystical and Political Dimensions of the Christian Faith* (ed. C. Geffré and G. Gutiérrez; New York: Herder & Herder, 1974), pp. 105-23.

—*The Liberation of Theology* (trans. J. Drury; Maryknoll: Orbis Books, 1976).

—*Faith and Ideologies, Jesus of Nazareth Yesterday and Today*, I (trans. J. Drury; Maryknoll: Orbis Books, 1984).

—*Theology and the Church: A Response to Cardinal Ratzinger and a Warning to the Whole Church* (trans. J.W. Dierksmeier; Minneapolis, MN: Seabury/Winston Press, 1985).

Seilhamer, F.H., 'The Role of Covenant in the Mission and Message of Amos', in *A Light Unto My Path: Old Testament Studies in Honor of Jacob M. Myers* (ed. H.N. Bream, R.D. Heim and C.A. Moore; Gettysburg Theology Studies, IV; Philadelphia: Temple University Press, 1974).

Shankman, P., 'The Thick and the Thin: On the Interpretive Theoretical Program of Clifford Geertz', *CurrAnth* 25 (1984), pp. 261-70, 276-79.

Shorter, A., *Toward a Theology of Inculturation* (Maryknoll: Orbis Books, 1988).

Sicre, J.L., *Los dioses olvidados. Poder y riqueza en los profetas preexílicos* (Etudios de Antiguo Testamento, 1; Madrid: Ediciones Cristiandad, 1979).

—*'Con los pobres de la tierra'. La justicia social en los profetas de Israel* (Madrid: Ediciones Cristiandad, 1984).

Sierra Pop, O.R., 'The Church and Social Conflicts in Guatemala', *SocCom* 30 (1983), pp. 317-48.

—'La iglesia católica entre el aperturismo y el conflicto social en Guatemala', *CrSoc* 103 (1990), pp. 41-57.

Silva, M., *Biblical Words & their Meaning: An Introduction to Lexical Semantics* (Grand Rapids: Zondervan, 1983).

Silvert, K.H., *Essays in Understanding Latin America* (Philadelphia: Institute for the Study of Human Issues, 1977).

Skinner, J., *Prophecy and Religion: Studies in the Life of Jeremiah* (Cambridge: Cambridge University Press, 1930).

Smalley, W.A., 'Recursion Patterns and the Sectioning of Amos', *BT* 30 (1979), pp. 118-27.

Smelik, K.A.D., 'The Meaning of Amos V 18-20', *VT* 36 (1986), pp. 246-48.

Smith, G.V., 'Amos 5.13—The Deadly Silence of the Prosperous', *JBL* 107 (1988), pp. 289-91.

—*Amos: A Commentary* (Library of Biblical Interpretation; Grand Rapids: Zondervan, 1989).

Snaith, N.H., *Notes on the Hebrew Text of Amos* (2 vols.; London: Epworth Press, 1945).

Snyder, G., 'The Law and Covenant in Amos', *RestQ* 25 (1982), pp. 158-66.

Soggin, J.A., 'Profezia e rivoluzione nell'Antico Testamento. L opera di Elie di Eliseo nella valutazione di Osea', *Prot* 25 (1970), pp. 1-14.

—*The Prophet Amos: A Translation and Commentary* (trans. J. Bowden; London: SCM Press, 1987).

Spencer, J., 'Writing within: Anthropology, Nationalism, and Culture in Sri Lanka', *CurrAnth* 31 (1990), pp. 283-300.

Spreafico, A., 'Amos: Struttura Formale e Spuntii per una Interpretazione', *RivBiblt* 29 (1981), pp. 147-76.

Spykman, G., *et al.*, *Let my People Live: Faith and Struggle in Central America* (Grand Rapids: Eerdmans, 1988).

Stager, L.E., 'The Finest Oil in Samaria', *JSS* 28 (1983), pp. 241-45.

Stek, J.H., 'The Stylistics of Hebrew Poetry: A (Re)New(ed) Focus of Study', *CalvTJ* 9 (1974), pp. 15-30.

Sternberg, M., 'Point of View and Indirections of Direct Speech', *Language and Style* 15.2 (1982), pp. 67-117.

—*The Poetics of Biblical Narrative: Ideological Literature and the Drama of Reading* (Indiana Literary Biblical Series; Bloomington, IN: Indiana University Press, 1985).

Story, C.I.K., 'Amos—Prophet of Praise', *VT* 39 (1980), pp. 67-80.

Stout, J., 'Virtue Among the Ruins: An Essay on MacIntyre', *NSys* 26 (1984), pp. 256-73.

—*Ethics after Babel: The Language of Morals and their Discontents* (Boston: Beacon Press, 1988).

Strawson, P.F., 'Social Morality and Individual Ideal', in *Christian Ethics and Contemporary Society* (ed. I.T. Ramsey; The Library of Philosophy and Theology; London: SCM Press, 1966), pp. 280-98.

Stroup, G.W., *The Promise of Narrative Theology: Recovering the Gospel in the Church* (Atlanta: John Knox, 1981).

Stuart, D., *Hosea–Jonah* (Word Biblical Commentary; Waco, TX: Word Books, 1987).

Suleiman, S.R., 'Introduction: Varieties of Audience-Oriented Criticism', in *The Reader in the Text: Essays on Audience and Interpretation* (ed. S.R. Suleiman and I. Crosman; Princeton, NJ: Princeton University Press, 1980), pp. 3-45.

Szabó, A., 'Textual Problems in Amos and Hosea', *VT* 25 (1975), pp. 500-24.

Tadmor, H., 'Azriyau of Yaudi', *SH* 8 (1961), pp. 232-71.

Talmon, S., 'The Textual Study of the Bible—A New Outlook', in *Qumran and the History of the Biblical Text* (ed. F.M. Cross and S. Talmon; Cambridge, MA: Harvard University Press, 1975), pp. 321-400.

Tamez, E., *Bible of the Oppressed* (trans. M.J. O'Connell; Maryknoll: Orbis Books, 1981).

Tannenbaum, F., *The Future of Democracy in Latin America* (ed. J. Maier and R.W. Weatherhead; New York: Alfred A. Knopf, 1974).

Taylor, M.K., 'Symbolic Dimensions in Cultural Anthropology', *CurrAnth* 26 (1985), pp. 167-85.

—*Beyond Explanation: Religious Dimensions in Cultural Anthropology* (Macon, GA: Mercer University Press, 1986).

Thiselton, A.C., *The Two Horizons: New Testament Hermeneutics and Philosophical Description with Special Reference to Heidegger, Bultmann, Gadamer, and Wittgenstein* (Grand Rapids: Eerdmans, 1980).

—'Reader-Response Hermeneutics, Action Models, and the Parables of Jesus', in *The Responsibility of Hermeneutics* (ed. R. Lundin, A.C. Thiselton and C. Walhout; Grand Rapids: Eerdmans, 1985), pp. 79-113.

Thompson, J.A., 'The Use of Repetition in the Prophecy of Joel', in *On Language, Culture and Religion: In Honor of Eugene A. Nida* (ed. M. Black and W.A. Smalley; The Hague: Mouton, 1974), pp. 101-10.

Todorov, T., 'Reading as Construction', in *The Reader in the Text: Essays on Audience and Interpretation* (ed. S.R. Suleiman and I. Crossman; Princeton, NJ: Princeton University Press, 1980), pp. 67-82.

Troeltsch, E., *The Social Teaching of the Christian Churches* (trans. O. Wyon; New York: Macmillan, 1931).

Tromp, N.J., 'Amos V 1-17: Towards a Stylistic and Rhetorical Analysis', *OTS* 23 (1984), pp. 56-84.

Tucker, G.M., 'The Role of the Prophets and the Role of the Church', in *Prophecy in Israel* (ed. D.L. Petersen; Issues in Religion and Theology, 10; Philadelphia: Fortress Press, 1987), pp. 159-74.

Uffenheimer, B., 'Ancient Hebrew Prophecy—Political Teaching and Practice', *Immanuel* 18 (1984), pp. 7-21.

Ureña, P.H., *A Concise History of Latin American Culture* (trans. G. Chase; London: Pall Mall Press, 1966).

Uslar-Pietri, A., 'El mestizaje y el Nuevo Mundo', in *Temas de filosofía latinoamericana* (ed. J.L. González Alvarez; Colección Antología, 6; Bogotá: Editorial El Buho, 1983), pp. 117-32.

Van der Wal, A., *Amos: A Classified Bibliography* (Amsterdam: Free University Press, 1983).

—'The Structure of Amos', *JSOT* 26 (1983), pp. 107-13.

Vélez, N., 'La lectura bíblica en las CEBs', *RIBLA* 1 (1988), pp. 8-29.

Van Leeuwen, C., 'The Prophecy of the *YOM YHWH* in Amos V 18-20', *OTS* 19 (1974), pp. 113-34.

Van Selms, A., 'Isaac in Amos', *OTWSA* 7-8 (1966), pp. 157-65.

Verhey, A., *The Great Reversal: Ethics and the New Testament* (Grand Rapids: Eerdmans, 1984).

Vermeylen, J., 'Les relectures deutéronomistes des livres d'Amos et de Michée', in *Du prophète Isaïe a l' Apocalyptique: Isaïe 1–35, miroir d'un demi-millénaire d'expérience religieuse en Israël*, II (Paris: n.p., 1978).

Vesco, J.L., 'Amos de Teqoa, defenseur de l'homme', *RB* 87 (1980), pp. 481-543.

Vigil, J.Ma. (ed.), *Nicaragua y los teólogos* (México: Siglo XXI, 1987).

Vijver, E., 'El éxodo: ¿un modelo para la ética social? Una respuesta crítica a la "Etica Comunitaria" de Enrique Dussel', *CuadTeol* 9 (1988), pp. 177-207.

Vollmer, J., *Geschichtliche Rückblicke und Motive in der Prophetie des Amos, Hosea und Jesaja* (BZAW, 119; Berlin: de Gruyter, 1971).

Vorlander, H., 'Religiosidad popular en el Antiguo Testamento' (trans. R. Godoy), *Conc* 206 (1986), pp. 7-86.

Walhout, C., 'Texts and Actions', in *The Responsibility of Hermeneutics* (ed. R. Lundin, A.C. Thiselton and C. Walhout; Grand Rapids: Eerdmans, 1985), pp. 31-77.

Walters, R. G., 'Signs of the Times: Clifford Geertz and Historians', *SocRes* 47 (1980), pp. 537-56.

Waltke, B.K., and M. O'Conner, *An Introduction to Biblical Hebrew Syntax* (Winona Lake, IN: Eisenbrauns, 1990).

Walzer, M., *The Revolution of the Saints: A Study in the Origins of Radical Politics* (London: Weidenfeld & Nicolson, 1965).

—*Interpretation and Social Criticism* (Cambridge, MA: Harvard University Press, 1987).

Ward, J.M., *Amos and Isaiah: Prophets of the Word of God* (Nashville: Abingdon Press, 1969).

Watson-Franke, M.B., and L.C. Watson, 'Understanding in Anthropology: A Philosophical Reminder', *CurrAnth* 16 (1975), pp. 247-62.

Watson, W.G.E., *Classical Hebrew Poetry: A Guide to its Techniques* (JSOTSup, 26; Sheffield: JSOT Press, 1984).

Watts, J.D.W., 'The Origin of the Book of Amos', *ExpTim* 66 (1955), pp. 109-112.

—*Vision and Prophecy in Amos* (Leiden: Brill, 1958).

Webb, B.G., *The Book of Judges: An Integrated Reading* (JSOTSup, 46; Sheffield: JSOT Press, 1987).

Weber, M., *Ancient Judaism* (ed. and trans. H.H. Gerth and D. Martindale; Glencoe: The Free Press, 1952).

—*Economy and Society: An Outline of Interpretive Sociology* (ed. G. Ross and C. Wittich; New York: Bedminster Press, 1968).

Weigert, A.J., *Sociology of Everyday Life* (New York: Longman, 1981).

Weinfeld, M., 'Divine Intervention in War in Ancient Israel and in the Ancient Near East', in *History, Historiography and Interpretation: Studies in Biblical and Cuneiform Literatures* (ed. H. Tadmor and M. Weinfeld; Jerusalem: Magnes Press, 1986), pp. 121-47.

Weippert, H., 'Amos. Seine Bilder und ihr Milieu', *OBO* 64 (1985), pp. 1-29.

West, G.O., 'The Succession Narrative as History: A Critical Discussion of the Debate in Light of Recent Work in the Philosophy of History' (unpublished MA thesis, University of Sheffield, 1986).

Westermann, C., *Basic Forms of Prophetic Speech* (trans. H.C. White; London: Lutterworth, 1967).

Whitelam, K.W., 'Recreating the History of Israel', *JSOT* 35 (1986), pp. 45-70.

Wicke, D.W., 'Two Perspectives (Amos 5.1-17)', *CurTM* 13 (1986), pp. 89-96.

Wilder, A.N., 'Story and Story-World', *Int* 37 (1983), pp. 353-64.

Williams, A.J., 'A Further Suggestion about Amos IV 1-3', *VT* 29 (1979), pp. 206-11.

Williams, B., *Ethics and the Limits of Philosophy* (London: Fontana/Collins, 1985).

Williams, J.G., 'The Alas-Oracles of the Eighth Century Prophets', *HUCA* 38 (1967), pp. 75-92.

—'The Social Location of Israelite Prophecy', *JAAR* 39 (1969), pp. 153-65.

Williams, R.J., *Hebrew Syntax: An Outline* (Toronto: University of Toronto Press, 2nd edn, 1976).

Willi-Plein, I., *Vorformen der Schriftexegese innerhalb des Alten Testaments— Untersuchungen zum literarischen Werden der auf Amos, Hosea und Micha zurückgehenden Bucher im hebräischen Zwölfprophetenbuch* (BZAW, 123; Berlin: de Gruyter, 1971).

Wilson, R.R., *Prophecy and Society in Ancient Israel* (Philadelphia: Fortress Press, 1980).

—*Sociological Approaches to the Old Testament* (Guides to Biblical Scholarship; Philadelphia: Fortress Press, 1984).

Wink, W., *The Bible in Human Transformation: Toward a New Paradigm for Biblical Study* (Philadelphia: Fortress Press, 1973).

Wolf, E.R., *Peasants* (Foundations of Modern Anthropology Series; Englewood Cliffs, NJ: Prentice–Hall, 1966).

—*Anthropology* (New York: Norton, 2nd edn, 1974).

—*Europe and the People without History* (Berkeley: University of California Press, 1982).

Wolff, H.W., *Amos the Prophet: The Man and his Background* (trans. F.R. McCurley; Philadelphia: Fortress Press, 1973).

—*Joel and Amos* (trans. W. Lanzen, S.D. McBride, Jr, and C.A. Muenchlow; Philadelphia: Fortress Press, 1977).

—*La Hora de Amós* (trans. F. M. Goñi; Salamanca: Ediciones Sí‌gueme, 1984).

Wolfram, S., 'Basic Differences of Thought', in *Modes of Thought: Essays on Thinking in Western and Non-Western Societies* (ed. R. Horton and R. Finnegan; London: Faber & Faber, 1973), pp. 357-74.

Wuthnow, R., *et al.*, *Cultural Analysis: The Work of Peter L. Berger, Mary Douglas and Jurgen Habermas* (London: Routledge & Kegan Paul, 1984).

—'Religion as a Sacred Canopy', in *Making Sense of Modern Times: Peter L. Berger and the Vision of Interpretive Sociology* (ed. J.D. Hunter and S.C. Ainlay; London: Routledge & Kegan Paul, 1986), pp. 121-42.

Yoder, J.H., 'Orientation in Midstream: A Response to the Responses', in *Freedom and Discipleship: Liberation Theology in an Anabaptist Perspective* (ed. D.S. Schipani; Maryknoll: Orbis Books, 1989), pp. 159-68.

Youngblood, R., 'LQR' in Amos 4.12', *JBL* 90 (1971), p. 98.

Younger, K.L., Jr, *Ancient Conquest Accounts: A Study in Ancient Near Eastern and Biblical History Writing* (JSOTSup, 98; Sheffield: JSOT Press, 1990).

Yuasa, K., 'The Image of Christ in Latin American Popular Religiosity', in *Preaching Jesus in the Two-Thirds World* (ed. V. Samuel and C. Sugden; Bangalore: Partnership in Mission–Asia, 1983), pp. 61-85.

Zalcman, L., 'Astronomical Illusions in Amos', *JBL* 100 (1981), pp. 53-58.

Zapata A., V., *Historia de la iglesia evangélica en Guatemala* (Guatemala: Caisa, 1982).

Zea, L., *Latin America and the World* (trans. F.K. Hendricks and B. Berler; Norman, OK: University of Oklahoma Press, 1969).

—*El pensamiento latinoamericano* (Biblioteca de Ciencia Política; Barcelona: Editorial Ariel, 3rd edn, 1976).

Zevit, Z., 'A Misunderstanding at Bethel, Amos VIII 12-17', *VT* 25 (1975), pp. 783-90.

—'Expressing Denial in Biblical Hebrew and Mishnaic Hebrew', *VT* 29 (1979), pp. 505-509.

Ziegler, J. (ed.), *Duodecim prophetae. Septuagint—Vetus Testamentum Graecum*

Auctoritate Academiae Litterarum Gottingensis editum (Göttingen: Vandenhoeck & Ruprecht, 1967).

Zijderveld, A.C., 'The Challenges of Modernity', in *Making Sense of Modern Times: Peter L. Berger and the Vision of Interpretive Sociology* (ed. J.D. Hunter and S.C. Ainlay; London: Routledge & Kegan Paul, 1986), pp. 57-75.

Zimmerli, W., 'Von Prophetenwort zum Prophetenbuch', *TLZ* 104 (1979), pp. 481-96.

INDEXES

INDEX OF AUTHORS

JOURNAL FOR THE STUDY OF THE OLD TESTAMENT

Supplement Series